The French Book Trade in Enlightenment Europe II

Also available from Bloomsbury

The French Book Trade in Enlightenment Europe I: Selling Enlightenment,
by Mark Curran
The Foreign Political Press in Nineteenth-Century London: Politics from a Distance,
edited by Constance Bantman and Ana Cláudia Suriani da Silva
London Calling: Britain, the BBC World Service and the Cold War, by Alban Webb

The French Book Trade in Enlightenment Europe II

Enlightenment Bestsellers

Simon Burrows

BLOOMSBURY ACADEMIC
LONDON • NEW YORK • OXFORD • NEW DELHI • SYDNEY

BLOOMSBURY ACADEMIC
Bloomsbury Publishing Plc
50 Bedford Square, London, WC1B 3DP, UK
1385 Broadway, New York, NY 10018, USA
29 Earlsfort Terrace, Dublin 2, Ireland

BLOOMSBURY, BLOOMSBURY ACADEMIC and the Diana logo are trademarks
of Bloomsbury Publishing Plc

First published in Great Britain 2018
Paperback edition published 2021

Copyright © Simon Burrows, 2018

Afterword © Simon Burrows and Jason Ensor

Simon Burrows has asserted his right under the Copyright, Designs and Patents Act,
1988, to be identified as Author of this work.

For legal purposes the Acknowledgements on p. x constitute an extension
of this copyright page.

All rights reserved. No part of this publication may be reproduced or transmitted in any
form or by any means, electronic or mechanical, including photocopying, recording, or
any information storage or retrieval system, without prior permission in writing from
the publishers.

Bloomsbury Publishing Plc does not have any control over, or responsibility for, any
third-party websites referred to or in this book. All internet addresses given in this
book were correct at the time of going to press. The author and publisher regret any
inconvenience caused if addresses have changed or sites have ceased to exist, but
can accept no responsibility for any such changes.

A catalogue record for this book is available from the British Library.

A catalog record for this book is available from the Library of Congress.

ISBN: HB: 978-1-4411-2601-6
PB: 978-1-3502-5081-9
ePDF: 978-1-4411-5913-7
eBook: 978-1-4411-8217-3

Typeset by Deanta Global Publishing Services, Chennai, India

To find out more about our authors and books visit www.bloomsbury.com
and sign up for our newsletters.

'For Hannah and Reuben'.

Contents

Illustrations, Maps, Charts and Tables	viii
Acknowledgements	x
Preface	xi
Prologue: *At the Shield of Minerva*	xv
1 The Elusive Enlightenment	1
2 The Book in Print Culture	17
3 Searching for Enlightenment in a Swiss Print Shop	35
4 The Intellectual Geography of the STN	49
5 Forgotten Bestsellers	67
6 Troubling Taxonomies	77
7 Harvesting the Literary Field	91
8 Of Cosmopolitan Reading and Novel Concerns	105
9 The Anatomy of the Illegal Sector	119
10 *Philosophie*, Science, Faith	137
11 From Swiss Politics to Revolutionary History	155
Conclusion	173
Afterword: The Future of FBTEE—Towards a Digital History of the Book	175
List of Online Appendices	181
Notes	182
Bibliography	223
Subject Index	239
Title Index	248

Illustrations, Maps, Charts and Tables

Figure

0.1 Léonard Defrance de Liège, *A l'Egide de Minerve. La Politique de tolérance de Joseph II favorisant les encyclopédistes*, Musée des Beaux-Arts de Dijon (inv. 3550–13). © Musée des Beaux-Arts de Dijon. Photo François Jay   xv

Map

4.1 Distribution of School Books by the STN, 1769–94   57

Charts

7.1 Surveys of popular reading in eighteenth-century France and Europe (categorized works only)   92
7.2 STN sales by Parisian category by edition type, 1769–94   99
7.3 Parisian categorized STN sales by Client Type, 1769–94   100
9.1 The structure of the French illegal and quasi-legal book trade, 1769–89 (excluding unlicensed innocuous works)   125
9.2 Comparative sales of pornographic works by the STN, 1769–87   135
11.1 STN 'Trade Sales' of political works as a percentage of all STN 'Trade Sales' to France; Switzerland; and All Europe, 1769–88   161
11.2 STN sales of works carrying keyword 'Du Barri' to France, 1769–94, adjusted to remove foreign wholesale clients   162

Tables

3.1 Ratios of STN acquisitions from Swiss sources by Edition Type   45
5.1 The STN all-time bestselling primary authors for global, trade and commercial lists compared   68

7.1	'Sales' of subcategories of the three leading Parisian categories in the STN database	93
8.1	Domestic readership for books about France and Switzerland	107
8.2	Loans of travel literature from Wigtown Library compared with STN sales data	113
8.3	Top ten works loaned by the Bristol Library, 1773–84, with occurrences in other datasets	115
8.4	'Cosmopolitan books' borrowed from the Bristol Library, 1773–84	116
9.1	Final total (estimates) of works, editions and copies of French-language libertine works produced in Europe, 1769–89	123
9.2	Categories of illegal work in the Bastille and Darnton's *Corpus*	126
9.3	Key categories of *livres philosophiques* traded by the STN as a proportion of all known *livres philosophiques*	127

Acknowledgements

This research was supported by the British Arts and Humanities Research Council's Research Grants (Standard) Scheme AH/E509363/1 and supplementary research under the Australian Research Council's Discovery Projects funding scheme (Project number DP160103488).

Preface

This book and its companion volume[1] were born of a wild goose chase, a search for a missing queen. Or rather elusive books about a queen. That queen was Marie-Antoinette. The books were salacious pamphlets (*libelles*) about her imaginary love life *published* before the Revolution. By early 2002, I was convinced such pamphlets never reached their public. Certainly some were written, and some were printed. A few even circulated in manuscript form. But I believed that until the French Revolution they were never available in print to the general readers.[2] To prove this hypothesis, I had to consider all available evidence, since to verify a negative proposition one must dispose of all possible counter-evidence. Thus in 2004 I went to Switzerland to examine the rolling stock inventories of the Société typographique de Neuchâtel (STN) publishing house in search of traces of the anti-Marie-Antoinette pamphlets. I found none.

However, I discovered something much more significant. After having completed my work in the stock inventories, in my last couple of hours in the STN archive I called up some of the STN's other accounting records. As I examined them I realized that the data they contained, together with the stock inventories, could, in theory, be used to create a database capable of mapping the STN's entire trade. It could trace from whence the books they traded came, where they were sent, and when. If such books were carefully catalogued and categorized, we might uncover trends in the dissemination of both books and the ideas that they contained. This data might then be cross-referenced with information in the STN's wonderful typed handlist of correspondents, which gave names, professions and places of residence.[3] Thus was born a theoretical blueprint for the path-breaking French Book Trade in Enlightenment Europe (FBTEE) digital humanities project.

Of course, what sounded simple on paper proved anything but easy in practice. On a pilot project in March 2006, Dr Mark Curran and I spent four days establishing beyond doubt and by multiple means that the various accounting documents could be reconciled with each other. We also conducted the detailed soundings and scopings to establish feasibility, time frame and what resourcing we would require. Armed with this information and the assistance of Dr Peter Millican and Dr Sarah Kattau of the Leeds Electronic Text Centre, we secured a grant from the British Arts and Humanities Research Council (AHRC) on which Dr Curran was named as postdoctoral research associate. Nevertheless, converting a rough blueprint into a meticulously structured relational database proved more complex and time-consuming than we had ever imagined; the data proved dirtier and more problematic than a short pilot could reveal; and the evidence the database provided challenged our original assumption – drawn from previous scholarship – that the STN records constituted a 'representative archive'. For the project, the implications of these discoveries were to prove profound. Contrary to the original plans, I would have to undertake the classification of the 4,000 titles in the database. Equally, when it came to the task of writing up our findings, it made sense to assign the first volume – which related to the STN's business practices and the supply side of the trade – to Dr Curran since that related best to the material on which he had worked.

Dr Curran's volume, *Selling Enlightenment*, surveys the STN's history and the structure, politics and organization of the book trade, laying bare the operation of eighteenth-century publishing and book-distribution networks as never before. It also undermines many of the foundational assumptions we drew from previous scholars of the STN. As a result, it deeply problematized the writing of this second volume, *Enlightenment Bestsellers*, which offers an in-depth study of the dissemination and reception of discourses and ideas. By examining the body of works traded by the STN, it explores what the STN archive can reveal about eighteenth-century print culture, the Enlightenment and that most vexed of historical questions: the cultural origins of the French Revolution. But to do so, it must first wrestle with the findings of Dr Curran's subtle and path-breaking study and establish afresh how we might tease out findings of wider significance from the STN data.

Fortunately, these problems also gave rise to significant opportunities. Over time it became clear that the solutions we adopted in response to these problems were of considerable interest to other digital humanists and computer scientists. These included our means of compensating for the unevenness of our dataset; for finding and defining 'representative' data and compensating for biases; our strategies for dealing with uncertainty; and the representation and plotting of eighteenth-century geopolitical space. As a result, our two companion volumes embed within them a tale of how digital humanities methods can lead us to better and more strongly grounded answers to old questions. Both studies are as much concerned with offering insights into new methods as interpreting a digital dataset which has been publicly available since June 2012.

In the course of writing and researching this book I enjoyed the support of many people and institutions, some of which are named above. First I must thank my wife Andrea and children Hannah and Reuben: they have lived with this project for as long as they can remember. Next come the members of the project team. Mark Curran's input facilitated almost every aspect of project design from its inception in 2006 to his departure in 2011. Too long to recount here, his involvement has been documented in full elsewhere.[4] Sarah Kattau's meticulous database design, formulated from a series of intense face-to-face interrogations, put flesh on my blueprint and ensured that our data structures were fit for purpose and potentially transferrable to other projects. Amyas (Henry) Merivale's user interface has been hailed by Robert Darnton as 'a joy to use'.[5] Finally, Vincent Hiribarren, who was hired initially to do digital mapping work, ended up completing work on the interface and providing endless technical support in the final months of the project. His energy, enthusiasm, initiative and drive ensured the successful completion of the AHRC-funded stage of the project and the transfer of the database, website and online interface to Australia, where it is now hosted by Western Sydney University. Thereafter Vincent has continued to contribute to the project's conceptual development.

Dr Jason Ensor, who from 2013 to 2017 was both my research collaborator and technical designer at Western Sydney, has made it possible to explore new issues and digitally record and mine new sources. An account of our collaboration and blueprint for future research is given in our joint-afterword to this volume. My readers and I owe him an enormous debt of gratitude, as we do Dr Catherine Bishop, Dr Juliette Reboul and Dr Louise Seaward, who patiently interpreted and entered new data on the *Permissions Simples, estampillage* of 1778–80 and Parisian booksellers' stock sales. Additionally, as an M.A. and Doctoral student at Leeds, Louise Seaward road tested the database. Without their work, this book would have been much poorer.

I am deeply grateful to the AHRC, which provided the foundational grant of £355,485. The University of Leeds gave supplementary financial support and a professorial dowry, which financed our mapping work. Western Sydney University ensured the project's future trajectory through the provision of a further $A150,000 of Research Infrastructure Funding and as the book was drawing to completion, the Australian Research Council (ARC) awarded $459,606 of further funding. Robert Darnton first indicated to scholars the value of the STN archive and consented to the inclusion of his statistics of demand in the FBTEE database. This book is inspired by his work, however much my conclusions may differ from his own.

I also thank those who were associated with the project informally, or as members of the project board, or by assisting with grant applications. Project board members David Adams (who commented extensively on my manuscript), Simon Dixon, Russell Goulbourne, Peter Millican and Jonathan Topham contributed their time, advice and collective wisdom. The staff of the Leeds Humanities Research Institute, particularly Gill Gray, Edward Kirby, Stuart Taberner and Matthew Treherne, also provided valuable support, as did research administrators in the School of History at the University of Leeds, notably Emily Abbey and Alice Potter.

I thank the Bibliothèque publique et universitaire de Neuchâtel and its personnel, for encouragement and support, particularly Michel Schlup and Thierry Châtelain, Marise Schmidt-Surdez and Michael Schmidt, not forgetting the hospitality of Marie Vuarraz (now Vuarraz-Curran). I also thank Geoffrey Forster of the Leeds Library, and staff at the Brotherton Library at the University of Leeds, notably Oliver Pickering, Jane Saunders, Chris Sheppard, and at the Western Sydney University library, above all Michael Gonzalez and Kaysha Russell. I would also like to thank the Musée des Beaux-Arts de Dijon for permission to reproduce Léonard Defrance's tableau, *A l'Egide de Minerve. La Politique de tolerance de Joseph II favorisant les encyclopédistes*.

I am also grateful to those who offered advice on I.T. or G.I.S., particularly Michael Pidd of the University of Sheffield's Humanities Research Institute; Catherine Nicole Coleman of the 'Mapping the Republic of Letters' team at Stanford University; Anna Clough of the University of Leeds; and Craig Pett, who served as our liaison with Gale-Cengage Australia. Equally, several colleagues have helped check or verify our information or identify non-French editions, notably Jeffrey Freedman, Andrew Brown, Rhiannon Daniels, Moritz Föllmer, Ian Moxon, Catherine Parisian, Jeffrey Ravel, David Smith and Anthony Wright.

My thanks also to organizers and participants at the many conferences and seminars where I have received feedback, in particular Pierre Serna and Antoine Lilti; the American Historical Association 2012 annual conference; the International Society for Eighteenth-Century Studies 2015 conference in Rotterdam; the Alliance of Digital

Humanities Organisations (2015); the Australian Association for Digital Humanities (2014); the Bibliographic Society; Alan Forrest and the International Commission on the History of the French Revolution; Dave Andress; Carol Armbruster and the Library of Congress; Laurence Brockliss and the Voltaire Foundation; Howard Hotson and the Cultures of Knowledge Project at Oxford; Robert Jensen-Rix (Aarhus) and his colleagues at the University of Copenhagen; John Chartres and the University of Leeds Eighteenth Century Group; the New Zealand Digital Symposium; Anne-Marie Mercier-Faivre and the LIRE team at Lyon-2; the American Society for Eighteenth Century Studies and Jeremy Popkin (who has also been an incisive yet sensitive reviewer); the organizers of the Rudé Seminars in Sydney (2010), Auckland (2012) and Geelong (2014), particularly Kirsty Carpenter and Jo Zizek; Eleanor Shevlin, Sydney Shep and the Society for the History of Authorship, Reading and Publishing (SHARP), especially the organizing committees for the Helsinki (2010), Washington (2011), Paris (2016) and Victoria B.C. (2017) conferences; the Society for the Study of French History and the Society for French Historical Studies; the organizers of the 'Collections and Compilations' at CRAASH, University of Cambridge (2008); Gillian Dow and the British Society for Romantic Studies (2013); Rafe Hallett and the Centre for the Comparative History of Print at Leeds; Ann Thomson and the AHRC/ANR Cultural Transfers in the Long Eighteenth Century network; Mark Towsey and the AHRC-funded 'Community Libraries' network; the Bibliographic Society of Australia and New Zealand; Jennifer Milam and the Sydney Intellectual History Network; FBTEE's close collaborator, Alicia Montoya, and the MEDIATE team at Radboud, who organized the second annual Digitizing Enlightenment symposium (2017); and the organizers of the Knowledge in Context colloquium in honour of Laurence Brockliss and Colin Jones (2017), the history seminar at Hong Kong University (2017) and first three Round the World Digital symposia (2013–15). Also to Julie Kalman and the anonymous referees at *French History and Civilization*.

Among the many other scholars at Leeds, Western Sydney and from around the world who provided advice or support, I would particularly like to thank Nigel Aston, Keith Baker, Dmitri Bovykine, David Burchell, Christophe Cave, Alexandra Cook; Dan Edelstein, Dena Goodman, John Gooch, Hugh Gough, Katie Halsey, Sarah Irving, Colin Jones, Gary Kates, Wallace Kirsop, Martyn Lyons, Angus Martin, Katie McDonough, Wayne McKenna, Robert Morrissey, Elena Muceni, Peter McPhee, Laure Philip, James Raven, Anna-Maria Rimm, Glenn Roe, Edward Spiers, Sean Takats and Richard Whiting. This book is all the better for their assistance; its remaining faults are entirely my own.

Simon Burrows
Digital Humanities Research Group
Western Sydney University
10 January 2018

Prologue: *At the Shield of Minerva*

Figure 0.1 Léonard Defrance de Liège, *A l'Egide de Minerve. La Politique de tolerance de Joseph II favorisant les encyclopédistes*, Musée des Beaux-Arts de Dijon (inv. 3550–13). © Musée des Beaux-Arts de Dijon. Photo François Jay.

Leonard DeFrance's painting *À l'Égide de Minerve* offers an invaluable window into the cosmopolitan Enlightenment's self-image. DeFrance's *tableau* depicts a public square in Liège in 1781. Now part of Belgium, Liège was in the eighteenth century the capital of an autonomous Roman Catholic ecclesiastical state, the Prince-Bishopric of Liège, where, if we can believe DeFrance, traditional religious ideas were making way for modern, Enlightenment values. In DeFrance's painting, freshly minted wall-posters advertise the works of arch-sceptics Helvétius, Condillac and Voltaire, symbolically replacing torn and tatty fliers for superannuated sermons. Beneath them, unperturbed by such sacrilege, clergymen of rival denominations are deep in conversation. A further poster, conspicuously announcing the emperor Joseph II's celebrated toleration edict, seems to demand such indifference of them. Behind the priests, merchants close a deal. Meanwhile a monk, clearly not oblivious to the charms of this world, flirts unashamedly with a young girl, a shop assistant perhaps, in a bookshop doorway. Besides her, and in their own way just as tantalizing, are several large parcels of books. Wrapped in brown paper, bearing addresses in Spain and Portugal, they bear the unmistakable *ballot* numbers used by book dealers, merchants and government officials across Europe to identify and trace individual consignments of goods. Perhaps they contain copies of works advertised here, including Montesquieu's *De l'esprit des Lois* or Rousseau's works, titles which seem to herald further political reform is coming to the Prince-Bishopric of Liège? And above the milling crowds, legitimizing and inspiring all this activity, is a sign proclaiming we are looking at the celebrated bookshop *À l'Égide de Minerve*. These events are taking place under the protective eye and shield of Minerva, the Roman goddess of reason and wisdom, patroness of the arts and trade. If DeFrance appears to immortalize a particular image of late Enlightenment culture and sociability, one blending urbane reason, scepticism, cosmopolitanism, toleration and religious latudinarianism laced with classical and pagan allegory, this is no coincidence. He intended his picture to epitomize a heroic, universalist Enlightenment, radiating reason and light.

DeFrance's *tableau* reminds us that the Enlightenment was above all about connections and networks. Under Minerva's protection, those of all faiths or none gather to discuss the latest intellectual fads, acquire classic Enlightenment writings or calmly debate matters of faith or politics. Ideas shaped in these gatherings or carried in these books will be recirculated, amplified and transformed in further formal and chance meetings in salons, coffee houses, masonic lodges, reading circles, taverns, subscription libraries, public squares, guild meetings, town halls, religious congregations and private homes. Some may find their way back into print in journals, pamphlets, printed sermons and books, to be carried once more around the circuits of Europe's burgeoning knowledge economy and public sphere.

The Prince-Bishopric of Liège is but one node in these communication circuits, which criss-cross Christian Europe from Lisbon and Madrid to Stockholm and Saint-Petersburg, from Edinburgh and Dublin to Naples and Budapest. Centred on the great arterial trade routes of the Rhine and Rhone corridors, and the metropolises of London, Paris and Amsterdam, they extend their tentacles to the cities of the North American seaboard, the Spanish American empire, even to India and lands beyond. But what books were most typically stacked high on the shelves of bookshops such as *À l'Égide de Minerve* or crammed into those enigmatic crates? The posters suggest that they carried the seeds of a popular and heroic Enlightenment around the European world. The current study attempts to peek inside bookshops and into book-crates as they wound their way around Europe, in order to assess the validity of this heroic vision of late Enlightenment culture. In the process it offers new insights into the francophone print culture of eighteenth-century Europe and challenges many of our notions of Enlightenment and the intellectual origins of late modernity.

1

The Elusive Enlightenment

How can we peek inside wooden crates (*ballots*) like those depicted in DeFrance's painting? Crates which, having traversed the highways and waterways of Europe, were emptied, broken up and consigned to the bonfire almost two and a half centuries ago? Why would we want to do so? What exactly are we looking for? What more can we hope to learn about the nature of the Enlightenment from such an endeavour? And how can we determine whether the crates we succeed in prizing open are somehow representative of the late-Enlightenment book trade anyway? These pressing and legitimate questions, already rendered more complex and problematic by Mark Curran's companion volume, *Selling Enlightenment*, will be addressed in this introductory chapter and those that follow. Only then will we be able to assess the significance of the books packed tight within the crates, and hence refine our vision of the literary, intellectual and cultural world of the late Enlightenment.

To interpret the content of the crates we will be taking a 'historical bibliometric' approach: we will be counting books.[1] But why count books at all? Such an endeavour may make sense when exploring the economics and mechanisms of the trade, as in the first volume of this study. But does 'historical bibliometrics' have the same value when examining the spread of discourses and ideas? Is there not a danger of becoming like the London-based Genevan bookseller Joseph de Boffe and getting to know books 'by the cubic foot'?[2] Or to put the same question in a different way, can the value or influence of a text really be measured by distribution figures? Should we not instead be looking at the literary merit and enduring reputation of a text, its assimilation by other authors, the integration of the ideas it propounds into the cultural mainstream? This is a classic question *mal posée* and for two reasons. First, because a desire to add historical bibliometric data to other evidence about the reception, impact, reputation and perceived literary merit of a text does not imply an effort to supplant or ignore conclusions drawn from those other sources, but rather a wish to enhance, nuance and further interrogate them. Second, because by combining and manipulating data about many hundreds of numbered *ballots*, we can discover something of popular reading and discourses that had wide cultural resonance in their own time. In particular, we can recover bestselling texts which although much read, and perhaps influential, have subsequently fallen from view. Such popular texts have much to tell us about the cultural life of an era.

Of course, historians have long used 'historical bibliometric' methods in their attempts to discover and describe the literary world of the Enlightenment or the common reader. They have scoured private library catalogues, will inventories, permission records and counted editions using powerful new online databases. They have examined booksellers' orders, book reviews and customs confiscations. But all these methods have significant drawbacks. Most fail to register the ephemeral, the flimsy, the worn out, and the disposable, including school textbooks, cheap religious or political tracts and trade publications. Many do not record clandestine publications, while others privilege them. Some sources are hierarchical, capturing only what was thought worth recording. The study of booksellers' orders, as we shall see, ignores a glaring gap between cultural supply and cultural demand in early modern Europe. Counting editions registers only editions that survive, often in public collections. It fails to reflect significant differences in print runs between and sometimes within different genres of publication. Peering into consignments of books promises to overcome most of these problems. If we can catch books in flight between their producers and consumers, hopefully we can gain a view of the whole market. We might in addition be able to identify differences between local markets and across time. But where are we to find such information?

Fortunately, the contents of many hundreds of book crates are recorded in the surviving accounting records of a Swiss bookseller, the Société typographique de Neuchâtel (STN), which traded across Europe from 1769 to 1794. These are the main crates – though not the only ones – examined in this book. The STN records inventory the contents, destination or origin, and dates of despatch or receipt for many such crates, as well as the customers who sent or ordered them, and, often, the middlemen and agents who handled them along the way. In total, the STN archive allows us to reconstruct the passage of more than 445,000 books around a network of 2,895 correspondents and business associates in 516 communities across Europe. This network extended from Edinburgh, Stockholm and St Petersburg in the north to Naples and Cadiz in the south; and from Lisbon in the west to Moscow in the east. At its heart, strategically close to its geographical central point, lay Neuchâtel itself, a highly literate town of just 3,000 inhabitants nestled in a micro-principality of 35,400 souls whose industrial development was based around lace and watchmaking.[3] Neuchâtel lay 418 kilometres south of Liège, the town depicted by DeFrance, where the STN's correspondents included the booksellers Anne-Catherine Bassompierre, Clément Plomteux, Orval-Demazeau, François Lemarié and the printer-bookselling partnership Jean-Jacques Tutot and C. J. Renoz.[4] Most of these individuals both published and traded in counterfeited clandestine Enlightenment classics by authors such as Voltaire and Montequieu or the materialists Helvétius, d'Holbach and Boulanger.[5] However, only one of the Liégois booksellers, Demazeau, did business with the STN and his orders contain few traces of such explosive forbidden material. They do, however, provide a window onto Enlightenment reading beyond the canonical works of the great *philosophes*.

In five consignments between March 1774 and 1776, the STN sent Demazeau 458 copies of sixty-eight titles. The books they despatched in crate number L.D. n. 48 on 27 March 1776 were fairly typical of his orders. Few of them are well-known today, though some of their authors occupy significant places in the Enlightenment literary canon. The crate contained two scandalous pamphlets relating to the high politics and sexual activities of Louis XV of France (ruled 1715–74); a British doctor's philosophic travel journal of a trip to Sicily and Malta; and a natural history of Switzerland. There is also a popular history textbook; an account of the present state of Portugal; and miscellaneous freshly issued tomes of the STN's lavish multivolume technical encyclopaedia, the *Descriptions des arts et métiers*. These were accompanied by a dissertation on Joan of Arc; a Christian conduct manual for young ladies; an unidentified work recorded as *Mémoires sur l'Angleterre*; and an anonymous attack on Voltaire's supposed religious hypocrisy entitled *Remonstrances du Père Adam à Voltaire pour être mises à la suite de sa confession*. There were also a handful of literary and dramatic works, several of which were political or historical in nature. Foremost among the dramatic pieces were fifteen copies of Beaumarchais' comic masterpiece *Le Barbier de Séville*; twelve copies of Voltaire's dark and ambivalent tragedy *Don Pèdre, roi de Castille*; eight copies of Du Rozoi's *Henri IV*; and ten copies of Louis-Sébastien Mercier's comedy *La Brouette de vinaigrier*. There were also novels and poetry by popular libertine writers Claude Dorat and the marquis de Luchet, both well-known for their *risqué* or mildly erotic writings. Finally, there were two copies of the *Dunciade*, a French translation of Alexander Pope's epic-comic masterpiece. Except for the plays and the *Dunciade*, Demazeau's crate contained just three to six copies of each work. Thus the full packing inventory for crate L.D. n. 48 would have read roughly as follows:

Beaumarchais, *Le Barbier de Séville*, 15 [copies]
Voltaire, *Don Pèdre, roi de Castille*, 12
Mercier, *La Brouette de vinaigrier*, 10
Du Rozoi, *Henri IV, drame lyrique en 3 actes et en prose*, 8
Brydone, *Voyage en Sicile et à Malthe*, 8
Gruner, *Histoire naturelle de la Suisse dans l'ancien monde*, 8
Dumouriez, *Etat présent du royaume de Portugal*, 6
Nougaret, (attrib.), *Mémoires authentiques de Mme la comtesse du Barri*, 6
Gregory, *Legs d'un père à ses filles*, 6
Anon, *Remonstrances du Père Adam à Voltaire*, 6
Luchet *Dissertation sur Jeanne d'Arc*, 5
Dorat, *Collection complète des œuvres de M. Dorat*, 4
Dorat, *Les Malheurs de l'inconstance*, 4
Mairobert, *Journal historique de la révolution opérée dans la constitution de la monarchie françoise par M. de Maupeou*, 3
Gessner, *Œuvres de Gessner*, 3
Millot, *Elémens d'histoire générale de Millot*, 3
Luchet, *Mémoires de Mme le baronee de S. Lys*, 3
Palissot, *La Dunciade*, 2
[*Mémoires sur l'Angleterre*], 2
Descriptions des arts et métiers, various volumes [comprising 0.7 of a full set]

What are we to make of the contents of this crate? Does it live up to the heroic Enlightenment of DeFrance's tableau? Should we expect it to? It was, after all, despatched five years before Joseph II promulgated his toleration patent and liberalized the censorship in the neighbouring Austrian Netherlands. A bookseller ordering a consignment of books in an adjacent ecclesiastical principality in such times might perhaps try to avoid the more caustic carriers of Enlightenment ideas. However, from 1772 to 1784, Liège was ruled by the liberal Prince-Bishop François-Charles, comte de Welbruck, who established enlightened programmes in education, public health, a local academy and public works for the indigent poor. The atmosphere, then, was conducive to Enlightenment ideas.

What emerges most strikingly as we unpack crate L.D. n. 48 is a refreshingly cosmopolitan collection of literature. The subjects or literary settings of the books it contained spanned much of Europe – Demazeau's customers' reading reveries would transport them to Spain, Portugal, Britain, France, Italy, Malta and Switzerland. Many of these works are surprisingly 'high brow', too, and often written by major writers – Mercier, Dorat, Beaumarchais and even Voltaire. Some commentators might also consider much of this literature socially subversive: Beaumarchais broke deeply entrenched literary protocols when he presented a sharp-witted and cunning valet, Figaro, as his comic hero, rather than his conniving aristocratic master, the comte d'Almaviva. In a scandalous sequel, *Le Mariage de Figaro*, he would go further, presenting Almaviva as an ungrateful wretch, whose attempts to invoke his *droit de seigneur* over Figaro's virginal fiancée provided the fulcrum on which the action turned. Also potentially subversive were the pamphlets about Louis XV, which pried into secrets of state formerly considered the king's business, exposing a nexus of cronyism at court and sexual–political corruption. The fabricated and highly novelistic *Mémoires authentiques de Mme la comtesse du Barri* went even further, inviting readers to erotic contemplation of 'the charms' of the royal mistress. There is anticlericalism and religious scepticism, too, particularly in Patrick Brydone's account of southern Italy and Malta, together with the destabilizing libertinism of de Luchet and Dorat.[6]

Yet although our crate contains a play by Voltaire, undisputed king of the *philosophes*, its contents do not quite live up to DeFrance's heroic image. It lacks the classic fare of the Enlightenment – Montesquieu's political works, Voltaire's polemics or religious scepticism, Helvétius or d'Holbach's corrosive atheistic texts, or Raynal's strident abolitionism – perhaps because local publishers like Bassompierre, Jean-Edmé Dufour, Jean-Louis Boubers and Plomteux already produced a plentiful supply at a competitive price.[7] There is, however, a *prima facie* case for seeing a more popular, accessible form of Enlightenment here. Many themes or tropes familiar to scholars of the *siècle des Lumières* are present: anticlericalism, religious scepticism, libertinism, cosmopolitanism and political reformism. It is their rich diversity of forms that is disorientating – together with the clear absence of Enlightenment classics. Were such works to be found in the STN's other ballots – and did they penetrate the more reactionary corners of Europe? To answer that we have to cast our net more widely and, following the crates depicted by Leonard DeFrance, look to parts of Europe without a strong indigenous Enlightenment publishing industry. The crates addressed to Lisbon stacked outside *À l'Égide de Minerve* hint that Portugal might be just such a place.

Like the Liège bookseller depicted by DeFrance, the STN traded with several book merchants in the Iberian peninsular. For example, on 26 October 1779, they despatched *ballot* V.F. n. 255 to Bertrand, *veuve et fils*, in Lisbon. This particular consignment would certainly not seem out of place in DeFrance's *tableau*, for its primary contents were volumes 18–35 of the work that more than any other epitomized the French Enlightenment: Diderot and d'Alembert's *Encyclopédie*.[8] As members of the consortium that produced the third edition, the STN were major suppliers of this work. This edition appeared in a cheap quarto format and hence reached a wider audience than the previous folio editions.[9] An enormous endeavour, the *Encyclopédie* tied up huge amounts of capital. For its publishers and retailers each sale was an important event. It made the Bertrands, who took three-and-a-half more copies from the STN over the years, valued customers. However, the *Encyclopédie* was not alone in the crate. It also contained a copy of Emer Vatel's *Questions de droit naturel*, a foundational text in international relations, and two recently printed copies of the sixth volume of the Lausanne edition of Antoine-Friedrich Busching's *Géographie*, which was still in the process of publication and would eventually run to twelve volumes. The STN accounts reveal that they had already sent copies of Busching's first five volumes in an earlier despatch, on 3 July, in *ballot* V.B. n. 143. That *ballot* also contained volumes 1–17 of their *Encyclopédie*. The October consignment was completing the partial sets sent earlier.

Reflecting the different preoccupations of eighteenth-century readers, the contents of these crates attest the variety and richness of Enlightenment print culture. They remind us, too, that the Enlightenment's leading figures were often controversial and even reviled in some quarters, their ideas and values deeply contested. The crate that transported Voltaire's *Don Pèdre* from Neuchâtel to Liège also contained pamphlets attacking its author. Libertine erotic novels and anticlerical travelogues were escorted by religiously inspired conduct literature.

Such glimpses of the popular and influential literature of the late Enlightenment intrigue and tantalize, but they are hard to interpret in isolation. The Enlightenment they represent remains elusive and just out of our reach. We still need to prise the lids off many more book crates to discover precisely what titles appealed to which readers where and when. This process will require more than just counting and reading books. We will also need to discover adequate methods to analyse our findings, through a close reading of individual texts and distant reading of key tropes. As a starting point, we need to gather data about many hundreds of crates.

Fortunately, we no longer need to visit the archives of the STN in the Bibliothèque Publique et Universitaire de Neuchâtel to discover what was hidden inside their crates. For the details of every consignment of books recorded in the STN account books have been carefully compiled into a single research database, which is now available online through Western Sydney University. The database gives bibliographical information on every book traded by the STN; the dates when copies were recorded entering or leaving its silos; the origins and destinations of those books; the names, professions, domiciles, gender, and details of the surviving correspondence of the customers who bought or supplied them; and *ballot* numbers when available. That information has been enriched by further data locating the places in the database geopolitically; categorizing the content of books; or grouping client professions into higher categories. Wherever necessary explanatory notes were also added.

As a result, this book reflects upon the development and application of new technologies and methodologies. The outcome of a uniquely rich digital project to map the dissemination of print in eighteenth-century Europe, it explains the hurdles and challenges inherent in our sources and methods and how they were overcome. Hopefully the kaleidoscope of eighteenth-century print culture and twenty-first century digital approaches it offers will be both illuminating and enriching. For it promises both a new gateway into the study of global culture across the print era and fresh insights into the Enlightenment. As a first step, however, we need to understand how the Enlightenment has been defined and viewed by historians. That is the purpose of the rest of this chapter.

The Enlightenment is a fundamentally contested term: it has many competing narratives. One of the most enduring remains the conviction that the Enlightenment was a religiously and politically radical movement that prepared the French Revolution by attacks on Christianity, which in turn undermined a sacralized Bourbon throne. This teleological (some would say fallacious) association of Enlightenment and Revolution has deep roots. Paradoxically, it predates the Revolution, as Darrin McMahon has shown.[10] Enlightenment sceptics, above all Roger Chartier, have (somewhat playfully) claimed that the French revolutionaries 'invented' the Enlightenment in order to establish their intellectual lineage.[11] McMahon provides compelling evidence to the contrary, suggesting that the construction of the French Enlightenment as a radical *philosophe* campaign to undermine the throne while attacking the altar can be traced back before 1789 to the literary and polemical writings of counter-Enlightenment publicists such as Augustin Barruel, Jacob Vernes and Charles-Louis Richard. These clerical pamphleteers denounced the impious works of the Baron d'Holbach and his *philosophe* associates in near apocalyptic terms. Drawing little if any distinction between the moderate deism of Voltaire and the full-blooded materialism of d'Holbach, Diderot and Boulanger, they suggested that the impending triumph of atheism would herald social and political disintegration. Their warnings had no more impact than those of Cassandra. However, after the Revolution, Barruel had the satisfaction of outlining the effects of the alleged *philosophe* conspiracy in his celebrated *Mémoires pour server à l'histoire du jacobinisme français*. Written in exile and published by the exiled neuchâtelois bookseller Pierre-François Fauche in Hamburg in 1797–8, Barruel's conspiracy theories contributed to establishing the idea that the Enlightenment was centred on a small band of Paris-based *philosophes* who were inherently opposed all organized religion, but particularly Catholicism. His claims had a wide resonance, particularly in counter-revolutionary circles. Even the most judicious of the revolutionary émigrés, the protestant Genevan political journalist Jacques Mallet Du Pan, accepted the theory in part, though he felt Barruel had cast his web too widely. In a combative polemical essay entitled 'Of the influence of philosophy on the origins of the French Revolution', Mallet absolved Voltaire, Rousseau and their acolytes of responsibility. The real criminals, he argued, were Diderot and Condorcet, who were 'promotors, partisans and protectors' of 'a class of opinions equally subversive of religion, morality and society'. These had spawned 'a crowd of fanatic pedants, sophists and demoniacs' who had 'seized upon the revolution as by right of conquest'.[12]

Although his tone is very different, Mallet's account bears striking similarities to the ideas of the most prolific and controversial of contemporary historians of the Enlightenment, Jonathan Israel.[13] Like Mallet, Israel draws a distinction between moderate enlighteners, such as Voltaire, and a small bunch of radicals, including Condorcet, Diderot, d'Holbach and Raynal. According to Israel, this bi-polarism was essential to the Enlightenment's nature and dates back deep into the seventeenth century. For the radical wing drew its inspiration and strength above all from the materialist thought of Dutch philosopher Baruch Spinoza (1632–77). Between radical and moderate poles there was little middle ground. According to Israel, Spinoza's great contribution was to argue that the universe was comprised of just one substance, matter. By disposing of the soul–matter duality of medieval thought, Spinoza's posthumously published *Ethics* (1677) left no room for God, the soul, miracles, revelation, divine providence, the afterlife or ecclesiastical authority. Such argumentation also led many thinkers ineluctably, if not inevitably, towards radicalism in politics as well. According to Israel, one-substance materialism tended to inspire a commitment to democratic, republican, egalitarian politics and human rights. Spinoza himself is notable, says Israel, as the first 'great democratic philosopher' and foundational advocate for freedom of thought and expression, as opposed to freedom of conscience.[14]

However, for almost a century after the publication of Spinoza's *Ethics*, the radical Enlightenment was marginalized by its more moderate cousin, and remained the preserve of a relatively small band of thinkers and intellectuals. They included several late-Enlightenment figures, most notably Condorcet, Diderot, d'Holbach and Raynal and Boulanger, Helvétius, Naigeon and Saint-Lambert. In contrast, while the moderate Enlightenment might loosely be described as secularist, it also harboured various types of deist, including many enlightened Christians. Its latitudinarian umbrella included the deist Voltaire and the adherents of Locke and Newton, Turgot, Leibniz and Wolff. In politics, the moderate Enlightenment shared the radicals' commitment to reason and empiricism and was generally reformist in a gradualist sense, but its adherents were quite happy to work with existing political authority. Indeed, most moderates embraced monarchy and many favoured enlightened absolutism. For this reason, Israel argues, the moderate Enlightenment proved incapable of radical reforms in an age characterized by widespread and growing popular discontent. By about 1770, the failure of moderate Enlightenment was becoming increasingly obvious. Constrained by the need to respect monarchy, social hierarchy and, indeed, religious authority, the reformers were 'unable to secure even a comprehensive toleration and extensive legal reform', let alone establish more representative forms of government or overturn serfdom and colonial slavery.

Thus Israel argues that by 1785 an initial enthusiasm for enlightened absolutism had 'cooled' among radical enlighteners, including Brissot, Condorcet and Gorani.[15] Further, the failure of reform allowed radical activists to seize the political initiative, by articulating critiques of government, religion and society that allowed them to capture widespread popular support, particularly in the French Revolution. A variety of one-substance materialists, including Brissot and Condorcet but also Mirabeau and the abbé Siéyès, were able to seize the helm of events. Their ideas were fundamental to the policies of the French Revolution of 1789 to 1792. Sadly, however, this small band of founding fathers of modern liberal democracy were quickly overthrown by the militant *sans culottes* and their Jacobin allies, who were inspired largely by the anti-Enlightenment ideology of Rousseau. The values of radical Enlightenment remained eclipsed too for much of the nineteenth and twentieth centuries, before emerging with renewed vigour to become established norms across most of the Western world after the horrors of the Second World War.

Israel's interpretation – set out at present over four formidable volumes and over 3,500 pages – has ignited heated controversy. It has, however, drawn up the battlelines in modern Enlightenment historiography in ways that might usefully illuminate our discussion. Before we do that, it is worth observing that the STN – and Neuchâtel more generally – has a particular relevance for Israel's theories. The STN was founded at the very moment that Israel suggests that the political failure of moderate Enlightenment was becoming clear and the radical Enlightenment re-emerging with new vigour. In Israel's telling, the renaissance of the radical Enlightenment began with the publication between 1751 and 1772 of Diderot and d'Alembert's *Encyclopédie* (a work generally seen as less radical than Israel portrays it).[16] However, the seven trumpets of Israel's materialist apocalypse were d'Holbach's *Système de la nature* (1770), *Bon Sens* (1772), *Système social* (1773), *Politique naturelle* (1773) and *Morale universelle* (1776); Helvétius' posthumous *De l'homme* (1773); and Raynal's *Histoire philosophique et politique des établissements et du commerce des Européens dans les Deux Indes* (1770), a 'project for world revolution' which 'won the general approval ... of the entire literary world'.[17] The earliest of these works was the *Système de la nature*, arguably the most important and intellectually coherent of all materialist polemics. First printed by Rey in Amsterdam in November 1769, it was rapidly pirated, not least by the nascent STN, who between December 1770 and April 1771 produced an edition for the Belgian publisher Jean-Louis Boubers.[18] As we have seen, the STN was also enmeshed in the *Encyclopédie* project as co-publisher of the third edition.[19] They also published an extremely successful edition of Raynal's *Histoire philosophique des Deux Indes*, and they traded in all the other works mentioned in this paragraph. The STN were thus heavily implicated in the revival of radical Enlightenment. Thereafter they also served as publisher for one of Israel's radical enlighteners, Brissot, who commissioned them to produce some of his pre-revolutionary works.[20] They also dealt extensively in those of another, Mirabeau, who published several libertine and political freethinking works with other Neuchâtel publishers.[21] The history of the STN therefore seems inextricably tied to the personnel and heyday of the 'radical Enlightenment', as defined by Israel. Thus the STN database can serve as an invaluable heuristic tool for evaluating his arguments.[22]

Some caution is necessary, however, in using the STN dissemination data to gauge the influence of radical Enlightenment. Although Israel has used STN statistics to argue for the importance of radical Enlightenment writers, in particular Raynal and d'Holbach, he has also insisted that prior to the Revolution, the radical Enlightenment was the preserve of intellectual elites. It would be 'absurd' to suggest, he argues, that it was a popular movement: moderate mainstream Enlightenment always commanded a greater audience.[23] Indeed, Israel contends that while the radical Enlightenment was the primary influence shaping the outcomes of the Revolution of 1789–92, it was not the cause of the initial revolutionary tumult. Israel has also argued that even among radical Enlightenment thinkers, the influence of Spinozism and one-substance materialism was not always acknowledged or recognized. For both reasons, Israel's intellectual history narrative of the origin of the French and other European revolutions of the period offers relatively little space for dissemination studies, or indeed the social, cultural or global–historical explanations that have dominated revolutionary historiography in recent years, including the plethora of works delineating the role of the public sphere. In that sense his is a very traditional intellectual history.

Not surprisingly perhaps, Israel's interpretation of the Enlightenment has triggered large scale debate. While even his critics generally admire his erudition, the global reach of his survey, and the scale of his ambition, particularly in attempting to uncover the link between Enlightenment and Revolution, many are scathing in their criticisms. It has been suggested that Israel's account vastly exaggerates the importance of Spinoza and the influence of his ideas (and indeed of ideas in general). Few accept the concept of an Enlightenment whose origins lie deep in the seventeenth century, which absorbs within it much of the 'scientific revolution', and whose original locus lies in the Netherlands rather than France. Dan Edelstein, whose path-breaking *The Enlightenment: A Genealogy* must be seen, at least in part, as a riposte to Israel, is adamant that the intellectual origins of the Enlightenment lie in France in a very particular academic debate – the dispute between the ancients and the moderns, and the intellectual confidence and values associated with the triumph of the latter. Edelstein does not deny the importance of divergent national Enlightenments, nor the historiography which has accreted around them since the publication by Roy Porter and Mikuláš Teich of the seminal essay collection *The Enlightenment in National Context* in 1981. He does, however, reaffirm that the Enlightenment was to a large extent French-inspired and, in its early days, a Francocentric phenomenon, just as most contemporaries believed.[24]

Commentators also have doubts about links between one-substance materialism and political radicalism. Alan Kors, author of the definitive study of d'Holbach's *coterie*, is adamant, for example, that the leading philosophical materialists were far from radical or democratic in their politics.[25] Other materialists, as Harvey Chisick notes, drew rather different, and perhaps more radical, conclusions from materialist premises: for La Mettrie they led to hedonism, while the Marquis de Sade advocated a radically amoral sexual libertarianism based on no standard beyond the fulfilment on one's physical urges, however depraved.[26] If these critiques are correct, the causal connection between radical Enlightenment and French Revolution appears to disintegrate. Other critics of the Israel thesis question whether Spinoza should be read as an atheist or even an unbeliever.[27] In the *Ethics*, Spinoza's account of a universal substance and consequential 'do-as-you-would-be-done-by' moral system can be read in pantheist terms, with God conceived as coextensive and consubstantial with all matter. This reading goes back at least as far as Pierre Bayle's *Dictionnaire historique et critique*, which was first published in 1697.[28]

Reviewers and critics have also highlighted that Israel's argument hinges upon the essential duality of the Enlightenment, its bifurcation into separate, distinct and diametrically opposed moderate mainstream and (long-marginalized) radical strands.

Yet both Israel and his critics recognize that the writings of some major Enlightenment figures incorporate moderate, radical and even anti-Enlightenment strands of thought. Some critics also emphasize major external influences on the Enlightenment, including religious thought and eastern philosophy. Carolina Armenteros points out that the Augustinian liberal current within Christianity could converge with Spinozism on issues such as 'self-government, egalitarianism and anti-slavery', as with the prominent revolutionary deputy, the abbé Grégoire, whose thought drew on civic humanism and the 'socially insurrectionary aspects' of Christ's teachings.[29] Nor were radicals entirely united among themselves. Diderot, for example, wrote a *Réfutation d'Helvétius* (1774), which highlighted political differences between the two men. Likewise, as Keith Baker points out, the supposed dichotomy between the moderate enlightener Turgot and his 'radical' acolyte Condorcet from the 1770s ignores significant nuances and similarities in political outlook, as well as Condorcet's rejection of Helvétius.[30] Such critiques suggest that to link the Revolution causationally to any one strand of Enlightenment thought involves dangerous oversimplification.

Many historians go further. Annalien de Dijn emphasizes the prevalence of monarchism across Europe, even among Enlightenment progressives, many of whom considered eighteenth-century monarchies as both liberal and modern. Conversely, she dismisses the view of the Enlightenment as politically, as well as religiously, radical, and hence the herald of both radical secularism and democratic political modernity. This she labels the 'Myth of Enlightenment'.[31] However, the intellectual tradition she denounces, which can be traced back to Barruel and his counter-Enlightenment allies, has deep roots and Israel is not alone in viewing the Enlightenment in those terms. His outlook is shared by Peter Gay and Robert Darnton, who have claims to be considered the greatest American post-war historians of the Enlightenment. Unlike Barruel, however, Gay, Israel and Darnton are united in celebrating – or as de Dijn might have it *mythologizing* – the Enlightenment as a progressive force and harbinger of the modern democratic west. Of these three 'mythmakers', it is Darnton, rather than Israel, who makes the boldest claims, for he finds a causative link between Enlightenment and the outbreak of the Revolution in the scribblings of a host of radicalized Grub Street hacks. It was their works, he contends, which sapped the ideological roots of the monarchy. Since Darnton's interpretation of the Enlightenment is indelibly linked to the STN, it merits our close attention.

Darnton's early work offers an exhilarating alternative to the vision Peter Gay outlined in *The Enlightenment. An Interpretation*, a work considered seminal in the late 1960s and 1970s. Gay's Enlightenment – which like Barruel's was predominantly a French affair – pitted a little band of *philosophes* against the forces of darkness: the Catholic Church and the confessional Bourbon state. It was, as Gay freely admitted, a history of the Enlightenment 'in its narrow sense – the Enlightenment of the *philosophes*'.[32] Gay's heroes were General Voltaire and his little troupe of bold and progressive lieutenants, d'Alembert, Condillac, Condorcet, Diderot, Montesquieu, Turgot, even Rousseau, whom Gay styled 'the party of humanity'. Their shock troops were the familiar texts of the Enlightenment literary canon: the *Encyclopédie*, Voltaire's *Dictionnaire philosophique* and *Candide*, Montesquieu's *Esprit des lois*, Rousseau's *Du Contrat Social* and so on. In such works, the *philosophes* 'undertook to devise forms – a social, ethical, political and aesthetic program – for the sake of freedom'.³³ Stirring stuff. However, in his seminal essay 'The High Enlightenment and the Low-Life of Literature', Darnton proposed a revolutionary new approach, calling for a literary history 'from below'.³⁴

In a nutshell, Darnton argued that historians and literary scholars should look beyond the canon of literary works habitually taught by university faculties and seek to recover texts important in their own time. More controversially, Darnton suggested that the cultural origins of the Revolution lay in the underground literary output of scores of literary hacks and would-be Voltaires, who found themselves excluded from the patronage networks which guarded on the path to fame and fortune in late ancien régime France. Unable to make an honest crust, such 'hacks' were driven to desperate expedients, publishing gutter pornography, salacious political *libelles*, anticlerical propaganda and not infrequently all three. Such works, he suggested, 'desacralized' the Old Regime, stripping it of its legitimacy in the eyes of its subjects, and began the political education of the revolutionary *sans culottes*, who unable to assimilate Rousseau in the original, avidly consumed pornographic popularizations such as Charles Théveneau de Morande's notorious *libelle* the *Gazetier cuirassé* (1771).³⁵ Forty years on, in *The Devil in the Holy Water* (2010), Darnton expanded these arguments in a formidable study of how the literature of character assassination and radical devaluation produced by Morande and his ilk operated and evolved from pre-revolutionary Grub Street into the French Revolution, reaching murderous new heights in the Terror. In Darnton's reading the literature of defamation holds the key to understanding much of the trajectory from Enlightenment to revolutionary excess.³⁶

Between 'The High Enlightenment and the Low-Life of Literature' and *The Devil in the Holy Water*, Darnton published his award-winning *Forbidden Best-Sellers of Pre-Revolutionary France* (1996), which was researched primarily in the STN archive.³⁷ It was this work which more than any other inspired the French Book Trade in Enlightenment Europe (FBTEE) project and hence the current book. Effectively, Darnton used *Forbidden Best-Sellers* to answer his own impassioned clarion call for a literary history 'from below', offering a case study of just how historians might proceed to identify and rehabilitate forgotten but historically significant texts. By studying the correspondence of a cherry-picked sample of French booksellers with the STN, Darnton felt confident that he had identified and assessed the most important works in the vast underground literature of the French Enlightenment, thereby providing an empirical underpinning to his earlier work. The centrepiece of his efforts was tables of the STN's bestselling *livres philosophiques* – the trade name for all freethinking illegal works – and their authors.³⁸ These, and his case studies of three titles from near the top of his bestseller tables, seemed to bear out his earlier suggestions that the French ancien régime had been undermined in a tidal wave of anticlericalism and political smut.

Close analysis of Darnton's claims raises a series of methodological questions. First, his methods measured bookseller orders rather than demand satisfied and failed to establish how closely the two coincided. Second, Darnton's statistics only comprehend the (highly) illegal sector, and it is not clear how significant this was as a proportion of the STN's whole trade with France, nor how French sales compared to the rest of

Europe. Finally, how representative or typical were the STN and their trade, even in comparison with the other cross-frontier publishing houses trading with France?[39]

Like much of the literature described here, Darnton's *œuvre* remains highly contentious and its relevance to our understanding of the Enlightenment contested. Some authors – Harvey Chisick, for example – have argued that Grub Street discourses were at best marginal to the Enlightenment mainstream; others such as Jeremy Popkin and Elizabeth Eisenstein style it an 'alternative to the Enlightenment' or the Enlightenment's 'other'.[40] To some extent these criticisms arise from questions of definition. But on another level they are susceptible to a degree of statistical analysis. We might, for example, be able to establish the size and composition of the illegal sector, and measure how far it accords with Darnton's descriptions. We might also analyse when and where the various genres of illegal literature enjoyed their heaviest sales, something that is not possible when using Darnton's statistics.[41] Herein lies one of the chief merits of the FBTEE database and current study.

This discussion of Enlightenment historiography is not intended to be definitive. Indeed, it has barely touched upon, or ignored entirely, some of the most important and innovative historians working in the field, including Keith Baker, Tim Blanning, Roger Chartier, Dan Gordon, Dena Goodman, Lynn Hunt, Colin Jones, Antoine Lilti, Thomas Munck, Dorinda Outram and Daniel Roche. Given the volume of material that now appears annually on the Enlightenment, any attempt at a comprehensive survey would indeed be a daunting task. Moreover, where Gay, Israel and to a certain extent Darnton stress the essential unity of the Enlightenment, much of the historiography of the last thirty-five years emphasizes fragmentation. We have different and sometimes competing national Enlightenments, high Enlightenments, Catholic Enlightenments, Protestant Enlightenments, Rosicrucian Enlightenments, counter and anti-Enlightenments. Faced with such complexity and contrasting visions, some might be tempted to abandon the Enlightenment entirely as a historical and analytical category, except perhaps as a loose label to describe the (short) eighteenth century. This would be rash, not least because so many contemporaries considered themselves to be enlightened and vigorously debated the meaning of Enlightenment. For practical purposes, it may make more sense to think of the Enlightenment as a loosely defined set of values inside a cultural system within which contemporaries made or evaluated claims to be enlightened. This is the preferred approach of this book. It allows us to conceptualize and discuss Enlightenment in general and particular Enlightenments without getting bogged down in ever-finer nuances of definition. This also enables us to use Israel, Darnton and Gay's work to set many of the broader parameters and themes for our discussion without allowing them to set the precise terms of debate.

Chapter 2 picks up on a theme that Israel's argument allows him to sidestep: the role of print culture in the Enlightenment and its wider contribution to the public sphere. Such an examination must for our purposes include a consideration of the book's place in print culture, and contrast books with other printed products. Having done that, Chapter 3 considers in more detail why and how we might search for Enlightenment in a single Swiss print shop, using the archives of the STN. This chapter and the two that follow necessarily revisit arguments set out by Mark Curran in the companion volume to this book, particularly his historiographically important, if unsurprising, revelation that the STN mostly sold Swiss books.⁴² It also sets out why a digital humanities approach should allow us to draw wider, more 'representative' conclusions from the STN data nevertheless. However, to interpret that data correctly, we need a proper appreciation of the different local markets that the STN served. Thus Chapter 4 surveys and explores 'the intellectual geography of the STN'. It offers extensive case studies of the STN's least explored markets, notably Britain and Sweden.⁴³ Further case studies appear throughout the two volumes of *The French Book Trade in Enlightenment Europe* and other existing studies.⁴⁴

The second part of the book examines the corpus of books traded by the STN and assesses their significance. Naturally enough it begins with a discussion of the works that the STN sales figures suggest might be considered 'Enlightenment bestsellers'. However, the quest to uncover a representative list of STN's 'bestsellers' proves unexpectedly complex, and so the fifth chapter also proposes an analytical framework for exploring the STN data. This framework will be applied in the chapters that follow.

An analysis based on bestsellers alone can only take us so far, since bestsellers only accounted for a minority of the STN's sales. To understand the full body of STN data, we need more inclusive and sophisticated tools to help us to categorize and comprehend the corpus of literature they sold. Chapter 6, 'Troubling taxonomies' explains the systems of book classification employed in the FBTEE database. This discussion serves as a prelude to Chapter 7, 'Harvesting the Literary Field', which examines the main contours of the literature sold by the STN and offers comparisons with the findings of other surveys of late eighteenth-century reading. This reveals suggestive differences between surveys, raising important questions for the four case-study chapters that follow.

Each case study looks at a different body or trope of the literature. Chapter 8 addresses the thorny question 'how central was cosmopolitanism to the European Enlightenment?' It assesses how international or cosmopolitan the STN literature and its audience might be considered, using a variety of measures, including a path-breaking study of the interpenetration of literature across digital datasets relating to different countries. This and the final two chapters draw inspiration from Dorinda Outram's conception of Enlightenment as a set of 'capsules of [intellectual] debates' or discussions, none of which can be uniquely situated to the Enlightenment era, but which came together with particular salience and prominence in the eighteenth century.⁴⁵ By treating cosmopolitanism in this way, we can discover how and how far readers could use books to encounter societies other than their own, both in and beyond Europe, and the genres in which these encounters might take place. Hence Chapter 8 is both a study in the sources of general knowledge and the frontiers of popular imagination.

The issue of frontiers and their porosity also looms large in Chapter 9, 'The Anatomy of the Illegal Sector'. Perhaps the most historiographically revisionist chapter in the study, it reveals the extent to which the STN's clandestine trade can be said to match Robert Darnton's depiction. It reveals a much more complex and nuanced picture than previous work, challenges central pillars of Darnton's theory of desacralization, and partially rehabilitates Peter Gay's view of Enlightenment. Conversely it begins an exploration of the real presence, or absence, of the Dutch philosopher Spinoza and his ideas in the STN corpus. This is a discussion that continues into our final two chapters. They concern the twin pillars of de Dijn's 'Myth of Enlightenment': radical religious ideas and revolutionary politics.

Chapter 10, 'Philosophie, Science, Faith', considers the extent to which faith and science are antagonistic or mutually supportive in the STN corpus. It also reassesses the prevalence and forms of religious faith present in and beyond this literature. This exploration builds on a growing reorientation towards the Christian in Enlightenment studies. Whereas Gay, Israel and Darnton insist on the animosity of Enlightenment – or in Israel's case 'radical Enlightenment' – to organized religion, a growing body of scholarship emphasizes that particularly beyond French borders, the Enlightenment and a more rational form of Christianity were not necessarily antithetical.[46] In British, German and Swiss contexts, to name but three, it has long been fashionable to talk of an enlightened Christianity, stripped of its more superstitious manifestations (including belief in miracles, transubstantiation and the intercession of Saints). Empowered by this analysis, some historians have even dared to smash the Ark of the Covenant and propose that France, too, witnessed a Christian Enlightenment. The arguments in favour of such an analysis look beyond the content of Christian writings to consider their rhetorical strategies, literary genres and modes of argument. Hence by the 1760s or 1770s it seems that the devil no longer had all the best tunes – Christian apologist writers such as Vernes and Barruel had turned the *philosophes* own strategies against them and were using plays and novels as vehicles for attacking materialist thought. Some Christian writers also vaunted their own *lumières*. Hence one recent prize-winning essay argues that while a Christian writer such as Georg von Holland instinctively understood that he was no Voltaire, 'he never for a moment considered himself less enlightened'.[47] Just how the Christian versus materialist dynamic played out in the STN corpus, which includes both the STN's piracy of d'Holbach's *Système de la nature* and the first edition of Holland's refutation *Réflexions philosophiques sur le Système de la nature*, is a topic worthy of our attention, as is the extent of religious and irreligious publishing more generally.

So, too, is the question of politics in print, the subject of the final chapter. Here of course Gay, Israel and Darnton are examples of a much longer tradition. Barruel and generations of historians who followed him were equally convinced of the political radicalism of Enlightenment thought. Among nineteenth-century liberals, who lauded Enlightenment ideology as containing the origins of their own credo, it was an article of faith that the Enlightenment had been above all a political movement built around liberal–constitutional and secularizing values. This commonplace view, held tenaciously by some intellectual historians well into the twentieth century,[48] is still embedded in many Western Civilisation primers. It was scarcely contradicted, too, by the rise of academic Marxism, the great intellectual movement of the early to mid-twentieth century. Many Marxist historians viewed the Enlightenment as the superficial expression of bourgeois self-interest, and hence barely worthy of serious study. In the political sphere, that self-interest took the form of liberal constitutionalism as enshrined in the French revolutionary Declaration of the Rights of Man and Citizen.[49] However, more recent commentators emphasize the general political conservatism of many Enlightenment thinkers including, as we have noted, d'Holbach and Diderot.[50]

This makes the political context of the STN particularly interesting, for if Neuchâtel itself had elected a Prussian overlord, many of its Swiss neighbours, and particularly Geneva, enjoyed republican forms of government. Moreover, from an early stage in the 'age of democratic revolutions', which lasted from around 1760 to 1848–9, Geneva was rocked by political clashes between the traditional oligarchic elite and more democratic elements. There was repeated turmoil from 1765 to 1770 and in 1782 a democrat revolt was only extinguished by the intervention of French and Bernese forces. These events find an echo in the STN's output, which includes political pamphlets produced on behalf of the defeated democratic *représentatif* party. Any appreciation of the political content of the STN corpus must consider the Swiss political context as well as French, Prussian and European dimensions. It must consider works on international relations, political theory; history primers; pamphlets on French finances, Genevan insurrections, and the French king's sex life, including the defamatory *libelles* on which Darnton sets so much store. Navigating from Swiss politics to French history in this way problematizes attempts to find explanations of revolutionary causation or outcomes in the political literature of the late Enlightenment. However, it promises to reveal a great deal about the political possibilities, passions and imagination of the revolutionary generation.

The approach outlined here may not provide a definitive definition of Enlightenment, as Peter Gay attempted. Nor will it reorientate our focus to specific bodies of texts or ideas, as Robert Darnton and Jonathan Israel have done. However, our peering into the STN's book crates may just offer correctives to all three of these historians, and a more nuanced survey of the dissemination and impact of francophone literary culture in the late Enlightenment.[51] It opens a window on a rather alien culture. To understand what we can view there we need to understand the place of the book in the larger culture of print. That is the subject of our next chapter.

2

The Book in Print Culture

In all probability, neither the proprietor of the Liège bookshop *À L'Égide de Minerve* nor the directors of the STN ever asked 'What is a book?' Nor would they have pondered the related but more complex question addressed by this chapter: 'What forces shaped eighteenth-century European print culture and how should we locate the book within that culture?' In all probability they also lost no sleep over other questions of definition which bemuse book historians. Are pamphlets books? What about four-page folded fliers? Or single leaf broadsides? Is a three-volume set one book or several? When does a book become a serial? When does a flier become a pamphlet? Can loose printed sheets be considered books? When does a reprint become a distinct edition, or a radically rewritten text a new work? These questions were foreign to their business concerns. The STN's approach to such matters was practical, commercially driven and hard-nosed. For their purposes (and ours) a book was whatever they chose to classify as such in their general accounts or advertise as a separate title in their catalogues. That tended to be any volume that might be sold independently, whether drawn from the STN's *fonds* (own editions) or their *livres d'assortissement* (miscellaneous stock from other publishers, sometimes also known in the STN accounts as *marchandise générale*).[1] Thus the 'books' sold by the STN and counted in the FBTEE database include pamphlet literature, almanacs or single miscellaneous volumes of periodicals. They ranged in length from four-page prepublication brochures through to multivolume histories or encyclopaedias. The database omits items the STN printed but did not sell commercially, such as one-off commissioned job printings of decrees or forms for the local administration, trade and calling cards, or hymnbooks commissioned by local churches. These were not sold individually, so are not treated as 'books' in the STN accounts or itemized as part of their *fonds*. Hence they slip below the FBTEE project's radar. This largely mirrors the practice of the Bourbon government. When it surveyed the output of printers across France, those recorded as exclusively producing *ouvrages du diocèse* or *ouvrages de la ville* – that is, works for the local churches or municipal authorities – generally escaped the scrutiny accorded to commercially orientated printers.[2] The products of such job printing are, as Mark Curran notes in *Selling Enlightenment*, the 'dark matter' of the FBTEE survey – we are aware that they exist, but the database does not capture or quantify them.[3] Wherever necessary we must uncover them by other means. But before we get dragged into that particular 'black hole', let us begin with material we can measure.

At first glance the FBTEE project appears to privilege books above all other forms of print – pamphlets, journalistic products and popular ephemera – as a means of studying the Enlightenment. Since much recent work on the public sphere and popular culture has concentrated on these alternative genres of print, this might seem a retrograde step. Such a conclusion would be wrong for at least three reasons. First, because books, narrowly defined, were the standard vehicle for conveying complex ideas. Second, the categories of book, pamphlet, serial publication and ephemera are far from watertight and frequently intersect. For example, book reviews and advertisements for new titles feature prominently in many serial productions (and were sometimes their entire *raison d'être*). Likewise, pamphlets and abridgements often carried the ideas of major books and authors to a wider public. But thirdly, and most importantly, because, as we have just seen, the STN thought rather in terms of marketable merchandise than books per se. The *marchandise générale* and *livres de fonds* recorded in their accounts included a broad selection of printed products.

The presence of a wide variety of print genres in the STN accounts enhances their attractiveness as a historical source. In recent decades, as historians have increasingly questioned the primacy of the book in their accounts of the cultural impact of print, there has been a rising interest in the material conditions and cultural environments in which ideas were produced, articulated and circulated. Whereas intellectual historians operating in the early twentieth century were often content to conceive their narratives around the movement and evolution of free-floating ideas between great texts, their successors have generally located the Enlightenment squarely within both a 'social history of ideas' and the 'literary field' from which it emerged. A seminal contribution to this discussion was the work of the German Marxist sociologist Jürgen Habermas, first published in 1962 and finally translated into English as *The Structural Transformation of the Public Sphere* in 1989.[4]

Habermas contends that the eighteenth century witnessed the emergence of a politically autonomous rational–critical 'bourgeois' public capable of critiquing and shaping the state's political decisions. For many historians this development appears to be the primary mechanism behind many of the most significant social, political and cultural changes of the era. Habermas describes how this new 'public sphere' operated through both printed products, above all newsprint, and new sociable institutions, notably *salons*, debating societies, scientific academies, reading circles, subscription libraries, masonic lodges and coffee houses, where the public gathered to discuss ideas and political news. Hence print and the new sociable institutions were deeply intertwined: printed texts informed debate in sociable forums, and sociable institutions often stocked or even published works pertinent to their discussions. Both were heavily implicated in the era's most momentous changes thereby shaping the emergence of political and economic modernity.

Veritable lakes of historians' ink have been drained assessing the validity of Habermas' ideas and questioning his assertions that the public sphere was bourgeois, robustly autonomous and inherently rational–critical.[5] Such discussions often overlook the fact that Habermas' primary purpose was political and sociological rather than historical. He wished to explore a perceived systematic corruption in the quality of public discourse across the late modern period, as market capitalism and the state seized control of the media apparatus in advanced Western societies.[6] In his model, the eighteenth-century public sphere served as a potential utopia, in which a limited, enlightened public engaged in rational–critical discussion to interface with the state through the print media and the new institutions of Enlightenment civil society. Whether or not Habermas thought he was offering a strictly accurate picture of historical reality is probably irrelevant here, for historians have found tremendous heuristic power in his theories and his central thesis remains broadly accepted. By the late eighteenth century an increasingly assertive, expanding public was influencing policy discussions. Indeed, policy makers were increasingly recognizing 'public opinion' as a legitimizing political force, thereby accepting the ideological and moral claims of its self-appointed spokesmen.

More significantly, Habermas' implies that journalism – a relatively new genre – rather than 'the book' was the most significant form of print in the new public sphere. Journalism offered readers and authors new forms of relationship with texts and one another. It gave readers a regular point of contact with news information, opinion and authorial insinuation; provided regular cycles of feedback (for example by repeat purchases); and offered new possibilities of interaction between the journalist and readers (for example through letters columns). This potentially turns on its head the assumption of many previous literary scholars and historians that the book is the more influential and important form. Is such a conclusion warranted? One place to begin such an enquiry might be with a survey of the relative quantity and vitality of books, pamphlets, newsprint and ephemera.

By the late eighteenth century, books were becoming ubiquitous in urban culture, and increasingly visible in many rural areas, too. The scale of book production was unprecedented, and relative price levels lower than ever. The most sophisticated estimates for the global level of book production come from the Dutch-based Global Historical Bibliometrics project. It calculates book output across Europe in the second half of the eighteenth century at 628 million copies. Of these, more or less a quarter, 157 million, was produced in France. The other major production centres were Great Britain (138.5 million books), Germany (117 million), Italy (75.5 million), and the Netherlands (53 million). Other regions with large native French-speaking populations lagged behind: the Belgians produced just 4.8 million books and the Swiss a mere 4.6 million, figures which imply that over its twenty-five-year history the STN produced around 10 per cent of the country's entire output.[7]

We can also estimate the European output of French titles over the core period of the STN's existence, from 1770 to 1790. In the most systematic bibliographic survey of French-language titles produced in the eighteenth century, Pierre Conlon identifies 1,576 first editions published in 1770, rising to 1,950 in 1786, in a range of genres broadly reminiscent of the STN's stock. Adding second and subsequent editions of the more popular works might increase these totals by 50 per cent. As the average print run for a single eighteenth-century edition has generally been estimated at under 1,000 copies,[8] these figures imply that across Europe, the total output of French books was perhaps 2,500,000 to 3,000,000 copies per year. If we further assume that French-language books produced abroad were roughly balanced by foreign-language titles produced inside the Bourbon realm, this equates to an annual rate of production of around one book per ten inhabitants of France.[9] This figure is broadly similar to the statistics offered by the Global Historical Bibliometrics project. The infrastructure and manpower to support such a rate of output would accommodate a rapid acceleration of publishing at the end of the period – driven by an explosion of pamphleteering in the French Revolution.[10]

These raw figures suggest that the audience for books was much more extensive than the readership for newspapers, at least in France, the STN's biggest market. French post office records indicate that in 1781 there were 45,000 newspaper subscribers among a population of 25 million, or one subscription per six hundred people.[11] Assuming, like most historians and contemporaries, between four to ten readers per copy, this equates to one newspaper reader for every sixty to 150 inhabitants. The French audience for books was hence many times greater than for newsprint, particularly as books, too, were often devoured by multiple readers. The same was probably true in Switzerland, where serial sales probably equalled one for every one hundred to two hundred inhabitants. In 1781, the country (including Geneva and Neuchâtel) boasted twelve newspapers, eleven advertisers and ten periodicals, but most had miniscule circulations.[12] Subscriptions to the STN's own *Journal helvétique* fluctuated at around three hundred.[13]

Elsewhere in Europe the social penetration of newspapers was significantly higher. Some estimates suggest that by the 1780s in Britain, Germany and the Netherlands they may have been consumed by one household in three or four. In contrast, in Russia, Sweden, Spain and Portugal and parts of Italy newsprint was even rarer than in France. In these regions newspapers were probably not a major means for sharing political information and opinion. For many Europeans – even literate ones – political knowledge continued to come through oral sources, particularly the pulpit, and 'books', particularly printed pamphlets.

Furthermore, journalistic texts were often inadequate as sources of topical political information or opinion. Across most of Europe editorial reporting was in its infancy. Most newspapers were digests of facts (news information) compiled from other sources. Objectivity was achieved by including reports of the same event from multiple sources. Many newspapers did not include local news at all, usually as a result of censorship restrictions, but also through custom. The traditional gazette form of newspaper excluded local news, offering instead a set of verbatim reports and documents received from across Europe in set order. The most reliable and ubiquitous reports were official bulletins and publications, which were fleshed out with reports from travellers and merchants' correspondence. In this publishing culture, those seeking to influence local opinion tended to use one-off pamphlets. This was particularly true in societies operating heavy censorship restrictions, since pamphlets could be produced clandestinely and anonymously for one-off consumption, whereas the journalist's activity was necessarily public. He (or occasionally she) relied on the public knowing where to subscribe for his product and generally needed the goodwill of the local authorities to circulate it through the posts. Only under conditions of revolutionary disruption or relative press freedom could journalists escape these shackles.[14]

Hence across much of Europe the political pamphlet remained the primary means of political communication right through to the French Revolution. Nevertheless, since many pamphlets were of only local significance, ephemeral, or produced and distributed clandestinely within closed patronage networks, only certain sorts of pamphlets feature prominently in the STN database. These include pamphlets relating to the Genevan banker Jacques Necker's handling of French finances and others stemming from the political affairs of Geneva itself. Among them are radical propaganda pamphlets produced following the troubles of 1782 and the personal pleadings of the Genevan economist Théodore Rilliet de Saussure, whose marital and family disputes took on political dimensions. The STN's presses pumped out thousands of these pamphlets to order, but many were never intended for pan-European circulation. Their significance was primarily local and ephemeral.

In contrast, pamphlets relating to the private life of Louis XV and its political ramifications had a longer shelf life and wider market. The Louis XV pamphlets, though certainly clandestine, often blurred the barriers between pamphlet and book. Some pretended to be serious histories, recording the alleged sources for their anecdotes, sometimes at considerable length: Mouffle d'Angerville *Vie privée de Louis XV* (1781) ran to four volumes (though it was usually bound as two). Moreover, their interest was transcontinental: the *Vie privée*, for example, was translated into English and German. Such works suggest that the booksellers' catch-all categories of *fonds* and *marchandise générale* may be more useful than any crude attempt to distinguish between 'pamphlets' and 'books'. Although both terms are used hereafter, 'pamphlets' and 'books' should not be considered mutually exclusive categories.

Who, then, read the books and pamphlets published or sold by the STN? Mostly it is difficult to be sure, because the STN primarily sold by mail order to booksellers and allied publishers. The end customers are generally unknown. However, we do know that book markets were expanding, and their growth was underpinned by rising popular literacy across most of Europe. Unfortunately, such rises defy precise or comparative measurement because literacy involves a wide spectrum of skills.[15] The surviving sources available to measure these skills vary widely in form and quality across and between societies. Swedish ecclesiastical surveys of parishioners' literacy reveal that almost the entire population could read key prescribed religious texts by the mid-eighteenth century, but there is little comparable material elsewhere.[16] By default, historians have fallen back on 'signature literacy', the ability to sign a marriage certificate or similar document, as their standard measure. This measure appears to provide unequivocal evidence of rising literacy in most European societies across the century.[17] Among French men, signature literacy rose from 21 per cent around 1700 to 50 per cent by 1789. By the Revolution, it was near universal among bridegrooms in Paris and the north-east. The majority of brides could also write. Figures for other major capitals in north-western Europe were equally impressive. In Amsterdam 85 per cent of grooms could sign their names. In London the figure was 92 per cent for grooms and 74 per cent for brides as early as the 1750s.

Such figures may overestimate the gulf between male and female readers, since reading and writing were taught as separate skills. In poorer families, girls were taught to read religious texts but never held a pen. The figures also mask regions of substantially lower literacy – often well below 20 per cent – in remote rural southern and western France, as well as Eastern Europe and the Mediterranean basin. In Russia, the Iberian peninsular, Southern Italy and much of central Europe literacy rates were lower still. This was an obstacle to the circulation of books and enlightened ideas.[18]

Yet even among populations with high levels of signature literacy, reading skills varied considerably. In Germany, one of Europe's most literate and urbanized societies, perhaps 10 per cent of the population could read with ease in 1750, rising to 25 per cent by 1800.[19] But were the newly literate sections of the population reading books? If so, were they the sort of books sold by the STN?

With the exception of a handful of *éditions de luxe* and multivolume sets, most of the STN's merchandise was intended for a popular market and affordable on a metropolitan labourer's wage. Falls in the cost of paper and production accompanied by rising living standards facilitated a rapid expansion in book ownership between 1750 and 1789. These developments are reflected in the annual production of books per capita, which across Europe as a whole almost doubled between the first half of the eighteenth century and the second. The Global Historical Bibliometrics project estimates that between 1751 and 1800, annual average output of books per thousand inhabitants hit 118 in France, 122 in Germany, 192 in Britain, 209 in Sweden and a staggering 488 in the Netherlands. In contrast, Spain's rate of output was only twenty-eight per thousand, Poland's around twenty-two and Russia's less than six. Italy (86.5 books per thousand inhabitants) and Ireland (78) occupied a middle ground. The relatively low annual rates of production for polyglot Belgium (44.5 books per thousand inhabitants) and Switzerland (32.3) might imply that both were net importers of books.[20]

Given these figures it is likely that in the more literate francophone regions the STN's fare sometimes reached urban workers and perhaps even rural readers. In Europe's most literate urban societies, book ownership was near universal: in Mainz and Frankfurt it reached almost 90 per cent.[21] However, few German-speaking workers read French books,[22] and in the STN's main market, France, lower class book ownership figures are less impressive (though perhaps more ambiguous). The testimony of Parisian will inventories from 1750 to 1790 records that just under 23 per cent of Parisians bequeathed books. Nevertheless, book ownership extended deep down the social ladder. By 1780, some 35 per cent of labourers and 40 per cent of domestic servants left books, compared with just 13 and 20 per cent respectively three decades earlier.[23] Book ownership was apparently higher in Nancy and western cities such as Angers, Caen, Nantes, Rennes and Rouen, with 33 to 36 per cent of inventories listing books.[24] In Orléans between 1750 and 1787, 56 per cent of will inventories contain books. Across the period 1677 to 1787, more than three quarters of elite homes owned books, and two fifths of artisanal foyers. By contrast, in Orléans' rural hinterlands books were only recorded in one in ten homes. Clearly books were becoming increasingly common possessions among urban folk and apparently more ubiquitous in many provincial centres than the metropolis.[25] Other, less enduring forms of print, such as cheap broadsides, short occasional pamphlets, ephemera, chapbooks and the *bibliothèque bleue* were doubtless more common still.

By the later eighteenth century, book ownership was by no means limited to the larger towns. In the small, bilingual Lorraine community of Saint-Avold (whose population tripled from 825 to 2,800 across the century), we have inventories for a third of those who died between 1750 and 1790: just under 26 per cent contain books.[26] At the same period many peasant families in wealthy, highly literate north-eastern France owned devotional material or other printed works. A survey of the

Franche-Comté in the decades before the Revolution revealed that 6 per cent of peasants left books and that four fifths of these peasant libraries included religious or devotional literature.[27] Evidence presented in Chapter 10 suggests that these figures may significantly underestimate rural book ownership. Provincial publishers such as the Besançon printer–bookseller Jean-Félix Charmet printed a conservative mix of religious and other traditional fare in volume sufficient to imply an extensive peasant market. Demand for Enlightenment works was, by comparison, limited.[28]

Occasionally, the STN's end consumers emerge into sight, for the company sometimes dealt directly with private individuals. Some of these were relatively prominent persons. Such customers were probably atypical of the general run of readers who made occasional purchases at the STN's trade counter in Neuchâtel or through retailers in cities like Geneva, Paris, Turin, Amsterdam, Liège or Lisbon. But others were locals who had accounts with the STN or ordered books by post. In some cases, we know these individuals only by name, but for most the archive supplies professional details. These were collected in the FBTEE database via John Jeanprêtre's marvellous handlist of STN correspondents. As a result, the STN archive gives us a rare comparative insight into the book orders and preferred reading of various professional groups, particularly in the Neuchâtel region. Such data needs to be handled with care, since it contains multiple potential distortions. In some cases, there are bulk orders for works, often placed by authors. Figures for the legal profession, for example, contain entire editions written and commissioned by the young *philosophe* and future revolutionary Jacques-Pierre Brissot de Warville. The data on Protestant clergy includes bulk orders from Pomaret, a pastor from Ganges in the Languedoc, who commissioned the STN to publish several works for the use of his flock. Equally, some professional titles mask individuals who dabbled in the book trade, sometimes extensively. Jeanprêtre and hence the FBTEE database list the Avignon printer–booksellers Joly *veuve et fils* as 'merchants', although they ordered at least 1,155 books from the STN and supplied them with a further 952. Conversely, Pourtalès and Cie – who handled over 2,300 copies of Théodore Rilliet's pamphlets – were not book dealers but Neuchâtel bankers acting on the author's behalf. However, if we filter out such occasional discrepancies and multiple purchases, the database offers valuable insights into the reading of individual clients and professional groups.

The medical men in the database are a case in point. Forty-three medics appear among the STN's clients and correspondents, listed variously as *chirurgien* (surgeon), *chirurgien-major* (surgeon major), *médécin* (doctor), *docteur en médecine* (doctor of medicine), *physicien* (physician) and *médecin charlatan* (medical charlatan). Twelve of them bought books from the STN and three supplied them, most notably the medical publicist Samuel Tissot, who sent the STN 114 copies of his *Traité d'épilepsie*. A bestsellers' table of the books these medical men purchased from the STN would result in a deeply misleading view of doctors' reading, however, because one of them, Dr Châtelain of La Neuveville, bought two hundred copies of Jean-Frédéric Ostervald's religious primer, the *Abrégé de l'histoire sainte et du catéchisme*. Another, Jean-Emmanuel Gilibert, took six copies of his own controversial *Anarchie médicinale*. However, if we set aside these two titles, and concentrate on what is left, a mere thirty-nine books, the results are informative.

These thirty-nine books were all acquired in single copies, suggesting that they were intended for personal use. The bulk were taken by a doctor named Vernier, about whom little is known. He was presumably local to Neuchâtel, since the STN records give his name and profession, but he is not listed among the STN's correspondents. We can surmise, however, that Vernier took his professional reading very seriously. His six orders to the STN, placed between October 1774 and May 1777, comprise three volumes of the *Journal de médecine, chirurgerie, pharmacie*, the *Mémoires de l'académie royale de chirurgie* and seventeen other medically related texts. These include one work in Latin, described merely as *Dissertation de Gummi*. This probably refers to a treatise by the Halle-trained physician Ernst Anton Nikolai concerning medical uses of the stimulant gum ammoniac.[29]

However, Vernier was clearly more comfortable reading French, as his other orders show. Among them were four treatises on venereal disease, a significant medical and social issue in eighteenth-century Europe. The most intriguing of these was the clinician-playwright Réné Guillaume Lefébure de Saint Ildephont's disarmingly appetizing and possibly self-defeating *Le médecin de soi-même, ou méthode simple et aisée pour guérir les maladies vénériennes: avec la recette d'un chocolat aphrodisiaque, aussi utile qu'agréable*.[30] There were also two tomes discussing Robert Sutton's closely guarded and secret method of variolation (inoculation) against smallpox; two works on cancers; and one each on childbirth; dysentery; caustic methods for treating hernias; the medical use of castor oil; and the pulse.[31] More intriguing was the macabre-sounding *Réflexions sur la triste sort de personnes qui, sous une apparence de mort ont été enterrée vivante*. To judge from its title, this might appear a prurient work of limited practical utility. Its subtitle, however, makes clear that it discussed resuscitation and was probably as useful to Vernier's medical practice as any other treatise he bought.[32] Finally there were three other works, all seemingly connected to medicine, Hilaire-Marin Rouelle's chemistry textbook *Tableau de l'analyse chymique* and two unidentified works listed in the STN's accounts as *Dissertation de Trisino* [?] and *Médecine commentaires*.

Vernier's orders from the STN appear to have been geared exclusively towards his professional practice. Unless he was a chocoholic or had a proclivity for promiscuous sex, it is unlikely that he ever read any of his purchases for pleasure, leisure, moral or religious instruction, or in pursuit of his wider interests. The same seems to apply to other medical men in our sample – a doctor named Vennes, for example, took five books from the STN, all on 9 July 1774. All were recent medical works.[33] In contrast, Dr Perrelet took books on land surveying and Millot's *Elémens d'histoire générale*, but he also bought copies of Girard Barthélemy's *Lupiologie, ou traité des tumeurs*, William Buchan's *Médecine domestique* and Joseph Priestley's *Expériences et observations sur les différentes espèces d'air*. Conspicuously absent from medical practitioners' purchases are the popularizing medical works of Samuel Tissot, whose books dominate the STN's medical bestsellers lists.[34] Instead their medical purchases seem to have been sourced direct from Paris by an STN keen to fulfil the needs of medical professionals in the vicinity of Neuchâtel. In many of these cases the STN supplied French translations of English works, but they also sourced German or Spanish texts. Thus the STN plugged local physicians into international networks of medical and scientific knowledge. But if these medical men also read for leisure purposes they were acquiring their general reading elsewhere.

Some other professional groups were equally focused in their purchases, among them the Protestant clergy. Their reading appears to have been serious, professional and religious. Conversely, Roman Catholic clergymen were unlikely to approach the STN for vocational reading. A publishing house based in a Swiss Protestant canton was not an obvious place to search out Catholic religious works that most could find closer to home. Unsurprisingly, the STN stocked few Catholic books, but those they did handle in limited quantity included baroque Counter-Reformation bestsellers such as Jacques Coret's *L'Ange conducteur dans la devotion chrétienne* and Dominique Bouhours and Denis-Xavier Clément's *La Journée du Chrétien sanctifiée par la prière et la méditation* or Thomas à Kempis' medieval spiritual handbook, *L'Imitation de Jésus Christ*. Sales of this last dwarfed – and continue to dwarf – those of all Christian literature save the *Bible* itself.[35]

Generally, the Catholic clergy who corresponded with the STN or bought their books were not doing so for devotional reasons. Many – twenty-five to be precise – were that uniquely ambiguous French archetype, the worldwise *abbé*. These included several important literary figures, among them the abbés Coyer and Sabatier de Castres; the Christian apologist Barruel; and *philosophes* of the calibre of the abbés André Morellet and Raynal. Most corresponded with the STN in their capacity as authors rather than customers, although Morellet received thirty-two copies of each volume of the *Descriptions des arts et métiers* as they rolled off the presses. Only the more obscure *abbés* took works on their own private accounts. The most prolific customer among them was the Paris-based abbé Joseph Grellet Desprades, a translator and member of the Academy of La Rochelle, whose only significant work, a poem on electricity, was published in the *Année littéraire*. In 1780–1, he took fifty-one titles from the STN, some clearly intended for distribution in Paris or Versailles, since they were in multiple copies. Not one of them was religious.

The STN sent Desprades seven *voyages* [travelogues], a large number of political, historical and pedagogical works, the complete works of Riccoboni, Molière, Dorat, Piron and the abbé Coyer, and a smattering of philosophical novels.[36] These last included some mild erotica and lightweight *philosophie*, including Marmontel's bestselling novel *Les Incas*, but no works of sexual–political scandal or anticlericalism. The same could not be said of the orders of the philosophically minded abbé Lesenne. A hack writer and pamphleteer, Lesenne purchased ten copies of a German novel attacking the religious fanaticism of the Lutheran clergy, *Intolérance ecclésiastique*.[37] Why did he want them? Were they intended as weapons of interdenominational warfare? It appears not. Although he intended them for friends in the clergy, Lesenne indicated that his clerical circle were freethinkers, not Catholic bigots.[38] Presumably these libertine clergymen also enjoyed the dozen copies of the *Anecdotes sur Madame la Comtesse du Barri* that he procured from the STN, as well as various other topical and political works.[39] These were, however, the raciest works ordered by a Catholic clergyman – none ordered genuinely pornographic works, religious polemics or materialist tracts. Nor, intriguingly, did they buy any classic Enlightenment text advertised in DeFrance's *À l'Égide de Minerve*.

The different demand patterns for Catholic and Protestant clergy demonstrate how cultural factors could shape reading preferences. Perhaps the most significant of these concern language. In France, the Swiss Romand and much of Belgium there was a native French-speaking audience for whom it was natural to read in French for leisure, educational, informational, religious, business or self-improvement purposes. While these areas took around 70 per cent of the STN's books, another 30 per cent went to regions where French was not the dominant language.[40] Although French was widely spoken by elites across Europe, the numbers of francophone readers in these areas was generally limited. Beyond the great metropolises of non-francophone Europe – notably London, Amsterdam and Vienna – few booksellers could survive on local demand for French books alone. What then was the nature of demand for French books in the non-francophone zones of Europe?

Such demand took many forms. Across most of Europe the STN supplied dealers who on-sold to French expatriate and other francophone communities. These included the vestiges of the seventeenth-century Huguenot diaspora; educators seeking French textbooks; other book dealers; merchants, travellers and adventurers; and a pan-European aristocratic elite for whom French served as a *lingua franca* and badge of culture and learning. Since the STN generally had at most a handful of major clients in each major centre, the nature of their business with each town also reflected the market niches of individual customers and the bewilderingly diverse range of legal, censorship and economic constraints under which they operated. These varied market conditions and the STN's client base are discussed in Chapter 4. Yet despite market fragmentation, when taken in combination and analysed systematically using digital tools, the STN's trade offers important insights into the eighteenth-century book trade and Enlightenment culture.

To uncover the reading culture of the Enlightenment, we must do more than trace readers. We also need to understand how books were consumed. In this context, Rolf Engelsing's proposal that the eighteenth century witnessed a 'reading revolution' has enjoyed wide currency. Enseling proposes that increases in production and the resultant wider dissemination of cheap print products promoted more critical reading habits, as readers became more fluid before and between texts, and more private in their reading habits.[41] According to Enseling, prior to the reading revolution readers generally had access to only a few texts, and these usually bore the imprint of religious or political authority. Such texts tended to be expensive and treated with reverence, since they gave access to truths required for eternal salvation, or more occasionally professional success or legal or political survival. Naturally, such texts were regarded as authoritative and seldom open to question. They were read intensively, repeatedly and frequently in public. By the late eighteenth century, however, solitary readers were accustomed to accessing, comparing and contrasting a greater number and variety of texts. This inculcated new critical habits, and these were eventually applied even to texts once considered authoritative. Eventually some readers began to treat even Holy Writ as if it were just another literary text, following in the footsteps of Pierre Bayle's *Dictionnaire historique et critique* and Voltaire's *Dictionnaire philosophique*. As the reading public grew more critical and engaged, it became accustomed also to questioning and even mistrusting received authority. Enlightenment habits of mind evolved as much from reading habits as reading matter.

Nevertheless, it would be misleading to suggest that all the STN's wares were designed for 'extensive' reading. Many clearly were not. School textbooks as well as religious primers continued to be produced in the form of catechisms, encouraging pupils to recite aloud authoritative answers to set questions.[42] Much devotional output was designed for traditional, intensive, public, ritual or meditative reading, and not infrequently all four. Many practical manuals and guidebooks were intended for reference and occasional study for practical purposes. So, in theory, was the STN's vast *Descriptions des arts et métiers*, with its detailed discussion of numerous crafts. Yet craftsmen were generally too poor to buy a luxury multivolume work, and few outside France would possess the exacting and precise vocabulary associated with the skills it described. The work's German market was limited to the aristocratic denizens of princely courts who, as Jeffrey Freedman has observed, probably valued it primarily for aesthetic reasons as an object of display.[43] Such comments suggest that if the reading revolution hypothesis is valid, it applies only within limited spheres, among those who enjoyed regular access to large selections of printed texts and possessed sophisticated reading techniques. For lower class and occasional readers, a doubling in output of books per capita appears insufficient to underpin the hypothesis of a general 'reading revolution'. For many readers, a widespread reverence for the printed word probably remained. Such reverence probably stemmed from both written content and a more general respect for learning, authors and the systems of quality control that generally precede print publication.

The STN's own quality control systems largely revolved around respect for established authors. They rarely gambled on unknown writers. Instead they republished works whose attractiveness had been tested in the marketplace, or endeavoured to be first into print with new works from established writers. Foremost of these was the playwright, novelist and pamphleteer, Louis Sébastien Mercier, who by the early 1780s was one of the brightest and most marketable figures in the French literary firmament. When Mercier first approached them, the STN's directors could probably hardly believe their luck. A popular writer whose celebrity might rival that of Beaumarchais was offering them an exclusive deal on a series of new manuscripts, albeit on terms that he dictated.[44]

On 19 January 1778, Mercier wrote to the STN in flattering terms. He admired some of their editions and wished to give them preference over other foreign publishing houses. To entice them further, he announced some clandestine *nouveautés*, promising 'Les uns sont susceptibles d'entrer en France, les autres ne le sont pas'. The first would be 'un ouvrage dramatique et politique' entitled *La Destruction de la Ligue, ou la réduction de Paris*. It was a tantalizing prospect, and if the STN sensed a future bestseller they were right. *La Destruction de la Ligue* would become their bestselling theatrical work.

An exclusive arrangement would not come cheap, naturally, and Mercier's opening gambit was not to propose terms but rather to ask what would the STN be prepared to pay? He sensed that his market power was such that rather than be bargained down, he would talk the STN up. To entice them further, he suggested 'Je pourrois même faire une edition complette de mes œuvres et surtout les pieces de theatre qui sont representées journellement avec quelque succès'. The ploy paid off: the STN was hooked. It was to prove a lucrative partnership. In all, the STN would trade some 45,718 units of

Mercier's works, including over 14,000 copies of his multivolume bestseller *Le Tableau de Paris* and 10,188 of *La Destruction de la Ligue*.[45] Mercier's works accounted for one in nine STN sales. In the 1780s, he was the author of one in every six books they sold.

The STN was assailed by authors wishing to do business with them, but few had the pulling power of Mercier. Instinctively cautious, the STN very rarely bought manuscripts from authors: the few exceptions include Rudolf Sinner de Ballaigues, Jean-Emmanuel Gilibert and Mercier himself.[46] Indeed, most authors had little to offer and dealing with them represented a high risk. It has been suggested that fewer than thirty authors were able to live wholly by the produce of their pens in eighteenth-century France, though this total obviously ignores journalists. The case of the abbé Lesenne is instructive here. During a correspondence spanning several years, he offered the STN numerous manuscripts and penned endless book proposals. The STN wanted none of them. Their main interest in Lesenne was his apparent links to the *philosophe* d'Alembert, his possible utility as a sales conduit, and the fleeting thought that he might edit their *Journal helvétique*.[47] Adventurers like Lesenne were ten a penny, but the chances that they would ever produce anything of commercial value were remote.

The STN did publish budding authors untested by the market, but only if they paid for the works on their own account. As Mark Curran has shown in *Selling Enlightenment*, by the early 1780s, this kind of publishing by commission had become an integral part of the STN's business model.[48] Commissioned publishing could also be an attractive option for authors, especially for foreign writers who for legal reasons feared publishing close to home, or for those wishing to print works which were not commercially viable. Legal considerations certainly motivated the French Protestant pastor Pomaret to commission the STN to print several of his own works for use among his congregations around Ganges. They also inspired the Maupoeuite magistrate Louis-Valentin Goëzman to employ the STN to print 1,000 copies of his controversial *Tableau de la monarchie française* and the minor *philosophe* Jacques Le Scene Desmaisons to order around 4,000 copies of his *Contrat conjugal*. Commissioning authors rank among the STN's most important clients.[49] Théodore Rilliet de Saussure commissioned their most distributed work while the budding *philosophe* and future revolutionary Jacques-Pierre Brissot de Warville employed the STN to print so many books that he became their largest single debtor.[50] His financial embarrassment and subsequent arrest on (unfounded) suspicions of producing pornographic pamphlets against Marie-Antoinette was a minor disaster for the STN.[51] Yet on other occasions the STN turned commissioned works to their advantage. When they printed an early edition of *Système de la nature* for the Belgian bookseller Boubers, for example, they creamed off five hundred copies for their own account.[52]

The STN's other favoured form of production was literary piracy. By producing their own editions of works with known market appeal, both tried and tested bestsellers and the latest *nouveautés* by established writers, they limited their risk. This was common practice, made easier by the limited existing forms of copyright protection, particularly in the international arena. It was not, however, entirely risk-free. Occasionally pirated works might be seized, usually for the benefit of the rights holders, particularly Parisian booksellers who aggressively guarded exclusive French publishing *privilèges* over many of the most lucrative titles.

Piracy of French books was a massive industry both outside and inside France. Roger Chartier and Robert Darnton have both estimated that 50 per cent of books circulating in France during the final decades of the *ancien régime* were 'illegal' in some way.[53] However, most 'illegal' books were pirated copies of otherwise innocuous works. So great was the problem that when the French government attempted to quash piracy in August 1777, they began by announcing an amnesty.[54] Every bookseller in the realm would be visited and given a chance to declare any pirated works and have them legalized by stamping. Records of *estampillage* visitations survive for about one third of the kingdom and are currently being added to the FBTEE database.[55]

Piracy, then, was central to Old Regime literary culture and a staple of the STN's business. Occasionally authors even assisted in pirating their own works. Voltaire connived with the STN to bring a pirated, corrected edition of his *Questions sur l'Encyclopédie* to market within weeks of the official edition.[56] Likewise, British author Patrick Brydone helped the STN to produce a more accurate translation of his *Voyage en Sicile et à Malthe* than the first Parisian translation.[57] Thus once the French clampdown on the pirate sector began to bite, the repercussions for the STN's business model were likely to be devastating.

The STN's stock was generally produced for a market which was neither free nor liberal. Almost everywhere in Europe the state imposed legal constraints on publishing, and these shaped what was written and sold. It would be wrong, however, to view censorship entirely in negative terms, and anachronistic to believe that most contemporaries did so. Censorship and book trade controls served many purposes and were often renegotiated between state and other stakeholders. Robert Darnton's study of the *Encyclopédie* and Louise Seaward's work on the STN's political correspondents have shown how the STN used political allies to negotiate a passage for their books, including pirated re-editions of useful works.[58] Censorship systems could be flexible, if inconsistent, hard to navigate and frustrating.[59] Equally, consignments of books might encounter a bewildering array of censorship arrangements on their travels; and even within a single polity there might be multiple authorities with competing responsibilities.

In France, the monarchy claimed the right of prepublication censorship. However, the higher clergy, the faculty of theology at the Sorbonne, and the *parlements* also claimed policing rights over the printed word. By the later eighteenth century the censorship authority of the Sorbonne and Assembly of the Clergy was waning, but the *parlements* were another matter. Many works the *parlements* suppressed were highly offensive to Louis XV's government. However, the *parlements* also proscribed pamphlets produced by their clerical enemies, which were immune from censorship. In the mid-1750s they also began condemning works which had passed through the royal censorship.[60] This was a step too far, especially in the hysterical atmosphere that followed Robert-François Damiens' attempt on Louis XV's life. On 16 April 1757, the Royal Council reasserted its supremacy, decreeing:

> All those convicted of having composed, having had composed, and having had printed writings that attack religion, disrupt minds, undermine our authority, and disturb the order and tranquillity of our territories, will be punished by death.[61]

This draconian policy was never enforced: the worst writers and publishers experienced was imprisonment. In reality, too, a dizzying array of gradations of illegality remained in place. These ranged from unauthorized editions of innocuous works through piracies to highly clandestine attacks on morality or the authority of state, church or scripture. In such an environment, even police, customs officers and book trade inspectors struggled to decide precisely what was illegal or permitted. As the Parisian confiscation registers show, books were frequently impounded only to be released following an official decision that they should be permitted to circulate.[62]

Censorship regimes varied enormously. In Neuchâtel itself the town executive, the *Quatre-Ministraux*, exercised a 'double censorship' over printed works on behalf of both municipality and state. In addition, the *Classe des pasteurs* still exercised a strong clerical authority in public and private affairs.[63] However, as long as the most noxious works were only sold for export, the authorities usually turned a blind eye to the STN's clandestine activities. Moreover, censorship violations were generally treated leniently, with very light sentences.[64] Many other states took a similar attitude provided clandestine books only passed through their territory. Despite dozens of customs barriers and inspection points along the Rhine, even the lewdest or most anticlerical works generally traversed Germany unmolested. The Rhineland states cared more about customs revenue than confiscating contraband. The same leniency did not always apply once books arrived at their destination. In the clerically dominated Imperial free city of Cologne, penalties for trading in irreligious, anticlerical or pornographic books were severe. In 1776, the local authorities intercepted and burned a large consignment of scandalous books sent from Neuchâtel by Samuel Fauche to the Cologne bookseller Simonin.[65] Yet a few hundred yards away in Münz, in the archbishopric of Cologne, another publisher–bookseller, Louis-François Mettra, plied a lively trade in *livres philosophiques* with impunity. Yet even there the regime was probably stricter than in Mettra's final asylum. When Rhine floodwaters inundated his business in February 1784, he shifted his base to nearby Neuwied, where he established a *Société typographique* and stepped-up his production of scandalous works.[66] Thereafter he exported books to the STN, over 5,000 in all.

With the exception of Britain and the Netherlands, few states were as liberal as Neuwied. Moreover, even limited liberalism could prove precarious. Joseph II began his reign by promoting press freedom, but took fright when faced with widespread political opposition. His reaction culminated in 1788 with the issuing of an Index of banned books and restoration of censorship.[67] In France the situation was slightly different. There, apparent laxity in policing the book trade gave Swiss publishers an opportunity to deal widely in pirated and clandestine publications. However, by the late 1770s this window of opportunity was closing and in 1783 it was slammed shut. On one level the story of the STN's rise, fall and eventual collapse is the story of France's policing of the external book trade. Traditionally, that policing has been viewed as ineffectual. However, by the 1760s the French government was filled with mercantilist alarm at the impact of foreign publishing on the domestic book trade. The measures they announced on 30 August 1777 against piracy and 12 June 1783 against the clandestine trade were intended to turn the tables, and largely succeeded.[68] They dealt a body blow to the STN, who responded to increasingly precarious balance sheets by trying to stimulate new markets across Europe, and forging business partnerships with other leading local publishers.[69] The French measures impacted similarly on other extraterritorial publishers.[70] It is therefore worth reflecting a little on French censorship practices.

The Bourbon state subjected most new books to prior censorship, a process that frequently spawned tortuous negotiations and resubmissions. During the final four decades of the *ancien régime*, the *Directeur de la librarie* employed between 122 and 189 censors, mostly men of letters. These were divided into specialist categories: 'Theology', 'Jurisprudence', 'Natural History', 'Agriculture', 'Medicine', 'Surgery', 'Chemistry', 'Mathematics and Physics', '*Belles-Lettres*, History etc.', 'Geography', 'Engraving', 'Architecture' and 'Genealogy'.[71] However, the lion's share of censorship work – which was not directly remunerated – was undertaken by just a few men.[72]

Censors were expected to judge both the literary and moral merit of manuscripts before recommending corrections. Their reports were often printed with the works they approved and thus served as a stamp of literary as well as official approbation.[73] Hence the system was not just about policing ideas. It was also a form of government-sanctioned editorial quality control, both shaping and enhancing literary output. Naturally, some sorts of publication had little need of literary checking, and this was reflected in censorship regulations. For posters, ephemera and theatrical works, a *permission de police* was sufficient, but for new books publishers must choose between a simple and cost-free *permission de sceau* or purchasing a *privilège*. The latter generally gave holders exclusive rights for between two and ten years.[74] However, not all *privilèges* were time limited. The University of Paris owned lucrative perpetual *privilèges* over a number of works, notably the scriptures and Thomas à Kempis' *L'Imitation de Jésus Christ*, already a Catholic bestseller for a third of a millennium.[75] These provided a perpetual revenue stream.

The denial of a *privilège* did not necessarily mean a book could not circulate legally in France, for many were granted '*permissions tacites*'. These were originally legal licences covering works produced abroad. However, in time they were also applied to editions produced in France but to which the government preferred not to grant a public stamp of approval. 'Tacitly permitted' works were usually obliged to carry a false foreign imprint, a requirement which placed subterfuge at the heart of the French book trade administration.[76] Faced with a complex, uneven and rather arbitrary system, publishers and authors resorted to rigorous self-censorship, often working closely with their censors to ensure that the final product was unobjectionable. Caution was all the more necessary because the censor's judgement was not definitive: his role was only advisory. Publishing permissions and *privilèges* could be withdrawn by the royal authorities. This posed a threat to both authors and censors. When the *privilège* for Claude-Adrien Helvétius' materialist classic *De l'Esprit* was cancelled after a concerted campaign by the Church, its censor Jean-Pierre Tercier was sacked.[77]

Censorship outcomes frequently depended on political and personal considerations, as in the Tercier case. Censors were active participants in the cultural life and patronage networks of the Old Regime. Their work offered ample opportunities to serve friends and clients; advance personal agendas; settle scores; or curry favour with powerful interest groups or patrons. In theory the identity of the censor was secret prior to publication. This increased the potential for malicious decisions or skulduggery. In practice anonymity was often breached and many authors requested to work with particular censors. Such flexibility ensured that, after suitable revisions, the vast majority of works were eventually cleared by the censors, whose names frequently appeared on signed approbation notices attached to authorized publications.[78] Most printed texts produced in France – and not infrequently pirated by the STN – were shaped by a symbiotic relationship between censor and author. Rather than viewing their relationship with the censors as essentially antagonistic, authors and the public generally shared the authorities' conviction that books harmful to religion, the state, good morals or individual reputations could be socially, politically or spiritually disruptive.

The French government also tried to secure the cooperation of the print trade using a system of licences to both police and enrich authorized printers and booksellers and hence tie them to the regime. The first licences were introduced in 1667, and from 1704 printer numbers were limited by law. In some towns this involved a reduction in licensed printers, and there was a further nationwide review in 1777.[79] Strict rules, set down in the 550-page *Code de la Librarie et imprimerie*, governed entry to the trade, production quality and the regulation and licencing of printed works.[80] This system allowed the government close control over licensed printers and booksellers while providing strong financial inducements to good behaviour, since licence-holders enjoyed monopoly or oligopoly rights within local communities. Printers' licences were particularly valuable, since they also conferred the right to sell books. As many printers and booksellers became wealthy local notables, most were satisfied with the *status quo*. There is little evidence that any wanted a free press prior to 1789.[81]

Books occupied an unstable, crucial and increasingly ubiquitous position as products and shapers of eighteenth-century print culture. Although we cannot draw hard and fast demarcations between books, pamphlets, serial publications and ephemera, it is clear that the elastic category of books fulfilled some particular social, intellectual and cultural functions that distinguished them from other genres of print. They were, for example, the leading genre for conveying, communicating and preserving complex ideas. Thus in the analysis that follows, books will serve as proxies for exploring the dissemination of the ideas and values they contain. More unexpectedly, books (including political pamphlets) were generally able to offer better analysis of politics and current affairs than newspapers. Books came in a bewildering range of genres, and were susceptible to multiple styles of reading for many different purposes. The most popular genres, moreover, were generally designed to be widely read across most of the social spectrum in a traditional intensive manner. Historians overly focused on the changes wrought by print have tended to overlook these continuities. Instead, they have concentrated on genres that they consider to be implicated in social, cultural and political change, notably Enlightenment classics, clandestine political pamphlets, *livres philosophiques* or serial literature. These were genres of print, moreover, that due to content, price and availability were, we might suspect, consumed primarily by aristocratic and urban middle-class readers. Such a mode of inquiry has its place. Major economic, social and political changes occurred across Europe across the last three decades of the century, and it is perfectly legitimate to seek both traces and origins of those changes in the world of elite print and a predominantly bourgeois public sphere. However, if we want a more rounded view of the cultural life, intellectual fecundity, popular reading and social imagination of the period, we must take a more holistic, less teleological, view of the print culture and literary output of the late eighteenth century. The FBTEE database empowers just such an approach, by allowing us to peer inside the book crates that emerged from the STN's silos and criss-crossed Europe before arriving in bookstores such as *À l'Égide de Minerve*. By exploring the contents of these crates, we should arrive at a more realistic view of the printed fare being received by booksellers and consumed by readers across Enlightenment Europe. But before we attempt to prise more of them open, we must address two closely linked questions. Why search for Enlightenment in a single Swiss printshop? And how should we do so?

3

Searching for Enlightenment in a Swiss Print Shop

How much can we learn about Enlightenment culture from studying the books traded by a single Swiss publisher? The question is a pressing one. At heart it boils down to another simpler question. How far can we treat data derived from the STN archive as representative? At least, that is how the question appeared to previous generations of scholars. Now, that way of phrasing it appears not so much *une question mal posée* as an outmoded methodological anxiety. For digital technologies allow us to manipulate our dataset in ways previously unthinkable and to interrogate carefully constructed subsets of data. Consequently, we should revise our question to read 'how might I best derive broadly representative or otherwise valuable insights from the FBTEE database?' The answer to this question is not a unitary one, for, as following chapters show, what constitutes the most appropriate or representative dataset varies according to our queries. But for now, let us begin by examining the original question. Why look at a single publisher? And why choose the STN?

At first the answer seemed simple. The STN archive, previous scholarship assured us, was the richest available for our purposes and had a broader representative value. To be sure, previous scholars felt obliged to establish the STN's representativeness, but generally overcame their doubts. Robert Darnton argued that the STN and most other eighteenth-century book dealers were ideologically neutral, profit-maximizing entrepreneurs. They would deal in any book that sold and, because publishers were also wholesalers, they dealt in editions produced by other houses as well as their own. To attract and keep customers, they sought to maximize their stocklists by exchanging books among themselves in the form of unbound sheets. Hence they could supply almost anything, sourced from anywhere, particularly as the most successful works tended to be widely pirated and available in multiple editions from multiple sources. Booksellers across Europe could thus draw on a general 'floating stock' of works to satisfy client demand. According to this 'floating stock' theory, the trade of a Swiss publishing house, the STN say, should look pretty similar to that of a Dutch house like Luchtmans, since both operated in relatively free publishing environments. To confirm his assumptions, Darnton created an elaborate system of 'controls' to show that the most frequently ordered libertine works in the STN's corpus of clandestine literature (the focus of his study) also featured among the books most seized at French customs or in police raids. This proved to his own satisfaction that the STN's 'forbidden bestsellers' list was broadly representative of demand for clandestine works in France as a whole.[1] More recently, on his website *robertdarnton.org* and its companion volume, *A Literary Tour de France* (2018), he extends these claims to the entire book trade, arguing that 'for a reliable view of the book trade, it is necessary to study the dossiers of dealers who established fairly close relations with the STN and ordered regularly from it.'[2] Where the dossiers are rich enough, as in the case of the Besançon bookseller Charles-Antoine Charmet, Darnton suggests that a single bookseller's correspondence might suffice and that 'by compiling statistics from documents of this kind, month after month, it is possible to enjoy a clear view of the demand for literature in a provincial capital.'[3]

Studies of the STN's French and German trading networks appear to buttress Darnton's argument that their order books were more broadly representative. Thierry Rigogne has established that the STN traded with three quarters of the eighty-eight biggest centres of book production and publishing across France. Their 270 clients in those towns accounted for 25 per cent of all French booksellers.[4] This was a large enough sample to suggest that their trade has a wider statistical relevance. Taking a different national context, Jeffrey Freedman argues that in Germany demand for French books came from a relatively limited and widely dispersed social elite. The STN's scattered German bookseller clients thus had to sell their stock across wide swathes of territory. Thus they represent German demand in general rather than local markets in towns where they were based.[5] Finally, estimates made during the FBTEE pilot project in 2006 suggested that the STN traded in perhaps 1–1.5 per cent of books circulating through the pan-European book trade. This was sufficient to make it a major player in the cosmopolitan French book trade and imply some representative value. All these studies bolstered confidence that the STN's trade was broadly 'typical' of extraterritorial publishing houses strung along the French border.

The STN was attractive for other reasons, too. Its data seemed tailor-made for a database project, both in terms of volume and content. During our pilot, optimistic initial projections suggested that the project could be finished – and even written up – in about four years. Preliminary soundings also suggested that at least one sixth of the STN's stock went to countries other than France and Switzerland. This promised rich opportunities for cross-cultural comparison. In fact, the final figure was closer to one quarter, but the spread was uneven chronologically and STN sales proved below preliminary projections.[6] The STN's accounts also allowed us to explore the sourcing of books, a topic little studied previously. All this work would be facilitated and enriched by the magnificent ancillary materials available in the Bibliothèque publique et universitaire de Neuchâtel, including John Jeanprêtre's superb typed and annotated handlist and supplementary card indexes of STN clients.[7] These were indispensable sources whose riches I had explored on earlier visits to Neuchâtel between 1990 and 2004. The survival of several of the STN's catalogues, which would help us to identify titles in advance, would simplify data entry work, as would pre-existing bibliographic studies of the STN, notably Michael Schmidt's published bibliographical list of STN editions.[8] Thus, although the FBTEE project turned up a number of booksellers accounts comparable to and in some cases more extensive than those of the STN, at this point in time, the STN remains the richest available Enlightenment period publisher's archive in terms of surviving sources and ease of working.[9] But there were other attractions stemming from the nature of the STN's business, its geography and its history.

One key attraction of working on the STN is that, in a political sense, Neuchâtel was neither French nor Swiss. As a Prussian-ruled principality, Neuchâtel benefited from relative political autonomy from 1707 to 1806 (and would do so again from 1814 to 1848). The principality's Prussian governors were frequently non-resident and their role was primarily to represent the Prussian crown. Meanwhile, many executive powers had devolved to Neuchâtel's Council of State.[10] Shielded by Prussian military protection and hands-off government, this was an ideal situation for an international publisher–wholesaler: it allowed the STN to trade in books that would be illegal in much of Europe, and to pump clandestine pirate works into France. However, this freedom had limits. As Mark Curran noted in the first volume of this study, the local civil and religious authorities could and occasionally did take action over illegal works, especially when pressured by foreign powers or local elites.[11] The STN might be given permission to publish the baron d'Holbach's *Système de la nature*, but only on condition it did not circulate within the principality. Nevertheless, the local Calvinist clergy reacted angrily to the publication and stripped one of the STN's three founding directors, Jean-Elie Bertrand, of his priesthood. A second director, Frédéric-Samuel Ostervald, felt constrained to resign the office of Banneret. On 22 August 1771 the work was condemned by the Council of State, which ordered all copies remaining on Neuchâtelois territory to be surrendered and burned. A public *auto da fé* followed on 26 September. This was sufficient to deter the STN from dabbling in the production of materialist works again.[12]

A handful of other works were also considered beyond the pale, notably Charles Théveneau de Morande's *Gazetier cuirassé* (1771), the most extreme and notorious collection of scurrilous anecdotes of Louis XV's court. Bertrand and Ostervald considered it too hot to handle. When a customs confiscation revealed that the STN's founding director, Samuel Fauche had forwarded copies in the company's *ballots* in defiance of their wishes, he was quickly shown the door.[13] Bertrand and Ostervald had good reason. Determined to close their border to the work, the French government pursued the *Gazetier cuirassé* with unprecedented vigour.[14] In Geneva, following French diplomatic pressure, the bookseller Jacques-Benjamin Téron was arrested and imprisoned for three weeks in January 1772 for handling the pamphlet. On release, he was threatened with harsher punishment in case of recidivism.[15] However, as the most corrosive materialist tract of the era and most reviled of political *libelles*, the *Système de la nature* and *Gazetier cuirassé* were two of the hottest works circulating in ancien régime France. Few other books were pursued so actively.

Equally fortuitous, the STN's existence coincided with a period of relative peace on continental Europe, and hence stable borders. Fortuitously, the only major war between the European powers during the STN's heyday was fought outside Europe, as the Americans sought independence. It did not impact on the map of the old world. To be sure, there were significant changes at the partitions of Poland in 1772 and 1793–95; on the Russo-Turkish frontier in 1774; and during the annexations and wars accompanying the French Revolution from 1790. However, such border changes, perhaps not entirely by chance, did not affect the STN dataset. This made international comparison much easier, although representing space in the FBTEE database and mapping tools was far from straightforward. The complex geopolitical realities of ancien régime Europe are notoriously difficult to capture cartographically, and raise some interesting dilemmas. Issues FBTEE needed to resolve included the visual and statistical representation of overlordship and shared sovereignty arrangements; non-contiguous territories; overlapping jurisdictions; and the representation of imperial and ecclesiastical lands.[16] The most problematic place in the FBTEE database was Neuchâtel itself, a consequence of Prussian overlordship. In consequence, it as decided to treat the geographically separate Prussian territories of Neuchâtel, Cleves and the territorially adjacent Prussian heartlands in Brandenburg, Saxony and East Prussia as three different sovereign entities. In the database and FBTEE maps they appear respectively as 'Prussia: Neuchâtel', 'Prussia: Cleves' and simply 'Prussia'. Each is treated as a statistically and cartographically discrete unit, and thus FBTEE's maps and statistical tables privilege actual geographic location over theoretical political unity. Similar solutions were adopted for other non-contiguous territories, notably the Austrian Habsburg Empire and the lands of the Duchy of Württemberg. Such disaggregation makes for more visually accurate mapping of the dissemination of the STN's wares across Europe. In this task, geography favoured the STN.

Centrally placed on the map of Europe, and with clients in every major Christian capital, the STN were better located than their Dutch rivals to conduct pan-European commerce, drawing on a long tradition of Neuchâtelois publishing.[17] While their trade did not reach every corner of the continent, and in both its early days and its decline was regionally circumscribed, between 1775 and 1787 the STN was trading into every large state and major region in Christian Europe (see Appendix 3.1). The STN's trade was relatively evenly divided between France, Switzerland and the rest of Europe. Ease of access to the heart of Europe meant that their stock could be drawn from the presses of Amsterdam and London; Paris and Frankfurt; Venice and Lyon. This held out the prospect of using the STN to undertake internationally comparative work. Perhaps it would even be possible to isolate distinctively French trends and link them to the cultural origins of the Revolution?

However, creating a database from the STN archives was fraught with difficulties, both practical and conceptual, many of which are discussed in my 'Designer notes' to the FBTEE database and throughout this book and its companion volume.[18] The first was how to integrate several discrete types of accounting sources, since the richest manuscripts in the STN archives, the daybooks (labelled variously as *journaux, copies de comptes, mains courantes* or *brouillards*), do not cover the entire period in which the publisher traded. We were thus forced to rely on stock inventories, order books and several ancillary documents to plug the gaps. In *Selling Enlightenment* Mark Curran explains how we were able to integrate information from these different sources, each of which was differently structured and most of which gave less complete data than the daybooks. To accomplish this task, Dr Curran first modelled how the different sources operated together in the accounting practice of the late eighteenth century, and this model was later checked against both secondary sources and popular accounting textbooks from the time.[19]

A second set of problems involved data interpretation, particularly for establishing bibliographic information. The STN sources were far from perfect in this regard. Although their catalogues, stock inventories, and Michel Schmidt's bibliography of STN editions enabled us to identify precisely many of the works that they traded, others proved more elusive, recorded in the STN accounts under short titles which were sometimes deliberately cryptic. Occasionally the STN's clerks even used coded titles to escape prying eyes. The most notorious of these was the *Système de la nature*, which was styled *l'ouvrage de Boubers*, after the Brussels bookseller who commissioned their edition. Another set of works were masked by numerical codes. These appeared in the letter book of the STN's touring agent Durand, who took the numbers from a set of catalogues that he carried with him. These catalogues, as it turned out, were not produced by the STN themselves, but by Louis Fauche-Borel, another Neuchâtel bookseller. Fortunately, Mark Curran discovered the 'Rosetta stone' for cracking this particular code, by matching the numbers and other compelling circumstantial evidence. Even then, because we lacked a final *supplement* to Fauche-Borel's catalogue, some titles remain tantalisingly out of reach, described in the database as 'Unidentified Durand Tour Works'. Nevertheless, we were able to identify the vast majority of works sold by the peripatetic Durand.[20]

It was not enough, however, to identify the works that the STN traded. To quantify the numbers of books traded by the STN, we also needed to pinpoint, as far as possible, precise editions. In particular, we needed to know whether they were comprised of just a few or many volumes, since the STN often dealt in incomplete sets, and sets of a single title might vary considerably in format and number of volumes. For example, STN clients could at various times order the works of Jean-Jacques Rousseau in editions comprising twelve octavo volumes (the Geneva and Neuchâtel edition of 1782–83); fifteen quarto volumes (Geneva, 1782–89); twenty-three octavo volumes (comprising eleven volumes published in Neuchâtel in 1775 and twelve supplementary volumes from an unidentified edition); thirty volumes (Geneva, date unknown); or thirty-one duodecimo volumes (Geneva, 1782). This matters, because in statistical terms a six volume partial set of the twelve-volume edition represents something different from six volumes of the thirty-volume set. As it was not always possible to identify precise editions, often we had to make do with recording the 'most likely' edition. For this and other reasons, the FBTEE statistics must be considered an amalgamation of probabilities, adding up at best to a 'fuzzy snapshot' of reality.[21]

But what does this 'fuzzy snapshot' show? A record of the act of purchasing rather than the experience of reading, the FBTEE evidence indicates primarily the sorts of things that booksellers believed that their customers aspired to read, possess or display. It can take us into a world of reading beyond the literary and cultural elites whose correspondence in the Republic of Letters provides so much of our evidence for the reception and interpretation of texts. It can expose areas of reading beyond well-known literary, political and religious texts. Some of the material thus exposed is humdrum and dry. Few twenty-first-century readers would stop long to contemplate, nor even seek to comprehend, François-Bertrand de Barrême's *Comptes faits*, an accounting self-help manual mainly comprised of mathematical tables. Yet despite only modest STN sales, this was a runaway bestseller. It may even have been the bestselling secular text of eighteenth-century France: thirty-two licensed editions comprising at least 69,300 copies were published in the decade 1778–89 alone.[22]

But the accolade of secular bestseller might equally lie with some cheap textbook, long lost from view, but a vital part of the educational culture that shaped the early training and foundational world view of the French revolutionary generation. Flimsy and cheaply produced, textbooks were usually discarded as they grew tatty or dated. Despite their formative power over young minds, they were seldom considered worth preserving. Printed in multiple editions in large print runs, the few that survive do so more often by chance than design. Yet such works provided a staple for many publishers. We can identify at least 116 of the works that passed through the STN's magazines as 'School books' (as textbooks were then known). Among them are several of their most popular titles, including the *Abrégé de l'histoire sainte et du catéchisme* by the Neuchâtelois Protestant divine Jean-Frédéric Ostervald and a series of introductory texts on geography and historical geography by his nephew Frédéric-Samuel Ostervald, one of the STN's founding partners. Between them, the Ostervald's alone sold almost 19,000 textbooks through the STN, accounting for almost 5 per cent of their trade by unit volume.

'Historical bibliometric' methods can also indicate what people were not reading or able to buy. Indeed, this insight helped to inspire the FBTEE project. For in 2004, I travelled to Neuchâtel intent on proving that scandalous pornographic works about the French queen Marie-Antoinette did not circulate in print prior to the French Revolution. This was at that time a historical heresy. A large historical literature existed on the anti-Marie-Antoinette pamphlets, much of it by prominent historians. Most of this scholarship implicated such works in the origins of the Revolution, suggesting they brought the regime into disrepute, desacralizing its symbols and deluging the monarchy in a tidal wave of scandal and smut.[23]

This supposition rested on the survival of a few copies of a handful of pre-revolutionary printed editions. By early 2002 I was convinced that although they were printed before the Revolution, they did not circulate at that period. To suppose otherwise implied a flawed understanding of the French ancien régime. To even imagine, let alone publish, such a pamphlet would be a crime of *lèse-majesté*, a strike against the precious Austro-French marriage alliance, and an outrage against the queen and the Habsburg family. The Habsburg and Bourbon monarchies would stop at nothing to prevent such '*ordures*' from circulating. Their tactics included extradition demands, prosecutions before foreign courts, kidnapping, assassination or paying off a pamphlet's authors or publishers and impounding their products in the Bastille. This last is what the *libellistes* were hoping for. But when the French court refused to pay, the *libellistes* never dreamed of publishing their works and provoking the wrath of Europe's two most powerful dynasties. Had they done so, few book dealers would have dared to sell or buy such fare.

The surviving copies of the anti-Marie-Antoinette pamphlets are thus either revolutionary reprints or rare original copies that, having escaped the Bastille's pulping room, were stored in that fortress until it was seized by a revolutionary mob on 14 July 1789. Thereafter entrepreneurial publishers rapidly reprinted the pamphlets, and their new editions frequently proclaimed that 'this work was discovered in the

Bastille'. An increasingly radical public had never seen anything quite like them. In the hate-fuelled atmosphere of revolutionary Paris, where the queen was detested for her Austrian origins and widely suspected links to counter-revolutionary hardliners intent on quashing the Revolution with military force, these pamphlets soon found imitators. The public bought them in their thousands, no longer fearing royal wrath. Thus a pornographic critique of the queen sprung fully formed into the revolutionary consciousness, where it was rapidly transformed into a literature yet more repellent, crude and hateful. Coarse revolutionary pamphlets were soon painting Marie-Antoinette as a rampaging Sadian nymphomaniac harpy capable of simultaneously indulging a cohort of Priapic lovers, libidinous lesbian playmates and an unquenchable thirst for Parisian blood. As attitudes against the queen hardened, revolutionary activists apparently internalized this absurd mythology. At her trial, Marie-Antoinette was accused of sexually abusing her own son while in gaol in the Temple.[24]

To carry my point (for one can seldom prove a negative), I had to dispose of, or explain away, all possible counter-evidence. This included the archives of the STN, which were known to contain unfilled orders for anti-Marie-Antoinette pamphlets from a bookseller called Bruzard de Mauvelain. On my 2004 visit I examined the STN's rolling stock inventories, which were arranged alphabetically by title, for traces of these *libelles*. To my delight, I found no mention of anti-Marie-Antoinette titles. I thus concluded that, like the police agents, underground newsletter writers, booksellers and other cultural intermediaries who had heard rumours of these pamphlets, and who had a professional interest in acquiring them, the STN never actually handled any. For the time being that conclusion remained provisional, however, since the surviving stock inventories spanned less than half the period when the STN was trading. Nevertheless, it was already clear that the placing of a bookseller's order for a particular book did not mean a publisher could supply it. Likewise, the existence of a book does not prove it circulated.

In the course of my examination of the STN's stock inventories and other accounting documents, I realized that the STN archive was a fine candidate for databasing. By bringing together data on sales, purchases, stocktakes, clients, books, trade routes and destinations, and enriching it with further standardized data on client professions, subject and genre taxonomies, and markers of illegality, it would be possible to trace and contrast the sales of Enlightenment works – and hence the dissemination of the different ideas and discourses they contained – around Switzerland, France and the rest of Europe. Moreover, because the STN's accounts were updated daily, it would be possible to pinpoint the movement of ideas precisely in time as well as space, and hopefully to discover major trends as a result. It was a mouth-watering prospect. At the very least, I hoped, it would allow us to develop a better understanding of the rhythms and international networks of the European book trade in the late eighteenth century, and to add nuance and depth to our view of the Enlightenment and popular reading. At best, it might help us to reassess the Enlightenment and its print culture. This latter challenge, daunting at any time, has been further problematized by FBTEE's findings on the book trade, as elaborated by Mark Curran in *Selling Enlightenment*.

From early in the project our initial assumption that the STN archive was representative of the wider book trade dissolved before our eyes. Instead it became clear that we were dealing with a distinctively Swiss archive. The first hint of this, which stemmed from my preliminary analysis of client professional data, was not unduly troubling. That data showed that the 'authors' and literary figures who corresponded with the STN were overwhelmingly based in either Switzerland or Paris, the heart of the French Enlightenment.[25] With some notable exceptions – above all the abbé Raynal, and (for a short while) Jacques-Pierre Brissot – the exiled writers who played such an important part in the French Enlightenment were absent. There were also a few French provincials or non-native French speakers.[26] This suggested that the literary and intellectual milieux with which the STN was enmeshed, and from which it drew its original book manuscripts, was predominantly either local to Neuchâtel or Parisian. In so far as the STN published original works or was influenced by its literary correspondents, it appeared embedded in closed Swiss-Parisian networks. As a cultural producer its output might be expected strongly to reflect such influences at the expense of wider European currents. The chapter on cosmopolitanism below explores how far that was indeed the case.

Soon, however, Mark Curran reported a more problematic issue emerging from our bibliographic and bibliometric data: the STN appeared to have traded almost exclusively in Swiss editions. A mere 5 per cent of books they traded could be positively identified as foreign printings.[27] Unless we could establish that the Swiss were publishing a standard Enlightenment fare, it seemed that the STN were peddling a distinctly Swiss Enlightenment. The former of these two hypotheses seemed unlikely: Dutch and British publishers were probably churning out rather more radical strains of French Enlightenment works. This, in turn, seemed to challenge the key premise of Darnton's argument, that the STN and other publisher–wholesalers of the Enlightenment era drew on a free-floating stock of books from around Europe, which they swapped with other publisher–wholesalers.[28] If the STN dealt only in Swiss books, the printed literature that they traded would probably diverge significantly from that of French publisher–booksellers in the Netherlands, Britain or the German Rhineland. In *Selling Enlightenment*, Dr Curran argues compellingly that this was indeed the case: rather than floating ethereally down the highways and byways of Europe, books ground their way slowly, haemorrhaging value by the mile. Couched in such terms, his point seems obvious. However, until we have comparable data from further archives, most notably the archives of the Luchtmans company of Leiden, it will remain uncertain just how significantly the Northern market diverged from the Swiss model.

In the interim, it is worth pondering why the 'floating stock' mirage shimmered so beguilingly in the first place. After all, one of our own central premises had been that a methodology based on records of physical stock movements would give a more accurate view of the book trade than Darnton's method, which was based on orders for immaterial titles. Moreover, the titles Darnton recorded through booksellers' orders were for generic works, rather than the actual editions the STN were able to deliver. Among them were orders from neophyte dealers such as Bruzard de Mauvelain who were credulous enough to believe the STN's sales patter that it could stock anything from anywhere.[29] Thus the work of Darnton and other scholars who studied booksellers' orders, by dint of their methodologies, reflected Mauvelain's (erroneous) belief in 'floating stock', failed to distinguish precisely what books were physically traded, and masked the Swiss origins of most of the STN's merchandise. Only once the FBTEE project began tracking physical stock movements and precise editions did it become transparent that the STN was unable to fulfil a significant portion of the orders it received or, for myriad reasons, chose not to supply every book ordered. Equally, booksellers orders did not reveal unordered books sent out to dealers 'on spec'.[30] These findings do not, of course, devalue studies of booksellers' orders as a means of exploring cultural demand. They do, however, raise important questions about their use in isolation to pronounce on cultural supply. In the eighteenth century, the two rarely married up.

Before FBTEE, the mirage of 'floating stock' seemed solid for two further reasons. The first is that because it uses analogue-era technologies, Darnton's work on the STN archive is asynchronous, whereas the FBTEE data can be chronologically calibrated. The FBTEE database allows users to examine the STN's trade in increments down to the individual day or edition. In contrast, Darnton's statistics in *Forbidden Best-Sellers* and the *Corpus of Clandestine Literature* treat the period 1769 to 1789 *en bloc* and offer bestseller tables only at the level of the generic work. The same static approach is taken in the 'best-seller' tables of most frequently ordered books published on his website in 2015.[31] Viewed from the long-term perspective of these tables, the more popular works in his sample – which were widely pirated and published in multiple editions across Europe – appeared omnipresent. But this was illusory because the 'floating stock' theory breaks down at the level of individual editions. Chapter 9 below shows that the STN traded almost all of the illegal titles most frequently ordered across the 1770s and 1780s at some point. In that sense the STN data has a wider representative relevance. However, the STN was not able to acquire any given work at any given moment, even when they were 'in print' somewhere in Europe. This distinction between short-term and long-term access to any particular title is vital to grasping how the book trade actually operated. It also helps to reconcile Mark Curran's insight that there was no generalized 'floating stock', which lies at the heart of the new understandings of the book trade advanced in *Selling Enlightenment*, with the insistence of the current volume that we can extract broadly representative, internationally comparative insights from the STN data.

A further reason the 'floating stock' mirage took so long to explode is that on the sales side the STN archive reveals that the STN conducted much long-distance commerce, and on a grand scale. At times, the company tried to sell whatever books it had everywhere it could across Christian Europe. This insight, too, helps reconcile the apparent contradiction of *Selling Enlightenment*'s portrayal of the STN as a seller of Swiss books with *Enlightenment Bestsellers*' quest for internationally comparative insights. As we have seen, the STN was a significant publishing operation, employing a strikingly large number of presses.[32] It traded in around 7 per cent of French-language editions produced in Europe between c. 1770 and 1787 and handled perhaps 1 per cent of all physical copies of French books circulating. In its heyday around 1780 these figures were even higher. This is enough to suggest a certain statistically representative value to the data.[33] Moreover, the company's long-distance trade was considerably more extensive than the Swiss-books hypothesis might seem to imply. As we have already noted, the STN's international market structure was relatively evenly divided between France, Switzerland and the rest of Europe. In all, over 60 per cent of the STN's outgoing trade went directly abroad (see Appendix 3.1), and seven eighths of these exports had destinations more than 200 kilometres from Neuchâtel. Until the FBTEE database suggested otherwise, it was not unreasonable to believe that the STN's supply networks were similarly dispersed.

In total, over a fifth of the STN's direct exports (51,000 units) went to places as distant from Neuchâtel as Russia, Poland, Scandinavia, Britain, the Iberian peninsular or the Low Countries. Almost as many more (44,000 units) were despatched to destinations in Germany, Italy or the Habsburg's central European territories. If the example of the Cramer brothers of Geneva is typical, a substantial portion of the books the STN sold to their Genevan and Neuchâtelois trading partners would also have been sold on abroad, most notably to France.[34] Likewise, a significant but indeterminate portion of the 25,000 books the STN despatched to the German-speaking Swiss towns of Berne, Basel and Zurich were forwarded to Germany, mainly for sale at the Leipzig's Easter book fair.[35] So how should we explain the apparent discrepancy between the STN's imports and their exports, since so few of their 'sales' can be positively identified as foreign editions?

This discrepancy is largely a statistical illusion based upon a false comparison. For we need to distinguish between the STN's retail trade in editions produced by other publishers and its wholesale trade in its own products. The STN's trade in its own editions accounted for 66 per cent of sales – all were, of course, Swiss editions.[36] If, however, we consider the STN as a retailer–wholesaler of other publishers' wares, the picture looks very different. Although the precise volume of the STN's trade in foreign books remains uncertain, because of the difficulty of precisely identifying editions or confirming places of publication, we can derive the likely proportion of foreign editions in the STN's stock.[37] First, there were the 31,311 units that the STN acquired directly from suppliers based outside the Swiss confederation and its perpetual allies, Geneva, Neuchâtel and the bishopric of Basel.[38] To these we might add a portion of the books supplied to the STN by their trading partners in Switzerland.[39] According to the database these include around 60,000 copies of (putatively) 'Swiss editions', 12,606 units of 'foreign' (non-Swiss) editions and 46,082 books with 'place of publication unknown'. How many of these were foreign imports? Due to false imprints, the sketchiness of the sources and the inconsistency and incompleteness of the bibliographic record we will never know. However, if we assume that the STN's Swiss suppliers traded imports and Swiss editions in broadly similar proportions to the STN itself, we can add about 10,000 units to our original total.[40] This method of calculation implies that around 41,000 of the books the STN acquired from other suppliers – well over a quarter of the total – were foreign editions.

This conclusion is reinforced by examining the acquisition patterns for books according to their putative provenance (Table 3.1). This reveals that, on average, the STN acquired individual Neuchâtelois and Swiss editions from their Swiss trading partners in significantly larger volumes than they did for supposedly 'foreign' imprints. The discrepancy – on average they took nine times as many copies of each Neuchâtel edition traded and five times as many of other Swiss editions – is enough to confirm that the bulk of 'foreign editions' were indeed imports from abroad. The

Table 3.1 Ratios of STN acquisitions from Swiss sources by Edition Type

Edition type	Copies	Titles	Av. copies/title
Foreign (non-Swiss) editions	9,815	633	15.5
Editions with unknown place of publication	46,082	845	54.5
Neuchâtel editions (non-STN)	6,166	46	134
Other Swiss editions (non-Neuchâtel)	42,470	589	72.1

main exception would appear to be works with a British imprint, many of which were almost certainly Swiss piracies, most notably 208 copies of each of Mairobert's *Espion anglois* and *Journal historique de la révolution opérée ... par M. de Maupeou*.[41] But British imprints, false or otherwise, only accounted for 1,797 of the 'foreign' books the STN acquired from Swiss trading partners, as recorded in the FBTEE database. Of the remaining 8,018 'foreign' books brought in from the same suppliers, the bulk were clearly imports. The STN's purchasing profile for editions of unknown provenance is also suggestive: on average they took only three quarters as many copies per work as for (non-Neuchâtel) Swiss editions. This profile might suggest that a significant minority of the 46,082 Swiss-sourced copies of these editions were imports – perhaps almost a quarter, to judge from the averages in Table 3.1. When we also factor in our 31,311 direct imports, this second approach would suggest that our 41,000 estimate is highly conservative. Such a conclusion would be bold, however, since the provenance of some editions is uncertain precisely *because* they were traded in low volumes, and hence were less likely to be recorded in the sources which supplied our bibliographic details – the STN's catalogues and, to a lesser extent, their stock books. Taken together, then, both methods of calculating the extent of the STN's trade in imported books indicate that a significant portion of their stock – comprising at least 9 to 10 per cent of all books passing through their magazines – was printed abroad.

It makes sense that a substantial proportion of the French Enlightenment book trade should involve long-distance commerce. Bibliophiles, scholars and lay readers were prepared to pay a premium if there were no locally produced version of a desired book, and in some cases sought out a particular edition. Marketing devices alert us to this: latest 'novelties', 'improved translations' and 'new', 'latest', 'corrected' editions, luxury versions 'on vellum', bound 'in morocco', or otherwise distinctive editions abound in eighteenth-century advertising. Savvy publishers and booksellers knew that consumers wanted these things and adjusted their behaviours accordingly. What is perhaps surprising is the extent to which editions produced in faraway places reached distant markets. Nevertheless, the STN tended to trade individual foreign editions in low volume, presumably reflecting both the cost of transportation and the fact that as they travelled from their point of origin, wholesalers tended to break up stock consignments into smaller bundles before selling them on.[42] Like blood being transmitted from the heart to the body, the consignments of any given title travelled in ever smaller volumes as they moved from the major arteries of the trade to the furthest capillaries.

As books moved further from their point of origin, they were also more likely to come into competition with rival, locally produced editions. Widespread piracy meant that most successful titles were reprinted in several places across Europe.[43] Other things being equal, these rival editions might be cheaper due to lower transport costs, better advertised close to their place of production, and quicker for dealers to stock. Piracy thus inhibited the geographical dissemination of physical books, but mainly because other versions of the same title were already widely available in a particular region. Not surprisingly, dealers like the STN preferred to draw their supplies from other local publishers but sell them over as wide an area as possible. The STN's preference for Swiss editions was inherent to the success of their business model, but their reach was international.

Thus while the STN data explodes once-and-for-all the 'floating stock' theory, in so far as the STN's inventory was overwhelmingly Swiss, we must not push the implications of this observation too far. For from a longer term or asynchronous perspective, the STN could and did source most successful secular works, regardless of where they were originally published. Indeed, our survey of the illegal trade suggests that it could and did at some time handle almost every clandestine work that ran to more than two or three of editions between 1770 and 1790.[44] Major differences in distribution patterns in different regions of Europe thus probably stemmed more from the nature of demand in each region (or, to be more precise, the preferences of the STN's local clientele) than from marked differences in the availability of titles. The challenge, then, is to isolate the factors that shaped demand – whether legal constraints, market expectations and desires, economic factors, taste or other cultural or chronological variables.

The chapters that follow analyse how demand varied between different markets and identify the editions and genres that travelled best, while noting that the STN had a particular market orientation. Most of their merchandise was aimed at a general, popular market. Although they poured vast resources into a handful of luxury editions, notably a heavily revised edition of the *Descriptions des arts et métiers* and the *Encyclopédie*, their day-to-day sales were cheap printings for a burgeoning market.[45] There is little reason to think that they were not a fairly typical enterprise in this respect. Of course, they had some business predilections. The religious market that they served was primarily Protestant and francophone. Moreover, although known to historians primarily as pushers of libertine pornography, political *libelles* and radical materialist works, the STN quickly took a hard-headed business decision not to publish such dangerous fare themselves. The personal impact of the *Système de la nature* and *Gazetier cuirassé* affairs on the STN's directors was probably too great to contemplate a repeat.[46] The STN enjoyed spectacular sales with Pidansat de Mairobert's salacious 'biographical' *Anecdotes sur Madame du Barri*, but the copies it sold came from elsewhere: most were probably printed by François Grasset in Lausanne.[47] Equally they left it to other Neuchâtel publishers to print Mirabeau's political and pornographic works. Not for them such fare as the *Errotika Biblion* (1783) and *Le Rideau Levé ou l'Education de Laure* (1788), a virgin's progress which commences with the eleven-year-old heroine being groomed and sexually molested by her own stepfather. Nevertheless, it is safe to conclude that, due to Prussian protection and a lax censorship regime, clandestine freethinking works were probably more prevalent *chez la STN* than in the general trade. Broadly speaking, the STN was free to hawk the entire literary output of late Enlightenment francophone Europe. They were in the business of marketing the bestselling popular books they could find.

However, the STN data is so rich and our digital tools sufficiently precise that we do not need to limit our analysis to the STN's trade *en bloc*. We can also look at distinct sections of the trade including, as we have seen, the origins and dissemination of books produced or bought from abroad. Such research is empowered by the eight options menus in the FBTEE database user interface, which serve to filter query outputs. The most important of these for present purposes is the 'edition type' menu, which can isolate editions by place of production. As a result, it is possible to compare, for example, the subject matter for books produced in France with those produced in Neuchâtel and the rest of Switzerland. This might give an indication of what sort of books were bought in by the STN from different parts of Europe. Chapter 7, 'Harvesting the Literary Field' contains just such an investigation. It shows that broadly speaking the STN was sourcing similar types of works in roughly (and sometimes remarkably) similar quantities from around Europe. At the level of subject taxonomic description, it does not appear that Swiss publishing differed significantly from French or Dutch publishing.[48] This finding should, however, be accompanied by our standard health warning. The places of publication ascribed to editions in the database can be problematic, primarily due to the widespread use of false imprints. Where such false imprints have been detected, a distinction has been recorded been 'stated' and 'actual' place of publication, and the 'option' menu filters search query results using the database field for the latter. Unfortunately, we cannot be sure that false imprints have always (or even usually) been picked up during the data entry process. However, by comparing provenance data to imprints, it seems that the books the STN bought from France were generally French editions, those purchased from the Netherlands Dutch editions and so forth.

Nevertheless, statistics derived from the database need to be treated with extreme caution. They contain multiple traps for the uninitiated. For example, one of the earliest searches I conducted was for the keyword 'American Revolution'. The initial results stunned me: 73 per cent of books ascribed this keyword went to France, and 57 per cent to Paris or Versailles, the political centres of the French Revolution in its early stages. Such figures might offer tentative support to the idea that the French and American Revolutions were 'sister revolutions', and that France perhaps became revolutionary in part because the French were better informed about, and more inspired by, the American Revolution. However, closer analysis revealed that sales figures for the 7,133 books bearing this keyword were dominated by two commissioned works, the anonymous *Extrait du journal d'un officier de la Marine de l'escadre de M. le comte d'Estaing* and Jacques-Pierre Brissot's *Testament politique de l'Angleterre*. The Versailles bookseller Poinçot ordered 1,800 copies of the former, while Brissot had 1,558 copies of the latter forwarded to him in Paris. Both were clearly handling their own distribution, quite probably through international networks.[49] Suddenly, the STN evidence for 'sister republics' seemed rather less compelling. The chapters that follow reveal many similar snares, and how to avoid them by carefully constructed search queries. As a result, we can view the STN data as revelatory of many of the larger contours of the pan-European trade in French books in the later Enlightenment, as well as many aspects of the Swiss local publishing trade, the French book market or long-distance commercial flows.

The main limitations of the STN data instead lie in the structural limitations and scale of the raw data rather than the Swiss biases of the STN. When the FBTEE project was launched, the scale of the dataset seemed its major advantage. One way the project was presented to its foundational funders, the British Arts and Humanities Research Council, was that our data would cover all Europe and every sector of the book trade. Hence the dataset would be about fifteen times larger than Darnton's survey of French clandestine demand, which recorded orders for 28,212 copies of 457 highly illegal *livres philosophiques*. The FBTEE database by contrast gives dissemination data on 413,710 copies of 3,601 works. It also gives supply data (some of it derived data on print runs) on 445,496 copies of those works. These numbers appear impressive, but as a means of measuring flows of books there is a problem. For our figures do not represent 413,710 individual sales or 445,496 book acquisitions. Instead, books tended to be traded in batches. The building blocks of the database are 70,584 discreet 'events' or 'transactions', each of which involves the 'in-flow', 'out-flow' or stocktaking of one or more copies of a particular edition of a specific work, usually to or from a named client based in an identifiable place and recorded on a stated date. Distributed in this way over a network of 2,895 clients in 516 towns, and with an average of over one-dozen copies per transaction, some of the fine-grained nuance we hoped to find becomes a little coarse and lumpy. Nor are sales distributed evenly across the sample.

Like modern publishing houses and booksellers, the STN derived the bulk of its sales from a limited number of titles (see Appendix 3.2). Just seventy-nine works account for half of all sales in the database. Eighty per cent of STN sales related to just 288 titles. At the other end of the demand curve, the STN disseminated a dozen copies or less of 1,114 of the 2,984 works with recorded 'sales'. Many of these have only one out transaction recorded against them. As a result, statistics drawn from global sales will inevitably be heavily skewed by a relatively small number of works that the STN traded in substantial numbers. Some of these were indeed international bestsellers, but others were primarily of local interest and almost all were published by the STN. In the analysis that follows, digital tools have been used to compensate for these inherent biases.

The take-home lesson from the examples given above, whether of the distribution pattern for works on the American Revolution, or the demand curve for STN books, is to reaffirm that the FBTEE database is best conceptualized as a digital representation of a collection of individual histories, all linked to a particular business archive. These histories interact and collide, as they narrate details of particular lives, tastes and businesses, about books, about places and about attempts to control books. Whenever we add new data, we add new narratives that might reveal or help to explain other histories. When we interrogate the database, we pull up new datasets, each of which offers a cumulative summary of multiple histories. Many of the tales thus revealed are primarily facets of the STN's own history; but others contain wider narratives of the business of books, the flow of ideas and cultural formation in the European Enlightenment.

4

The Intellectual Geography of the STN

Although the STN dreamed of using bookshops like *À l'Égide de Minerve* to reach a broad popular market across Europe, in reality they traded with a variety of local markets. In each they formed distinctive partnerships with one or more clients. In most, they reached only a limited proportion of available dealers. Thus our view of specific local markets is filtered through, and distorted by, a restricted and sometimes idiosyncratic client base. Moreover, as Mark Curran has shown in *Selling Enlightenment*, across a quarter-century long existence, the STN underwent a series of market reorientations. In many places, particularly at the European periphery, the STN's client base grew only slowly. Beyond their Swiss and French hinterlands, the heyday of their international market came late in their history. To accurately comprehend the STN's market, we therefore need to understand the distinctive contours and evolution of their local markets and the client dealers and readers of which they were comprised. Detailed case studies of London and Stockholm illustrate just how far local clients and market conditions might affect the nature of their trade with a particular capital city and its national hinterland.

As the nascent STN scoured Europe for markets, some places seemed more propitious than others. Britain proved more difficult than most. As early as 1769, indicating challenges to come, the leading London bookseller William Owen declined the first fruits of the STN's presses, remarking frankly, 'J'ai raison de conclure que c'est une chose très incertaine que la vente de ces livres dans cette ville, et qu'ils ne me conviendra [*sic*] nullement d'envoyer des orders.'[1] He would, however, happily take and promote books on commission on the STN's account. The STN ignored his offer.

It was a similar story with other leading booksellers. In February 1770, the STN's correspondent, Samuel Roulet, forwarded the names of London's seven principal dealers in foreign books, but warned:

> le peu de consumation de livres pour les françois, italiens, allemans &c., porte obstacle à la vente des livres dont vous cherchés à désposer, & surtout les fraix exhorbitans de transport & droits de Neuchâtel à Londres bornent beaucoup les affaires entre ces 2 places.

Roulet had for some time been trying to persuade these booksellers to do business with the STN and had spoken to several of them. Unfortunately 'ces messieurs m'ont dit qu'ils ne pourront guerre [*sic*] faire d'affaires avec vous pour les raisons cy dessus'. He also advised the STN against making any arrangements akin to that proposed by Owen, noting '& si quelqu'un vous en demande, il faut que le papier et l'impression soient parfaits, car tout ce qui n'est pas tel en ce genre est consideré icy comme parfait rebus'.[2]

So it was that the STN never entered into commercial relations with James Robson in New Bond Street, nor Thomas Davies in Great Russell Street, nor Thomas Payne in News Gate, Castle Street, nor Miller or John Nourse or Beckett and de Hondt in the Strand.[3] The sole bookseller on Roulet's list with whom they enjoyed any success was Peter Elmsley, through whom they placed several copies of the *Encyclopédie* and *Descriptions des arts et métiers*.[4] The problem was not one of cost and distance, however, but market orientation. For as the merchants Agassiz and Rougemont explained:

> ce seroit avec plaisir, messieurs, que nous saisirions les occasions d'être utiles à votre établissement, mais il nous sera difficile d'y réussir, n'aiant pas de relations avec les libraires que vous désignés. Nous devons d'ailleurs vous prévenir que la chereté des droits d'entrée sur les livres étrangers engage ordinairement ceux qui en font commerce à préférer les meilleures éditions qu'ils peuvent se procurer.[5]

British customs duties, it seems, significantly impacted upon the market for cheap foreign imports. With a catalogue comprising mainly popular editions and a distant home base, the STN was ill-equipped for the London market. Generally, established booksellers there could access editions printed in Britain and the Netherlands more quickly and more cheaply. Hence the Amsterdam firm Luchtmans was far more successful in snaring the London booksellers targeted by the STN: their clients included Robson, Payne and Elmsley. In the 1780s they also did business with Woodyer in Cambridge, Prince in Oxford, Fischer in Rochester, Elliot in Edinburgh and Hallhead in Dublin.[6] Foreign booksellers could prosper in the British trade, but they needed more attractive fare than the STN. Other Swiss publishers had managed this in the past. As Voltaire's publishers in the 1750s and 1760s, the Cramer brothers forged alliances with Nourse and the *huguenot* bookseller Paul Vaillant (c. 1715–1802), a correspondent and agent of Voltaire, who became sheriff of London but retired from the trade around 1770.[7] The STN may have hoped that their handful of *éditions de luxe* would prise open distant markets. Unfortunately, demand in London was insufficient to entice the major dealers to sell them on commission. To be sure, the Swiss pastor D. H. Durand managed to place thirteen copies of the quarto edition of the *Encyclopédie*. However, this edition, produced and marketed by a consortium including the STN, was apparently neither sufficiently luxurious nor sufficiently economical to appeal strongly to the bifurcated London market.[8] Bibliophile and aristocratic demand was probably already saturated by the various folio editions produced between the 1750s and 1778, while for humbler purchasers there was the cheaper octavo edition produced by the *Sociétés typographiques* of Berne and Lausanne from 1778 to 1782. Although savage price-cutting brought the price of the Neuchâtelois product down sharply from 384 *livres* to 240 *livres* by the early 1780s, this remained far from competitive.[9] The London-based Genevan exile, François d'Ivernois, reported that he could get the octavo edition for less than half the 225 *livres* demanded by the STN.[10] Faced with the London market, the STN was caught between a rock and a hard place.

Of course, d'Ivernois's testimony is self-interested. A long-established client of the STN, he was bargaining for better terms. In the same letter he rejects a 25 per cent discount on sales of their *Descriptions des arts et métiers* as inadequate and asks for their best possible price on Raynal's *Histoire philosophique des Deux Indes*.[11] Although these negotiations proved fruitless, it is the displaced refugee d'Ivernois, rather than prosperous merchants from the bookselling quarter around The Strand or Great Russell Street, who is typical of the STN's London clients.

The four London traders who did purchase STN wares were all marginal figures. James de Winter, who placed his sole order in December 1785, requested fifty-two copies of just seventeen titles. Top of his wish list were six copies of the *Contes moraux* of Marmontel, perhaps the bestselling *philosophe* novelist of the late 1770s and 1780s, and four each of the *Dictionnaire de l'Académie*, Voltaire's *Théatre*, Raynal's *Histoire philosophique des Deux Indes* and its supplementary *Recueil de diverses pièces servant de supplément à l'Histoire philosophique* and, more intriguingly, two different editions of the *Droit des gens portative*.[12] These look like sure-fire sellers rather than speculative purchases. Accompanying orders for two or three copies of several multivolume complete works, which presumably were unavailable in cheaper local editions, also suggests a certain market knowledge and perhaps pre-orders from customers. De Winter's request included Rollin's *Histoire ancienne* and *Histoire romaine*; the *Mémoires de Sully*; and sets of the collected works of Crébillon *fils*; Boileau; Rousseau ('grand' and 'petit' duodecimo editions of 30 and 31 volumes respectively); Henry Fielding (presumably for the benefit of French readers unable to manage the original); and the bestselling medical writer Tissot.[13] With the exception of the *Dictionnaire de l'Academie* and the *Mémoires de Sully*, the STN despatched everything de Winter requested on 17 January 1786. A month later, they sent a second consignment, which exactly replicated the first. Was this second despatch sent in error? Since de Winter's correspondence dries up after December 1785, there is no evidence that he placed the mirror order, nor gave the STN any repeat business. Perhaps he decided to stop dealing with the STN following this mistake? Perhaps he ceased trading? If so, he at least cleared his account, for his name is absent from a list of STN debtors and creditors produced in 1792. The STN were not so fortunate with their other London clients, Louis Huguenin du Mitand, Jean-Baptiste Arnal and Edward Lyde.

Huguenin, an educational writer, grammarian and schoolmaster, prided himself on his well-to-do Parisian origins and Swiss connections. However, by the early 1780s the family fortune was exhausted. Thus in the preface to the fourth edition of his *A New Treatise on the Method of Teaching Languages* (1782), Huguenin advertised 'genteel accommodation' in his home for up to eight boys, who would be taught languages and 'attended by capital masters in the different arts of Writing, Drawing, Dancing, Fencing, &c. for 100 Guineas a Year and 6 Guineas entrance'.[14] Nevertheless, Huguenin, who was frequently creative with the truth, boasted in his first letter to STN that he occupied a home costing 130 *Louis d'or* (about £110). The same letter, written in November 1782, claimed he had access to the homes of the British nobility and ran a 'petit magasin' with a rapid turnover of new and old books. Nevertheless, he asked the STN for six to nine months credit.[15] In all, Huguenin ordered 220 copies of eighty-two works from the STN.

Requesting credit was hardly unusual, but when the Paris banker Perregaux, via whom Huguenin proposed to make payment, denied knowing him, the STN began to have second thoughts. They demanded guarantors and refused payment in unmatured letters of credit. Huguenin was outraged: he was not, he protested, some 'pauvre diable' forced to survive on borrowed money. He had a 'bon table', three horses and a carriage, about 20,000 *livres* from *rentes*, a turnover of 30,000 *livres* at his bookshop and no need of the STN's business. The STN, hardened merchants, were unlikely to listen to such protestations. But they would heed the advice of the merchant Jean-Baptiste d'Arnal, formerly a partner in Arnal *frères*, their Lyon bankers. In 1781, d'Arnal settled in London where he attempted to place copies of the STN's most important works with booksellers.[16] In May 1783, d'Arnal informed the STN that he believed Huguenin was an *'honnête homme'* and capable of fulfilling his engagements but, since they were little acquainted, advised them to seek other *bona fides*. Doubts partially dispelled, the STN fulfilled Huguenin's first and only order on 30 July 1783. They soon regretted their hastiness. On 6 January 1784, Huguenin informed them that following a financial reverse he had retired from the book trade and was trying to settle with his creditors. He advised the STN to send a power of attorney (*procuration*) to allow their agents to sign his 'acte' of insolvency.[17] Although the STN did just that, it availed them little. On 1 October 1784, Rougemont and Agassiz, the merchants appointed to chase their bad debts in London, reported that Huguenin had disappeared. He had moved home leaving a false address.

The bad news did not stop there. The same letter reported that Rougemont and Agassiz could not locate Edward Lyde. This was a rude shock. Between March 1778 and October 1779, Lyde had lodged orders for 1,543 copies of one hundred works.[18] In all, the STN sent him almost nine hundred books and he still owed them 932 *livres* (about £ 39). The figure appears on a list of debtors drawn up in 1785, when the STN was itself in trouble. Huguenin also appears on that list, owing 629 *livres* and seveteen *sous*. Huguenin is listed again in 1792, still owing this sum. On both occasions the STN rated his credit as 'mauvais'.[19] Lyde's debt was presumably settled, however, for he does not appear on the 1792 list.

London was marginal to the STN in numerous ways. Having failed to penetrate the capital's leading book stores, they could barely gain a precarious toehold in the English market. England accounted for less than 0.3 per cent of the STN's sales, and only 0.25 per cent of their *Encyclopédies*.[20] This outcome was the result of commercial conditions and the hard-nosed business decisions of several key individuals. This is the context against which we should evaluate Darnton's famous discovery that the STN sold almost as many copies of their *Encyclopédie* (direct) to Dublin (where they traded with leading bookseller and pirate publisher Luke White) as to London, albeit that sales in these cities were limited twelve and thirteen respectively.[21] The STN did slightly better in indirect dealings with the Genevan-born London bookseller David Boissière. Boissière arrived in London and set up shop in about 1770, just too late to appear on Roulet's list. By 1782, d'Arnal described him as the 'principal libraire français à Londres'.[22] Boissière never dealt with the STN directly, but received their works through a middleman, Pierre Gosse junior in The Hague.[23]

The STN's sales to London might be considered too small even to merit a bestseller's list. Reflecting the decisions and client bases of a handful of marginal bookdealers, it reveals little about the scale of the London market and its overall preferences for French literature. For despite the pronouncements of Samuel Roulet, William Owen, or Agassiz and Rougemont, London's demand for French works was quite substantial. It took a sizeable proportion of the local output of French books, which as David Shaw has observed, accounted for 'one out of every ninety editions printed in London' between 1500 and 1800.[24] Besides those already mentioned, the trade supported numerous dealers who, at the very least, sold French books as a side line. In the 1770s and 1780s, M. de Lorme traded in Dover Street, Piccadilly, while in 1781 John Peter Lyton published a French edition of the *Vie privée de Louis XV*. The Swiss bookseller Joseph de Boffe had set up shop by 1786. His business, as the partnership De Boffe and Dulau, survived beyond the Second World War. In addition, various *marchands de nouveautés*, who presumably also sold French books, served as vendor outlets for the London-based French international newspaper *Le Courier de l'Europe*, including Henry Brookes in Coventry Street; Garrett in Panton Street; Shepperson and Reynolds in Oxford Street; and Axtell of Finch Lane.[25] Demand for French books was sufficient that between 1776 and 1782, de Lorme also ran a circulating library, as did John Boosey, whose bookshop and lending library specialized in French, Spanish, Italian, Danish, German, Dutch and Russian titles.[26] Foreign lending libraries also existed in provincial cities: for example, Leeds boasted an independent foreign library from about 1778 to 1814.[27]

It would be rash to assume that the STN's paltry sales to the British capital reflect the stock of the city's book merchants, particularly as their London trade only spans an eight-year period (March 1778 to February 1786). Yet the STN's London bestseller list does indicate the sort of safe-bet, tried and tested works that appealed to small-time dealers dependent for their livelihoods on a mix of French expatriate, British aristocratic and local school book markets. Its top ten, accounting for 41 per cent of the 1,155 books the STN despatched to London, is as follows:

1. *Mémoires du maréchal de Berwick*, 130 copies
2. Millot, *Elémens d'histoire générale*, 52 copies
3. Frederick II, *Eloge de Voltaire par le Roi de Prusse*, 50 copies
4. *Catalogue raisonné des manuscrits conservés dans la Bibliothèque de la ville et république de Geneve*, 50 copies
5. Voltaire, *Histoire de Charles XII*, 49 copies
6. Restaut, *Abrégé des principes de la grammaire Françoise*, 40 copies
7. Marmontel, *Les Incas*, 34 copies
8. *Œuvres de Rousseau*, 30.3 copies
9. *Lettre de Mr. de Voltaire à l'Académie française*, 22 copies
10. Alemán, *Histoire de Guzman d'Alfarache*, 21 copies

London's bestseller list is not particularly staid in its choice of literature, as perhaps befits the capital one of Europe's freest states. Alongside two popular textbooks (Millot's history, Restaut's grammar) and Alemán's moralizing picaresque novel (which was first published in 1599–1604), it includes five works associated with the *philosophes*. Three of these were by or relating to Voltaire, but Marmontel's philosophic novel *Les Incas* and the works of Rousseau also feature. The popularity of Marmontel's works in London is further attested by Edward Lyde's advice that the STN should reprint his enormously successful historical novel *Bélisaire*.[28] In combination with the *Encyclopédie*, which with twenty sales (slightly more than Darnton found in his survey) occupies eleventh place on the list, these figures suggest that the British market included some sophisticated readers who wanted access to the best of French Enlightenment literature.

The list also has a local British flavour, albeit with a twist: it is headed by the *Mémoires* of French Jacobite hero the Maréchal de Berwick. And, due no doubt to its statistically limited sample, it also contains a curiosity – Edward Lyde's apparently inexplicable purchase of fifty copies of Jean Senebier's *Catalogue raisonné des manuscrits conservés dans la Bibliothèque de la ville et république de Genève* (1779). Presumably Lyde's customers included a cross section of British cognoscenti, for Chirol's octavo edition was certainly no *édition de luxe*.

This survey of the British trade suggests that a complex interplay between market conditions, individual book dealers, local audiences and timing helped to determine the reception of the STN's wares, even in its freest and most limited markets. In more closely policed states, markets were also shaped by the effects of censorship. The intellectual geography of the STN's market is thus extremely complicated, and comparative insights it provides need careful evaluation.

The STN's market-orientation went through several phases, each of which affected its competitiveness in different places.[29] By the early 1780s, finding it increasingly hard to sell pirated or clandestine wares in France, which had hitherto been its primary market, the STN was having to look elsewhere. Fortunately, by 1783 the STN had developed one advantage that it lacked earlier in its history: stock – in increasing variety. On one level an expanding catalogue of back titles represented commercial failings. Publishers aimed to sell books, and each title lingering in the STN's stockpiles unsold represented unrealized – and perhaps unrealizable – capital. But they also gave clients a much wider choice, making the STN more attractive as a one-stop shop. With over 1,500 titles in its magazines, by 1787 the STN combined range of choice with depth of stock.[30] This made it increasingly attractive for clients in distant markets such as Sweden, where the STN secured a handful of major clients from 22 June 1782 to 1 October 1788.

On paper, Sweden was an attractive market. In 1781 the French printers' bible, the *Almanach de la librairie*, listed more book dealers in Stockholm than Amsterdam, Berlin, Madrid or Rome.[31] However, Swedish booksellers depended on a limited elite clientele and faced long delays if their chosen supplier could not send the titles that they ordered. The problems they faced are exemplified in a letter of 11 September 1787 from the Stockholm-based bookseller and director of the Royal Library, Charles G. Ulf. It requests that the STN expedite a new order via Wismar to beat the winter closure of navigation. Ulf adds:

> Pendant tout cet été le trafique de livres a été fort modique à cause du séjour à la campagne qu'ont fait la Cour et les chalands de marque, après leur retour en ville, j'espère que la circulation se raminera et à mesure de mes recouvremens, je ferai tous mes efforts, pour satisfaire ma promesse à Mr Durand l'ainé et me conserver votre confiance par des remises successives.[32]

Faced with a limited but wealthy market, Swedish booksellers tended to order many items in small numbers. For example, in her six large orders, all placed between 6 July 1784 and 23 November 1786, Ulf's former business partner Elsa Fougt, the bookseller to the Swedish court,[33] received 2,212 copies of 654 separate titles. With an average of just under three-and-a-half copies per title, Fougt's demand curve was so flat that it includes only seventeen titles with total orders of a dozen or more copies. The work she took in most numbers was Jean-Marie-Jérôme Fleuriot's romantic novel *Amours, ou lettres d'Alexis et Justine par M***** published by Jérome Witel in Verrières: the STN sent her a mere twenty-six copies. This amounted to just 1.17 per cent of her total purchases.

A composite bestsellers table of the STN's three Swedish bookselling clients proves similarly flat. In total, Fougt, Ulf and Antoine Adolphe Fyrberg took 6,267 copies of STN merchandise.[34] Their combined top ten bestseller list indicates that they served a very different market to London. It reads:

1. Mercier, *Tableau de Paris*, 77 copies
2. Genlis, *Adèle et Théodore ou Lettres sur l'éducation*, 62 copies
3. Leprince de Beaumont, *Magasin des enfans*, 59 copies
4. Mirabeau, *Le Libertin de qualité*, 55 copies
5. Rilliet, *Inceste avoué à un mari*, 50 copies
6. Rilliet, *Planta gagnant sa vie en honnête homme*, 50 copies
7. *Pièces importantes à la dernière révolution de Genève*, 50 copies
8. Imbert, *Chronique scandaleuse*, 38.6 copies
9. Millot, *Elémens d'histoire générale*, 38 copies
10. Fleuriot, *Amours ou lettres d'Alexis et Justine*, 36 copies

The STN's London and Swedish top ten bestseller lists have only one work in common. That work is Millot's history textbook, *Elémens d'histoire générale*, which the STN printed and sold in significant numbers. However, three other works on the Swedish list were STN 'bestsellers'. First among them was Mercier's celebrated *Tableau de Paris*, which, if we ignore commissioned titles, was the STN's top-selling work of all time. Likewise, *Planta gagnant sa vie en honnête homme* was the work they printed and distributed in greatest numbers. Finally, the *Pièces importantes à la dernière révolution de Genève* was an important commissioned political pamphlet which they printed and distributed in bulk. All these works are discussed in later chapters. Their presence here is indicative of wider European patterns.

A more distinctive feature of the STN's Swedish market is a predilection for scandalous works, two of which, Mirabeau's pornographic novel *Ma Conversion ou le libertin de qualité* and Guillaume Imbert's notorious *Chronique scandaleuse*, gatecrash the top ten. Slightly further down the list come Chloderos de Laclos's classic erotic novelistic depiction of aristocratic libertine decadence, *Les Liaisons dangereuses*, and the Marquis de Luchet's libertine satirical novel *Le Vicomte de Barjac*. The STN sent twenty-eight copies of both to Stockholm. The Swedish market also absorbed two dozen copies of the *Mémoires de Suzon, sœur de D… B… portier des Chartreux* and *Histoire de Marguerite fille de Suzon, nièce de Dxx Bxxxxx*. To the initiated these titles smacked of the illicit pleasures of anticlerical libertine pornography. The cryptic 'D.B.' in both titles is the hero of the *Histoire de Dom Bougre, portier des Chartreux*, a clandestine classic brimming with bawdy tales of monastic orgies, sex and buggery.

This and other evidence hints at the existence of a small but significant libertine group among the Swedish aristocratic elite, who avidly consumed French scandalous works and pornography. This might explain why Sweden was the only country to support a translation of Théveneau de Morande's notorious *Gazetier cuirassé*.[35] Clandestine works seemed able to enter the country easily enough. A letter from Ulf instructing the STN on how to smuggle Raynal's *Histoire philosophique des Deux Indes*, Cleland's *La Fille de joie*, the *Académie des Dames*, the *Histoire de Dom B.* and d'Argens notorious materialist anticlerical novel *Thérèse philosophe*, suggests that inspectors seldom looked beyond the packing inventories. It observed:

> Il n'est pas nécessaire de les cacher dans d'autres livres tout ce qu'il y a observer, c'est de ne les point mettre à la facture et qu'à l'avenir vous voulez bien me faire tous les envois en caisses et de placer Rainal [Raynal] et les autres articles prohibés au fond.[36]

The STN never carried out this order, for Ulf died shortly afterwards owing them over 9,300 *livres*.[37] This sum was never recovered. The STN's claim on Ulf's estate lapsed after they failed to send Schön and Cie, their agents in Stockholm, a power of attorney in time to be included on his list of creditors. As late as 1792, Ulf was listed as their second biggest debtor.[38] They were luckier with Elsa Fougt. When faced with financial difficulties, she placed merchandise received from the STN on deposit with Schön until the debt was redeemed.[39] Although Fyrberg sent repeated remittances, eventually he, too, fell behind on payments. By 1792 he owed 2,838 *livres* and the STN rated his credit '*douteux*'.[40] As in London, their affairs had gone badly wrong. Their Stockholm clients had appeared solidly established but this proved an illusion.

Sweden's French book trade was always precariously balanced. The small aristocratic client base on which Fougt, Fyrberg and Ulf depended made them vulnerable and limited their orders. This explains the low sales figures for Swedish bestsellers and the relative prominence of another category of book: works related to education. This includes textbooks such as Millot's history, pedagogical works, books aimed at children and novels on educational themes. The second and third placed works on the Swedish bestsellers list, Madame de Genlis's didactic novel *Adèle et Théodore ou Lettres sur l'éducation* and Jeanne-Marie Leprince de Beaumont's *Magasin des enfans* both fall into these categories. So, too, do seven other works in the top twenty-five.[41]

The Swedish nobility may have been typical of Europe's francophone elites in their pedagogical preferences, particularly in favouring de Genlis and Leprince de Beaumont. A survey of Dutch auction catalogues for 254 eighteenth-century private libraries, both local and foreign, found Leprince de Beaumont's works present in 50 per cent, a total second only to Voltaire. Madame de Genlis featured in 32 per cent.[42] The prominence of these bestselling pedagogical tools in the STN's Swedish trade points to another, more significant, conclusion. In peripheral countries like Sweden, although demand for French-language 'school books' and pedagogic treatises was relatively high, local printers could not offload the large print runs required to sustain mass production of cheap educational texts. Instead, dealers drew their stocks from the French-speaking heartlands, where they were printed in bulk primarily for local markets, but at a unit price that could undercut small print runs in peripheral markets.

A map of the STN's distribution of school books reinforces these conclusions (see Map 4.1). While Switzerland took a disproportionate number of school books (19,762 units or 62.7 per cent), and the French a further 17.5 per cent, over half the remainder (2,660 units) went to Eastern Europe (Poland and Russia). This exceeded combined textbook sales to the German, Italian, Dutch and Belgian zones, suggesting that these countries comprised an inner core of partially or non-francophone territories whose domestic markets could support local mass production of cheap textbook editions (and probably other cheap mass-produced genres such as religious texts). Poland and Russia by contrast were part of an outer periphery that, lacking extensive domestic markets, had to import such works.[43] This inflated prices, but not sufficiently to justify more expensive local production. Michel Schlup suggests that transport costs for the journey to Russia were normally about 20 per cent of the value of books, though with smaller consignments that could rise to 40 per cent. A portion of this cost was borne by the STN, who paid transport costs as far as the first seaport. This was generally Amsterdam if the books were shipped to Saint Petersburg via the Rhine, or Lübeck if they travelled overland, a route which the STN came to favour more over time. In addition, there was the cost of maritime insurance, generally calculated at 2.2 per cent of value.[44]

The STN's four top-selling titles in Russia were all school books. Nor were the works in question – Pierre Restaut's *Abrégé des principes de la grammaire Françoise*; Ostervald's *Géographie elémentaire* and *Géographie*; and Mathurin Veyssière de

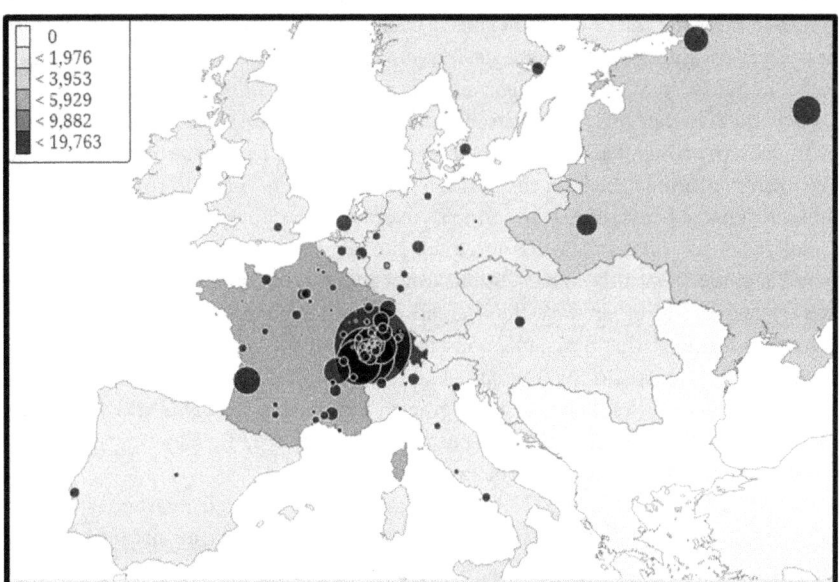

Map 4.1 Distribution of School Books by the STN, 1769–94.

Lacroze's *Abrégé élémentaire de l'histoire universelle* – the only educational texts selling well to Russia.[45] Textbooks or didactic works aimed at the young occupy many further slots in the Russian bestseller charts. Elsewhere in the top twenty-five are Johann Christoph Gottsched's widely admired, *Maître de la langue allemande*, Millot's *Elémens d'histoire générale*, Hübner's *Histoires de la Bible* and several of Leprince de Beaumont's compilations. In part this was a consequence of the vagaries of the Russian market. The STN's trade with the Tsarina's Empire was confined to the twin capitals, St Petersburg and Moscow. These were the only cities large enough to support an educated clientele for the STN's merchandise, and home to the country's only institutions of higher education. The STN's Russian clients included dealers connected to the world of education, notably J.-J. Weitbrecht, head of the printshop of the Army Cadet Corps in St Petersburg, and Christian Rüdiger, director of the Imperial Bookshop at the University of Moscow.[46] Between them Rüdiger and Weitbrecht took over 60 per cent of books the STN despatched to Russia.

Given the limited and aristocratic nature of the Russian market, these dealers, like the Swedish booksellers, rarely took more than six to ten copies of each title. However, they made an exception for educational textbooks, which they might order fifty at a time. Due to the tyranny of distance and climate, repeat orders were few and far between. Navigation of the Baltic was seldom open much more than five months, so Russian dealers tended to place and receive just one order per year, usually in late April or May.[47] Occasionally, a second order might follow as late as October or November, but these consignments needed to overwinter en route. This did not favour repeat purchases of the latest fashionable *nouveautés*, which even when reordered might be unavailable by the time the STN received a second request. Hence besides textbooks, the works the STN sent to Russia in greatest numbers were their own mass-printed editions, some of which may have been sent 'on spec'.[48] Similar to the Swedish bestsellers list they include Mercier's *Tableau de Paris*; three pamphlets by Théodore Rilliet de Saussure; and *Pièces importantes à la dernière révolution de Genève*.

Beyond these categories the bestselling STN work in Russia was a French translation of the German bookseller Friedrich Nikolai's novel *L'Intolérance ecclésiastique*. Weitbrecht informed the STN that Nikolai's novel owed its vogue to royal favour: 'J'ai présenté à notre Souveraine [Catherine II] avec d'autres nouveautés un exemplaire de l'intolérance [i.e. *Intolérance ecclésiastique*], etc. Elle en a beaucoup ri, et cela a mis le livre à la mode.'[49] But although traditional royal approbation might occasionally dictate literary fashion, in other ways the Russian market largely resembled others. Michel Schlup has argued that Russian booksellers ordered all kinds of works, including Enlightenment texts and *livres philosophiques*. The STN database indicates that they took marginally less erotica and pornography, highbrow *philosophie* and anticlerical literature than the general run of STN customers, but not once we allow for the Russian dealers' predilection for school books and didactic works.[50]

Local niche markets for STN products can also be detected in frontier regions. Perhaps not surprisingly, these were major consumers of dictionaries and instructional language materials. This is particularly apparent in the sales patterns for French and German language dictionaries, which outside (bilingual) Switzerland are clustered in major capital cities and around the Rhineland (see Appendix 1.1).

Practical manuals dealing with agriculture, exclusively or in part, also have a distinctive distribution pattern that appears to reflect their market (see Appendix 1.2). In all, some thirty-six 'agricultural manuals' appear in the STN database, and these are headed by *L'Art de faire le vin* (499 copies sold), *L'Art de la Vigne* (234 sales) and *Le Jardin potager mis à la portée de tout le monde* (199 sales). They also include books on animal husbandary, veterinary medicine and arboriculture. Relatively few copies of such works sold to Western capitals or the mountainmen of the Swiss Romand. Far more went to smaller provincial centres, probably for purchase by local landowners. Besançon (ninety-four copies) took more agricultural manuals than Lyon and Paris combined. Indeed, the STN sold only two copies of such works in the French capital, although they sold forty-one copies to Versailles, presumably to courtiers keen to improve their estates or, perhaps, their wine cellars.

Distinctive markets of another kind existed in Geneva and the Dutch republic, particularly in The Hague. There, STN wholesale clients plied long-distance mail-order businesses similar to the STN. For that reason, bulk sales of works to these destinations, as well as to a few other Swiss houses, must be seen as part of an *entrepôt* trade, with the final destinations for books ordered typically far from the places to which the STN initially shipped them.[51] Books sent to The Hague to Pierre Gosse *fils* as likely as not were shipped onwards to London where, as we have noted, Gosse enjoyed an exclusive arrangement and business partnership with David Boissière.[52] One of Boissière's surviving catalogues, produced in about 1775, contains twenty-four Neuchâtel editions, including nineteen published by the STN. All nineteen appear to have been traded in substantial numbers by Gosse between 1769 and 1775.[53] Likewise, with some obvious exceptions, books sent to Geneva were mostly intended for distribution in France, particularly in Lyon and the South.[54] The likely scale of this trade is indicated by Giles Barber's study of the *Grand Livre* of the Genevan publishers Cramer *frères* in the period 1755–66. Just under half of their international business by value was shipped to France. In marked contrast to the STN's commerce, a large portion of their stock was shipped to Paris.[55] If Cramer was typical, the Genevan international wholesalers also sent a far larger proportion of their stock to the Iberian peninsula than did the STN.[56]

Even the STN's direct trade with France – their biggest and most important foreign market for most of their history – might best be conceived as a series of niche markets, each formed around particular communities and clusters of clients. The Parisian market, for example, proved impossible to crack. Particularly before the 30 August 1777 reforms, the Parisian printers jealously guarded their monopolies over much of the kingdom's book production against interlopers. Parisian book dealers were also closely policed: it was difficult to get large consignments of books into the city without facing inspection by the local *chambre syndicale* (bookseller's guild). Not surprisingly, few Parisian dealers were keen to do business with a foreign pirate publishing house, and so the STN made little progress despite the efforts of their local agent, Quandet de Laschenal. The STN corresponded with less than 10 per cent of the three hundred printers and booksellers trading in Paris between 1769 and 1789, and only succeeded in establishing low-volume trading links with a handful of these.[57] Although they shipped significant consignments of books to Paris, some 38,570 units in total, the vast majority – 28,653 units – were commissioned editions for clients such as Brissot,

Göezman, or Le Scene Desmaisons, and destined to be on-sold. As we shall see, not all these consignments reached their intended destinations.[58]

Of the remaining 10,000 units, only a few thousand went to Parisian booksellers. More than half went to Quandet de Lachenal and eight hundred more to the authors Mercier, Brissot and Simon-Nicolas-Henri Linguet. The STN's largest Parisian bookseller clients were Nicolas-Léger Moutard on the *rue des Mathurins* who, if we ignore commissioned editions, took around 1,500 units, and Louis François Barrois (a.k.a. Barrois *l'aîné*), Jacques-François Valade, Edme-Marie-Pierre Desauges and Cugnet, who each took less than two hundred. Generally, Parisian clients, whether booksellers, authors or distribution agents, cared little for pirate editions and the STN's general stock. Of 3,600 titles traded by the STN, Parisian customers took just 375. The vast majority of books sent to them were freshly printed by the STN. Just 1,401 copies of non-STN titles were despatched to the French capital.

From the late 1770s, French trading conditions became even tougher, as the new inspection regime introduced by the decrees of 30 August 1777 squeezed the STN's clandestine trade. The decrees established a much tighter system of inspection over consignments of imported books and attached a centrally paid inspector to each of the country's twenty *chambre syndicales*. Before the decrees, dealers such as Charles-Antoine Charmet in Besançon used their positions in the *chambres syndicales* to protect and promote the STN's clandestine trade, often abetted by the local authorities. Charmet himself enjoyed the protection and connivance of the local intendant Charles-André de Lacoré, but, following the appointment of an independent inspector, he decided that the risks of the clandestine trade now outweighed the rewards.[59] In February 1778, he duly informed the STN that he could no longer participate in their smuggling operations.[60] Other leading dealers followed suit.[61] The measures hit the pirate trade, too, by cancelling *privilèges* relating to a large number of bestselling or classic works and placing them in the public domain. Henceforth the government would, against a small fee, allow French publishers to produce new editions of these works.[62] This cut the ground from under the foreign pirate trade and helped to re-energize provincial publishing.

The STN kept its flagging business with France afloat by sending an agent, Favager, to whip up new custom. Beginning in July 1778, Favager's tour brought a flurry of business, but few of his new clients placed repeat orders.[63] Nevertheless, the period 1779–82 was the heyday of the STN trade, and saw them pump more books into France than at any other period, including pirated editions. However, trade volumes with France were already falling back when the *Arrêt* of 12 June 1783 brought this golden age to an abrupt close. The *Arrêt* ordered all books entering the kingdom to be inspected in Paris.[64] This delivered a coup de grâce to the Neuchâtelois and their fellow Swiss publishing houses, whose wares needed to take a more circuitous detour than their Dutch, Belgian or Rhenish competitors, adding to their costs and time delays, and wrecking their comparative advantages in the marketplace. Unfortunately, their protests fell on deaf ears.[65] The measure was finally repealed as being 'destructive du commerce de librairie' in mid-1787, following the death of its architect, the foreign minister Vergennes.[66] By then the damage was done. The STN's attempts to stir up new business in France by their touring salesman, Durand, proved abortive. As he progressed from July 1787 to November 1788 through Southern France, Italy and the German lands, the gathering revolutionary crisis was already beginning to shift French readers' focus towards locally produced political pamphlets and journalistic products at the expense of books in general and foreign books in particular. In 1788, our admittedly incomplete data records only 174 sales to France (out of 10,786). Between 23 May 1790 and 22 August 1793, a period for which records are complete, the figure falls to 38 (from 5,919). The STN limped on into the revolutionary era, but its remit was increasingly circumscribed in terms of sales and geographic reach, especially after the outbreak of the revolutionary wars in 1792. Its last recorded sales were on 20 May 1794 when it shipped a large consignment of its remaining stock to Durand, Ravanel et Compagnie in Lausanne.[67]

One of the STN's more significant and enduring bonds with France was through its Protestant co-religionists. Before 1788, French Protestants were unable to publish their own liturgical and religious works, and following an edict of 1686, all printers had to be avowed Catholics of good morals.[68] Thus many French Protestants, particularly in the South, looked to the Switzerland for religious books and an outlet for printing their own pious works. Hence a map of sales of Protestant scriptures and religious texts closely follows the famous Protestant Arc, from Geneva and Neuchâtel in the East through Nîmes and Montpellier to Bordeaux, La Rochelle and Rochefort in the West (see Appendix 1.3). On this route is the small town of Ganges, the destination for the commissioned religious works printed by the STN for the local pastor, Pomaret. Ganges thus took more religious books from the STN than any other city in France, and her total trade rivalled that of more prominent towns in its region, notably Nîmes and Montpellier.

The STN's trade with other French towns also had distinctive characteristics, usually shaped by the dealers who traded with them, usually for a few years at most. The Besançon bookseller Charles-Antoine Charmet and his wife are rare exceptions. They corresponded with the STN for over fifteen years, longer than any other French clients. During that time the STN despatched crates containing over 7,000 books to the Charmets' shop. Were they representative of Besançon's general book trade? As noted in Chapter 3, Robert Darnton certainly thinks so. But looks can deceive, and 7,000 books contributed little to the city's overall sales: Charmet's own brother occasionally printed editions in runs of 4,000 copies. As we shall see, Charles-Antoine used the STN to fill niche demand, and this was apparently far from typical of Besançon's overall sales.[69] It is dangerous therefore to assume that the STN's wholesale trade with a single town, let alone a single dealer, can tell us a great deal about the nature of a place's readership or intellectual climate. Moreover, as our case studies demonstrate, the STN's trade with peripheral regions was too limited to permit all but the most tentative conclusions about comparative reading tastes across Europe. Conversely, at the core of the STN's trading networks – in France and the Swiss romande – raw trade figures can be distorted by the presence of large *entrepôt* centres and middlemen. Thus an unexpected conclusion of the FBTEE project was that for some purposes the dataset was too small to draw reliable internationally comparative conclusions. Often the best we could do was to filter out the middlemen (using our options menus) and run a three-way comparison between France, Switzerland and the rest of Europe.

Nevertheless, the search for informative 'fuzzy snapshots' of demand within particular towns and regions was not entirely hopeless.

Where then might we hope to find for an accurate, representative snapshot of a local market? One possibility might be Germany, where the STN sold over 17,000 units, or 23,000 if we include the integral lands of the Austrian and Hungarian crown.[70] As we have noted, Jeffrey Freedman's study of the STN's German market contends that because no town in the Holy Roman Empire save for Vienna had sufficient demand to support a specialist French bookseller, the STN's German clients served large hinterlands. The demand that he detects came from a relatively limited elite: aristocratic circles at Germany's many princely courts and urban middle class readers, often organized in *sociétés littéraires* or reading circles.[71] Analysing the German market is made more complex by the many possible definitions of Germany available for the eighteenth century. If we take Germany to mean the Holy Roman Empire and thus include Belgium, much of Austrian Empire including Vienna and Prague, and the bishopric of Basel in northern Switzerland, the STN sales list looks truly radical. Its top ten bestsellers include d'Holbach's *Système de la nature* at number two, Voltaire's riposte *Dieu. Réponse de M. de Voltaire au Système de la nature* at number three and Voltaire's *Questions sur l'Encyclopédie* at number nine. But many copies of those works disappear if we adopt a *Kleindeutsch* solution, including the majority of copies of the *Système de la nature*, which were destined for Boubers in Brussels. Yet if we try to break German demand down by individual towns, we must generally rely on the assumption that the trade of a single local dealer is representative of the wider trade of a region.

Italy seems a bit more promising, since it is easier to define geographically and geopolitically. The STN's 20,230 unit sales there were broadly dispersed among fifteen different towns.[72] Thus sales figures for Italy, being spread fairly evenly across the country, may have a broader representative value. This hypothesis is supported by the STN's list of the twenty all-time Italian bestsellers, which has a relatively flat demand curve and includes several works not published by the STN (see Appendix 3.3). Moreover, almost all the Italian bestsellers are familiar from other chapters of this book. The exceptions are two works of local interest to Italian readers, since they treated local dignitaries, who were respectively a viceroy of Sicily and a Venetian patrician and diplomat. The *Apologie du marquis de Fogliani* and Louis Godard's *Discours oratoire contenant l'éloge de S.E.M. le chevalier André Tron* were both printed on commission by the STN. The *Discours* was printed for Guiseppe Rondi in Bergamo in March 1774, the *Apologie* for Rondi and his business partners six months later. No extant copy of either edition has been found.[73] The list fairly bristles too with Enlightenment works and intellectually heavyweight *livres philosophiques*, including works by Voltaire, Marmontel and the abbé Raynal. Scandalous or sexually libertine works are conspicuously absent. Moreover, the list is replete with overtly political works in multiple genres, including those relating to Tron and Fogliani, Mercier's play *La Destruction de la Ligue* and utopian fantasy *L'An 2440*; Vatel's *Droit des gens*, Raynal's *Histoire philosophique des Deux Indes* and Mably's *De La Législation*; as well as Marmontel's *Les Incas*, Fénélon's *Avantures de Télémaque* and the *Pièces importantes à la dernière revolution de Genève*. If this was their typical reading fare, the Italians were surely the most politically engaged people in Europe.

But was it? More likely we can link many of these books to francophone urban elites – who suggestively were the social group most receptive to the French rule during the revolutionary triennium. Moreover, at the level of individual Italian towns, it is hard to judge whether the FBTEE database gives a representative view of local markets. For example, the STN's 4,306 sales to Turin went predominantly to just two, quite different dealers. Reycends, *frères*, were long-term clients of the STN: they bought over 1,700 books between January 1772 and May 1787. In contrast, Charles-Marie Toscanelli took around 1,780 books in just ten months between December 1787 and October 1788. There are thus deep chronological and possibly personal biases in the Turin data.

Neuchâtel itself probably offers our best chance to uncover directly 'popular' tastes in a single town. There a group of clients bought books for everyday use across the STN's shop counter.[74] The archival records cover some 3,761 units of 616 titles sold across the counter during almost the whole of the STN's existence.[75] These sales can be isolated in the database using the 'Client type' menu and subjected to close analysis. Unfortunately, the identities of buyers are rarely mentioned. Mostly they are described as 'unknown clients paying cash'. However, rare exceptions provide a fleeting glimpse of daily life and concerns.

On 6 June 1774, the STN accounts record the counter sale of *Leçons du Clavecin* to Mademoiselle Bondely.[76] Why did the STN's clerks record this detail? We do not know.[77] It suggests a familiarity with the family, so perhaps Mademoiselle Bondely was the daughter of another STN client, Madame Bondely (whose place of residence is not given, and was thus presumably local to Neuchâtel and known to the publishers). If books give an insight into their readers, we might imagine that theirs was a rather austere existence made tolerable by fantasies of lottery wins and the daughter's keyboard playing, for Madame Bondely's only known purchases from the STN were a *Traité de la vie sobre* and a *Livre de rêves, ou l'Oneiroscopie. Application des songes aux numéros de la Loterie royale de France*.[78] Alternatively, perhaps these entries relate to the (unmarried) Swiss *salonnière* Julie Suzanne Bondeli (1732–78), who spent the last ten years of her life in quiet retirement in Neuchâtel.[79] Might she, too, have appreciated a life of sobriety and musical interludes while daydreaming of spending a fortune?

The STN's trade-counter customers mostly bought only one copy at a time, suggesting that they visited the STN magazine purposefully to collect some personal reading.[80] There are also, however, a number of suggestive instances of bulk over-the-counter sales. The titles taken on such occasions may well be revealing of collective reading practices or communal activity. Almanacs were a common mass purchase: six were sold to a single customer on 16 April 1774 and another took nine copies of the *Almanach de Neuchâtel* on 4 November 1773. Religious works were also commonly purchased *en bloc*. On 31 March 1773 the STN's trade counter sold nine copies of the *Sermons de Bertrand*, a work which did particularly well there.[81] Another favourite was the *Abrégé de l'histoire sainte et du catéchisme*.[82] On 15 January 1774 the STN sold five copies over the counter, and on 12 February they shifted twenty-one more along with thirteen *Recueil des passages du Nouveau Testament*. Twelve more *Abrégés* were sold on 9 May 1774 with six *Cantiques sacrés*. Seven more sold on 11 July and thirty-nine on 18 December. Textbooks also sold in job lots: five *Géographie elémentaire* were sold on 31 May 1774 and six more on 6 June. So, too, in the year of his death, did funeral orations for Louis XV. Fourteen copies of the *Eloge de Louis XV* were sold on 11 July 1774 and five of an *Eloge funèbre de Louis XV* on 16 October. Thirteen more sold on 18 December. Most intriguingly, on 6 June 1774, a customer bought two copies of the pornographic *L'Arretin*. Presumably only one copy was for his or her personal use. This raises interesting questions about communal purchases of erotica.

Over-the-trade-counter purchases allow us to reconstruct the reading of a discrete group of Neuchâtelois clients in detail (for a full top twenty listing see Appendix 3.4). They indicate a striking localism in the Neuchâtelois customers' favoured reading and authors. The authors that dominate are mostly local men: the two Ostervalds and two Bertrands alone were responsible for eight of the twenty bestsellers. The subject matter for many trade-counter bestsellers was also of local interest, including Frédéric-Samuel Ostervald's *Description des montagnes et des vallées qui font partie de la principauté de Neuchâtel et Valangin*, Elie Bertrand's *Thévenon*, Hertzberg's *Collection de pièces intéressantes et authentiques concernant la vie et les derniers jours de Frédéric le Grand* and, more tangentially, the *Compte rendu* of Genevan-boy-made-good Jacques Necker.

Equally striking is the religious nature of popular reading in Neuchâtel. The *Psalms* (mostly with musical scores) and the *New Testament* (in integral text and a digest of key passages) are both present, as is a French translation of Johann Hübner's monumentally popular Lutheran *Biblische Historien*. This was 'the most widely used school Bible and children's Bible' in early eighteenth-century Germany and Switzerland and clocked up at least 274 editions and fifteen translations between its first publication in 1714 and final edition in 1902.[83] Religion also features in the shape of the Neuchâtelois' number one bestseller, Jean-Frédéric Ostervald's *Abrégé de l'histoire sainte et du catéchisme* and Jean-Elie Bertrand's *Sermons*.

Several trade-counter bestsellers aimed at a youthful audience, either as school textbooks or for religious instruction, or both. These include J.-F. Ostervald's *Abrégé de l'histoire sainte et du catéchisme*, F.-S. Ostervald's various geographies and historical geographies, Restaut's celebrated *Abrégé des principes de la grammaire Françoise*, Millot's *Elémens d'histoire générale*, Fougereux's *Abrégé de l'histoire poétique, ou Introduction à la mythologie par demandes et par réponses*, John Gregory's *Legs d'un père à ses filles*, a Christian conduct manual for young women and, of course, Hübner's *Histoires de la Bible*. The bestseller list also includes an anthology of *Lectures pour les enfans* by leading seventeenth-century and eighteenth-century authors.

Conspicuously absent from Neuchâtelois counter-trade sales, if we ignore extracts by Voltaire, Marmontel, Montesquieu and Saint-Lambert in the *Lectures pour les enfans*, is even a whiff of Enlightenment *philosophie*. A work by the anti-*philosophe* Simon-Nicolas-Henri Linguet makes the cut, but it is a pamphlet product of his battles with the French government for permission to circulate his works rather than debates with rival thinkers. Nor, with the single exception of the *Lettre de M. Linguet à Monsieur de Vergennes* does any of the libertine clandestine works that Robert Darnton so memorably traced through magazines of the STN make the bestseller list. The highest selling heavyweight philosophical work is Raynal's *Histoire philosophique des Deux Indes*, which with just eleven counter sales ranks at number seventy. Politics, foreign travel, fiction, novels, plays and poetry are also missing from the picture, and in their place we find the workaday (almanacs), spiritual and educational literature, and works of local interest.

Is this evidence that Neuchâtel was a Swiss provincial backwater, immune to the Enlightenment that was supposedly a major part of the STN's stock-in-trade? Or were the town's ordinary readers typical of their peers in smaller communities across Switzerland and Europe? Is it possible that cheap devotional editions and school books were the sales mainstay for even the most adventurous of Swiss publishers? If so, was Enlightenment a mainly metropolitan phenomenon which, beyond the great cultural capitals of Europe, interested only small elites? And was religious reading more deeply entrenched than previous surveys based on private libraries and will bequests have suggested? Furthermore, were reading audiences more parochial and less open to cosmopolitan influences than we have been led to expect? What too was the place of fiction, drama and lightweight reading in the literary diet and can their importance be overstated? These are challenging and iconoclastic questions, and certainly cannot be adequately answered on the basis of the reading habits of a limited sample of small-town readers in a remote and mountainous Prussian-Swiss principality. However, through the evidence of the STN database and related datasets, as well as close readings of some of the books they contain, it should be possible to place the Neuchâtelois evidence into a wider context. And to contextualize the preferences of the Neuchâtelois, it seems appropriate to begin by examining the STN's global bestsellers list and revisiting the book at its apex.

5

Forgotten Bestsellers

Sex, betrayal, incest, marital breakdown, political intrigue, courtroom drama and a colourful cast of characters: Théodore Rilliet de Saussure's *Planta gagnant sa vie en honnête homme* had them all. To modern eyes, it contains all the ingredients of a blockbuster bestseller or Hollywood movie. And Rilliet swore that it was all true. The tale opens with a tearful wedding-night confession. In the bombshell revelation that would tear their lives apart, Ursula von Planta admitted to Rilliet, her new husband, that she had borne her own brother an illegitimate love child. Rilliet, a member of the Genevan Grand Council of 200, who somewhat scandalously was already a divorcee, was shocked but initially made the best of it. The couple, who married in 1773, were still together in Paris in the winter of 1775, when Rilliet learned that several people in Geneva were aware of the love child. Deeply humiliated, he repudiated Ursula and sued her brother, the baron Friedrich von Planta. Planta counter-sued for defamation. The Grand Council found against Rilliet, who on 24 August 1780 was gaoled, stripped of his Genevan citizenship, and ordered to pay damages and settle an annuity on Ursula.[1] Rilliet's pamphlet, the last of several he penned during this epic struggle, was written to protest his innocence and the searing injustice of a decision that added political disgrace to sexual betrayal. Sadly, this unedifying tale has no happy ending. Rilliet died suddenly shortly afterwards in circumstances which suggest a heart attack or perhaps, as Mark Curran has proposed, foul play.[2] Ursula retired into obscurity. As for Planta, he became embroiled in further scandal. His testimony in the celebrated Diamond Necklace trial would help clear Cardinal Louis de Rohan.

In the age of the 'misery memoir', few eyebrows will be raised at the sight of a work like *Planta gagnant sa vie* standing at the apex of our STN 'bestseller's table' (see Table 5.1). Its presence there seemed great news for the French Book Trade in Enlightenment Europe project. A little-known pamphlet by an obscure Genevan economist seemed to have outsold anything in the STN's stock by Voltaire, Rousseau, d'Holbach, Louis-Sébastien Mercier or Madame Riccoboni. Better still, though illegal in France, the pamphlet does not register in Darnton's rival bestseller tables in *Forbidden Best-Sellers*. We could hardly have hoped for a more exciting and explosive find. Or so it seemed. But there was a problem.

There is, of course, something spellbinding about the idea of a bestseller. Bestseller lists indicate what texts, music or other products are popular, and presumably desirable. Thus they help us to organize and understand our world. They offer us tantalizing glimpses of the common knowledge, shared tastes, inner lives and secret desires of our

Table 5.1 The STN all-time bestselling primary authors for global, trade and commercial lists compared[3]

	Global list		Trade list		Commercial list	
Rank	Author	Sales	Author	Sales	Author	Sales
1	Mercier	44,452	Mercier	18,999	Voltaire	8,426
2	Rilliet de Saussure	22,055	Voltaire	14,671	Bible	5,264
3	Voltaire	14,671	F.-S. Ostervald	12,434	Tissot	3,703
4	Brissot	12,912	Bible	11,147	Mercier	3,222
5	F.-S. Ostervald	12,434	J.-F. Ostervald	6,930	Dorat	2,536
6	Bible	11,147	Riccoboni	5,541	J.-J. Rousseau	2,132
7	J.-F. Ostervald	6,930	Dorat	5,212	Leprince de Beaumont	1,857
8	Riccoboni	5,541	Necker	5,184	Mairobert	1,853
9	Dorat	5,212	Elie Bertrand	4,235	Genlis	1,585
10	Necker	5,184	Millot	3,831	Berquin	1,538

fellow beings. They provide insights into our shared experiences and, when published, serve to stimulate consumer culture by indicating the most popular new products. It would perhaps be natural to assume, moreover, that because a text sells well, it is also influential. The quest for bestsellers thus lay at the very heart of the FBTEE project. Books would serve as a proxy for the ideas they contained and offer us fresh insights into the intellectual culture and lived experience of the eighteenth century. Of course, few would be so naïve as to believe that there was a direct correlation between the sales of a text and its cultural or historical significance. René Descartes' *Discourse on Method* sold only a couple of hundred copies in his lifetime, yet the impact of Cartesianism is undeniable and the book is still widely studied. Equally, Mrs Elizabeth Meeke, the outright bestselling novelist of early nineteenth-century Britain, left so little trace that even her identity was uncertain until recently. Her works were quickly forgotten.[4] Yet a work's presence in the bestseller lists, particularly if it is neither ephemeral nor fictitious, might still serve, in absence of other evidence, as a kind of shorthand for influence, and a means of reconstructing the *mentalités* of the STN's long-dead readers. Even ephemeral works might tap into and reflect the cultural mood of a particular moment. The STN's bestselling works might therefore be seen as a shortcut to understanding the significance of the STN's trade, particularly as their top-twenty 'bestsellers' account for more than a quarter (26.6 per cent) of all the works they despatched. By uncovering the works and authors that the STN's readers consumed in most abundance, we might uncover their mental worlds and better comprehend the Enlightenment universe. It is a tantalizing prospect. The reality is not quite so simple, however. For how are we to define a bestseller from the STN data?

The STN's most printed work is a case in point. It heads what we might call the 'global list' of STN bestsellers – that is to say the list of works that the STN despatched to their clients in the greatest quantities. The STN sent out many thousand copies of *Planta gagnant sa vie en honnête homme* but, as explained in the companion volume to this study, very few were sold on the open market.⁵ Instead most copies went to Rilliet himself, who shortly after the publication of the original eighty-one-page edition hatched the idea of flooding Geneva with a second, cheaply produced, six-page edition. To judge by the numbers, he probably intended to send one to every household.⁶ As an object exercise in scandal-mongering pamphleteering, this second edition of *Planta gagnant sa vie* seems revelatory of the scale of the literate audience in Geneva and the vitality of the city's public sphere, at least as Rilliet understood them. But it does not tell us much about market demand. Nor, it seems, did Rilliet's cheap propaganda edition reach its intended audience. Rilliet's death came just days after the STN sent him thousands of copies and it seems his heirs had them destroyed. Not a single copy of this second edition is known to have survived. So while the STN did 'sell' the pamphlets, it was primarily as a commissioned edition and not on the open market. That such a work could be produced in greater numbers than any of the company's commercial publications is revealing. It suggests we need to exercise caution about our 'sales' figures in general. The works that the STN printed or distributed in most abundance were not necessarily market orientated or commercially successful. Nevertheless, it is instructive to see which books the STN distributed in greatest number. This STN global 'bestsellers' list, spanning the years 1769 to 1794, reads as follows:

1. Rilliet, *Planta gagnant sa vie en honnête homme*, 16,787 copies
2. Mercier, *Tableau de Paris*, 14,076 copies
3. Mercier, *La Destruction de la ligue*, 10,188 copies
4. *Pièces importantes à la dernière révolution de Genève*, 8,428 copies
5. Frédéric Ostervald, *Abrégé de l'histoire sainte et du catéchisme*, 6,815 copies
6. Samuel Ostervald, *Géographie*, 6,397 copies
7. The *Bible*, 5,323 copies
8. Le Scène Desmaisons, *Contrat conjugal*, 4,164 copies
9. Mercier, *Mon Bonnet de nuit*, 4,043 copies
10. *Collection complète des œuvres de Madame Riccoboni*, 3,843 copies

Some of these 'bestselling' titles had a genuine popular appeal. Chief among them was Mercier's celebrated *Tableau de Paris*. Whereas Rilliet's work was a flimsy propaganda pamphlet, the *Tableau de Paris* was a sprawling multivolume blockbuster, appearing in instalments between 1781 and 1788. Attempting to capture the spirit and flavour of Parisian life, it contained hundreds of short, vivid essays covering any topic that caught Mercier's fancy. Capturing the spirit of the times, he wrote on street lighting and quack remedies; lunatic asylums and the policing of theatres; second-hand markets and the young maniacs whose irresponsible coach driving made crossing Parisian streets a risk to life and limb. Mercier wrote both as a participant and an ethnographer about a city he both loved passionately and wished to reform. His work enjoyed a genuine vogue across Europe and was soon translated, in digest, into various languages. It has been mined ever since by historians seeking striking descriptions of the *ancien régime* on its deathbed.

Technically illegal inside France, the *Tableau de Paris* was not the sort of work to seriously irritate the Bourbon government. It was able to circulate fairly freely but its author felt safer publishing from exile in the safe haven of Neuchâtel. As a result, the Neuchâtelois were able to get successive and progressively bigger editions of the *Tableau de Paris* to market first, and several other local publishing houses seem to have been involved in printing and distributing the STN editions. Indeed, the STN's four-volume edition of 1782 was commissioned by their Neuchâtelois trading partner Jonas Fauche.[7] Thus, although the *Tableau de Paris* was a genuine publishing sensation and significant commercial venture, we lack information about the final destination for most of the volumes they despatched. Out of the 14,076 copies they distributed, 10,500 were sold to Fauche and his associates, doubtless for resale to other destinations. Again, an interpretational problem prevents us seeing where the books ended up.

Mercier was a house author for the STN, which partially explains his dominance of the bestseller chart. From 1779 onwards, he was a sure-fire cash cow for the company, who could get his works to market well before rival counterfeit editions could appear. This was an ideal commercial scenario. As a result, the company printed and sold large numbers of his key works, which occupy second, third, ninth and eighteenth positions in the STN's global top twenty. They include, in third place, the *Destruction de la Ligue*, a hard-hitting political drama about the wars of religion, a work he had promised when he first wrote to them in January 1779.[8] However, once again close inspection reveals unexpected complexities. Again the bulk of the STN's print run was taken by Jonas Fauche, Ch. S. Favre *et compagnie*. They took a staggering 8,500 copies on 15 April 1782. Once again we are in the presence of a commissioned printing: Fauche and Favre were partners in the work's publication and speculated heavily on the work's explosive appeal. Few of their copies were destined for Neuchâtel. Although we know that the Paris police impounded some of Fauche and Favre's copies, probably only temporarily, we can only speculate where the bulk of them ended up.[9]

In fourth place on our global bestsellers' list is the blandly titled *Pièces importantes à la dernière révolution de Genève*, a work which was nevertheless politically charged. A topical pamphlet, it dealt with the civil unrest in Geneva. It was published in the wake of French, Bernese and Sardinian military intervention and the expulsion of the leaders of the Genevan democratic *représentant* party on 1-2 July 1782. As a piece of *représentant* propaganda, it was produced semi-clandestinely, appearing under the false Genevan imprint of Jean-Leonard Pellet.[10] As a further precaution, the STN accounted for it under a false title. In their records it appears as the *Mémoire apologétique des Genevois*. It was worth the subterfuge. Sales of a first impression were brisk and impressive. This original edition, apparently a commercial venture, was rushed into print. On its first day in the marketplace, 25 July 1782, the STN despatched 925 copies to dealers across Switzerland and Europe. Many hundreds more left their silos in the following week and on 24 September 1782, 1,200 copies were sent to the STN's agent in Paris, Quandet de Lachenal. A fortnight later, 5,000 more were sent to David Chauvet in Geneva, a number high enough to suggest a second, commissioned printing.[11]

The subject matter of the remaining works on the STN's 'global' bestsellers' list suggests that their audience had diverse tastes. Religious works play a prominent part in the top ten. There is an abridged Protestant *Catechism* produced by Neuchâtelois Calvinist divine Jean-Frédéric Ostervald in fifth place and the *Bible*, of which the STN produced several Protestant editions, occupies seventh position. A popular school geography textbook, written by STN partner Frédéric-Samuel Ostervald; a collection of sentimental novels by Madame Riccoboni, which were enormously popular in their day; and a miscellany of essays and short stories by Mercier flesh out the list. Finally, there is a discourse on divorce laws, Jacques Le Scène Desmaisons, *Contrat conjugal, ou loix du mariage, de la répudiation et du divorce, avec une dissertation sur l'origine et le droit de dispenses*. The STN printed at least 4,166 copies of this work, but only twenty-five found their way to market. The rest were confiscated en route (see below Chapter 9).

Despite their diversity in form, length and subject matter, the STN's top ten global bestselling works tend to have common features. All were published by the STN and several, including *Planta gagnant sa vie en honnête homme*, the *Contrat conjugal*, and possibly the *Destruction de la ligue* and a second printing of the enigmatic *Pièces importantes sur la dernière révolution de Genève*, were commissioned editions. However, with the exception of the Planta pamphlet, even these commissioned works appear genuine commercial speculations on which publishers or authors risked print runs many times the eighteenth-century norm of 750 to 1,000 copies. But for Le Scène Desmaisons' treatise and certain works by Mercier, who is usually portrayed more as a Rousseauian than a *philosophe*, the global 'top ten' also appears to contain precious little Enlightenment.

Are these works typical of STN sales? If so, how much further down the STN's bestseller lists do we have to descend before we find works widely considered to be mainstream Enlightenment texts? Not very far, as it turns out. Nevertheless, most of the works occupying positions eleven to twenty on the global bestseller list have a remarkable similarity to those in the top ten. Indeed, the extent to which most mirror a specific work in the top ten is almost uncanny.[12] The second tier contains another of Rilliet's pamphlets concerning his *procès romanesque*; *Psalms* in place of the *Bible*; a second of Ostervald's geography textbooks and, in place of the *Abrégé de l'histoire sainte et du catéchisme*, a secular history textbook by Millot. Instead of a contentious secular text on divorce, the second tier contains Christin's polemical attack on the serf-holding Abbaye de Saint-Claude, a work of *philosophie* sometimes attributed to Voltaire. There is also another of Mercier's political works, a topical tract entitled *Le Philosophe au Port-au-Bled*.[13] Finally, the 'complete works' of the racey popular writer Dorat replace those of Riccoboni. These second-tier bestsellers have a stronger emphasis on politics and social issues, however, for they also include a pamphlet by Necker and, in twelfth place, Raynal's sprawling abolitionist tract, the *Histoire philosophique des Deux Indes*. This is the highest ranking work of heavy-duty *philosophie* in our table. Compiled from multiple sources, including colonial officials, Raynal's colourful, if uneven account, provided the French with their main indigenous ideological impetus towards ending the slave trade.[14]

To Raynal and Christin's abolitionist polemics, we can add Voltaire's *Questions sur l'Encyclopédie*, the great *philosophe*'s most highly ranked work. It weighs in at a heady nineteenth place. The *Questions sur l'encyclopédie*, which the nascent STN published between 1770 and 1772, was an important commercial venture. It involved piracy, guile and the collaboration of Voltaire himself, who assisted the STN to publish their edition behind the back of his official publisher, Cramer. When the STN edition's title-page boasted that this 'nouvelle édition' was 'Soigneusement revue, corrigée & augmentée', it was alluding to improvements made by the hand of the master, who annotated copies of Cramer's proofs and passed them to the pirates. This cloak-and-dagger operation enjoyed the complicity of the local censors, who consented to the edition's being produced in Neuchâtel 'sous la reserve qu'il ne sera ni vendu ni débité dans l'Etat, mais uniquement pour le faire transporter d'ailleurs, ou on a permission de les faire parvenir'.[15] Extending across nine volumes, and running the dangers associated with the clandestine trade, the *Questions sur l'encyclopédie* involved a major investment and risk for the newly established Neuchâtelois publishers. Comprising miscellaneous philosophical essays, many of them loosely inspired by Diderot and d'Alembert's *Encyclopédie*, the *Questions* also doubled as a continuation of Voltaire's *Dictionnaire philosophique portatif*. Among the many essays in the *Questions* was Voltaire's deistic response to d'Holbach. Entitled 'Dieu. Réponse au Système de la nature', the STN published it as a short pamphlet to advertise the wider venture. Here at last, then, is some typical Enlightenment fare, sandwiched between our Rilliets, Riccobonis, Dorats, Merciers and Ostervalds.

One reason for the faint representation of the Enlightenment might be the prevalence among our bestsellers of vanity or commissioned editions. These distort our picture of general demand for the STN's products, particularly as some commissioned editions were never intended for commercial sale, only sold in low volumes, or never reached the market. It remains a moot point, for example, whether the second edition of *Planta gagnant sa vie* should count towards a bestseller table at all. So what happens if we exclude commissioned works to concentrate on a 'trade' top twenty instead? This 'trade' list, reproduced below, includes all editions produced primarily for wholesale or retail sale. As such, it is still headed primarily, in the parlance of the trade, by the STN's own *fonds*, that is to say, their own editions:

1. Frédéric Ostervald, *Abrégé de l'histoire sainte et du catéchisme*, 6,815 copies
2. Samuel Ostervald, *Géographie*, 6,397 copies
3. The *Bible*, 5,323 copies
4. Mercier, *Mon Bonnet de nuit*, 4,043 copies
5. *Collection complète des œuvres de Madame Riccoboni*, 3,843 copies
6. Samuel Ostervald, *Géographie élémentaire*, 3,822 copies
7. Raynal, *Histoire philosophique des Deux Indes*, 3,694 copies
8. Necker, *Mémoire donné au roi en 1778*, 2,922 copies
9. *Pseaumes*, 2,888 copies
10. Christin, *Dissertation sur l'établissement de l'Abbaye de S. Claude*, 2,710 copies
11. Millot, *Elémens d'histoire générale*, 2,584.4 copies
12. Mercier, *Le Philosophe du Port-au-Bled*, 2,581 copies
13. Voltaire, *Questions sur l'Encyclopédie*, 2,523.4 copies
14. *Collection complète des œuvres de M. Dorat*, 2,507.7 copies
15. *Dieu. Réponse de M. de Voltaire au Système de la nature*, 2,327 copies
16. Vatel, *Droit des Gens*, 2,281.5 copies
17. Linguet, *Requête au Conseil du Roi*, 2,227 copies
18. *Descriptions des arts et métiers*, 2,219.3 copies
19. Calonne, *Les Comments*, 2,133 copies
20. Grimoard, *Lettre du marquis de Caraccioli à M. d'Alembert*, 2,063 copies

This STN 'trade' list looks somewhat different from our global listing, particularly beyond the top ten. Its upper ranges are dominated by religious works, Samuel Ostervald's geography textbooks, and anthologies of Mercier and Riccoboni's fiction. However, mainstream Enlightenment works are beginning to climb. Foremost among them is Raynal's *Histoire philosophique des Deux Indes*, now at number seven, closely followed by Christin's *Dissertation sur l'établissement de l'Abbaye de S. Claude*; the *Questions sur l'Encyclopédie*; and Voltaire's short anti-materialist pamphlet *Dieu. Réponse de M. de Voltaire au Système de la nature*. Altogether these four works account for just over a sixth of the 'sales' of top-twenty trade works.[16] Our 'trade' bestseller list also includes works of literature and political economy by the STN's pet Rousseauist, Mercier; a tract by the anti-*philosophe* journalist, Linguet; a foundational work of international relations theory, Emer Vatel's *Droit des gens*; and works on French finances by Philippe-Henri Grimoard and the French finance ministers Jacques Necker and Charles-Alexandre de Calonne. These, too, could potentially be seen as Enlightenment works.

The prevalence of works of political economy is noteworthy. All concern a single issue: the debates over French finances precipitated by the Swiss-born *contrôleur-général* Jacques Necker. These French financial debates generated more heat than light. From the moment that he published his celebrated *Compte rendu des finances* of 1781, which purported to prove that the French government was solvent despite fighting the American War of Independence on credit, Necker cemented an ill-deserved reputation as a financial wizard. Time would show that his rosy financial picture was over-optimistic. From 1786 the financial debate erupted with fresh urgency as Necker and his rival Calonne blamed one another for the fiscal *débâcle* that would bring the Bourbon monarchy to its knees. Perhaps unsurprisingly, pamphlets related to these debates occupy three places among our top-twenty bestsellers. Strangely, the *Compte rendu* itself is not among them, but Calonne's twenty-page riposte, *Les Comments* features strongly, as does Necker's earlier *Mémoire donné au roi par M. Necker en 1778* and Grimoard's *Lettre du marquis de Caraccioli à M. d'Alembert*. Also present is Mercier's short topical pamphlet *Le Philosophe au Port-au-Bled*, which briefly addresses financial issues. A further pamphlet, Pierre-Augustin Robert de Saint-Vincent's *Observations modestes d'un citoyen sur les opérations de finances de M. Necker* is bubbling under in twenty-first position.

Both the STN's global and trade bestseller lists are dominated by STN editions. This is not surprising. Ideally, the publishing house needed to shift 100 per cent of its own editions, whereas with other publishers' works it only tended to buy in what it required to satisfy customer orders or thought it could sell. Thus while many hundreds or even thousands of copies of its own editions passed through its magazines, it often only handled a few dozen copies of even the most successful works produced by other publishers. Clients knew this. Unless a work appeared in the STN's catalogues, they were unlikely to order it.[17] Even when the STN did advertise a work through their catalogues, clients would only expect them to have access to significant copies if the STN or local allied publishing houses had printed the work. Thus, if we want a bestseller list that better represents the contours of the wider book trade, we might choose to exclude STN *fonds* and generate a 'commercial list'. Again, this can be done in the database at the touch of a button by using the options menu to delist all STN editions. *Et voilà*:

1. *Pseaumes*, 2,888 copies
2. *Collection complète des œuvres de M. Dorat*, 2,201 copies
3. Mercier, *L'An deux mille quatre cent quarante*, 2,006 copies
4. *Le Nouveau Testament*, 1,631 copies
5. Pidansat de Mairobert, *Anecdotes sur Madame du Barri*, 1,489 copies
6. Leprince de Beaumont, *Magasin des enfans*, 1,381 copies
7. Berquin, *Lectures pour les enfans*, 1,378 copies
8. Rousseau, *Œuvres*, 1,312.2 copies
9. Tissot, *Avis au peuple sur sa santé*, 961 copies
10. Jean-Rudolphe Ostervald, *Nourriture de l'âme*, 936 copies
11. Raynal, *Histoire philosophique des Deux Indes*, 749.7 copies
12. The *Bible*, 739 copies
13. Gottsched, *Maître de la langue allemande*, 701 copies
14. Trembley, *Instructions d'un père à ses enfans*, 672 copies
15. Tissot, *Onanisme*, 642 copies
16. Anon, *Histoire et vie de l'Arrétin*, 629 copies
17. Genlis, *Adèle et Théodore ou Lettres sur l'éducation*, 626 copies
18. Alletz (attrib.), *Albert moderne*, 615
19. Goudar, *Considérations sur les causes de l'ancienne foiblesse de l'Empire de Russie*, 580 copies
20. Tissot, *Traité de l'épilepsie*, 566 copies

This operation, to be sure, still gives a bestseller list dominated by Swiss editions that the STN traded *en nombre*. But since other Swiss publishers, like the STN, tended to reprint pirate editions of popular works whenever they caught the whiff of commercial success, this may not present much of a problem. By eliminating STN editions, we reduce our sample size to just 136,957 units, a little under a third of books traded by the STN. However, since these works tended to sell in smaller consignments than the STN's own works, the sales picture is made up of numerous relatively fine grains. We also get a much flatter demand curve. Sales of the twentieth work on this 'commercial list' are a fifth that of the *Psalms*, which occupy top spot. The work in one-hundredth place on the commercial listing, Marmontel's philosophic novel *Bélisaire*, has sales just under 10 per cent of the *Psalms*. Moreover, as we shall see, the general popularity of many works on this new list can be verified against other sources.

The differences between this new 'commercial' bestseller list and the 'global' and 'trade' tables are striking, although there are also similarities. Biblical texts retain their importance, with editions of the *Psalms*, *New Testament* and *Bible* all holding spots in the top dozen. A further pious work, Jean-Rudolphe Ostervald's *Nourriture de l'Ame* also occupies a prominent position. But alongside spiritual health and well-being, this list reveals an obsession with mundane physical health issues. It lists three works by the Swiss physician Samuel Tissot, whose popular medical treatises were bestsellers across Europe. A fourth work on the list, a popular compendium of recipes, *L'Albert moderne*, named after a medieval book of secrets, also offers numerous remedies and much medical advice. Between them these four medical works outsold the *Bible* and *New Testament*. A third evident preoccupation of this list is the education, moral instruction and rearing of children. No less than four works on the list, many of them already familiar to us, address this topic. They include Genlis's didactic novel *Adèle et Théodore ou lettres sur l'éducation*, Leprince de Beaumont's *Magasin des enfans* and the anthology of *Lectures pour les enfans*. They also include a work of Christian instruction by the spiritually inclined Swiss naturalist Abraham Trembley: *Instructions d'un père à ses enfans, sur la religion naturelle et révélée*. Textbooks and educational primers are less evident on this list than our previous bestseller tables, and with good reason. As school books were produced cheaply with large print runs for local sale, we would not expect the STN to be buying them in bulk from other publishers. The exception is language texts, which were often produced in more robust form so that they could serve as reference works. One such work appears on our commercial bestsellers' list: Gottsched's *Maître de la langue Allemande*.

Perhaps the most surprising aspect of the commercial bestseller list is the absence of *philosophie*. The only works of *philosophie* left in the commercial top twenty are, predictably enough, Raynal's *Histoire philosophique des Deux Indes* and Rousseau's *Œuvres*. Tellingly, Voltaire is missing. His highest listings are the sceptical and anticlerical *Examen important de Milord Bolingbroke* at number thirty and the pornographic satire on Joan of Arc, *La Pucelle d'Orléans*, at thirty-five. In his place, a different form of so-called 'philosophical work' appears high on the commercial bestseller table: the highly illegal, clandestine libertine titles made familiar through the works of Robert Darnton. Foremost among them are Mercier's utopian futuristic thought experiment, *L'An 2440* and Pidansat de Mairobert's scandalous life of the king's mistress, *Anecdotes sur Madame la Comtesse Du Barri*. Both rank among Darnton's foremost clandestine bestsellers and feature among the three texts chosen for his anthology of forbidden works in *Forbidden Best-Sellers*. Our list also features a third clandestine bestseller, the anonymous erotic *Vie et histoire de l'Arretin*, whose title celebrates the life of Pietro Aretino, the Italian Renaissance satirist frequently considered the father of modern pornography. These three libertine works are highly placed on the commercial list, at positions three, five and fifteen respectively. On this listing, between them they outsold the *Bible* and *New Testament* combined. Nor were the *Vie de l'Arretin* and *Anecdotes sur Madame du Barri* the only works dealing with sex on the list. Tissot's *Onanisme* was a medical tract on the dangers of what contemporaries euphemistically referred to as self-pollution (i.e. masturbation) and Dorat's *Œuvres* – the runner-up to the *Psalms* – contained numerous *galant* or erotic poems.

Taken in the round, the STN's 'commercial' bestseller list seems notable for its mundanity, earthiness and concern with everyday issues of living, loving, nurturing and dying. *Belles-Lettres* are conspicuous by their relative absence. Heavyweight philosophy, social commentary, history and high politics are, with the notable exceptions of Raynal's *Histoire philosophique* and the publicist Ange Goudar's *Considérations sur les causes de l'ancienne foiblesse de l'Empire de Russie*, almost nowhere to be seen. Where such things are present, it tends to be in attenuated and easily digestible form: Mercier's utopian fantasy; Mairobert's fictionalized exposé of the royal mistress; Dorat's light verse. Instead, we have education, health, religion and copulation vying for centre stage. If this is the choicest crop of its literary field, the late Enlightenment looks somewhat different to many textbook treatments. It would also be unfamiliar terrain to Peter Gay or Jonathan Israel, though some of its key features have been mapped by Robert Darnton.

We can, of course, play similar games with the STN's authors, creating 'global', 'trade' and 'commercial' bestseller lists (see Table 5.1). When we do this for 'primary authors', Peter Gay might rest a little more comfortably, for Voltaire now gatecrashes our story. The highest 'new entrant' in the 'commercial' authors table, he occupies the number one spot, knocking Biblical texts (*Bibles*, *New Testaments*, and *Psalms*) into second place. Voltaire's works sold more than twice as many copies as those of Samuel Tissot, who occupies third spot. However, Voltaire does not owe his success to a handful of bestsellers, but rather to his prolific output: the STN database lists 125 of his works. Yet with this sole exception, most of our commercial authors penned works that occupy places near the summit of our bestselling book chart. Tissot, Mercier, Dorat, Jean-Jacques Rousseau and Pidansat de Mairobert, together with the educational writers and anthologists Genlis, Leprince de Beaumont and Arnaud Berquin all produced titles which feature among our twenty bestselling titles. Our picture of the classic Enlightenment, on the evidence of the STN's bestselling author tables, should be one dominated by Voltaire. Only a handful of other leading Enlightenment figures appear in the STN's top fifty 'commercial' authors, and, even in combination, he outsold them: Rousseau (at no. 6), d'Holbach (no. 16), Raynal (no. 20), Helvétius (no. 21), Marmontel (no. 27), Frederick the Great (no. 32). The popular reading of the late Enlightenment was primarily built around other authors, other genres.

Of course, the bestselling titles analysed here only account a sixth of the STN's 'commercial market'; the bestselling authors account for around a quarter. Moreover, clandestine works and their authors were almost certainly over-represented in the STN's trade, if only because, unlike many foreign publishers and book dealers, they could generally trade them without fear. As a result, we need to ask whether the STN bestseller figures are representative of their wider trade, and to try to better establish the size contours of the clandestine sector, particularly within France. To do so will require more specialized analytical tools than we have used in our exploration of the STN's 'global', 'trade' and 'commercial' bestseller lists. The chapters which follow discuss and apply those tools to the entire crop of the STN's 'literary field'. This process will require both close and distant reading approaches, to appraise sales patterns and discover what types of works sold best. But before we can proceed, we need to adopt taxonomic systems that allow us to comprehend the subject matter and genres of books sold by the STN.

6

Troubling Taxonomies

When Joseph d'Hémery thought about books, he divided them into the practical categories that assisted him in his job. Was a work pirated? Had an edition received a *permission*? Was it a threat to public order, good morals or religion? Was its author among the known troublemakers listed in his personal files? Above all, as the police inspector charged for over three decades from 1748 with policing the Paris book trade, he thought in terms of the fundamental categories of legality and illegality.[1]

The directors of the STN and their clients also had to consider the categories of legality and illegality as they planned their business strategies. Books which might get them or their clients into trouble with the authorities required special handling, sending via trusted middlemen or roundabout routes, hiding at the bottom of crates, or, if unbound, interleaving with legal books to escape the attention of customs officers and book trade inspectors. The costs and risks of stocking or sending such works needed to be weighed against profit margins and the likely demand for works carrying the cachet of clandestinity.

Making such assessments required the STN's directors and clients to classify books by other criteria than their position on a blurry spectrum of legality and illegality. They had also, like any other commercial publisher, to think about the marketability of the author, the text and the subject matter. Did the work have the fresh appeal of *nouveauté* or was it perhaps past its sell-by date? Was its author tried and tested in the marketplace? Was the edition attractive enough to compete on price or presentation with others on the market?

The intellectual categories into which policemen, publishers, booksellers and customers pigeonholed books reflected real-world conditions and had practical consequences. They affected consumer demand, commercial decisions and policing priorities. These preliminary observations highlight that categorization is one of the fundamental tools by which we humans understand and control our world. By linking similar items together into categories, we can relate, narrate, measure, quantify, assess and direct our efforts more effectively. Nevertheless, our categories are subjective labels rather than concrete things.

This caveat is important because the categories we use and the taxonomic schemes and hierarchical arrangements into which we fit them can affect our very thinking. They may be practical, but they are also inherently political. Hence when Linnaeus's *Systema naturae* (1735) treated *Homo sapiens* as animals and categorized them among the primates, he promoted an intellectual revolution in thinking about humanity's place in the universe. It had profound theological implications as well as biological ones. Thinking of humans as monkeys gave rise to new evolutionary conceptions of human origins and appeared to challenge Biblical assertions that 'Man' was formed in God's own image. Similarly, the categories and hierarchies of knowledge adopted by d'Alembert and Diderot in the *Encyclopédie* served to relegate theology from its prominent place as queen of the sciences to a sub-branch of philosophy, in which Church doctrine, 'holy mysteries' and other aspects of orthodox religion not susceptible to empirical demonstration would become almost invisible.[2] Their subtle reshaping of the 'tree of knowledge' was a key strategy in the struggle to scotch superstition and *écraser l'infâme*.

Any attempt to taxonomize books must therefore be handled with extreme care. The systems of categorization that we adopt will both empower and limit the sorts of questions we can ask of our data. On the one hand, we risk imposing twenty-first century concepts of knowledge onto an eighteenth-century corpus of texts, and thereby missing key intellectual currents, experiences and relationships that shaped ancien régime culture and thinking. Conversely, if we adopt taxonomic systems from the eighteenth century, we lose much of the analytical power of hindsight to raise and answer new questions. We may even find ourselves implicated in the power struggles of *philosophes* and anti-*philosophes*.

A further conundrum concerns the relational model implied by a tree metaphor used to describe many taxonomic systems. This model for describing knowledge systems, made popular by d'Alembert and Diderot and their intellectual forebears Chambers and Bacon, places each book on a single branch of the tree of knowledge. This is helpful for locating books in a library or catalogue, or if we wish to make comparisons that weight all books equally. But it risks significant loss of nuance by fitting each of the complex and subtle texts of the Enlightenment into a single box. Yet the alternative approach of ascribing a series of keywords to each work also has significant drawbacks, particularly when drawing up statistics. As different books carry different numbers of keywords, some will have more influence on statistical tables than others. Moreover, such systems are necessarily complex and require more effort and specialist knowledge to apply.

To mitigate these problems, the STN database incorporates multiple taxonomic systems. Some are inherent in the bibliographic data: for example, the database and online user interface can group works by author for most analytical functions. As we have seen in Chapter 5, the 'options menus' also allow works to be categorized in terms of provenance ('edition type'). This allows users to sort them according to their countries of (putative) publication, and in the case of Neuchâtel editions, whether or not they were published by the STN. It is also possible to group editions by their actual or original languages of publication. Moreover, since we shared Joseph d'Hémery's objective of tracing the illegal sector, we included a database field and an 'options menu' which allow users to sort and filter works according to a number of markers of illegality. Without this facility, the analysis of 'The Anatomy of the Illegal Sector' in Chapter 9 would have been impossible.

The most fundamental tools for understanding the STN's literary field were the subject taxonomies. Here it proved possible to 'have our cake and eat it'. We adopted both the standard tree system used by eighteenth-century booksellers and library cataloguers and a bespoke twenty-first-century keyword system. The former respected and reflected eighteenth-century patterns of thinking about books. Moreover, because 100 per cent of works would be represented exactly once each, we could use the tree system to prepare pie charts and similar data representations. In contrast, our twenty-first century system was purpose-built, because we concluded that modern 'off-the-peg' library classification systems were poorly adapted to the task and difficult to apply rigorously.[3] It uses multiple keywords to describe and analyse the STN corpus.

When aggregated across all books, the taxonomic schemes we adopted gave a detailed idea of what the STN sold, by subject, language, geographic provenance, certain ideological tendencies, various measures of illegality and often, with literary works, by genre. Such data can give significant new insights into popular reading in 1770s and 1780s francophone Europe. But before we can analyse the data, we need to understand the taxonomic systems used. This is where our old friend the baron d'Holbach can assist. We will begin our digression into the subject taxonomies used in the FBTEE database by exploring the arch-materialist's own library.

When d'Holbach died on 21 January 1789, the library he left behind included, as we would expect, many heterodox works. The fortuitous timing of his death means that we have a printed auction catalogue recording most of the books the library contained. The catalogue was prepared by the Parisian bookseller Guillaume de Bure l'aîné at the very moment that police control over the book trade was breaking down. Nevertheless, the catalogue bears the marks of *ancien régime* censorship, which required sale catalogues to be inspected to ensure that they did not advertise reprehensible works. Hence it was signed off in the traditional manner 'Lu et approuvé ce 24 octobre 1789' by 'Mérigot jeune', an 'adjoint' in the Parisian booksellers' guild, perhaps the last catalogue ever to go through this process. By that date we might suspect that this was a mere formality, following the fall of the Bastille in July, the proclamation of freedom of expression in the Declaration of the Rights of Man and Citizen in August and the return of the monarchy to Paris in the October days. After September, books were no longer being seized at customs. However, the absence of the most hardcore materialist works from d'Holbach's library catalogue – notably the *Système de la nature*, Helvétius' *De l'Homme* and the materialist classics of La Mettrie, Diderot, Boulanger and Naigeon – suggests that de Bure, Mérigot or d'Holbach's family preferred to err on the side of caution. Nevertheless, de Bure's catalogue does advertise a great many works that only a few months earlier would have almost certainly been confiscated by the police or spirited away by d'Holbach's heirs. They include a significant number of religiously sceptical or heterodox works (and their refutations) and we can see exactly how they were classified. This is just as well, because to the uninitiated it is far from clear whether many such works belong in the category *Théologie hétérodoxe* or in *Métaphysique*. This was one of several conundrums facing users of the Parisian booksellers' classification system, which de Bure used for d'Holbach's library catalogue.

The Parisian booksellers' system was widely used by bibliographers, booksellers and cataloguers of private libraries.[4] It has also been used by book historians, and this facilitates comparative insights.[5] The system grew out of late seventeenth-century attempts to categorize knowledge, particularly those of the abbé Garnier, Prosper

Marchand and Ishmael Bouillaud, whose impressive achievement was to embrace all human knowledge and creative writing within just five overarching containers: *Théologie, Jurisprudence, Histoire, Philosophie* and *Belles-Lettres*. However, Bouillaud's category *Philosophie* proved an unwieldy and imprecise catch-all, so in one of his most significant innovations, the bookseller Gabriel Martin replaced it with the more precise though still capacious category *Sciences et Arts*.[6] The resultant Parisian booksellers' system had widespread appeal to contemporaries, for as Charles Nodier remarked: 'It is simple, clear, easy. It can include, without strain, all the capricious and innumerable subdivisions which it has pleased human fancy to introduce into the literary form of books.'[7] Not surprisingly, the system was, as Edward Edwards remarked in 1859, 'embodied in catalogues which have become classics in their kind', most notably those produced by the system's chief innovators, Martin himself, who published an unprecedented series of catalogues between 1711 and 1760, and Guillaume-François de Bure (1732–84), a cousin of the bookseller who produced the d'Holbach catalogue.[8]

In total, d'Holbach's library catalogue lists 2,777 items, mostly in French and Latin, but also in Italian and English. A supplementary list contains a further 179 'German books', though their titles, too, are in French or Latin. Both lists use the Parisian booksellers' system to subdivide and describe the books on offer. However, the shorter 'German' list, like many commercial book catalogues of the era, only uses the main headings of the system. The main catalogue begins, as was customary, with *Théologie*, which takes precedence even in the arch-atheist d'Holbach's catalogue. Under this heading are found 268 works. It then continues through *Jurisprudence* (85 works), *Sciences et Arts* (777 works), *Belles-Lettres* (849 works) and finally *Histoire*, the largest category with 977 works. These five overarching categories embraced every work in the library, as was intended. In order to achieve this, the cataloguing system incorporated some associations that might strike the modern reader as odd. It followed a long-established convention by listing works on travel (*Voyages*) and geography, as well as chronology, genealogy and heraldry, under *Histoire*. General reference works belonged under *Belles-Lettres*, being seen as a form of dictionary, and thus ranked alongside works of creative literature, grammars and philology.

The range of subjects categorized as *Sciences et Arts* is even more disconcerting. Among its many branches, it included the pure and applied sciences alongside the mechanical, practical, decorative and visual arts, equitation, dancing and *Arts pyrotechniques*. It also embraced *Philosophie*, whose several sub-branches covered economics and finance as well as politics and the somewhat puzzling concatenation *Logique et morale* ('logic and moral philosophy'). However, some works relating to the performing arts – particularly dramatic works – belonged in *Belles-Lettres*. There they were usually invisible within the category *Poétique* (poetry), since prose drama was almost unknown in France at the moment when the Parisian system was first drawn up. By the late eighteenth century, however, the rise of prose drama made this conflation of drama and poetry a little incongruous. De Bure himself recognized this. His catalogue of d'Holbach's library includes separate categories for *Poëtes dramatiques François*, *Poëtes dramatiques latins anciens* and the more specific *Poëtes tragiques grecs*, a category elastic enough to embrace Aristophanes' comedies. Italian, German and English dramatical works were, perhaps because they were few in number, lumped together with poetry under the headings *Poëtes Italiens* and *Pöetes Allemands et Anglois* respectively. The existence of such headings is testimony to the flexibility of the Parisian booksellers' system, and the fact that it has no single or definitive iteration. Instead booksellers and cataloguers adapted the system to their needs and the contours of the libraries with which they were working. Hence d'Holbach's library catalogue contains various headings not encountered in many other catalogues. *Belles-Lettres*, for example, includes, among other subcategories: *Mythologie, Fables et Apologues, Facéties, Plaisanteries, &c., Contes et nouvelles, Satiriques, invectives, défenses, apologies &c.* and even *Dissertations critiques, allégoriques, enjouées, &c.*

Creating specialist subheadings was relatively easy. A bigger problem was that some books might fit under multiple headings. Chief among them were works of speculative theology, especially religiously sceptical tracts, which occupied an ambiguous status in the Parisian system. *Théologie* was supposed to include scriptures and religious works of all sorts, and so the d'Holbach catalogue includes under *Théologie polémique*: Thomas Woolston's *A Discourse on the Miracles of Our Saviour*; the abbé Bergier's Christian apologetic responses to deism and materialism; and refutations of the *Système de la nature*, including Holland's *Réflexions philosophiques sur le Système de la nature*.[9] The category *Théologie hétérodoxe*, however, contained further freethinking works by Collins, Toland and even Spinoza's *Tractatus theologico-politicus et alia opera*. Yet other sceptical speculative works contesting the nature or reality of God or the soul, or exploring the nature of existence were listed instead under *Métaphysique*. They appear in a variety of subcategories, notably *De Dieu, de son existence, de sa Providence, &c., De l'Ame, de son immortalité, de l'esprit de l'homme, &c., Traités de l'homme & de ses facultés, de sa vie et de sa mort &c.* It is here that Guillaume de Bure lists the works of Shaftesbury, Condillac or Leibniz. Yet although these categories blurred into one another, *Métaphysique* was not a branch of *Théologie* or even *Philosophie*. Instead it existed as an independent subsection of the broad and eclectic category *Sciences et Arts*.

Such ambiguities and flexibilities may not have unduly concerned library cataloguers and booksellers in the eighteenth century but they were disconcerting for digital researchers in the twenty-first. Intending to quantify sections of the book trade, the FBTEE project needed a system that could be applied rigorously, with precision. Thus, early in the project, Mark Curran prepared a report on the strengths and ambiguities in the system and, since, in all probability, no two catalogues had ever contained exactly the same set of subheadings, an iteration of the system appropriate for our use. The results were encouraging: the report noted that although in every catalogue he had consulted some books cropped up in surprising places,[10] the main ambiguous areas were ones we had already identified – the problematic placement of sceptical works and the fact that 'Ecclesiastical history' occasionally appeared as a category under *Théologie* rather than *Histoire*. The latter problem required nothing more than an executive decision: in our database 'Ecclesiastical history' would be a branch of 'History'. The issue of placing sceptical works was somewhat more difficult, but Dr Curran – a specialist in the controversies surrounding d'Holbach – offered a tidy, conceptually operable solution. Sceptical works targeted primarily at the teachings of Christianity, he suggested, should be placed under *Théologie hétérodoxe*, while their

Christian apologetic adversaries would be placed separately in *Théologie polémique*. Philosophic works that went beyond attacking Christianity and attempted to build their own systems, or speculated on the nature of God and the soul, would belong in *Sciences et Arts* under *Métaphysique*. Beyond that, our principle was to keep the system reasonably simple, primarily in order to avoid difficulties and ambiguities. As a result, we decided to ignore the innumerable subcategories of literature that crept into de Bure's catalogue of d'Holbach's library and the many and abstruse divisions sometimes encountered under *Théologie*.

The FBTEE version of the Parisian system proved eminently workable. Ultimately, save for a few works that were uncategorizable due to incomplete information, nearly every work was placed. When I finished the categorization process, I had to add just three extra categories (some of them authentic) to accommodate a rump of about twenty works – *Franc-maçonnerie*, *Jeux* and *Bibliographie*. There are, of course, shortcomings in our version of the Parisian system. Some were the result of our own decisions: lumping together all prose fiction under the catch-all designation *Romans* may have reflected the practice of many late eighteenth-century booksellers, but it also created a large and rather amorphous category. The grouping of both plays and poetry under the category *Poétique* also limited the forms of analysis we could take using Parisian categories, while again reflecting standard Enlightenment practice. In addition, modern users will be surprised at the arrangement and hierarchical interrelationships of certain topics. The placement of *Voyages* as a branch of *Histoire* is surprising, perhaps, but not as disconcerting to a scientifically grounded world view as learning that *Astrologie* is a branch of *Mathématique*. Yet such apparent anomalies have a valuable heuristic function. They serve to remind us that the men and women of the Enlightenment organized the world in radically different ways to ourselves. As such the Parisian categorizations are a tool to help us approach our archive in ways more familiar to its original creators.[11]

In contrast, when it came to developing a twenty-first-century taxonomy, we decided to create our own system. This would give the twin advantages of providing automatic familiarity with a system we had designed and creative flexibility to add new words and structures. On the other hand, the system would be unfamiliar to users, and so each keyword would need to be carefully defined.[12] But how do you create a taxonomic system for a body of works from scratch? Indeed, was there not a certain presumption (and ambition) in attempting to reinvent the wheel (on project-funded time) when librarians and bibliographers have been working on these problems productively for generations?

To answer these objections, it is necessary to go back to first principles. What were the priorities that had driven us to decide to develop our own system? The ultimate aim of the keywords was to allow each printed work encountered through the STN accounting records to be defined as richly as possible in just a few words. We hoped, while keeping it relatively simple, to be able to capture and describe subject, theme, genre, and in some cases ideological tendencies or erotic intensity. We were very aware that scholars have been interested in all these aspects of the literature we were describing, and that literary scholars might be searching for different things in literary works than historians looking at, say, political texts.

Unlike the tree structure of the Parisian system, which has a fixed place for everything and set hierarchical structures, we hoped that our keyword system would be flexible to apply, and that no relationship between keywords would be so rigid as to be definitive. Nevertheless, as a starting point, we identified a number of key domains of knowledge or literary activity, and then listed themes, topics, genres that might occur within them. Likewise, we isolated a number of ideological tendencies that might work alongside them (e.g. *Philosophie*, Works of Religiosity, Sceptical Works, AntiClerical Works and Libertine works). And because it is a key issue in the book history of our period, the system closely defined a hierarchy of terms dealing with the sexual side of human relationships. Overlapping descriptive labels classified works variously along a spectrum, ranging from 'romantic literature' and tame or not-so-tame treatments of [multiple] 'amorous adventures' through genuinely 'erotic works'[13] to sexually explicit 'pornographic works'. Such pornography was defined narrowly and precisely, following Lynn Hunt, as 'works offering explicit descriptions of human genitalia or sexual acts for the purpose of provoking sexual arousal in the reader'.[14]

Once we had a draft framework for our classification system, we did a hypothetical 'dry run' through many of the titles listed for a single year (1771) in Pierre Conlon's bibliography of eighteenth-century France, in order to identify further keywords, themes and conceptual issues that might arise when we tried to apply the system to a diverse body of eighteenth-century texts.[15] In addition, we recognized that we would need to develop 'tags' to describe key people or places, whether in factual works such as history or travel literature, or works of creative literature. That said, the people in the keyword system are almost all either real persons or mythical ones from ancient legend. Generally, I did not index fictional characters and only tended to classify the main protagonists of factually based works, trying to limit tags to key historical individuals or otherwise significant persons: people who, in all likelihood, would appear in multiple works. Rather than create a finite ontology, we kept our system open: if need arises I continue, even ten years on, to add and define new key words as I work through new datasets.

Naturally, such a system involves implicit hierarchies. Most works on 'medicine' tended also to be works of 'science'. Most, but not all. A play satirizing doctors, for example, treated 'medicine' but was not considered a work of 'science'. So rather than the tree system of the Parisian booksellers, our keyword system is perhaps best conceived of as a tangled bush, and one wrapped in, and connected by, varying lengths of string. There are common and almost obligatory interrelationships, but also discontinuities and unexpected linkages.

One distinction we avoided was the binary divide between 'fiction' and 'non-fiction', which our pilot concluded would be difficult to apply in practice. We preferred instead to isolate [creative] 'Literature', which could thus accommodate historical plays and epics, and incorporates all 'Prose Fiction', 'Poetry' and 'Drama', which are its three main sub-branches. Works of 'literature' tended to be described primarily and necessarily in terms of 'genre', rather than content. However, our need to establish the existence and type of erotic charge led to some time-consuming excursions into texts suspected of harbouring accounts of amorous encounters. Digital searches for erotically charged terms (*baiser*, *lèvres*, 'bras' &c.) could sometimes shorten the quest, but the need to scroll virtually or thumb physically through yellowing pages in search of sex scenes proved a significant drag on project time. Contrary to popular belief among my Leeds colleagues, this proved a frustrating pastime, particularly as I had over 3,600 works to categorize. Indeed, the experience proved the wisdom of our general decision to avoid keywords that would require a deep engagement with text. Fortunately, most of those that did – primarily our ideological keywords and the genre category of 'school book' – seldom required us to look much beyond prefaces or introductions. In practice, most other content queries could be resolved by inspecting extended titles, tables of contents, prefaces and introductions.

It is one thing to develop taxonomic schemas; it is quite another to apply them consistently, particularly when faced with thousands of complex texts and only about nine months pro rata to complete the work. So how did I ascribe categories? The short answer is, after much work and to the best of my ability given the time and resources! In retrospect the book classification process appears the most naïve aspect of the original FBTEE grant application. It estimated that we would have to categorize 3,300 (the final total was 3,600) different works – or superbooks in FBTEE parlance – and that two thirds of them would be categorized using reference works. One thousand more, it suggested, would require a more thorough hour-long physical examination of title page and content-skimming. A rump of two hundred would need closer reading. The application proposed that a single person would peruse these 1,200 books, primarily in the British Library and Bibliothèque nationale de France. Even had all the required books been held by these twin national repositories, this would still have been a logistical and managerial challenge. As any seasoned humanities researcher knows, library delivery systems, other readers' borrowings, daily lending limits, works missing from shelves, restoration work and a plethora of other problems can derail any research plan. When that plan involves consulting 1,200 books, the potential pitfalls are myriad.

Fortunately, technology came to the rescue: namely Gallica and Google Books. By the time that I started categorizing books early in 2010, the majority of our titles were already consultable online – several hundreds of them in the very editions traded by the STN. As a result, my year's categorization work was conducted almost entirely from my home office. Only a few identifiable works required physical examination. When I finally emerged again into the world in mid-2011, I had categorized every work we had encountered in the STN archive. So how was this monumental task accomplished?

For practical purposes, I had approximately fifteen to twenty minutes per work. In that time, I needed to research the work, ascribe keywords and record any supplementary data or errors found in our bibliographic records during the process. The classification process thus had the added function of allowing bibliographic checking. These tasks were accomplished with the aid of a purpose designed 'keyword editor', which had inbuilt computer-moderated systems to help the user identify related keywords. It incorporated a scroll down list of all keywords in the database, and whenever one of them was selected a tick-box data display would appear. For every keyword it offered lists of hierarchically and conceptually related keywords plus a computer generated list of the most popular associated terms. The system also offered a short separate menu listing of all the ideological tags in the database, so that they could be consulted for each work, and facilities for creating new words and calling up all works with a given keyword. This was particularly useful for retrospective tasks, such as identifying works which needed to be ascribed a newly created keyword. The system was designed to meet a specific need but it was intuitive, efficient and proved more than adequate to the job.

The basic principle behind the classification work was that it was undertaken on a 'best available information' basis. The information used in the process might therefore come from a number of sources. Wherever possible I consulted the texts of the works themselves, usually in digital form. In most cases a perusal of tables of contents, prefatory material and introductions was all that was necessary. Only occasionally was deeper reading required, usually in my search for representative love scenes, ideological tendencies or evidence that a book had been marketed or used as a textbook. However, when such texts were not available to me, I could usually glean more than adequate information from a combination of contemporary review journals; keyword categories or other details in online library catalogues (although in isolation these often proved untrustworthy and inconsistent); digitized antiquarian book dealers and auctioneers catalogues; miscellaneous bibliographic sources encountered online (which proved particularly helpful for identifying erotica); references from Google Scholar; biographical resources concerning authors; miscellaneous references in books or online. As a last resort, book might be classified on the basis of title alone.

For my categorization of prose literature and dramatic works, potentially the two most difficult genres to describe consistently using these methods, I was able to draw on two superb and near definitive bibliographic resources. When classifying prose fiction, Angus Martin, Vivienne Mylne and Richard Frautschi's magnificent *Bibliographie du genre romanesque français, 1751-1800* proved invaluable. It lists every novelistic work published by year, and for those published for the first time between 1751 and 1800 a brief, formulaic content breakdown.[16] For dramatic works, my standard source was the online César database.[17] This contains data on several thousand French dramatic works written or produced in the seventeenth and eighteenth centuries. These are classified by form and content. However, this classification is derived from the title or title page of the play itself – there has been no attempt at standardization. Fortunately, most playwrights of the time conformed to fairly standard conventions when describing their works – most are 'drames', 'tragédies', 'comédies', 'opéras', 'ballets' and so forth, with a few 'parades', 'vaudevilles', 'tragi-comédies' etc. thrown in. Most of these terms map directly on to equivalent keyword terms in the STN database. A few works also add further useful descriptors, perhaps noting that they are historically based or contain 'ariettes' or other songs or musical forms. The César database also gives supplementary information, including whether a play is written in verse or prose, and as a result this information is given as standard for dramatic works in the STN database. By using these bibliographic resources, FBTEE was able to adopt a highly standardized approach to categorizing novels and plays, and describe them in far more detail than would have otherwise been possible.

This digression on taxonomic systems has served two purposes. First, to help the reader understand the application and nuances of our categorization systems. But it also aims to establish the extent to which readers and users of the database may place confidence in our work. When we began thinking about categorization systems, I assumed that reviewers and the historical and literary professions would be dissatisfied with our achievement in this area. After all, any taxonomic system is bound to have practical and conceptual drawbacks. Users need therefore to be aware of limitations in our taxonomic decisions and the unevenness of the source material on which they were based. Some key judgements had to be made on incomplete information. In many cases categorization is dependent on what was 'detected' about the text on relatively cursory inspection or secondary reports. Without reading a text cover to cover I cannot be absolutely sure that it qualifies as merely 'erotic' rather than 'pornographic'. Even then, unless it is the precise edition the STN traded, how can I be sure that it was not a bowdlerized or rewritten version? To some extent our categories must remain tentative, the numbers indicative. But they remain the best we have.

The system will not appeal to everyone. It may not be adapted to the particular queries they have in mind, to their patterns of thought or the needs of their discipline. Hopefully in such cases, the sheer breadth of keywords available will afford some compensation. Although we have created tools to help users navigate the system, it can be unfamiliar and complex. Certainly it would be difficult to apply it in an exactly analogous way in another project. However, it is probably at least as rigorously and consistently applied and more richly descriptive than most existing systems used in large bibliographic projects. It can also be supplemented with data from other means of navigation: the Parisian system, our markers of illegality and author queries. All provide proxy means of approaching certain groups of texts.

What would we design differently were we to start again? That question is far from esoteric. As I write, more than 3,000 further titles are waiting to be classified in the FBTEE-2.0 database expansions. Certainly there are some minor technical points I would adjust in the database structures and data entry processes. These need not detain us here.[18] There are also some weak points in the keywords system. It did not do very well at handling 'Emotions and Sentiments' (an overarching keyword added retrospectively), and it was weak for works aimed at or debating issues around women, gender and social life. This largely reflects our data and methodology – while the literature sold by the STN often dealt with emotions or gender issues, and could certainly reveal a great deal about both, relatively few works treated them discernibly as their central preoccupations. Just 0.9 per cent of STN sales (3,718 units) were classified as treating 'Emotions and sentiments' and 1.9 per cent (7,843 books) were given the classification 'Gender relations'. Works classified as addressing the 'Education of Women' account for 2,423 sales; those categorized as 'Women's Literature' 2,371 sales; and those relating to the 'Nature of Women' 488 sales. Clearly, on the level at which we pursued our classification work, the 'second sex' were relatively invisible.

However, women, emotions and sentiments were very much present on the pages of novels, in particular sentimental fiction, a popular genre which the STN sold in substantial numbers. They traded over 1,000 copies each of Dorat's *Les Malheurs de l'inconstance*, Mercier's *Jezzenemours*, Pfiel's *L'Homme sauvage* and Louise de Keralio's *Adelaïde, ou mémoires de la marquise de M**** and almost 4,000 copies of the *Collection complète des œuvres de Madame Riccoboni*. In so far as this literature systematically portrayed strong heroines who seized control their own destiny, much of it was subtly socially revolutionary.[19] Sadly the practicalities of the classification process could not capture female lead protagonists, nor identify the many novels written in a female voice, a strategy which might variously serve as a narrative device, help women readers identify with the characters, or convey an erotic charge. Had we had the time to allow a close reading of every text we encountered, women would surely have been more visible in our keyword ranking tables. Recent advances in data-mining and topic-modelling techniques and the ubiquity of digital texts make the identification of themes buried within texts more feasible as I write in 2017 than they were in 2007 when we drew up our original schema, or even 2010–11, when the classification work was carried out. The application of these techniques to digitized texts might in future projects make it more practical to look for material relating to women, female characters, emotions or sentiments in conduct and travel literature, poetic erotica, popular medical texts and other types of published work.

A further statistically significant problem was the habitual ascription of a large number of disparate keywords to travel literature describing alien peoples and their governments, beliefs, mores, practices and social and cultural institutions. For example, William Macintosh's *Voyages en Europe, en Asie et en Afrique*, which sold only eight copies, carries no less than seventeen keywords, including 'travel' and 'voyages' and the standard terms for a variety of geographical regions, but also 'political institutions', 'national customs', 'social mores', 'economics', 'commerce', 'colonial policy', 'international relations', 'military affairs' and 'American Revolution'. The all-embracing keyword 'Travel and Description' (belatedly noted in some library catalogues) would probably be a better way to handle many such cases, while leaving terms like 'political institutions', 'social mores' and 'national customs' for more specialized works. The same applies to certain sorts of household and agricultural reference manuals, which contain multiple keywords for miscellaneous information ranging from 'recipes' for 'cookery', 'distillation', 'medical remedies' or 'dyes' to 'animal nutrition'. To take but one example, Louis Liger's *La Nouvelle maison rustique*, which notched up ten STN sales, carries eighteen keywords, including 'Agronomy', 'Cookery', 'Fishing', 'Food and Beverages', 'Gardening', 'Hunting', 'Medical Remedies' and 'Veterinary Science'. While such lengthy lists of keywords were at times unwieldy, their overall effect was to create a richly informative set of descriptors for the vast and varied literature sold by the STN. This allows us to harvest formidable new insights into the popular literature of the late Enlightenment while working in the STN's literary field.

However, before we reap the literary field, it is worth asking what should we expect to find growing there? There are several ways to answer this question. The first might probe a little deeper into d'Holbach's library, which is that of a gentleman scholar and radical *philosophe*. As a connoisseur of certain types of clandestine literature, we might ask whether his taste reflected the general demand patterns of the STN's clientele? If this were the case, we might expect the distribution of STN sales between the main Parisian categories to mirror the distribution of books in his library, which comprises 33 per cent works of *Histoire*, 29 per cent *Belles-Lettres*, 26 per cent *Science and Arts*, 9 per cent *Théologie* and 3 per cent *Jurisprudence* (see Appendix 2.1).

Perhaps, however, a better comparator for the STN's trade might be found in the trade catalogue of a major dealer trading in French books in a foreign city with a relatively free press, someone who was willing and able to trade in a full range of legal and illegal titles. The London-based Swiss bookseller David Boissière produced just such a catalogue in 1774/5. For our purposes it has the advantage of being extensive (it contains some 3,700 works, approximately 10 per cent of all French titles published in the previous twenty years).[20] It is also organized according to a simplified version of the Parisian booksellers' system. That Boissière adjusted the system is no surprise, given that the system's flexibility.[21] For a general bookseller like Boissière, it made sense to direct his clients to a few coherent sections. Those he used map on closely to the main headings of the standard Parisian system. Intriguingly, the distribution of French-language works in his general catalogue is significantly different to those in d'Holbach's library. Fully three quarters of the titles he stocked are classified as either *Belles-Lettres* (41 per cent) or *Sciences et Arts* (34 per cent).[22] Conversely a mere 13.5 per cent of titles stocked by Boissière were *Histoire*, a category which of course included geography and travel literature. His stocks of *Théologie* (7.5 per cent of titles) and *Jurisprudence* (4 per cent) were not substantially different to d'Holbach's holdings. With an equivalent number of individual works to the FBTEE database, and twice as many French titles in stock as the STN traded in their heyday, we might ask whether Boissière's catalogue more closely reflects the shape of the literary market? How closely, too, does it compare with other surveys of the book trade or popular reading?[23]

The answer is striking. The literature listed in Boissière's stock catalogue has an entirely different shape to the literature scholars have discovered in private library catalogues or reviews in key journals (see Chart 7.1). None of these surveys suggests that *Belles-Lettres* comprised anywhere near 41 per cent of printed output in the French language, while the amount of *Histoire* sold by Boissière looks surprisingly low. Maybe this should not surprise us. Boissière was, after all, catering for a London audience in which English gentry rubbed shoulders with foreign exiles and French ne-er-do-wells.[24] Moreover, booksellers' catalogues are a problematic source for measuring demand. Successful titles which flew off the shelves and sold out rapidly may not have remained in stock long enough to feature in catalogue listings. In contrast, flops or tired ephemera, which often sat dead weight on the shelves, might feature year after year.[25] However, as Boissière first entered the trade only about three years before he produced his catalogue, his inventory may well have been fresher than most.

But neither do surveys of books in permission registers, reviews in learned journals, or private libraries, agree among themselves. Robert Darnton has graphed the results of several such surveys that first appeared in the work of Daniel Mornet or the path-breaking *Livre et société* volumes edited by François Furet. They are reproduced in modified form in the first nine bars of Chart 7.1, where they can be compared with the data in d'Holbach and Bossière's catalogues.[26] The amount of *Science et Arts* revealed in the surveys Darnton collated fluctuates wildly. However, it seems that in general science books were more talked about in the journals than bought and read by the public. *Law [Jurisprudence]* accounted for around 20 per cent of books owned by France's *Parlementaire* magistrates, but only 3 to 4 per cent of general private library holdings. There, at least, Boissière's stock seems to reflect the tastes of a wider public. Religion [*Théologie*] features prominently among official publishing *permissions*, yet comparatively few religious works were reviewed in the *Journal des Savants* or even the

Jesuit-run *Mémoires de Trévoux*. Religious fare was surprisingly popular in the libraries of many *Parlementaires*, accounting for 15 to 20 per cent of their holdings, though more so in provincial Brittany than sophisticated, metropolitan Paris. D'Holbach's library does not seem atypical in this regard. However, theology was apparently less popular in Daniel Mornet's general survey of five hundred libraries, although a smaller proportion of Mornet's books are categorized at all.²⁷ The high number of religious permissions and comparatively small number of religious works in surviving libraries points to two tentative hypotheses. Either religious works generally had relatively small print runs, or they were significantly more ephemeral than other sorts of printed works. Indeed, we might speculate that both propositions were true. The chapter on science and religion, below, explores whether this was indeed the case.

Finally, *Histoire* accounted for around 12 per cent of *permissions*, but this seems to understate its popularity with readers. All the library surveys reveal holdings in excess of this level and among Parisian *Parlementaires* the average was over 35 per cent. *Histoire* accounted for a similar proportion of the works reviewed in journals. This suggests both that works of *Histoire* often had large print runs and were perhaps considered less disposable than other sorts of literature, particularly modish, ephemeral, creative writing such as novels. One suspects many of these were eventually thrown away, explaining perhaps the low library ratings for *Belles-Lettres*, at least in comparison with the Boissière catalogue.

The disparate results given by these surveys suggest that none of the various approaches they exemplify is likely to reveal the shape of popular reading with any degree of accuracy. Elite libraries, official permission registers, review journals, and the catalogues of individual booksellers are all problematic sources for measuring the sorts of books that were actually in circulation. If we really want to know what was being read, it seems likely that our best bet is indeed to turn to book trade sources. We might start by harvesting the literary field of the STN.

7

Harvesting the Literary Field

What types of literature precisely did the STN sell, and did they match DeFrance's portrayal of the international book trade in *À L'Égide de Minerve*? The STN's bestsellers have provided some clues, but they represent only the visible part of the sales iceberg. Armed with our twin classification systems, we can now analyse the STN's 'global', 'trade' and 'commercial' sales. This involves a sweeping 'distant reading' approach to delineate the contours of the STN trade and late eighteenth-century print culture more generally. Our various taxonomic labels, when aggregated across all books, give a detailed view of what they sold by subject, by certain ideological tendencies and, often with literary works, by genre. In the process, the data gives new insights into the market for popular reading in European francophone communities in the 1770s and 1780s. Because FBTEE uses the Parisian booksellers' system, we can also compare the STN data to other surveys of the world of print in the final decades of the French *ancien régime*. As we have noted, such surveys have generally failed to reach consistent conclusions. Part of any discrepancies may stem from choices made during the classification process, but at the level of the five basic categories there were relatively few areas of overlap. The margin of error between surveys is thus relatively small, so some meaningful conclusions can be drawn.

The results of a comparative survey are striking and suggestive (see Chart 7.1).[1] In contrast to the findings of statistical surveys of library holdings and journal reviews, and in spite of the relative lack of fictional titles among the STN's bestsellers, *Belles-Lettres* is comfortably the most prominent Parisian category by sales in the STN database. It accounts for 33.5 per cent of their global trade. The STN's customers, it seems, were reading more works of creative literature than previous surveys have implied. Is it possible, then, that works in literary genres were more disposable than others, and hence less likely to end up in the permanent libraries of institutions or elite readers? And did they individually lack the appeal to make it to the pinnacle of the STN bestseller lists?

The second highest Parisian category in the FBTEE database was *Histoire*, with 27.5 per cent of sales. Nevertheless, *Histoire* was a more prominent category in Mornet's survey of five hundred libraries, where it accounted for half of all categorized holdings, and in the collections of Parisian *parlementaire* magistrates. Here we might tentatively conclude the opposite. Works in this category, many of which were multivolume works of record or reference, were more likely to be preserved, particularly by learned or cultured gentlemen and aristocratic families. *Histoire* also apparently received disproportionate coverage in heavyweight review journals such as the *Journal des*

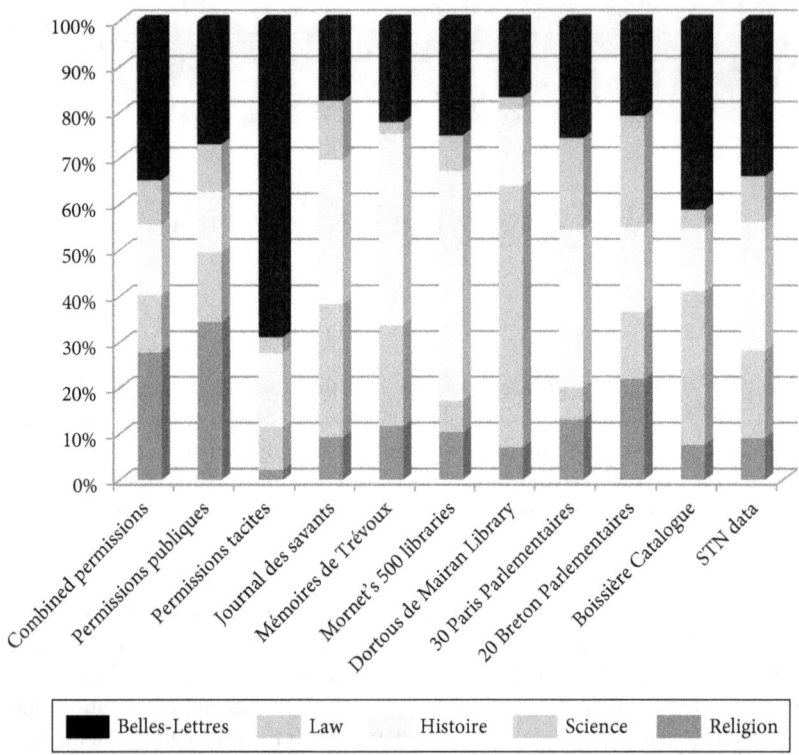

Chart 7.1 Surveys of popular reading in eighteenth-century France and Europe (categorized works only). The first nine bars of this graph are adapted from a chart in Darnton, 'Reading, Writing and Publishing', p. 180. Uncategorized works are excluded and range as high as 27.5 per cent in the surveys of Permissions and a staggering 42 per cent in Mornet's survey. In contrast only 1 per cent of STN sales were 'uncategorizable'.

Savants and *Mémoires de Trévoux*, perhaps reflecting the significance with which it was viewed. Yet tellingly, it accounted for only one eighth of titles in Boissière's stock.

At 19.5 per cent of STN sales, *Sciences et Arts* also rates highly within the STN global data, as well as in learned reviews. It was much less prevalent in the general run of private libraries and the *Permissions registers*. Was this because the STN was selling a lot of scientific works, or carrying works relating to the Arts, or both? The lowest two categories in the STN data are Law (*Jurisprudence*) and Theology. Works classified as 'Law' account for a respectable 10 per cent, a frequency broadly consistent with the permissions registers but comfortably exceeding figures for Mornet's general library survey. The proportion of theological works among STN sales seems suspiciously low at just 9 per cent, though it is not inconsistent with Mornet's survey. Perhaps it reflects the Protestant orientation of the religious books traded by the STN?

The answers to many of these questions become clearer if we interrogate the data a little further. If we go down to the next level of categories, the shape of the STN's global trade is more evident (see Table 7.1). The STN's buoyant sales of *Belles-Lettres* were not driven by novels [*Romans*] alone, but also, and in near equal measure, by *Poétique*. There was also a strong showing for *Polygraphes anciens et modernes*, a category which comprises single-author anthologies in multiple genres (sometimes mixing creative writing and non-fiction). So were volumes of poetry as popular with the STN's readers as novels? Probably not, for there is something missing from our picture. As we have noted, when the Parisian system was devised prose drama was virtually unknown in France. Thus *Poétique* also includes drama, both in verse and prose. The STN sold significantly more drama than most rival publishing houses, its sales-volume driven by the popularity of Louis-Sébastien Mercier's theatrical pieces. Conversely, sales analysis of the STN's stock of *livres d'assortissement* suggests that they probably printed rather less novels than most rival or allied houses.[2]

Just as *Belles-Lettres* was driven by sales of novels, poetry and collected works, the success of *Histoire* was significantly boosted by the STN's sales of *Géographie* and *Voyages*, although History was the predominant subcategory. Likewise, *Sciences et Arts* relied on sales of two subcategories that we might hesitate to associate with either – *Philosophie*, which accounted for 43,740 sales and *Métaphysique*, which contributed 7,202 more. In this context, *Philosophie* is a general category, which includes *Logique et morale* and the lives and works of *Philosophes anciens* and *modernes*, as well as a series of categories concerning political theory, economics, commerce and finance.

Table 7.1 'Sales' of subcategories of the three leading Parisian categories in the STN database

Category	1st level subcategory	Units distributed by STN	% of all units distributed
Belles-Lettres	Romans	53,346	13.01
	Poétique	42,817	10.44
	Polygraphes anciens & modernes	32,260	7.87
	Grammaires & dictionnaires	6,821	1.66
	Rhétorique	2,057	0.5
	Bibliographie	275	0.07
	Philology	136	0.03
Histoire	History (all subcategories)	70,758	17.25
	Voyages	22,405	5.46
	Geography and Maps	17,215	4.2
	Other subcategories	1,429	0.35
Science et Arts	Philosophie	43,740	10.66
	Médecine, Chirurgie	9,666	2.36
	Histoire naturelle	8,055	1.96
	Arts	7,797	1.9
	Métaphysique	7,202	1.76
	Mathématique	1,982	0.48
	Other subcategories	104	0.03
Total		328,065	79.99

Métaphysique is more specific, embracing works treating the existence of God or the Soul as intellectual problems rather than revealed or demonstrable religious truths. Intriguingly, these two widely drawn philosophical categories *Philosophie* and *Métaphysique* account for around two thirds of all sales in the *Arts et Sciences* category. The sciences and the mechanical and visual arts by contrast sold relatively poorly.

Macro-level analysis of Parisian categories, however suggestive, can only take us so far. Answering nuanced questions about demand and reception requires more precise keyword descriptors to reveal more about the flavour of a work and its ideological tendencies. This is where an analysis of the frequency and dissemination patterns for the keywords we have applied to the STN data comes into its own. They tell us much more about the books the STN sold and differences between groups of readers, especially in terms of international comparison. When we aggregate the sales of books ascribed our most popular keywords, it reveals a richer and more complex range of preoccupations than were visible in our dissection of the Parisian system (see Appendix 3.5 for details).

As with the Parisian categories, the overarching significance of creative literature is again apparent. The keyword 'Literature' was assigned to over one quarter of all STN book sales (112,993 units). Other FBTEE keywords give us a clearer picture of the shape of this 'Literature'. The substantial majority, 65,819 units, were works of 'Prose Fiction'; 35,045 were dramatic works; and about 10,000 were works in other literary genres. The significance of books about or, in the case of fiction, set in, France (87,285 units) and Switzerland (41,174 units) is also apparent. The near numerical equivalence of works relating to 'Politics' (71,662 units) and those on 'Religion' (69,334 units) is also intriguing: it suggests a balance of concern between heavenly and earthly cities.

Equally striking is the near-perfect balance between 'Works of Religiosity', our rather ungainly term for works on any subject written with a clear or explicit Christian religious inspiration, and '*Philosophie*', our category for works matching a classic Peter Gay style definition of Enlightenment – stressing that it was cosmopolitan, sceptical, tolerant, humanitarian and generally favoured more representative forms of government ((54,248 and 49,888 units respectively). Works classified as '*Philosophie*' accounted for some 11 per cent of the STN's global trade and almost 40 per cent of its illegal trade. If this measurement is used as our proxy for Enlightenment, relatively little of the literature sold by the STN might be considered 'enlightened'. This was something noted by Robert Darnton in a review of the FBTEE database in which he commented, on the basis of a survey of our bestselling texts and authors, that '"Enlightenment Europe" as seen by the statistics of the *FBTEE* is a Europe without much Enlightenment'.[3] But such a conclusion ignores lessons Darnton himself taught us. It limits the canon to a few authors and texts, when in fact a whole gamut of books in multiple and mixed genres conveyed Enlightenment to the most unlikely places, including the pulpit and the boudoir.[4] Jeremy Popkin took a rather different lesson from FBTEE's findings, particularly on the illegal sector, commenting:

> To be told that the majority even of the illegal books sold in French-speaking Europe in the late eighteenth century were relatively serious works of philosophy and political commentary takes us back, in some ways, to the Enlightenment of our grandparents, when Voltaire, Montesquieu, and Rousseau were still names

to conjure with and Théveneau de Morande, *Thérèse philosophe* and Pidansat de Mairobert were unheard of, even by specialists.[5]

Moreover, if the STN statistics reinforce the importance of Peter Gay's style of *philosophie* over other forms of enlightened discourse, they may nevertheless understate the general prevalence of the *philosophes*' works in the international book trade, and for three reasons. First, for analytical purposes in the FBTEE database the term '*Philosophie*' has been applied narrowly on the basis of content. It does not, for example, cover all the works of Voltaire. Second, although the STN is notorious for dealing in illegal works, for most of its history, as we have noted, it did so rather cautiously. As a result, it appears to have published rather less *philosophie* than the general run of Swiss international publishers. The company did trade in such material, but much of it was bought in: for example, the only works by Voltaire that they printed were *Dieu* and the *Questions sur l'Encyclopédie*. Thirdly, there are other ways to measure and assess the presence of 'Enlightenment' in the STN's trade. These might include both a 'distant reading' of the STN's corpus and trade patterns and a close reading of some of their bestselling texts.

Equally, the FBTEE database figures certainly understate the STN's own religious output, as their general accounts do not list details of books commissioned by local churches for liturgical purposes. Thus, many of the most essential and intensively used religious texts they produced seem to have escaped our purview. A later chapter will consider whether other sources used to study the circulation of books also tend to under-report religious titles. Suffice to note here that the STN itself probably sold faith and *philosophie* in near equal amounts.

The significance of schoolbooks to the trade is also evident from the keyword statistics, though such works tend to be absent from most studies of reading and ownership. Generally, textbooks tend to be ephemeral and many of the most popular have not come down to us. Fortunately, the STN database offers significant insights into this oft-overlooked and hard to detect sector of the market. The 126 works identified as schoolbooks accounted for 31,661 unit sales, 7.65 per cent of the STN's trade by volume, but probably proportionately far less by sales revenue. In the main, such books taught sacred or secular History (twenty-six titles, 3.35 per cent of sales), Geography (nine titles, 3.36 per cent of sales) or both (i.e. historical geography), Languages (thirty-two titles, 1.01 per cent of sales) or the Christian Religion (seventeen titles, 1 per cent of sales). Science textbooks were marginal to the STN's school book trade (twenty-six titles, 0.18 per cent of sales). For the STN, schoolbooks were a sideline, though a handful of titles figure prominently in our bestseller lists. Nevertheless, schoolbook sales, as we have seen, formed a significant portion of the STN's trade with some more distant markets as well as in and around Neuchâtel.

The prominence in global sales figures of works classified under 'Law' (over 47,500 units) and Economics (30,000 units) is also worthy of comment, though many jurisprudential works were commissioned by Brissot or produced in the context of Théodore Rilliet's struggles with his wife, brother-in-law and the Genevan authorities. The impact of the Rilliet corpus is a sobering reminder that in assessing and comparing keyword distribution patterns we need to consider the impact of bestsellers in our data.

For example, our top four global bestsellers each account for over 2 per cent of total STN sales. This weighting can substantially affect our keyword counts. By dispatching over 16,700 copies of Rilliet's *Planta gagnant sa vie en honnête homme* from the STN's Neuchâtel premises, the STN's clerks inadvertently boosted our tally counts by 4.1 per cent for every keyword we applied to the pamphlet. This rockets the improbable-sounding keyword combination 'Geneva', 'Scandal' and 'Incest' up our keyword tables. It has a similar effect on the terms 'Causes célèbres', 'Criminal Law', 'Illegitimacy', 'Judicial Mémoires', 'Judicial proceedings', 'Law', 'Rilliet affair' and 'Switzerland' as well as the Parisian classification 'Droit étranger'. Sales of Mercier's *Tableau de Paris* provide a 3.4 per cent boost to the keywords 'France', 'National Character', 'National Customs', 'Paris', 'Social issues' and 'Social mores' and, in the Parisian booksellers' system, the miscellaneous writers category *Polygraphes anciens et modernes*. A few key works therefore had a disproportionate effect on our keyword counts. Significantly, most of these works were commissioned editions, and all were published by the STN. As in our previous analyses, it might therefore make sense to filter out one or both of these categories. This will smooth out our results (by removing those few titles which distort our dataset) and cancal out the effects of the STN's own publishing biases.[6]

First let us strip out all 'vanity press' commissioned works – most notably Brissot's works – from our sales figures. This leaves us the STN's trade sales, in which *Belles-Lettres* accounted for just under 35 per cent of units sold; *Histoire* for almost 30 per cent; and the catch-all *Sciences et Arts*, 21 per cent. Hence, when compared to the global bestsellers list, all three major Parisian categories have expanded, as has *Théologie*, which now accounts for 10.5 per cent of sales. In contrast *Jurisprudence* collapses to a mere 2.8 per cent, following the removal of Brissot's commissioned legal works from our dataset. Tellingly, more than half of the STN's 'trade' sales were works which might provide entertainment or distraction besides, in some cases, edification: creative literature, history and travel writing. These dominated the STN trade sales. We might assume they were the staples of the market.

When we filter out the rest of the STN's own editions as well as 'commissioned works' there is a further significant shift. Among the *'livres d'assortissement'* that now comprise our entire dataset, over two fifths (40.17 per cent) of unit sales have been classified as *Belles-Lettres*. This figure is broadly consistent with our title count for Boissière's catalogue, which was also a product of the long range international trade. However, the match with Boissière's catalogue is much less precise for other categories. *Science et Arts* now weighs in at 22.78 per cent while *Histoire* has declined significantly to 21.67 per cent. *Théologie* remains relatively stable at 10.45 per cent and *Jurisprudence* barely registers on 2.66. These results are nevertheless highly suggestive, particularly as the 'commercial list' is the dataset which probably best reflects the generality of works flowing through the arterial networks of the long-distance French extraterritorial publishing trade. Having stripped out the works which reflect the STN directors' own commercial, political and intellectual predilictions, we are left with a heavy dose of *Belles-Lettrres*. Works in this category seem to have travelled better – or at least in greater numbers – than other genres.

We can add nuance to this picture by examining the incidence of keywords allocated for commercial sales and comparing them those with equivalent figures for the STN's global trade (see Appendix 3.8). The keyword 'Literature', which was assigned to a little over one quarter of global sales (27.55 per cent), rises to over one third (36.47 per cent) on the commercial list. Similarly, the proportion of works tackling 'Religion' rises by almost one quarter (from 16.9 per cent to 20.7 per cent), and those on 'Christianity' even more steeply. 'Works of Religiosity' and 'Theology' both rise by one fifth, but this is matched by a similar climb in the proportion of works carrying the keyword '*Philosophie*'. In contrast, areas where the STN specialized – dramatic works, 'Geography' and 'Economics' – all fall sharply, as does 'Law'. There is also a mild decline in the proportion of works dealing with 'Politics'. This is sharper in the field of 'Current Affairs', which comprised the bulk of political works, than for 'Political Theory'. Intriguingly there are also a few areas where figures are remarkably consistent between 'global' and the 'commercial' sales, notably 'Romantic Fiction' and 'Philosophy'.

Several subjects on which the STN published little appear considerably more significant when considered as a proportion of their *livres d'assortissement*. Among these commercial sales, 'Science' (at 11.1 per cent) is almost twice as prevalent as among the STN's global sales figures. Likewise, 'Lives and Letters', an umbrella category for biographical works and memoirs, jumps by almost half (from 6.56 per cent to 9.75 per cent). This may be significant to our story, since one particular genre of biographical literature, the scandalous memoir or '*vie privée*', has been associated with the emergence of the practices of personal denigration and violent invective that would shape the political culture of the French Revolution.[7] This is a topic that we will explore further in our final chapter.

However, the most substantial changes are in other genres notoriously associated with the clandestine trade, 'Erotic Works', 'Anticlerical Works', 'Libertine Texts' and 'Pornographic Works'. All these categories more than double their market share, with 'Pornographic Works' tripling from 1.95 per cent of 'global sales' to 5.83 per cent of 'commercial sales'. This is important in our discussion of the anatomy of the illegal sector in Chapter 9 and reflects that fact that the STN did not publish such works themselves.

If (as argued in Chapter 6) the STN's 'commercial sales' broadly mirror the shape of a pan-European market, the international French book trade was dominated by creative literature. It accounted for almost two in five sales. Works related to 'Religion' may have accounted for one fifth and the vast bulk of these were religiously inspired. About one in seven books was infused with the spirit of *philosophie* and one in eight had erotic qualities. Around half of erotic works were also pornographic in the narrow sense. About the same number were infused with sexual libertinism. About one in six works tackled political issues, and one in nine treated current affairs, history or science. Biographical genres were also important, and seemed to account for about one in ten works sold via these international networks.

So far, this chapter has painted the STN's sales with broad strokes while highlighting caveats about its representativeness. How, then, are other scholars going to make sense of the FBTEE data and how might they compensate for distortions, biases and problems in the database? These are pressing problems and building digital tools to help resolve them significantly delayed publication of the project. The most important solution was our system of filters or 'options menus', which can be applied individually or cumulatively. These have already been described and one of them, the 'Edition Types' option menu, was employed to create our 'trade' and 'commercial' sales figures. Each of the eight options is carefully outlined on a single web page in the database's user interface, which explains how it operates and why it might be helpful. A user worried about the distorting effect on our keyword tables of including 'commissioned works' such as Rilliet's *Planta gagnant sa vie en honnête homme*, can use the 'Edition types' menu to exclude 'STN commissioned works'. One obsessed with clandestine literature can limit searches to the illegal sector using the 'Markers of illegality' menu. Others might distinguish between small retail traders and the wholesale market using the 'Client types menu'. Users can even explore the impact of women in the book trade using the 'Client gender' menu.[8]

Such faceted searching allows us to move beyond the STN archive as we find it, to explore multiple sectors of the trade and conduct sophisticated comparative studies. For example, by isolating books by origin, or to be more precise edition type, we can contrast the literature produced by the STN with that sourced from elsewhere in Switzerland, France or other parts of Europe. When we do that some interesting nuances emerge (see Chart 7.2). For example, it confirms that the STN produced far more *Jurisprudence* than the norm, much of it on Brissot's account. Likewise, they produced considerably less science than other Swiss publishers.[9] It appears, too, that the Swiss produced less *Belles-Lettres* than French-language publishers elsewhere, and that the STN's prodigious trade in *Histoire* was fuelled by its own publications, notably the geography textbooks and historical geographies written by Frédéric-Samuel Ostervald.[10]

Things get more interesting if we move from books supplied to the STN to books demanded from them, for as Chart 7.3 shows there were significant divergences between different markets. Between 1769 and 1794, the French took a little less *Histoire* (27.3 per cent), and marginally more *Sciences et Arts* (23.75 per cent), *Théologie* (11.3 per cent) and *Jurisprudence* (3.1 per cent) than the STN's clients generally. The deviation in each case is around 10 per cent, enough to appear statistically significant. What should we make of this? The deviation is probably not enough to support a general theory. It suggests that *Belles-Lettres* and *Histoire* were more popular in France than do most other surveys. But the figures perhaps also indicate that French readers were more interested in serious, highbrow genres (i.e. *Sciences et Arts*, *Théologie*, *Jurisprudence*) than francophone readers elsewhere?

The data also allows us to further dissect the tastes of those Neuchâtelois who bought books over the STN's trade counter (see Chart 7.3). As we have already noted,[11] the STN sold about 6,000 books this way, mostly in parcels of one or two, suggesting that they were going to individuals intent on reading them. In general, these Neuchâtelois appear to have been a conservative bunch. They took more '*Théologie*' proportionately than any other STN client group defined here (24.5 per cent); they also took a lot of *Histoire* (29.1 per cent). In contrast, the Neuchâtelois were lukewarm towards creative literature (20.4 per cent) and *Sciences et Arts* (13.25 per cent), which included philosophy. Thus they appear to have shunned subjects and genres associated with the transmission of the most dynamic and radical aspects of Enlightenment and proto-romantic thought. These were tendencies shared, though to a lesser degree, by their compatriots elsewhere

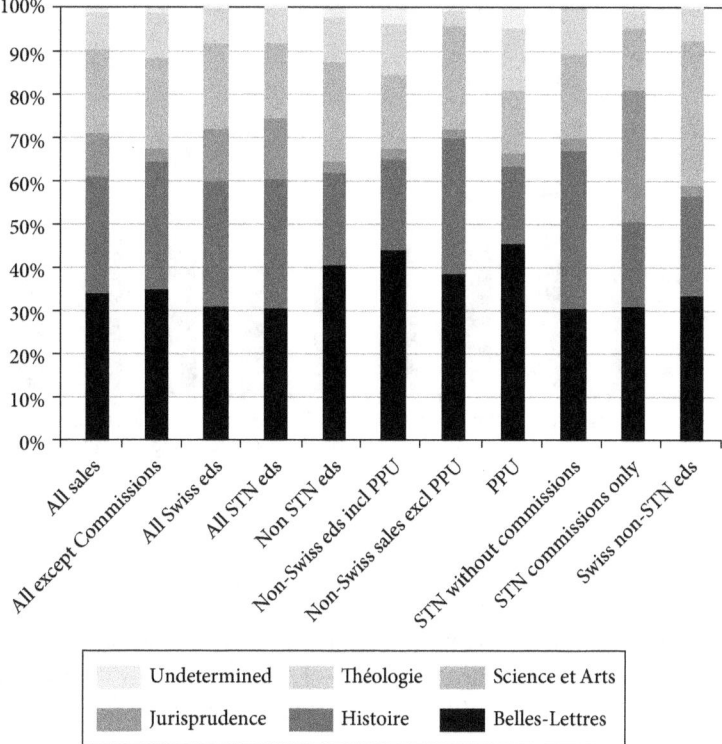

Chart 7.2 STN sales by Parisian category by edition type, 1769-94. (PPU = Place of Publication Unknown). The first column of the chart represents 'global' sales; the second 'trade' sales, and the fifth 'commercial sales'.

in Switzerland, where the STN's retail customers took more *Théologie* and *Histoire* but less *Belles-Lettres* and *Sciences et Arts* than clients in France and elsewhere in Europe. Some of this is explicable. The STN produced a lot of Calvinist devotional works for local sale, as well as Swiss and French historical works that had wide local appeal. Their textbooks on French and sacred history, geography and historical geography were also intended primarily for sale locally, although some copies sold as far afield as Russia.

When I conceived the FBTEE project, I hoped that such comparative insights would allow us to map the tastes of francophone readers across Europe. Ten years on, I confess that such hopes were rather naïve and optimistic. However, the problem is not so much in the quality and conceptualization of the data but the scale of the building blocks on which the database draws. As noted in Chapter 3, the average sale or purchase transaction in the STN database records the transfer of over a dozen copies. Moreover, in many towns or regions, just one or two key correspondents dominate the purchase or sales records. Thus, in any given region, the STN database is generally composed of a set of distinctive case studies, and the representativeness of each of them is open to question. However, to draw solid internationally comparative

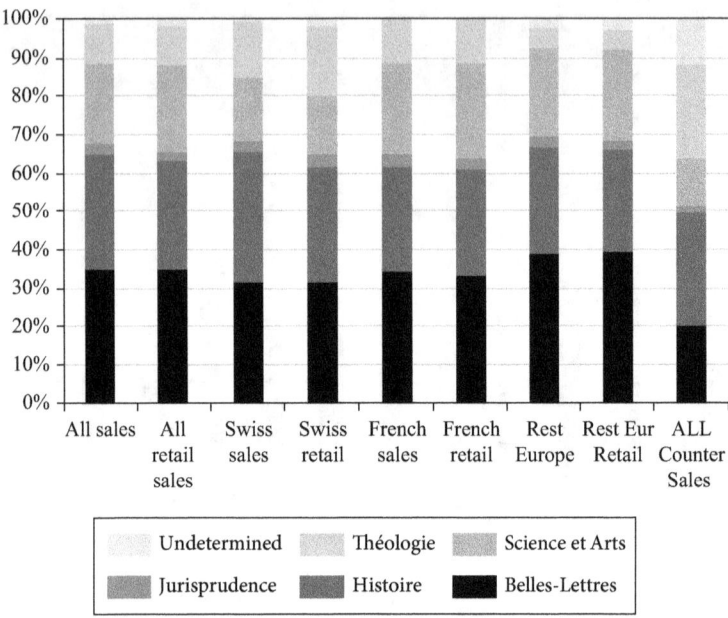

Chart 7.3 Parisian categorized STN sales by Client Type, 1769–94 Commissioned editions are excluded from figures, with the exception of sixty over the counter sales. Retail sales also exclude 'Swiss Wholesale' and 'French Wholesale' clients.

conclusions, we need to amalgamate large numbers of case studies. Sadly, this is not possible for many individual countries, particularly if we wish to break up the data further and consider only the 'commercial sector' or to look for annualized trends. For these purposes, Britain's 2,189 or the Iberian peninsula's 2,991 global unit sales are clearly inadequate. But equally it is doubtful whether the 21,790 recorded sales to Eastern Europe (Russia and Poland), 20,320 sales to Italy or 17,220 sales to Germany taken individually, offer large enough samples. As a result, most of the internationally comparative work that follows juxtaposes just three geographic entities: the Helvetic zone (equivalent to modern Switzerland), the [Bourbon] kingdom of France, and the 'Rest of Europe'.[12]

Yet even a tri-partite division reveals some telling differences in distribution patterns (see the Appendix 3.9). For this purpose, the most revealing and appropriate dataset with which to work is the STN's 'trade' list. Since our purpose is to analyse the comparative distribution of our keywords across the STN's various markets, it does not matter that this list includes many STN editions, so long as 'commissioned editions' and the biases they bring into the data are excluded. As the largest dataset meeting this criterion, the STN's 'trade list' can be considered the most 'representative' for this purpose. Helpfully, this list is finely balanced between our three geographic entities, with the smallest entity (Rest of Europe) contributing 30.5 per cent of the sales, and the largest (the Swiss zone) just 36.1 per cent. Thus the percentage scores for each entity (revealed in Appendix 3.9) also approximate crudely to absolute relativities in sales volumes. By looking at the variance – the difference between lowest and highest selling markets – it is possible to see significant patterns at a glance. Indeed, our variance figures reveal that demand patterns diverged significantly across subject materials and genres. While some genres and subjects seem to have been demanded equally across all markets, others were several times more popular in some markets than others.

The flattest patterns of keyword distribution apply generally to the most ideologically neutral and/or heterogeneous types of works: 'Miscellaneous essays', 'Collected works', 'Short stories' and perhaps, more surprisingly, given the presence of Mercier's plays, 'Drama'. That these categories show the smallest divergences (between 6 and 16 per cent across our three markets) is in itself significant and appears to validate our methodology. Genres that had a general or non-specific appeal, or which anthologized in single collections works on many subjects or with multiple ideological tendencies, appear to have had much the same appeal everywhere. So too, did the other capacious general literary genres 'Literature' and 'Prose Fiction' (both had variances of around 21 to 22 per cent). With genres that lacked such general or non-specific appeal, however, more significant divergences occur between markets.

The most significant of these divergences are visible exactly where we might expect. They apply to 'Protestant texts' (333 per cent) and to 'School Books' (313 per cent), both genres in which publishers were geared to serve mass localized market demand by printing cheap editions in huge volumes.[13] As a proportion of sales, the Swiss took more than four times as many 'School books' as the French, and four and a third times more 'Protestant texts' than the 'Rest of Europe'. Nevertheless, the scale of the STN's trade in religious literature with the French Protestant arc is worthy of note: distinctively Protestant works accounted for 7 per cent of 'trade' sales to France. In their 'global' figures, this demand would be supplemented by Pomaret's commissioned works for the Protestants of Ganges. In total, 10,017 of 29,631 'Protestant texts' traded by the STN were sent directly to France. The most numerically significant were the *Bible* (1,611 copies) and *New Testament* (589 copies) together wish a triptych of Pomaret's commissioned works and three texts by Neuchâtelois divines. The former comprised Pomaret's *Le Bon père* (1,004 copies), *Le Chrétien par conviction et sentiment* (780 copies), and *Le Catéchumène instruit sous une forme nouvelle* (612 copies).[14] The latter included Jean-Elie Bertrand's *Sermons sur différens textes de l'Ecriture Sainte* (548 copies); Jean-Frédéric Ostervald's *Abrégé de l'histoire sainte et du catéchisme* (674 copies) and his son Jean-Rudolphe's *Nourriture de l'âme* (493 copies). Until 1787 most of our Protestant texts works were technically illegal in France. However, they are generally not listed as illegal works in the FBTEE database because few appear in the police and secondary sources from which we drew our 'markers of illegality'.[15] Nevertheless, the STN evidence suggests such works comprised a significant subset of the extraterritorial publishers' clandestine trade with France, perhaps as much as 20 per cent. Outside of Calvinist regions of France and Switzerland, the STN's Protestant trade was predictably much more limited. In contrast, sales of the works tagged with the denominationally non-specific category 'Theology' sold in relatively similar volume in each of our three markets: the variance was below 20 per cent and the Swiss were the STN's worst customers for this sort of work.

After 'Protestant Works' and 'School Books', the categories with the largest variances between markets are 'Financial Administration', 'Geography', *Philosophie*, 'Erotic works' and 'Economics'. High sales of works tagged 'Financial administration' to France can be explained. Most such books relate to the political–economic policies of one man – the Genevan-born French finance minister Jacques Necker – and the controversies to which they gave rise.[16] Such financial pamphlets commanded a wide interest in France, and also attracted attention in Switzerland, the country of Necker's birth. However, the STN evidence suggests they drew little interest abroad and that their sales were ephemeral. Financial pamphlets relating to Necker dominate the STN's 'trade' bestseller table for the year 1781, occupying eight of the top ten positions (see Appendix 3.11). These eight works accounted for an astonishing 49.96 per cent of STN trade sales in that year. The vast majority of copies went to clients in France or Switzerland. These figures capture the surge of the public interest generated by the debate over Necker's celebrated *Compte-rendu*. They also demonstrate that the vogues and political preoccupations of a particular moment (and particularly those of the late 1770s and 1780s when the STN's sales were at a peak) can be heavily reflected in the STN's overall bestseller tables.

The passion for financial pamphlets soon passed, but this raises important questions about temporality. The chapters that follow will show the significance of trends over time and the need to be attentive to the changing contours of the STN's trade. For now, suffice to observe that trade patterns were not constant and contained considerable chronological as well as geographic divergences. To a quite remarkable extent, demand for the Necker pamphlets was confined chronologically to the years 1781 and 1782 and geographically to France and Switzerland.[17]

High variance figures for the keywords, 'Economics' and 'Geography' can be tied to particular subgenres of each and phenomena we have discussed already. A high proportion of the books tagged as 'Economics' are also tagged 'Financial Administration', and this Neckerana almost entirely explains the high proportion of 'Economics'-related books going to France.[18] Equally, the distribution pattern for books tagged as 'Geography' is shaped by the prevalence of 'School Books'. Altogether, Frédéric-Samuel Ostervald's geographical and historical geographical textbooks alone notched up over 12,000 sales, and Anton Busching's *Introduction à la connoissance géographique et politique des Etats de l'Europe* added 1,133 more.[19] The bulk of these works were sold in and around Neuchâtel.

Our variance figures also imply that French readers were much more interested in '*Philosophie*' and 'Erotic works' than readers elsewhere. These two genres were both tied to the illegal sector and have been linked to revolutionary causation. To discover that they were substantially more in vogue in France than elsewhere may thus be historiographically significant. However, the extent of these French predilections may be exaggerated by the particularities of the Swiss market, which seems to have been peculiarly resistant to both *Philosophie* and erotica. Thus while French readers apparently consumed substantially more of both genres than those elsewhere, the 'Rest of Europe' also bought marginally more 'Erotic works' and *Philosophie* than the market average. In the case of 'Erotica', low Swiss demand may reflect the fact that the STN printed few erotic works. The STN's partner houses probably sourced most of their erotica direct from known publishers.[20] In contrast, FBTEE statistics suggest the STN was reasonably active as a publisher of *Philosophie*, albeit with an output below the industry average.[21] Given the legal controls and changing legislative and practical rigour applied to policing erotica and 'Philosophie', extreme caution is needed in trying to interpret this data. There is prima facie case here that the French market for both genres was exceptionally active. This requires further interrogation when we explore the illegal sector as a whole.[22]

If the French liked their erotica, they appear to have had less time for 'Romantic' and 'Sentimental' fictions than francophone readers elsewhere. The Swiss, by contrast, were drawn to both these genres. Intriguingly, the Swiss were also heavy consumers of another escapist genre which French readers apparently shunned: 'Travel' literature. In all three genres the divergences were in a middle range of around forty to 85 per cent, a margin which appears big enough to be statistically significant. Similar variance rates apply to many other significant keywords, including most of those relating to religious content ('Religion', 'Christianity', 'Work of Religiosity'), 'Science' or 'History', 'Politics' and 'Current Affairs'. Not surprisingly, perhaps, the Swiss and French interest in works relating to 'Religion' and 'Christianity' ran almost neck and neck, whereas the Swiss were significantly more liable to purchase religiously inspired 'Works of Religiosity'. All three of these categories were of much less interest to readers from the 'Rest of Europe'. In contrast, readers in the 'Rest of Europe' were significantly more interested in acquiring works we tagged as 'Science' or 'Philosophy'.

French readers had a strong preference for works on 'Politics' and more especially 'Current Affairs' than their counterparts in Switzerland or other European countries. To a considerable extent this seems to have reflected French parochial interests. A significant number of works related to 'Current Affairs' dealt with the debates unleashed by Necker's financial policy. In contrast, it was the Swiss who consumed most 'History', even though only a small proportion of historical works related to Switzerland (just 4,288 out of the 56,160 'History' sales). Yet paradoxically, the biographical genre 'Lives and Letters', which was usually political or historical in content, was apparently consumed most avidly by readers in the 'Rest of Europe', albeit by a relatively slender margin (the variance is under 35 per cent).[23] In the final chapter of this book, 'From Swiss Politics to French History' we will attempt to tease out some of the complex interrelationships between historico-political genres.

As if this story of national difference were not complex enough, distribution patterns were far from constant. These, in turn, reflected seismic shifts in the STN's strategic focus, particularly in the aftermath of the French Council's decrees of 30 August 1777, which smashed their smuggling infrastructure, and of 12 June 1783, which hobbled their pirate trade. The impact of the STN's changing strategies and market reorientations are visible when we cross-reference STN book sales with our keyword attributions across a series of five-year bands (see Appendix 3.12). In the early years of the STN's history, when Switzerland was the key market, they sold markedly less 'Literature' but significantly more works related to 'Religion' and religious controversy. These were not all spiritual texts or 'Works of Religiosity' such as the *Abrégé de l'histoire sainte et du catéchisme* (4,702 sales in 1769–74) or the *Bible* (2,232 sales). They also included refutations of d'Holbach's works, including Voltaire's pamphlet *Dieu* (2,327 sales) and Holland's *Réflexions philosophiques sur le Système de le nature* (1,161 sales), and 'Philosophie' attacking church practices, notably Christin's *Dissertation sur l'établissement de l'Abbaye de S. Claude* (2,690 sales). Nevertheless, at this period

STN's sales were significantly boosted by religiously inspired and Protestant works, as well as textbooks. All were guaranteed to sell well locally. But the STN were also dabbling in *philosophie*, a market from which they would later retreat. In part this was a conscious decision following the *Système de la nature* affair. However, *philosophie* was probably less in vogue once the controversies surrounding d'Holbach's corpus cooled, particularly following the deaths of Voltaire and Rousseau in 1778 and French book trade regulations of August 1777. Indeed, for the period 1780 to 1784, *philosophie*'s market share slipped to just 6.18 per cent of STN sales. For those same years, 'Politics', 'Economics', 'Current Affairs' and 'Financial Administration' perform strongly in our keyword sales charts as a result of the 'Jacques Necker' effect. However, the popularity of other genres remained relatively stable: for example, works of 'Literature' enjoyed a remarkably consistent market share of 34.8 to 37.4 per cent across the final twenty years of the STN's existence. Nevertheless, the importance of 'Prose Fiction' rose over time, reflecting a general increase in the availability of novels.[24]

This analysis has revealed that a study of bestsellers can only ever provide a partial picture of the literary field of a major publisher. Had we limited our discussion to such texts, we may well have missed the importance of creative literature or *Belles-Lettres* to the STN's overall sales figures, or failed to spot the growing importance of the novel genre. We might also miss the significance of *Philosophie* in the marketplace, or believe it to have been eclipsed, on certain measures, by erotica and the clandestine literature uncovered and memorably described by Robert Darnton.

By treating the literary landscape of the STN *en bloc* through distant reading methods and then breaking it down chronologically and geographically, we have revealed a more complex topography. In many places it is an alien vision. The literary landscape of the late Enlightenment bears only a passing resemblance to that imagined by Darnton or Israel. But neither does it live up to the scenarios outlined by any number of other scholars, including such luminaries as Daniel Mornet, Peter Gay or François Furet. Nor, despite the richness of the STN dataset, and the digital tools at our disposal, is it clear how far the books passing back and forth through the STN's international or clandestine book trade networks were typical of general retail stocks and personal libraries. The STN data reveals that alongside cosmopolitan long-distance book trade networks there existed more localized circuits for the distribution, for example, of mass-produced religious print, political pamphlets and schoolbooks. This hypothesis will be explored further in the chapters that follow. Equally there are indications of national tendencies and chronological trends that reflected and shaped intellectual traditions and political cultures across Europe.

Thus the remainder of this book will attempt to understand developments across the period 1769 to 1789, using the evidence of the STN data and other bibliometric measures to give indicative answers to four questions posed by this analysis. How cosmopolitan was the print culture of the late Enlightenment? What was the true complexion of the illegal sector? How widespread was Enlightenment materialism and conversely to what extent does the printed record suggest religion was in decline? Finally, what does the FBTEE evidence suggest were the key political currents of the later Enlightenment? In the process we might hope to establish the cultural and intellectual history of the period on firmer foundations than has hitherto been possible.

8

Of Cosmopolitan Reading and Novel Concerns[1]

Having harvested the STN's literary field, it is time to examine its fruits in more detail. To begin, we might ask how far they match up to the cosmopolitan Enlightenment's self-depiction in Leonard DeFrance's *À l'Égide de Minerve*? DeFrance intended his tableau to epitomize a heroic Enlightenment which blended urbane reason, scepticism, cosmopolitan universalism, toleration and religious latitudinarianism. To begin, this chapter examines the universality of the booksellers' stock. Did the books in their stores really link together an imagined community of cosmopolitan 'citizens of the world', persons who were equally happy in London, Paris, Liège, Warsaw, Naples, Lisbon or Seville? Were the books themselves like wandering 'cosmopolites' – of no fixed abode yet strangers nowhere? Did they convey and help forge a common universalist culture across borders, or are they implicated in more complex transfers or conversations that were diluted or transformed in the transition process? This chapter will show how digital historical bibliometric approaches can help shape new answers to these questions.

This work is still very much in its infancy. It responds to Jeffrey Freedman's path-breaking 2010 study of the STN's trade with Germany, *Books without Borders*. Freedman's introduction argues the case for freeing book history from the 'dominant national model' in which it has so often been treated, not least because national funding council priorities and academic specialisms have tended to promote 'nationalistic' approaches to the history of print culture.[2] Freedman stresses that the 'national model' poorly reflects the realities of diffusion, which 'cannot be folded neatly into the geography of nations', let alone the patchwork of states comprising eighteenth-century Germany. French books were particularly significant in this regard, partly because French was by the eighteenth century the language of European elites, but also because publication in French conferred the *imprimatur* of cultural respectability. Indeed, many works were translated into other European languages after their French translations, rather than their original versions. Rather than vectors for reinforcing French cultural superiority, Freedman finds the French books circulating through Enlightenment Europe's transnational trade to be 'European as much as they were French'.[3] Nor could a national model cope with the peregrinations of booksellers and printworkers, whose mobility in travelling to the great European book fairs of Leipzig or Frankfurt, or when seeking out customers, employers, safe havens or new markets in which to publish has long been recognized.[4] Yet, as Freedman remarked, previous work on the international dimensions of the French trade had generally focussed on the production of French books abroad for the French market. He therefore set out to study 'how booksellers mediated the transmission of literature across the frontiers of language, nation and culture'.[5]

The approach taken here expands on Freedman's enquiry by asking the extent of the European book trade's cosmopolitanism, or how far readers across Europe were exposed to and consumed books with foreign origins and subject matter? An underlying concern is to reveal how far we may talk of a common Enlightenment reading culture across Europe, and how far we should continue to compartmentalize the Enlightenment into separate national contexts. This is a debate that has raged among historians since the publication of Roy Porter and Mikuláš Teich's edited collection, *The Enlightenment in National Context* in 1981. Historical bibliometric evidence, taken in isolation, is unlikely to resolve this issue definitively. It can, however, establish the parameters for future debate, by revealing the extent to which European publics were plugged into a single reading community, based on common knowledge networks and fictional fare. By comparing database evidence of book trade and publishing patterns with digital resources on reading habits, book ownership, library holdings and borrowing across the Enlightenment world, it should become possible to develop a much better idea of what reading publics in Naples, Lisbon, Lyon, Vienna, Edinburgh, Stockholm, Boston and smaller towns across Europe and the Americas read in common, and where and how their reading fare diverged. The starting point for this discussion will be the STN evidence, but, in an innovative new approach, this will then be compared with the evidence of other databases.

Taken on its own terms, the STN database archive offers a major resource for tracking the movement of books, discourses and ideas across national, linguistic, religious and cultural frontiers. And by a combination of distant and close reading, it allows us to assess whether the Enlightenment's international book trade was geared to form and address cosmopolitan 'citizens of the world'. A first step might be to re-examine the degree to which the STN's trade was internationalized. In its set up phase and final death throes, the STN's trade was mainly with Swiss local dealers. However, as we have seen, across its entire history, approximately 39 per cent of its sales went to Switzerland (many of them to partner houses in Geneva, Berne or Lausanne who on-sold them abroad); almost 37 per cent went to France; and almost one quarter of sales to the rest of Europe. Of the books it bought in, something over one quarter came direct from trading partners outside Switzerland, while, allowing for false imprints, approaching 30 per cent were also foreign editions. In short, the vast majority of books traded by the STN physically crossed Swiss borders at least once before they finally reached retail customers. In all, these probably accounted for at least 80 to 85 per cent of unit sales.

A substantial proportion of books also bridged linguistic frontiers. In total, about 11.4 per cent of the works sold by the STN were translated works. The majority of these (5.9 per cent) were translated from the English, mostly for the STN, and a further 3.8 per cent translated from German. Translations from Italian and Latin comprised respectively 0.8 and 0.3 per cent of sales. While over 99 per cent of the STN's sales were French-language editions, we have also identified sales of Latin-language works (927 copies), Italian editions (180 copies) and German works (95 copies). In this the STN may have been atypical compared to foreign book dealers elsewhere – even a cursory dip into the archives of the Luchtman's company of Leiden reveals that in addition to French and Dutch titles, they were dealing in substantial numbers of German and Latin works. Their extensive catalogues confirm that they were trading in English and Italian ones as well.[6]

Almost 500 copies of bilingual texts can also be traced passing through the STN magazines. These were mostly French-other language dictionaries and grammars, but also included a handful of French–Latin, French–Italian or French–Spanish parallel texts. There are even Greek–Latin editions – one copy each of Plutarch's works and Xenophon's *Cyropaedia*.[7] None of these foreign-language or bilingual works was printed by the STN, and thus they are probably under-represented in STN sales figures compared to the broad run of the international trade.[8] Hence, one way or another, the vast majority of the books handled by the STN and similar international publisher-wholesaler organizations had crossed linguistic or national frontiers physically or metaphorically, and in many cases both.

Could the same be said of subject matter? Did it transport readers' imaginations across frontiers and into new realms? Is there evidence to suggest that readers preferred to read voyages or fictitious tales of the far away? Or was their reading more parochial? One way to address these questions might be to consider the subject taxonomic keywords in the FBTEE database related to travel or geography. Nineteen of these keyword tags are attached to works which achieved total aggregate sales of more than 5,000 units. Such keywords might therefore be subjected to further scrutiny. The most numerically significant of these keywords were 'France', which we attached to works with unit sales of some 87,285 units, 'Switzerland' (41,174 units), 'Geneva' (32,437 units) and 'Travel' (23,975 units).[9]

While there is considerable overlap between these keywords – since several might be attached to a single work – works ascribed one or more of the keywords 'France', 'Switzerland' or 'Travel' accounted for 144,857 unit sales, well over one third of all STN sales. Clearly, voracious readers of the STN's wares were likely to encounter many places in their reading, whether they preferred escapist fiction or practical literatures.

Who read literary and non-fiction works about France? Was it predominantly French readers or foreigners? The results appear unambiguous (see Table 8.1). The French took more than their share of books on France, and the Swiss more of those on Switzerland. In both cases we can detect a marginal preference for reading non-fiction treatments of one's homeland over fiction set there. This tendency was especially marked among the French. Their reading, particularly in terms of non-fiction, had a discernible trend towards the parochial. Nevertheless, we should be cautious here. A few bestsellers can skew our sample, particularly for literature. Mercier's sprawling journalistic *Tableau de Paris* contributes some 14,076 units of the literature on 'France'. The historical drama *La Destruction de la ligue* added 10,188 more.

Table 8.1 Domestic readership for books about France and Switzerland. Figures for non-commissioned works only. Helvetic zone versus France.

Keyword	Keyword alone	Keyword and literature	Keyword 'but not' literature
France	47.43	38.19	49.18
Switzerland	45.77	43.65	46.54

Of particular interest to this discussion is travel literature, a rapidly expanding genre in the later Enlightenment. This broad category covers anything from travellers' guidebooks and the gazetteers, which by the later eighteenth century covered much of Europe, though to journeys of exploration across Siberia, Africa or the Pacific Ocean. Travel literature is conspicuous in the STN sales figures – the STN sold 23,975 units, almost 6 per cent of total sales. In general, this literature was popular throughout Europe and distributed in proportions broadly similar to the STN's general sales pattern. The big outliers were Switzerland, which took almost 25 per cent more travel literature than might have been expected, and France, which took commensurately less.[10]

Once again, the evidence of the STN database seems to suggest that readers in France, the supposed heartland of a cosmopolitan Enlightenment, were more parochial readers than those in Switzerland or the 'Rest of Europe', and less interested in encountering other places and cultures. This may partly have been because the French looked to the STN for particular types of work – for example, illegal works, a category in which most travel or spatially related keywords (other than the omnipresent keyword 'France') are conspicuously absent. However, this seems insufficient to explain the whole phenomenon. Perhaps instead it is to do with class. After all, the STN's business model aimed to shift large numbers of cheap popular editions to retailers catering for a general audience. In France and some parts of Belgium and Switzerland, where French was the native language, this general readership was probably less affluent or leisured than francophone readers elsewhere across Europe, who belonged to a cultured and educated elite. Such educated readers were probably more likely to buy voyages, novels and travel guides than the common run of readers in France. That may explain why French readers only took 25.8 per cent of all travel literature sold by the STN, and roughly the same proportion of the STN's top-selling travel book, Patrick Brydone's *Voyage en Sicile et à Malthe*.[11] As a result, the *Voyage en Sicile et à Malthe* merits further analysis, as a work with representatively broad appeal.

However, the STN's edition of Brydone's travelogue was not the first French translation to hit the market, and was begun without the author's permission. Brydone, a Scottish doctor who was at the time visiting Lausanne, learned what was afoot from an advertisement in the STN's newspaper, the *Journal Helvétique*. He at once wrote to the publishers, informing them that he had just read de Meunier's translation, which had recently been published in Paris:

> et quoique il y a des passages bien traduit; j'y ai trouvé une nombre prodigieuse des fautes, et de contresens, qui m'a fort etonné, et m'a fait le plus vif chagrin. Je n'y parois pas seulement pecher contre les principes de la bonne physique; mais souvent contre le sens commun.[12]

Noting significant gaps in the translation, he went on to ask:

> Puis je vous supplier donc messieurs de retarder s'il est possible votre publication, avant que je suis en etat de vous envoyer au moins les corrections les plus necessaires. J'y travaille actuellement, et avant que je puisse recevoir reponse a cette lettre, j'aurois probablement fini le premier volume.

The STN were eager to oblige and reap the commercial benefits of being able to boast that their improved translation had been approved by the author himself. Brydone, good to his word, did his best to assist them, though like many a gentleman traveller he was often hard to pin down. There were frequent delays as he took tours of Switzerland or complained of the tiresomeness of his task.[13] Perhaps to buy time and keep the STN's interest, he speaks of fending off offers from other would-be translators.[14] Nevertheless, when the STN's edition finally appeared, Brydone was disappointed. In particular, he was irritated that the STN advertised his involvement.[15] Moreover, when the final volume came out, Brydone was touring the Austrian empire and noted that in Vienna and many towns on his route he had found the STN's edition banned. Only a few copies circulated clandestinely.[16] Finally, he complained that his Parisian translator had removed all the humorous passages ['les passages qui pouvoient faire sourire son lecteur'], although they were the best part of the original.[17] Why was this? Could it be that the bans and the humour be interrelated?

On the surface, the STN edition of Brydone's text was about as international a venture as the Enlightenment might muster. A Scottish doctor's account of a journey in Italy and Malta, originally published in English in London by Strahan and Cadell, then translated into French in Paris, before being retouched and corrected in Switzerland. It thus linked many of the major centres of the European Enlightenment – Edinburgh, London, Paris, Lausanne/Neuchâtel with a corner of the Mediterranean periphery. Was it also an exemplar of the sort cosmopolitanism we might associate with a citizen of the world – urbane, sceptical, tolerant? This brings us back to Brydone's allegation that de Meunier had removed the humour.

It is not immediately apparent where in Brydone's narrative the humour might lie. The modern reader is likely to be struck by the amount of space given over to three things: vulcanology, antiquities (which Brydone insists were not his main concern) and meteorological readings. To be fair, Brydone was a doctor, scientist and member of the Royal Society, so these interests might be expected, particularly as his meteorological observations are sometimes linked to the health effects of the Italian climate. But there was not much humour in these subjects. Neither were there many belly laughs in his descriptions of the towns, harbours and monumental buildings, the local flora, the seasickness he and his companions experienced, or the enervating effects of the *sirocco*. Nor, despite some mordant irony, were his tales of the honourable brigands assigned to escort his company through rural Sicily likely to have readers rolling in the aisles. Instead, Brydone reserved his acerbic wit for something altogether different, and perhaps altogether more predictable.

The first clues appear at the start of his *Avertissement*. There the STN's editor tells how he considered translating Brydone's work when it first appeared, but abandoned the idea on learning that a translation was being prepared at Paris. He continues: 'Pouvois-je croire que l'on écouteroit encore, dans notre siècle, ces aveugles préjugés qui ont fait le malheur de nos peres.'[18] He then elaborates on this apparent non sequitur,

> comment supposer que, dans une ville qui se pique d'être le centre de la philosophie, on se crût permis de défigurer un auteur, de lui faire tenir un langage qu'il désavoue, de mettre sous son nom des choses qu'il n'a point dites, & cela par un beau zele de religion?[19]

This short passage thus reveals what Brydone's correspondence had obscured. The main issue in Brydone's squabble with de Meunier is religion. In the eyes of his 'editor', Brydone has done nothing to offend:

> Un écrivain étranger à la France, vivant dans un pays où le système protestant est la religion dominante, parle, non point en homme prévenu, mais en philosophe impartial, des abus de la superstition; il dit ce qu'aucun catholique romain, éclairé et de bonne foi, ne s'avisera de nier: & l'on tremble que les observations d'un homme sage ne portent atteinte à la religion romaine![20]

Thus his task as editor had been as follows:

> J'ai cru devoir rétablir tout ce que le censeur de Paris avoit jugé à propos de supprimer; &, quoique bon protestant, je ne l'aurois pas fait, si ces passages retranchés avoient contenu la moindre indécence contre la religion catholique romaine.[21]

These passages invoke the existence, at least on a rhetorical level, of a Catholic cosmopolite. This paragon of 'enlightened' civilisation is a Catholic of 'good faith' who disdains 'superstition' to such an extent that he would not deny anything Brydone might say, nor find any affront to the Roman Church therein. Is this credible? To formulate an answer, we must review what Brydone has to say about Roman Catholic practices. His stance soon becomes apparent. Brydone's complaint that de Meunier removed the 'humorous' passages is a euphemism. For these passages, replete with an acerbic mockery reminiscent of Voltaire or Gibbon relate to just one subject. Religion.

Brydone's first aside has a predictable enough target: monasticism. At Messina, Brydone recounts how he and his companions visited a convent, and chatted with several entertaining and pretty young nuns through a grille. He cannot help adding that none of them had 'la sincerité de convenir que sa situation fût malheureuse', in marked contrast to nuns he had encountered in Portugal. Instead, each declared that she would not change her 'prison contre l'état le plus brillant de la vie'. Nevertheless, he declares that 'quelques-unes avoient sur le visage une douce mélancolie qui démentoit leurs discours' and insists that they would have spoken very differently in a private 'tête à tête'.[22] Brydone reports he was saddened to see a beautiful young woman 'faire le sacrifice de ses charmes, & abandoner le monde & tous ses plaisirs, pour passer ses jours dans la mortification' and was stricken with melancholy on leaving 'ces tristes grilles, barrière impénétrable que la tendre pitié ne peut renverser'.[23]

After this visit, Brydone and his companions encountered a festival for Saint Francis. Fortuitously, they arrived just as the Saint's statue was carried through the crowds and replaced in his chapel, where, according to Brydone 'il fait tous les jours un grand nombre de miracles pour tous ceux qui ont beaucoup d'argent et beaucoup de foi'. Venality, credulity, inhumanity – Brydone is filling the reformation and Enlightenment charge sheet against Catholicism, and in ways that might challenge revealed religious faith more generally. And there is more. Twenty pages later, Brydone describes an ingenious machine depicting the Virgin Mary and the Trinity, wherein a number of wheels contained models of a choir of children dressed as winged heavenly beings 'suivant les différens degrés de la hierarchie'. When the wheels turned the children sang. Sadly, Brydone had been unable to lay eyes on the sacred vehicle, which he believed the inhabitants had hidden from him and his companions, fearing ridicule. But this festival was as nothing compared to that for Saint Rosalie at Palermo, which 'passe pour le plus beau spectacle de l'Europe' because the inhabitants of Palermo spare no expense, being 'superstitieux et fort inventifs'.[24]

Brydone makes clear that such superstition and expenses avail the locals little. In an aside discussing eruptions of boiling water, he remarks that when Vesuvius erupted a century earlier, an 'inondation extraordinaire englouit dans un instant environ cinq cents personnes qui alloient en procession au pied de la montagne pour implorer S. Janvier'.[25] Likewise, he mockingly suggests that when Catania acquired a lava-spit and much needed harbour following an eruption, it was 'sans doute par l'intercession de sainte Agathe'. Unfortunately, when a subsequent eruption destroyed the harbour, 'Le voile miraculeux de sainte Agathe, regardé comme le plus grand trésor de Catane, & qui passoit pour un remede infaillible contre les tremblemens de terre & les volcans, semble avoir perdu sa vertu'.[26] As a result, Brydone notes, the people of Catania moaned about their saints. Yet still they believe that pieces of cloth blessed by the bishop provide miraculous protection against eruptions and earthquakes.[27] Whenever these expedients fail, the people say it was for lack of faith, for they can also relate occasions when homes have been saved due to the magic veil.

Ironic asides against the circular arguments of the credulous are just one part of Brydone's assault. He also mocks transubstantiation and traces the pagan origins of many saints' cults, popular Catholic practices, rites and religious buildings. Indeed, Brydone claimed that if the high priest of a pagan temple were to return to earth to resume his functions, 'il n'auroit qu'à se familiariser avec quelques nouveaux noms, & apprendre par coeur la messe, les *pater* et les *ave*'.[28] Finally, to round off his attacks, he invokes Enlightenment science, noting the private observations of his friend, the vulcanologist and priest father Recupero, whose studies of Etna's lava flows led him to reject the Mosaic chronology of the origins of the earth, much to the chagrin of his ultra-orthodox bishop.[29]

Brydone's targets went far beyond the superstitious practices of Catholic peasants. Contrary to statements in his prefatory material, they were not limited to things beyond the formal teaching of the Roman Catholic Church. On the contrary, they attacked historic claims and traditions of the church and the literal truth of scripture. These might be things that enlightened latitudinarian Protestants could stomach, but for more literally minded Christians of all denominations, Brydone's swipes must have smacked of sacrilege. While geared specifically to Catholic credulity, they sapped beliefs dear to other Christian denominations. As with Voltaire's *Philosophical Dictionary*, whose strategies Brydone mirrored, attacks on one faith raised suggestive questions about the claims of all revealed religion. Such a sceptical attitude operates on many levels. On one, it signals Brydone's claims to be a cosmopolite *philosophe*. But on another, his observations could be presented as representing a position generally accepted by (enlightened) Protestants, and admitted, according to his editor, by all Catholics of good faith, at least in private. There are inherent tensions here between Brydone's cosmopolitanism, sectarianism and nationalism that invite multiple readings.

Where then does this leave us? What image of cosmopolitanism can we take from Brydone's text? Is it or its author a true citizen of the world, equally at ease with, and curious about, different cultures and peoples? Again the balance sheet is open. Brydone is curious, to be sure, though keener to denounce than to accommodate superstition. But some places are outside his comfort zone. His introduction notes that his Italian friends thought his voyage was impossible given the lack of decent inns and the bandit-infested country.[30] Likewise, his accounts of the bandit-guards he was given by the viceroy of Massena mix fascination and gratitude with revulsion.[31] This is not a society where he feels at home or relaxed, and he is deeply condescending about the religion, superstition and practices of most of its inhabitants, including those who pass for *savants*. The cosmopolitan 'citizen of the world' may be intrigued by Sicily, but he is only truly comfortable in the *civis*, in proximity to his fellow cosmopolites and the pleasures of civilisation, such as the orchestra of Naples.[32] Conversely, Brydone's cosmopolitan condescension apparently had little appeal to southern Italians. Although the STN sold over 6,000 books to Tuscany, Rome and Naples, Brydone's masterpiece was not among them. Instead, it found its main markets in the Protestant regions of Switzerland, France and Germany and cosmopolitan centres such as Paris and Warsaw (see Appendix 1.4).

So was the STN corpus a set of books of 'no fixed abode' which are 'strangers nowhere'? Certainly the popular literature of the later Enlightenment, as peddled by businesses like the STN, was deeply international, criss-crossing physical and linguistic borders, and allowing readers to encounter and imagine the world within the comfort of their armchairs. But, as Brydone's work reminds us, those encounters often took place within cultural settings and frames of reference that domesticated and reinterpreted texts whose authors were often less comfortable with 'otherness', less tolerant and more nationalistic than their philosophic pretensions might suggest. Such then were the lenses that guided the STN's readers and helped to frame the ways in which they (re)imagined a universe in which not all world citizens were equal.

Despite these caveats about the processes of translation and cultural transfer, it is worth exploring how far European readers drew on a common stock of texts, knowledge and ideas. To what extent, in other words, did publishers and readers across Europe tap into a common literature and culture? But how can we answer such a question? One fruitful approach might be to begin by considering the reading fare of common readers in a remote corner of Europe who, far from the wholesalers of Liège or Neuchâtel consumed books primarily in their mother tongue. Wigtown in the Scottish county of Galloway seems as good a place as any. A community of but a few hundred souls, Wigtown was by the 1790s home to a small subscription library, but had little to distinguish it from many other small Scottish lowland or northern English towns. But for the historian, it has one distinctive advantage: the borrowing records of the library (though not its catalogue) survive for much of the second half of the 1790s. These records, logging 898 loans for fifty-six titles to forty-three borrowers across the period 4 January 1796 to 20 November 1799, have been extensively studied by Dr Mark Towsey and compiled into a single spreadsheet.[33] This spreadsheet, which Dr Towsey has kindly supplied, makes it possible to compare the borrowings of Wigtown readers with the stock of the STN to establish how far we can talk of a common reading culture between late Scottish Enlightenment readers and customers for the STN's wares.

Before we begin, however, we should note a few peculiarities of the Wigtown library. First, not a single religious title appears in the loan records. This may reflect a conscious decision not to stock religious fare. Second, subscribers to Wigtown library were generally well educated: almost half were clergymen, lawyers and doctors.[34] But there were also merchants, a tailor, a miller, a vintner[35] and five women: indeed, women accounted for 151 loans.[36] The library's members suggested what it should stock, and mostly chose works first published in or before the heyday of the STN in the 1770s and 80s. Of seven titles in the Wigtown records first published after 1791, none, unsurprisingly, feature in the STN records.[37] Nor do the British periodicals stocked by the library.[38]

This leaves forty-four titles that might feasibly appear in both Wigtown library and STN records. Twenty-six do so, including both literary classics and non-fiction.[39] Under Towsey's classifications, this common material falls into just three genres: travels, novels and histories.[40] The most popular travel literature included William Coxe's *Travels into Poland, Russia, Sweden and Denmark*; John Moore's *A View of Society and Manners in France, Switzerland and Germany*; Claude-Etienne Savary's *Letters on Egypt*; and Volney's *Travels through Syria and Egypt*. All were borrowed at least ten times (see Table 8.2). French editions of each also sold respectably among the STN's clientele.[41] Sterne's *Sentimental Journey* was less popular with Wigtown's borrowers, but better received among STN customers. But most popular of all with readers in Wigtown and STN customers alike were the voyages of Cook in the Pacific: in various titles and versions, they notched up fifty-two borrowings and 2,615 STN sales. Remarkably, all nine travel narratives borrowed from Wigtown Library were either first published in or translated into French, and eight were sold by the STN.[42] Travel narratives, it seems, enjoyed universal appeal across Enlightenment Europe, transporting readers' imaginations across much of Europe, Africa, the Pacific and the near Orient.

Table 8.2 Loans of travel literature from Wigtown Library compared with STN sales data

Title	Wigtown loans (borrowers)	STN sales
Combined *Voyages* of Cook (all, various versions)	52(11)	2,615
Coxe, *Travels into Poland, Russia, Sweden and Denmark*	22(10)	39
Moore, *A View of Society and Manners in France, Switzerland and Germany* (4 vols)	12(7)	299/406
Savary, *Letters on Egypt*	11(7)	32
Volney, *Travels through Syria and Egypt*	10(7)	66
Bruce, *Travels to Discover the Source of the Nile* (14 vols)	8(8)	1
Savary, *Letters on Greece*	8(6)	0
Sterne, *Sentimental Journey*	3(3)	385

Some of the most popular novels in the Wigtown borrower records were equally cosmopolitan. Rousseau's *Eloisa (Julie, ou la Nouvelle Héloise)* was loaned eighteen times. *Don Quixote*, first published early in the seventeenth century, chalked up eight Wigtown loans and 165 STN sales. Its early eighteenth-century French comparator, Le Sage's *The History and Adventures of Gil Blas of Santillane*, achieved ten loans and fifty-two STN sales. French political novels were less popular among Wigtown's readers, although two classic titles, Fénélon's *Telemarchus* and Marmontel's *Belisarius*, were borrowed on a handful of occasions. Conversely, many English novels popular in Wigtown Library also appear prominently in the STN accounts, including Henry Fielding's *Works* and Smollett's *Adventures of Roderick Random* and *Adventures of Peregrine Pickle*.[43] In total, works also sold by the STN accounted for 117 of the 185 loans of novels from Wigtown Library. This equates to a 63 per cent overlap.[44] Moreover, by the late 1790s, French editions existed for every single novel in the Wigtown Library.[45]

Similarly, much historical literature in Wigtown Library was also sold by the STN. Just over half of all loans of historical works at Wigtown involved such books (176 out of 343). A significant proportion of borrowings were for the various volumes of Gibbon's *Decline and Fall of the Roman Empire*, which were signed out seventy-nine times by sixteen different readers.[46] However, the English translation of Raynal's *Histoire philosophique des Deux Indes* was taken out twenty-one times by six borrowers.[47] These figures stand up well besides Scottish Enlightenment classics such as Hume's *History of England*, or Robertson's *The History of the Reign of the Emperor Charles V* and *The History of Scotland, during the reigns of Queen Mary and of King James VI* or Robert Watson's *The History of the Reign of Philip the Second, King of Spain*. The STN sold all these works in French-language editions, albeit in modest quantities.[48]

Several other historical works loaned by Wigtown Library were also available in French. They included Robert Henry's multivolume *History of Great Britain*, which clocked up fifty-three loans from fourteen borrowers. Its French edition appeared from 1789. Likewise, John Gillies, *The History of Ancient Greece, its Colonies, and Conquests* was first published in English in 1786 and French in 1787.[49] Smollett's *Continuation of the Complete History of England* was available in several French versions. Watson's *The History of the Reign of Philip the Third, King of Spain* (1793) was also translated, but not until 1809.[50]

The only histories found in the Wigtown library that were never translated into French were multivolume general histories of Scotland by the journalists Robert Heron and William Guthrie;[51] a *History of Edinburgh*; and two studies focusing on particular periods in British history, George Lyttelton, *The History of the life of King Henry the Second* and George Pettit Andrews, *History of Great Britain*, which covers only Tudor period. Given their specialized, chronologically limited or local focus, these works held little appeal to commercially minded French publishers and translators.[52]

The Wigtown Library records strongly suggest that the associational readers who formed British subscription libraries read a common stock of books with educated francophone readers. In fact, five out of every six of Wigtown Library's loans relate to works available in full or part in French editions. Moreover, almost half of untranslated borrowings were for periodicals such as the *Critical Review* or *Annual Register*. Such serial publications were rarely translated, but their literary news and reviews informed reader choices and library orders and frequently discussed translations of foreign works. They, too, were vectors of Enlightenment cosmopolitanism.

Of course, Wigtown's was a small-town library stocked with bestsellers requested by the well-educated middling class of subscribers and a handful of aristocratic patrons. It is therefore fair to ask whether the same patterns apply in a larger library in a more socially diverse British centre, such as the Bristol, whose subscription library's loan registers for the period 1773–84 have been collated by Paul Kaufman?[53] Bristol Library's holdings span the whole range of eighteenth-century knowledge. In all, Kaufman's study tabulates 13,497 borrowings of 900 items.[54] Using the classification model in the 1782 catalogue, the most popular categories for loans were 'History, Antiquities and Geography' (6,121 loans) and '*Belles-Lettres*' (3,313 loans).[55] These accounted for two thirds of all loans, suggesting that the Wigtown library was right to concentrate on supplying works of history, geography and literature. Nevertheless, almost one third of Bristol Library borrowings were for books classified under other categories.[56]

Kaufman's 'top ten' borrowings were mostly familiar to the STN's clientele (see Table 8.3). The most borrowed work was John Hawkesworth's *Voyages*, an account of the voyages of Byron, Carteret, Wallis and Cook. The STN and Société typographique de Lausanne published the *Voyages* in a joint edition.[57] The STN printed 1,008 copies and bought in a few dozen more. The Bristol Library loaned the *Voyages* 201 times. The second most borrowed work, Patrick Brydone's *Tour through Sicily and Malta*, was, of course, the STN's bestselling piece of travel literature. Four other works on the Bristol Library's top ten were big commercial successes for the STN. Three were British works: Laurence Sterne's *Life and Opinions of Tristram Shandy*; Henry Fielding's *Works*; Robertson's *History of the Reign of the Emperor Charles V*. The fourth was Raynal's *Histoire philosophique des Deux-Indes*. It ranked twelfth on the STN's all-time bestseller

Table 8.3 Top ten works loaned by the Bristol Library, 1773–84, with occurrences in other datasets

Author	Title	Bristol loans	STN sales	Wigtown loans
Hawkesworth	Voyages	201	1,008+	No
Brydone	Tour through Sicily	192	1,792	No
Chesterfield	Letters	185	23	No
Hume	History of England	180	7	31
Raynal	Philosophical History of Two Indies	173	3,694	21
Goldsmith	History of the Earth	150	Others by author	Others by author
Robertson	Charles V	131	82	19
Sterne	Tristram Shandy	127	1,191	Others by author
Lyttleton	Henry II	121	Others by author	12
Fielding	Works	120	186+ per vol	53

list and was the fifth most borrowed work in the Bristol Library, which held both English and French editions.[58] Lord Chesterfield's *Letters to his Son* and Hume's *History of England* were also available in French translation to STN customers, but sold only a handful of copies.[59] Thus eight of Bristol Library's 'top ten' works were sold by the STN. The Swiss publishers also traded in works by the authors of the other two.

Can we find similar 'cosmopolitan' trends across the range of works borrowed from the Bristol Library? Preliminary analysis of the 900 works loaned by the library showed that 359 were either available in whole or part from the STN; held in French or Latin editions; translated from other languages;[60] or written by authors who had other works available through the STN. Several works fell into multiple categories. These 359 items accounted for 7,002 borrowings, well over half of all loans (see Table 8.4). An as yet undetermined number of further loaned titles also had foreign-language editions. Hence, despite more diverse holdings than Wigtown, the Bristol Library's collection was equally as cosmopolitan, as were the borrowing choices of its approximately 137 members.[61]

A second way to assess the scale of cosmopolitan reading is to identify and examine sources that comprehend the literary output of a whole society. We might consider, for example, the number of books translated into and out of the local language. For Germany much of that work has already been done. Thanks to Hans Jürgen Lüsebrink, René Nohr and Rolf Reichardt, we know of 2,678 translations of French works into German during the final two decades before the revolution (1770–88), many of them in multiple editions.[62] If we assume, following the Global Historical Bibliometrics project, that approximately 50 million books were printed in Germany in this period, it is clear that these translations comprised a significant proportion of books circulating in German-speaking lands (probably around 10–15 per cent).[63] Translations into German direct from other languages, as well as works printed in Latin or non-German tongues, including French, also circulated in significant numbers.[64]

Can we arrive at a similar view for English-language publishing? One approach is to analyse the most comprehensive (if not definitive) digital collection of eighteenth-century British works available, Gale-Cengage's Eighteenth-Century Collections Online (ECCO).[65] This vast collection, which spans 220,000 volumes of 180,000 works published in Britain (including English-speaking North America) or in the English language from across the eighteenth century.[66] Significantly, ECCO aspired to offer a comprehensive collection of all extant works meeting these criteria, and in many cases

Table 8.4 'Cosmopolitan books' borrowed from the Bristol Library, 1773–84

Type of 'Cosmopolitan Work'	Borrowings from Bristol Library
Work found in both STN data and Bristol Library	4,802
Work appears on in Bristol Library, but STN traded other titles by the same author	1,326
Works identified as translated from other languages	751
Works in French not found in STN dataset	39
Latin titles	84
Works with French editions not listed above	Undetermined

supplies multiple editions.⁶⁷ However, while ECCO's bibliographic metadata, drawn primarily from library MARC records, is extremely valuable, it does not have fields for all the information needed to quantify cross-cultural publishing.⁶⁸ Significant further work is needed to identify translations into English from the metadata notes fields, and to locate books were translated out of English into other languages using the Worldcat collective library database.

As a result, my analysis draws on a sampling of just over 1 per cent of the ECCO metadata records, comprising 2,077 records in total. These records, an arbitrary sample, comprise the first editions whose details were downloaded into spreadsheet form as part of FBTEE's attempt to transfer, store and sample ECCO metadata. They are drawn from across the eighteenth century, have titles beginning with letters from across the alphabet, and appear to cover all major topics areas and genres. Nevertheless, the sample contains some particular biases. In particular, it has disproportionate amounts of history, biography, geography and travels, and relatively few religious and scientific works. In this sense it mirrors the Wigtown data.

Almost one third of the ECCO metadata sample was composed of Almanacs, Calendars and Yearbooks.⁶⁹ In addition, there were large numbers of works that might be considered ephemeral, in the sense that they were unlikely to be either translated or held in subscription libraries.⁷⁰ Once all these items – 874 in total – were removed, the proportion of 'cosmopolitan' works in the ECCO sample appears comparable with our other datasets. Of the remaining 1203 items, just under half – 583 items – exist in foreign-language versions. About one third of these were actual foreign-language works; another third were works translated into English; and a final third were English works for which foreign-language editions exist.⁷¹ There were in addition four items containing parallel texts.

A significant number of these 583 items appear in the STN or Wigtown data. The historical works in the ECCO sample, for example, include a five-volume translation of one of the STN's bestselling school books, Millot's *Elémens d'histoire générale*, published at Salem in 1796. It is one of nine English-language editions digitized in ECCO.⁷² John Barrow's multivolume textbook, *A New and Impartial History of England*, which STN sold in French translation to Geneva, St Petersburg and Vienna, is also present.⁷³ The sample also includes French editions of Raynal's *Histoire du parlement d'Angleterre* and Hume's *Histoire de la Maison de Stuart*, as well as English and French versions of Montesquieu's *Reflections on the causes of the rise and fall of the Roman Empire*.⁷⁴ Also present are Voltaire's *The History of the Russian Empire under Peter the Great*; Vertot's *History of the Knights Hospitallers* and *History of the Revolution in Sweden*; and two eight-volume Dublin editions of Hume's *History of England*.⁷⁵ All of these works were sold by the STN in French-language editions. So was Robertson's *History of the Reign of the Emperor Charles V*: the ECCO sample includes English-language editions published in Philadelphia and Basel.⁷⁶ There are also three-volume octavo English-language editions of another STN bestseller, Robertson's *History of America* published in Vienna and Leipzig.⁷⁷ A handful of classical historical works also appear in both the ECCO sample and STN data,⁷⁸ as did a number of biographical texts.⁷⁹ There is then, a very high degree of interpenetration between our datasets. Many of the historical works found in our ECCO metadata sample were also borrowed in Wigtown or Bristol and ordered by the STN's clients. Nevertheless, 113 historical works in the ECCO sample did not get translated, including some that were far from parochial in focus.

Several novels in the ECCO metadata sample also feature in the STN database in French translation. These include London editions of Fanny Burney's *Evelina* and Richardson's *Clarissa*;[80] a 1793-4 New York printing of *Cecilia, or memoirs of an heiress*; two versions of *The history of Sir Charles Grandison* and one of Eliza Haywood's didactic novel *The Fortunate Foundlings*, which was adapted into French by Crébillon *fils*.[81] Another foundling, Fielding's *Tom Jones*, surfaces in two different editions in the ECCO data, as does Sterne's *Tristram Shandy* (in both English and French editions). The STN dealt in all these titles. Equally, our ECCO sample features a number of French works in English translation, including Le Sage's *Bachelor of Salamanca*; Prévost's *The Dean of Coleraine*; Barthélemi's, *The Travels of Anacharsis the Younger, in Greece* and Crébillon *fils*' erotic masterpiece, *The Wanderings of the Heart and Mind*.[82] Conversely ECCO lists a French edition of Fielding's *Histoire de Jonathan Wild le Grand*, published with a (presumably false) London imprint and available via *veuve* Duchesne in Paris.[83] These titles all feature in the STN database, sometimes prominently.

Many travel works in the ECCO sample are also familiar from STN data. These include the various voyages of Cook,[84] Bougainville,[85] and the French sea captain Pierre-Marie-François Pagès,[86] Carsten Niebuhr's *Travels through Arabia, and other countries in the East*,[87] the Marquis de Chastellux's *Travels in North-America*, and William Coxe's *Travels in Switzerland*.[88] Erotica mimicking travel literature also crossed language frontiers: the ECCO sample contains Thomas Stretser's *A new description of Merryland. Containing, a topographical, geographical, and natural history of that country*, first published in 1741 and later translated into French.[89] This last, however, was not an STN title. Finally, extracts of Brydone's voyage appear in *The Present state of Sicily and Malta, Extracted from Mr. Brydone, Mr. Swinburne, and other modern travellers* (London, 1788).

That writers like Brydone could, and often did, attempt to promote and perpetuate the religious and cultural prejudices; that their words and sentiments were often abridged, lost, mangled or deliberately distorted in the processes of editing and translation; and that independent-minded readers reinterpreted and adapted to their own world view the ideas they encountered in their reading are truths beyond dispute. Yet these caveats pale into insignificance alongside the wider importance of the cosmopolitan content and international dissemination of the STN's merchandise. For travel, biographical, historical and novelesque writings formed part of a common literary culture that transcended national and linguistic borders and helped transport readers to far-flung corners of Europe, Mediterranean islands, Russia's relentless Asian steppe-lands and remote corners of the Americas, the Caribbean, Africa, Arabia and the Pacific. They represent a common European culture and incorporated an increasingly globalized vision. Between the pages of cosmopolitan books which respected few borders, Enlightenment popular readers could, at least in the peregrinations of the imagination, become *concitoyens* of a rapidly expanding world. Readers of this book, meanwhile, should prepare to transport themselves to another place altogether.

9

The Anatomy of the Illegal Sector

Working in Hell had its perks. Above all, Hell [*Enfer*] always had plenty of space for newcomers. And by the early 1990s that was useful if you spent your mornings working elsewhere. Come early afternoon, all the places in the *Salle Richelieu* of the old *Bibliothèque nationale de France* had long been occupied, leaving dozens of latecomers thronging in the library foyer waiting forlornly for a seat. But if you worked in Hell, you could jump the queue and waltz into the Salle, before veering right and climbing the staircase to the infernal reading room.

Time spent in Hell was unusually pleasurable, too. For Hell was where scholars went to examine musty yellowing erotica, the once-banned pornographic books that nineteenth-century librarians sought to hide from mere mortals. It was also home to reels of obscure microfilmed newspapers. I first ascended to Hell to read the latter – short-lived and long-forgotten titles such as the *Journal de Middlesex*, of which only two isolated numbers survive.[1] Later I went there to read less wholesome fare such as *Les Amours de Charlot et Toinette* and the *Portefeuille d'un talon rouge*,[2] which contain pornographic attacks on Queen Marie-Antoinette. Both survive in only handful of pre-revolutionary copies. Thus I came to associate *Enfer* with rare and even unique items, and that made me start asking some iconoclastic questions. Questions that would challenge the assumptions of many distinguished scholars who had taken the path to Hell before me: Lynn Hunt, Roger Chartier, Antoine de Baecque, Chantal Thomas and, above all, Robert Darnton.[3] Why if such books were so rare had so much been written of them and their consequences? How many such titles were there? And how did they fit into the wider corpus of clandestine books and the illicit trade?

Unfortunately, the literature was disarmingly vague on these points. Despite an outpouring of academic work on the illegal sector, particularly the hardcore pornographic attacks on the monarchy, the truth was that no one really knew.[4] The general conviction seemed to be that the illegal sector was vast. But that was not particularly helpful, since illegality spanned everything from innocuous works that had not bothered to go through the censorship apparatus, through pirate editions, to hardcore pornography and proselytizing atheist materialist works.[5] This chapter seeks to confront this uncertainty and establish the broad shape of the illegal sector. But how? Perhaps the best place to start is with a single work and one of the largest editions the STN ever produced. That work was Jacques Le Scène Desmaisons's *Contrat conjugal*.

On 29 September 1782, the STN despatched 4,141 copies of Desmaisons's book to Paris for the Lyon bookseller Pierre Duplain *l'aîné*. The consignment departed in five crates, numbered DP n.161–5. These books never reached their intended destination.[6] In November they were seized en route at Versailles.[7] Five months later, and still in their original crates, they were transported to the Bastille on the king's orders, along with further crates containing other, more serious contraband books.[8] One contained a veritable muster roll of the old regime's most notorious pornographic masterpieces: *Thérèse philosophe*; *L'Académie des Dames*; *La Chandelle d'Arras*; *L'Arretin Moderne*; *Le Balai, Poeme*; *Le Compère Mathieu*. It also contained the politically scandalous *Gazetier cuirassé* and the abolitionist *Supplément à l'abbé Raynal*. Others were chock-full with the most celebrated *chroniques scandaleuses*, notably *Le Chroniqueur ou l'Espion des Boulevards*, *L'Espion dévalisé*, *L'Observateur François à Amsterdam* and the *Lettres hollandaises ou Correspondance politique*. The *Procès du Comte du Barri avec Madame la comtesse de Tournon* and *La Pucelle libertine*, equally sensational, also featured.[9]

With a handful of exceptions, mostly political works such as Mirabeau's *Lettres de cachet*, the *Tableau historique de Laurent Ganganelli* (i.e. Pope Clément XIII), a *Mémoire aux souverains de l'Europe* and a couple of digests of Raynal, whose political radicalism has already been noted, most of these works were erotically charged, and many were outrightly pornographic. The inclusion of the *Contrat conjugal* alongside such titillating or political fare therefore seems at first sight rather odd. Steeped in the language of Enlightenment, justice, humanity, reason, nature and the law of contract, the *Contrat conjugal* made an impassioned case for divorce, while examining alternative practices for negating unhappy unions drawn from across time and space.

Desmaisons argued that marriage should be seen in entirely secular terms as a free civil contract between parties with equal rights. Hence it should be dissolvable by mutual consent, or whenever one partner felt unable to meet his or her contractual obligations. This was preferable to the misery, frustrated desire or culpable infidelities that might otherwise accompany an unsatisfactory union. Desmaisons contended that there was nothing in the nature of marriage to suggest that it was indissoluble, nor was it useful to the body politic or its individual members for it to be so. Moreover, for individuals to promise to be 'immuable' in their wishes was 'insensé, contraire à la nature, à la raison, à l'experience'.[10] Divorce was infinitely preferable to the prevailing and unequal practice of repudiation, or the banishing of wayward wives to convents, as practised in France and some other Catholic countries. This was, besides, something that Desmaisons found repellent because it made separation dependent upon commission of a 'crime'. But he also protested on grounds of gender equality: why were wives not also able to incarcerate their husbands? Divorce was also preferable to the English practice of legal separation – an abominable hybrid of repudiation and divorce that left women vulnerable in legal and moral limbo.

Nevertheless, Desmaisons felt that marriages should not be abandoned lightly, observing that divorce had sufficient inconveniences that few would do so. Indeed, he suggested that safeguards be put in place so that both spouses had time to reflect, including an obligatory three-month cooling-off period after legally requesting a divorce.[11] Such secular liberalism, accompanied by explicit pleas for readers to free themselves of cultural and religious prejudice to reflect rationally on the issues, was too much for the French government. *Contrat conjugal*'s discussion of the laws surrounding marriage and divorce was placed on a par with pornography and political smut. It was duly impounded and pulped in the Bastille as a threat to public morals. Four copies survived this *auto-da-fé*. They would be discovered and catalogued in the Bastille's secret *dépôt* after the storming of the fortress on 14 July 1789. The ensuing revolution would enact many of Desmaisons' ideas.[12]

That the *Contrat conjugal* had strange and varied banned books for bedfellows as it awaited its destruction is perhaps not surprising. For practical purposes, as Robert Darnton has revealed, French booksellers often lumped together politically and religiously scandalous works with erotica, pornography and Enlightenment philosophy under the catch-all term *livres philosophiques*.[13] These reportedly 'sold like hot cakes'.[14] Such a conclusion is based on widespread evidence from the STN archives and elsewhere. The cry for 'philosophical books' came to the STN from across the Bourbon kingdom, from big-time printer–booksellers and fly-by-night dealers and *colporteurs* on the margins of the trade. Time and again, booksellers such as Charles-Antoine Charmet in Besançon, Petit in Rheims, Mauvelain in Troyes and, most improbably of all, Paul Malherbe *l'aîné* in the sleepy little Poitevin town of Loudun assured the STN that they wanted this sort of stock above all else. 'Would you have any philosophical things?' asked Manoury from Caen, 'It is my main line.'[15] From Nantes, Augustin-Jean Mallasis wrote, 'Send me as quickly as you can – that is by return mail – a catalogue of all your forbidden books, and I will sell a great many for you.'[16] 'My line is all philosophical,' chimed in Regnault of Lyon, 'so I want almost nothing except that kind.'[17] Finally, Malherbe assured them that 'pedlars are extremely eager to get books of this kind. They make more on them than on others, because they charge whatever they fancy.'[18] Hence the *Contrat conjugal* and the works that accompanied it to the Bastille have long been seen as the tip of an iceberg of illegal works. And because these works were chased so vigorously by the authorities, it was natural to assume that they were the most corrosive and subversive printed agents for change circulating in late eighteenth-century France.

Yet the mass seizure of the *Contrat conjugal* raises interesting questions. How effective was French policing – traditionally seen as close to ineffectual – at preventing books getting to market? How often were whole consignments arrested in transit? How big was the market for *livres philosophiques*? Which was more typical of the forbidden 'philosophical' literature – titillating pornographic smut such as the *Académie des Dames*; sordid politically scandalous works like the *Gazetier cuirassé*; highbrow Voltairean or d'Holbachian *philosophie*; or specialized legal–moral treatises like the *Contrat conjugal*? And who tended to read *livres philosophiques*, since they were clearly expensive? Were they, as Darnton suggested in one of his early essays, aimed at the future revolutionary *canaille*, serving to begin the 'political education' of a common people who were unable to assimilate Rousseau?[19] Clearly these were not the intended readers of a work like *Contrat conjugal*. So were most 'philosophical books' perhaps aimed at a more limited elite – that is, at people with the spending power to shrug off prices inflated by the costs of the clandestine book trade and the education and insider-knowledge to decode the complex political allusions of the *Gazetier cuirassé* or the dry and abstruse materialism of d'Holbach and his ilk?[20] And if these books had a subversive appeal and impact, how did the complexion of the market for *livres philosophiques* in pre-revolutionary France differ from markets in other countries, where there were no such indigenous disturbances?

Our first challenge is to gauge the scale of the market for these highly illegal works. Is it possible to arrive at a realistic estimate of the numbers of banned books circulating in pre-revolutionary France? At first sight, the task looks hopeless. The complexity of the regulations and the way they operated; the clandestinity of the trade; and contemporary confusion about what precisely was and was not legal confront us at every turn. Hence Chartier and Darnton's estimates that half of all books circulating in pre-revolutionary France were somehow illegal does not get us very far, since it lumps together very different market segments.[21] Raymond Birn offers a similar figure in more precise language, suggesting half of all books disseminated in France between 1750 and 1789 were 'tacitly permitted', 'produced abroad' or 'clandestine'. However, it remains unclear how far piracy features in his last two categories.[22] The problem remains – was the illegal sector of the trade composed primarily of *livres philosophiques*, works which the regime rightly or wrongly considered subversive of religion, state or society? Or was it made up primarily of pirated editions of legally permitted works – including orthodox religious works, school textbooks and 'how to' manuals – together with other fare so innocuous that its suppliers had not bothered to address formal censorship channels?

And yet, the problem can be approached bibliometrically, via the work of Robert Darnton and his near namesake, the late Robert Dawson.[23] For Darnton's *Corpus of Clandestine Literature* provides us with a painstaking and self-consistent bibliographic list of 718 works which book dealers and the book police considered to be reprehensible.[24] This *Corpus* was compiled using a wide sampling of French booksellers' orders in the STN archives; clandestine manuscript catalogues of *livres philosophiques*; and records of confiscations of books in police raids and customs seizures. The data published by Darnton also contains a preliminary (but by no means comprehensive) census of editions. However, Darnton's survey is not exhaustive, and certainly does not include every title that got into trouble with the authorities. It is thus helpful to cross reference it with another list of banned books, an inventory of titles found in the Bastille and drawn up for the revolutionary authorities by the Versailles bookseller Poinçot after the fortress was stormed in 1789. Once it is stripped of periodical works and books that Dawson identifies as piracies or 'not illegal', it lists 370 putatively 'illegal' titles, only 150 of which appear in Darnton's *Corpus* (see Appendix 3.18).[25] However, those works which did appear on both lists tended to be the works which, according to Darnton, circulated in the greatest number of editions.[26] The strength of these correlations suggests that the Bastille library and *Corpus* taken in combination do indeed broadly reflect of the shape of the highly illegal sector in the last couple of decades of the ancien régime.

By cross-referencing the Bastille inventory with Darnton's list and establishing the proportion of overlap, it is possible to estimate the volume of libertine works missing from both lists – that is to say works that either got into serious trouble with the authorities on the grounds of content but are not recorded by Darnton or Poinçot, or works that might have done so had they been discovered. Moreover, by entering them on a spreadsheet and conducting surveys of the number of editions visible in Worldcat, and making adjustments for missing data, it was possible to arrive at consistent, transparently calculated empirically based estimates for the number of editions and copies of libertine works produced in the period 1769 to 1789. These figures are summarized in Table 9.1 below.

The complex series of calculations and adjustments by which these estimates were derived are explained and discussed in Appendix 5. These calculations suggest that around 4,366,000 French-language *livres philosophiques* were produced in Europe in the two decades prior to the French Revolution. Of these, assuming the STN's own trade pattern was typical, around two thirds were destined for France, whether directly or having passed through the hands of other extraterritorial publisher–wholesale traders in Neuchâtel, Geneva, the Swiss confederation, Belgium, the United Provinces or the German Rhineland.[27] Some were even produced – at considerable risk – inside France. Thus we might estimate total number of *livres philosophiques* entering circulation in France between 1769 and 1789 at around 2,910,000. This would appear to equate to around 5 to 6 per cent of all new books circulating in the Bourbon realm.[28] This, however, was just a small portion of the total trade in illegal books.

The remainder – and, by all available measurements, far greater proportion – of the 'illegal sector' was comprised of generally innocuous fare, mostly piracies and works published without formal permissions. These circulated in much more significant volumes than *livres philosophiques*, certainly in France. The scale of the pirate trade is visible in the surviving documents relating to the stamping and legalization of pirated books in 1778 to 1780, following the decrees of 30 August 1777. Given the draconian penalties that would apply to undeclared works under the new inspection regime, booksellers everywhere had strong incentives to comply, despite the modest stamping fee. And comply they did. Records of the *estampillage* operation survive for some 122 French printers and booksellers in eight of the country's twenty *Chambres syndicales* (guilds). In all they declared just over 416,000 pirated books.[29] Given that a nationwide survey of printers conducted the same year (1777) listed 305 licensed printers across the country and that the 1781 *Almanach de la Librairie* adds around 676 booksellers, this implies that across the country around 3,200,000 items of pirated stock would have been surrendered for stamping.[30] It was a monumental exercise.

Although we lack accurate records of stock turnover, we might nevertheless use these figures to derive a crude estimate of the total output of pirated works. A publisher like the STN would hope to clear most of its stock of a popular title within a few months of printing, perhaps sooner. To speculate that these pirated copies

Table 9.1 Final total (estimates) of works, editions and copies of French-language libertine works produced in Europe, 1769–89

Place where libertine work is encountered	Number of works produced 1769–89	Estimated total editions	Estimated total print runs (copies)
Bastille list and *Corpus*	150	936	936,000
Corpus only	568	1,488	1,488,000
Bastille list only	220	566	566,000
Neither Bastille or *Corpus*	829	1,376	1,376,000
Totals	1,767	4,366	4,366,000

represented no more than a couple of years' output does not seem unreasonable. We might also note that in the decade following the creation of the new *permission simple*, which was introduced by a second decree of 30 August 1777 and placed a portion of previously privileged works into the public domain, France's printers and publishers asked for printing *permissions* for some 3,000,000 copies.[31] This number may understate the books printed under licence, since a reproduction fee was payable and there was little to prevent fraudulent under-reporting. Conversely, however, a significant proportion of the licensed editions were never published, and so the two probably balance out.[32]

Likewise, many printers did not apply for licences and continued printing pirate editions, despite theoretically severe penalties.[33] A survey of one popular religious title, *La Journée du Chrétien sanctifiée par la prière*, found that only one third of editions went through the *permission simple* process.[34] This proportion seems to have been fairly typical. On that basis, titles appearing in the *permission simple* records would have accounted for as many as 9,000,000 copies of books printed across the period 1777-89, two thirds of them in pirated editions. This suggests that around 12,000,000 pirated copies of those works were printed across the period 1769 to the French Revolution. This only represents a portion of the total of the pirated trade, however. Of the books recorded as stamped in the 1778-80 *estampillage* process, just under 56.5 per cent were copies of titles found in the *permission simple* registers. The other 43.5 per cent were not. This implies that pirate publishers printed a further 11,550,000 pirated copies of works which were not licensed under the *permission simple*.[35] At a crude estimate, the total output of pirated French books between 1769 and 1789 was around 23,550,000 units. This implies an average stock-turnover time of just over thirty months, a rather conservative figure.[36] In short, if libertine literature accounted for around 2,910,000 books, the French pirate sector was eight times as large. These libertine and pirate books, when added to an estimated 3,663,000 copies of the 3,663 editions works produced under *permissions tacites* between 1769 and 1787, comprised the French market for clandestine or semi-clandestine works.[37] At around 30 million books, according to our calculations, it equates to almost exactly half of our estimated total output for French books for the period 1770 to 1790 (see Chapter 2 above). Yet taken as a corpus, these pirated and tacitly permitted works were generally very different in nature to the libertine books that ended up in the Bastille or traded through illicit stock catalogues.[38] A summary breakdown of the illegal and quasi-legal sector in France between 1769 and 1789 based on these figures is given in Chart 9.1. It provides a dramatic visualization of the limited extent of the libertine book trade in contrast to other parts of the clandestine trade. However, it is this libertine sector, these *livres philosophiques*, that concern us here.[39]

Since previous work has argued or assumed that the STN's trade in libertine works was typical of the wider trade in *livres philosophiques*, our exploration should first confirm whether the available evidence supports this interpretation. A first stage in this process is to compare the STN's stock with the supply statistics for the rest of Darnton's *Corpus of Clandestine Literature*. This can be done fairly simply, by correlating his estimates for the number of editions circulating between 1769 and 1789 with the number of works in the STN's stock.

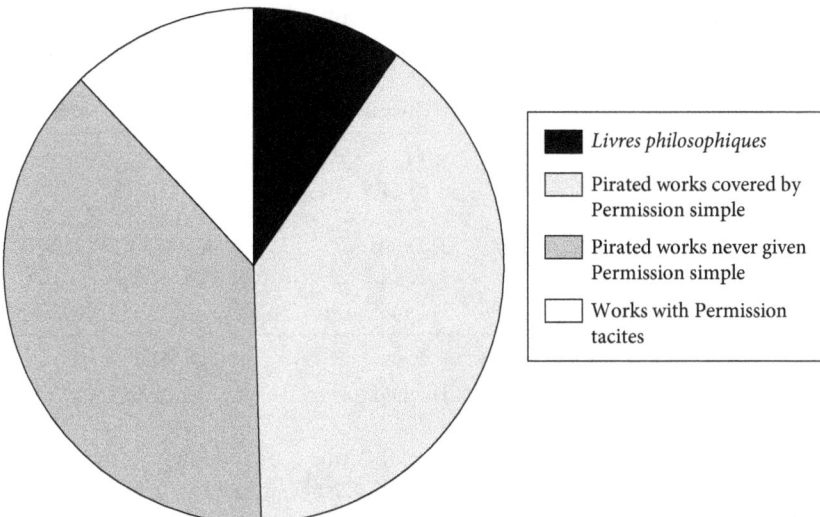

Chart 9.1 The structure of the French illegal and quasi-legal book trade, 1769–89 (excluding unlicensed innocuous works).

The STN habitually stocked most (69 per cent) of the libertine works in Darnton's *Corpus* that ran to multiple editions across the period 1769–89 (see Appendix 3.18). Of forty-seven works which ran to (approximately) seven or more editions, the STN sold forty-three. In contrast, of the 328 libertine works with only a single edition, they traded only 127, eleven of which they published themselves. Moreover, there are very strong correlations between edition counts for libertine works and STN sales. Appendix 3.18 calculates that of the aforementioned 127 single-edition works, the STN sold less than one hundred copies of 124. In contrast, of the eighteen libertine works with (approximate) edition counts of eleven or more, the STN traded seventeen works and sold over one hundred copies in ten cases. In four instances they sold over 1,000 copies. The corollary thus seems clear: if illegal works were available in multiple editions, the STN was indeed able to source copies (in general from a locally produced edition). The STN might not have been able to stock literally anything from anywhere at any time, but they could and did habitually at some time stock most of the illegal works in highest demand. And the STN tended to sell the works with most editions in the greatest numbers. What the STN could not do was stock anything from anywhere in Europe at any given time.

Nevertheless, the suspicion remains that books clandestinely traded by extraterritorial publishers such as the STN did not represent the entire range of philosophic works, particularly those available in France. To test this hypothesis, the subject content of books in the Bastille's secret *dépôt* was compared with titles in Darnton's *Corpus of Clandestine Literature*, using categories familiar to the book police. They generally sought out books inimical to religion, the state or public morals, so these were the main categories used, together with a catch-all term 'general *philosophie*' (largely used in this context for miscellaneous collected works of Enlightenment

Table 9.2 Categories of illegal work in the Bastille and Darnton's *Corpus*

Primary category of work	Total works	Works in Corpus	Works in Bastille	STN 'sales'[40]
Offends Morality (M)	213	181 (25.2%)	74 (19.9%)	35,258 (28.6%)
General *Philosophie* (P)	70	57 (7.9%)	25 (6.7%)	9,666 (7.8%)
Offends Religion (R)	266	234 (32.5%)	71 (19.1%)	28,118 (22.7%)
Offends State (S)	350	217 (30.2%)	191 (51.5%)	43,435 (35.3%)
Other (O)	39	30 (4.2%)	10 (2.7%)	6,767 (5.5%)
Totals	938	719	371	123,244

authors) and a small group of works labelled 'other'. The results of this survey are shown in tabular form in Table 9.2.[41]

The standout news of Table 9.2 is clear. The title-census derived from Darnton's *Corpus* diverges in significant ways from the Bastille inventory. In particular, the Bastille inventory contains a substantially greater proportion of political titles than Darnton's *Corpus*, and commensurately less works offensive to religion and morality. Net STN sales are likewise substantially slanted towards works offensive to morality and away from political works. Closer investigation of key subcategories of these three types of reprehensible work suggests why this might be the case (see Table 9.3 below).

As Table 9.3 reveals, the STN stocked a relatively high proportion of the (known) erotic and pornographic titles on the market. The erotica they did not handle tended, moreover, to be relatively soft-core works, primarily anthologies of risqué libertine poetry. They stocked an even more significant proportion of the much smaller corpus of works denouncing penal despotism or demanding legal reform. Conversely, they dealt in relatively few of the far more numerous pamphlets and books treating high politics, political economy or the polemical struggles between the Crown and French *Parlements*. Equally, the STN handled few banned works relating to internal Catholic controversies, debates about religious minorities or toleration, and perhaps more surprisingly, world and comparative religions. On these religious topics and the *Parlements* they sold just a few dozen books per year.[42]

The likely reason for these biases is that pamphlets relating to French internal politics and religious controversies tended to be produced within France for clandestine circulation under the protection and patronage of powerful factional groupings.[43] Many circulated primarily at court and in Paris and were not intended for commercial sale. Such, at least, is the testimony of the French police chief Lenoir, who held office for much of the 1770s and 1780s.[44] These sorts of political and religious works were thus unlikely to reach the STN, clog up the arteries of the international book trade, or be found in the official accounts of police raids on commercial book stores or the registers of customs confiscations. However, they were prone to seizure and confiscation by the police, so feature more prominently in the Bastille than among Darnton's *Corpus of Clandestine Literature*.

It is probable, moreover, that such *pamphlets de circonstance* feature disproportionately among the many hypothetical 'unknown' libertine works that feature in neither Poinçot's Bastille inventory nor Darnton's *Corpus of Clandestine*

Table 9.3 Key categories of *livres philosophiques* traded by the STN as a proportion of all known *livres philosophiques* (Corpus and Bastille lists). NB. The table shows only those categories which diverged furthest from the STN average and contained over fifteen titles[45]

Category	Definition	All titles in category	Titles traded by STN	Traded titles as a % of all works in category	Total copies traded
S7	Despotic systems, prisons, lettres de cachet, legal reform	17	11	64.7	1,029
M1	Pornography, erotica & sexual scandal	142	79	55.6	11,298
S2	High Politics, Political Economy & Finance	69	24	34.7	15,591
R7	Toleration & Religious minorities, Protestants and Jews	20	6	30	372
R8	World and Comparative Religion, Sociology of Religion, Paganism	17	4	23.5	153
R5	Catholic controversies & Heterodox works; Jansenism & Jesuits	19	3	15.8	86
S6	*Parlements*	20	1	5	142
All	All known *livres philosophiques*	938	414	44.1	123,244

Literature (see Table 9.1 above). Conversely, the ribald anticlerical pamphlets, *libertine* novels and endless anthologies of *risqué* poetry that comprised the standard erotic fare for eighteenth-century readers were nakedly commercial products. Naturally, they appear ubiquitous in the ledgers of the STN and records of customs confiscations and police raids.[46] It seems fair to suggest, therefore, that there existed extensive networks of Catholic/Jansenist controversialist and high political factional pamphleteering whose products were very significantly under-represented in the STN figures. We should bear these biases in mind in the discussion that follows.

Despite these caveats, banned political works sold well for the STN. However, they were not the sort of political works emphasized by previous scholarship (see Appendix 3.19). In *Forbidden Best-Sellers* and elsewhere, Robert Darnton has stressed the importance of desacralizing political *libelles* in undermining the French monarchy, and this line, as we have noted, has been widely accepted in scholarly literature on the origins of the Revolution. But, in fact, the STN sales data suggests that this sort of work was a distinctly minority interest. Works dealing with court scandal account for a grand total of just 3,123 units from the 123,244 *livres philosophiques* they distributed, and one work, Mairobert's blockbuster *Anecdotes sur Madame la comtesse du Barri* accounted for almost half of this total. The *libelle* genre was outsold tenfold by other genres of forbidden political works, most notably 'High Politics, Political Economy & Finance' (15,591 units); 'War, International Relations, Colonies, Foreign Powers' (8,463 units); and 'Political Philosophy' (7,690 units).[47] In sheer numerical terms, the importance of political *libelles* has been overstated.

The significance of highbrow *philosophie* is similarly inescapable. The category of 'general *philosophie*' comprising collected works and titles with miscellaneous philosophic subject matter comprises 9,622 units. 'Metaphysics, Natural Religion, Materialism, Deism, & the Soul', a category which includes the atheistic and sceptical output of d'Holbach and his associates, accounts for a further 9,353. To this we must add many of the 1,685 copies of works categorized as 'Biblical History & Criticism', which mostly comprise philosophic challenges to the Biblical record. Christian refutations of materialist and deist works unacceptable to the authorities offer 1,361 more unit sales. Taken as a whole then, the STN shifted about 22,000 illegal units of the *philosophes*' general works or clandestine titles concerning materialism and the existence of God. Alongside these sorts of numbers, the STN sales record implies that anticlerical works (at 3,107 units) were relatively unimportant. Religious desacralization, if it was occurring, was doing so primarily on a metaphysical rather than a pornographic level. Works which operated on both levels, such as the marquis d'Argens' erotic masterpiece *Thérèse philosophe*, were rare indeed.[48]

These tendencies are equally clear if we turn to the keywords applied to illegal works in the FBTEE database itself (see Appendix 3.20). This measure gives a more fine-tuned overview, since each work has been ascribed multiple keywords. Hence a novel containing graphic descriptions of monks and nuns indulging in sexual acts can be defined as both an 'anticlerical work' and a 'pornographic' one, as well as a work of 'Literature' and 'Prose fiction'. On our previous table it appears only under the category 'M1: Pornography, erotica & sexual scandal'. Such a fine-grained reading might be expected to uncover substantially more works containing political smut or religiously sceptical, anticlerical, anti-aristocratic or sexually licentious scenes, particularly if such categories overlap in the literature. However, this is not the case. Again we see a prevalence of *philosophie*, religion and politics in the table, but sceptical works, erotica and scandal (whether relating to royalty, the court or anyone else) are, by comparison, small subsets. Well over one quarter (29.25 per cent) of the *livres philosophiques* traded by the STN were considered highbrow *philosophie*, but less than 10 per cent had any erotic content, and only 8 per cent were noticeably anticlerical. Just under one eighth (15,214 units) might be considered sceptical works, but less than half of these contain sustained discussions of 'atheism' or 'materialism'.[49] Of these, only 3,914 are tagged as 'atheist works'. In short, although the STN carried a high proportion of the available metaphysical philosophical works, their trade in key radical Enlightenment texts was limited.[50] The one-substance materialist atheism described by Jonathan Israel was far from omni-present: on these figures it accounted for less than one in thirty *livres philosophiques* sold by the STN. And as we have already noted, *livres philosophiques* of all sorts made up around five per cent of the total French book market.

Discrepancies between Darnton's figures, which are based on a wide sampling of French booksellers' orders and the FBTEE European sales statistics (see Appendix 3.19) give rise to important questions. Above all, do the figures point to a major divergence between the French and wider European trades? Or do they merely emphasize the difficulty of matching cultural demand to cultural supply in eighteenth-century Europe, particularly when trading clandestine products across large distances? To answer these questions, we need to return to the database and to keyword analysis. But before we do so, we need to examine the identity of the structure of the illegal market and the STN's illegal bestsellers. The STN's global bestseller list for illegal titles found in Darnton's *Corpus* or Poinçot's inventory of the Bastille's secret *dépôt* reads as follows:

1. Mercier, *Tableau de Paris*, 14,076 copies
2. J.-F. Ostervald, *Abrégé de l'histoire sainte et du catéchisme*, 6,815 copies
3. Desmaisons, *Contrat conjugal*, 4,164 copies
4. Mercier, *Mon Bonnet de nuit*, 4,043 copies
5. Raynal, *Histoire philosophique des Deux Indes*, 3,694 copies
6. Christin, *Dissertation sur l'établissement de l'Abbaye de S. Claude*, 2,710 copies
7. Mercier, *Le Philosophe du Port-au-bled*, 2,581 copies
8. Voltaire, *Questions sur l'Encyclopédie*, 2,523 copies
9. Voltaire, *Dieu. Réponse de M. de Voltaire au Système de la nature*, 2,327 copies
10. Brissot, *De La Vérité*, 2,260 copies

Even a cursory glance at this list shows that it is replete with familiar titles by familiar house authors. These few titles and authors dominated the STN's illegal trade. All of them are already known to us. Between them the top ten titles accounted for almost two in every five *livres philosophiques* the STN despatched (39.17 per cent). The top twenty titles accounted for well over half the market (54.9 per cent) and the top fifty for over three quarters (75.9 per cent). One bestseller alone, Mercier's *Tableau de Paris*, accounted for almost one in eight of STN illegal sales (12.2 per cent); a religious primer, included because such Protestant works were banned in France, was responsible for more than one in twenty (5.9 per cent). Moreover, the STN printed editions of the top thirteen works on the list, including client-commissioned editions of *Contrat conjugal*, Brissot's *De La Vérité* and the *Tableau de Paris*. At least one these editions, as we have noted, was confiscated *en bloc* before it reached market. This suggests that focusing too closely on the STN's global bestseller list can introduce significant distortions into our image of the illegal book trade.[51]

Given the STN's conscious decision to leave to others the risks of publishing pornography, anticlerical works and (post-*Système de la nature*) hardcore materialism, we might also suspect that our view would be rather anodyne. For the purposes of our analysis, it would be better then to exclude the STN editions altogether and consider instead the 'commercial' sector. This gives us a rather flatter market spread: the top ten works account for less than one quarter of the market (22.3 per cent), the top twenty for under a third (32.4 per cent). It also creates a list of bestsellers much more familiar to readers of *Forbidden Best-Sellers*: indeed it is topped by the same two works as Darnton's own list, Mercier's 'utopian fantasy' *L'An 2440*, with 2,006 sales, and Mairobert's tale of a royal 'whore's progress', the *Anecdotes sur Madame du*

Barri, with 1,489.⁵² The rest of the STN's 'commercial top ten' illegal bestsellers reads as follows:

3. J.-J. Rousseau, *Œuvres de Rousseau*, 1,312 copies
4. Raynal, *Histoire philosophique des Deux Indes*, 750 copies
5. Aretino, *Histoire et vie de l'Arrétin*, 629 copies
6. Alletz (attrib.), *Albert moderne*, 615 copies
7. Voltaire et al., *Lettre philosophique par M. de V****, 553 copies
8. Cleland, *La Fille de joye*, 530 copies
9. Rilliet, *Requête au Grand conseil de la République de Genève*, 520 copies
10. Koppen, *Plus secrets mystères des hauts grades de la maçonnerie dévoilés*, 518 copies

Many of the other works heading this list seem equally familiar from Darnton's *Corpus*, including Rousseau's works, Aretino's erotica, Cleland's 'whore biography' *Fanny Hill* and Raynal's *Histoire philosophique des Deux Indes*. Further down the table, in seventeenth position, we would discover another philosophic treatment of the non-European inhabitants of the Americas, de Pauw's *Recherches philosophiques sur les Américains* and considerably more pornography. The *Ecole des filles*, *Venus dans le cloître*, Mirabeau's *Libertin de qualité* and the erotic poetry of *La Lyre gaillarde* all make the top twenty, as do two works of erotic fiction of *La Vicomte de Barjac* and *La Belle Allemande ou les galanteries de Thérèse* and Voltaire's satirical, scurrilous mock-epic treatment of Joan of Arc, *La Pucelle*. More puzzling perhaps are two books that smack of illicit secrets and even the occult – Karl-Friedrich Koppen's revelations of the supposed crusading and Christian origins of freemasonic ritual and the *Albert moderne*, usually attributed to Pons-Augustin Alletz, which presents itself as an update of a popular medieval 'book of secrets'.⁵³ There is enough here already to suggest the STN was a major wholesaler of erotica and *philosophie*, as well as some more intriguing genres of illegal work. Nevertheless, religiously sceptical and materialist works remain surprisingly rare among the leading 'commercial' bestsellers, the notable exception being Voltaire's *Examen important de Milord Bolingbroke* at number eleven. Moreover, only one work in the top twenty relates to scandal at the royal court. The question remains, did any types of illegal work sell disproportionately well in France, and if so, is there prima facie evidence to suggest that these works contributed to desacralization or promoting radical Enlightenment?

This issue is best approached by comparing keyword statistics on the STN's 'commercial sector', to see what sorts of works sold relatively well inside France. Of particular interest here are works ascribed keywords associated with the alleged desacralization literature, most notably: 'amorous adventures' (a term used to broadly represent the French term *aventures galantes*); 'libertine texts'; 'erotic works'; 'pornographic works'; 'sceptical works'; 'anticlerical works'; and, when used in conjunction with the word 'scandal', 'royal mistresses', 'court and courtiers' and 'Louis XV'. All these categories seem to have sold disproportionately well in France compared to the rest of Europe. Moreover, although the sales figures for 'commercial' works are much lower than our 'global' statistics, 'commercial' works tended to be traded in smaller blocks across more works, meaning that the figures are generally more 'representative' and less prone to distortions than those derived by querying the 'global' trade.

The STN's 'commercial sector' statistics reveal that French readers' had a particularly strong appetite for sexually licentious works. France was the destination for almost half (49.4 per cent) of 'commercial sector' sales of *livres philosophiques*, as opposed to just under 36 per cent of total sales of books. But within that sector it also took more *aventures galantes*, libertine works, erotica and pornography (see Appendix 3.21). Almost one sixth of *livres philosophiques* (16 per cent) despatched to France carried the keyword 'pornographic works'. This compares to just over one thirtieth (3.72 per cent) of books taken by Swiss clients and 13.35 per cent for the rest of Europe. Moreover, in so far as there is a continuum of keywords relating to amorous activities, ranging from works depicting characters in multiple romantic or sexual liaisons ('Amorous adventures'), through works with 'Erotic' content to sexually explicit 'pornographic works', there is a further trend in evidence.[54] For the French not only took proportionately more of these materials than the subjects of other countries, they also seem to have preferred hardcore materials. When compared to readers elsewhere, French readers took more tales of 'amorous adventures' by a ratio of 57:43. The ratio for 'erotic works' was 61:39 and for 'pornographic works' 65:35. The French apparently liked their erotica to be spicier and more explicit. The French also took marginally more sexually 'Libertine texts', that is to say books that depicted and promoted sexually aggressive attitudes, particularly among dominant males.[55]

These preferences are equally evident if we turn from disembodied keywords to material books. In the STN's French 'commercial' bestseller list for *livres philosophiques* under the ancien régime, most of the titles overlap with the European 'commercial' top ten. It reads:

1. Mairobert, *Anecdotes sur Mme la comtesse du Barri*, 954 copies
2. Mercier, *L'An deux mille quatre cent quarante*, 904 copies
3. Aretino, *Histoire et vie de l'Arrétin*, 545 copies
4. Voltaire et al., *Lettre philosophique de M. de V****, 486 copies
5. Cleland, *La Fille de joye*, 468 copies
6. Raynal, *Histoire philosophique des Deux Indes*, 441 copies
7. Rousseau, *Œuvres de Rousseau*, 416 copies
8. Anon, *L'Ecole des filles*, 407 copies
9. Anon, *La Lyre gaillarde*, 331 copies
10. Voltaire, *Examen important de milord Bolingbroke*, 330 copies

However, there are subtle and important differences between the French and European lists. The erotically charged *Anecdotes sur Mme la comtesse du Barri*, *Histoire et vie de l'Aretin* and *Fille de Joye* are all further up the French chart, while the *Ecole des filles* and *Lyre gaillarde* gatecrash the top ten. There are a further six erotic works in the French top twenty, plus *La Fille naturelle*, a novel by libertine writer Nicolas Rétif de la Bretonne, the man who coined the modern usage of the word pornography.

What does this mean? Perhaps it indicates merely that eighteenth-century readers preferred to experience orgasmic fantasies in their mother tongue. However, that does not explain the startlingly low figures for 'erotic works', 'libertine works' and, above all, pornography, on the STN's Swiss market, which served francophone regions almost exclusively. Clearly, then, the STN bibliometric evidence suggests that libertinism and sexually licentious reading were more strongly embedded among French readers than those elsewhere. And if sexual libertinism was as closely connected with philosophical and political freethinking as some commentators suggest, this discovery has wider ramifications.[56] Equally, we might conclude that the Calvinist Swiss were measurably more sexually strait-laced. While Swiss publishers might produce and profit from this sort of material, their compatriots did not read it, whether from taste or because it was socially unacceptable to consume such material. But the Swiss figures are so low that they also indicate that rival wholesalers tended to source such works direct from the publishers, rather than the STN, and that in all probability very few Swiss retail booksellers handled this sort of material.

Sexually licentious works are not the only genre in which the French tastes were distinctly more liberal than those of the Swiss and other foreign readers. Similar trends can be seen when we turn to freethinking religious and metaphysical works. Across all these categories French dealers took a much greater proportion than those elsewhere (see Appendix 3.22).[57] The numbers of texts involved are relatively low, so it may be risky to read too much into this. It seems clear nevertheless that the French were significantly keener on both religiously sceptical philosophical works, and on works that were anticlerical or downright disrespectfully 'irreligious'. As traditional Enlightenment historiography suggests, religious scepticism seems to have penetrated more deeply into French society than elsewhere, abetted by the fashionability of the *philosophes* in elite circles. Nevertheless, such fare was far from ubiquitous. Many readers probably never laid eyes on materialist works, let alone assimilated their arguments into their world view. As we have already noted, materialist works probably made up no more than one in three hundred books printed in French across Europe in the two decades prior to the French Revolution. Yet it seems that these works were more in vogue in France than elsewhere. This finding is potentially consistent with both Darnton's account of the role of religious scepticism in the desacralization of the monarchy or Israel's attempts to link 'one substance materialism' to Revolution via a radically enlightened intellectual elite.

The French were also the major consumers of those allegedly more direct motors of the desacralization of the monarchy – anti-aristocratic pamphlets and salacious political *libelles* against King Louis XV and his mistresses, most notably *la Pompadour* and *la Du Barri*. Such works were in reality few in number. Despite their remarkable presence in the historical literature, the STN sold only thirty-two titles carrying the keyword 'Louis XV', and, prior to 1789, only twelve bearing the keywords 'Louis XV' and 'scandal'. These dozen works are almost all familiar to scholars. To Mairobert's *Anecdotes* we can add, in descending order of sales, *La Vie privée de Louis XV*, *Mémoires de Louis XV*, the *Fastes de Louis XV*, the *Mémoires authentiques de Mme la comtesse du Barri*, *La Gazette de Cythère*, the *Lettres de Mme la marquise de Pompadour*, the allegorical roman-à-clef *Amours de Zeokinizul, roi des Kofirans*, the *Galerie de l'ancienne cour*, the *Mémoires de Pompadour* and *Lettres originales de Madame la comtesse du Barri*. In all, these dozen works sold some 2,610 units. Mairobert's *Anecdotes* accounted for over half of these.

A thirteenth work, Morande's *Gazetier cuirassé* was too hot for the STN to handle, at least until the French Revolution. They finally acquired a handful of copies in May 1790. Likewise, the STN did not trade a single work carrying the hypnotic keyword combination 'Marie-Antoinette' and 'scandal' before 1789.[58] As I had long suspected, such works indeed seem not to have circulated at this period.

Suggestively, none of the court *libelles* dealt with the reign of Louis XVI. Nor with the exception of the cryptic and anagrammatically titled *Amours de Zeokinizul*, which dated from the 1740s, did these *libelles* treat royal favourites in office at time of publication. The Pompadour *libelles* dated to final years of Louis XV's reign, after the death of the mistress, while the main Louis and du Barri *libelles* date to the years following the king's death in 1774. The sole exception is the novelistic *Mémoires authentiques de Mme la comtesse du Barri*, which offers an almost entirely fabricated account of the favourite's early life.[59] The historically orientated *Anecdotes de l'ancienne cour* appeared only in 1786. The dates of these works are significant. They indicate that the heyday of the supposedly desacralizing *libelles* was in the 1760s and 1770s; their subject matter was a king who died in 1774 and mistresses who had already fallen from grace and were in some cases already dead. Whatever readers made of them, they were not, then, attacks on a government in office or mistress currently in favour. Moreover, as they attacked persons not systems, they did not represent a direct challenge to Louis XVI, whose virtuous private life, restoration of the *Parlements* and early foreign policy successes marked him out as a very different ruler.

In all probability, neither the intended political nor actual sociological impact of these works was harmful to monarchy per se. In a society steeped in Biblical culture and histories offering sharp dichotomies between good and bad rulers, parables of dysfunctional and recently deceased monarchs, formed part of a narrative of cyclical restoration and renewal. One virtue of monarchic systems was that tyranny did not last for ever, and the crown generally passed by peaceful and agreed means from one ruler to another. The *libelles* reminded readers of these truths.

Moreover, in eighteenth-century France, where power was generally circumscribed within an accepted legal framework, even tyranny was relative and limited. True, the monarchy retained powers of arbitrary arrest and imprisonment which to enlightened eyes looked increasingly despotic. However, these were nothing new, and indeed most persons detained arbitrarily were wayward sons, daughters or wives held at the behest of their families for infringing moral codes.[60] There is, moreover, as Rolf Reichardt and Hans-Jürgen Lüsebrink have shown, little evidence that the French penal apparatus was seen or portrayed as systematically despotic prior to the appearance in 1774 of the *Remarques historiques sur le Château de la Bastille*, a pamphlet variously attributed to Brossais du Perray or Théveneau de Morande.[61] Instead, the personal charge sheet against Louis XV was primarily that he allied with the hated Austrians; suffered disastrous military defeats (some said as God's punishment for his sexual sins); quashed impeachment proceedings against an unpopular minister (d'Aiguillon); purged the obstreperous *Parlements* (an action many considered to have removed the last bulwark against royal despotism); and took inappropriate mistresses including a succession of Nesle sisters (which in the eyes of contemporaries amounted to incest), a mere *bourgeoise* (Pompadour), and a common courtesan (Du Barri). These were unfortunate, politically unpopular and sometimes ill-advised choices rather than the acts of a brutal tyrant.

More troublingly, in an age where religious conformity sat uncomfortably against burgeoning Enlightenment, Louis XV continued his predecessor's clampdown on the Jansenists. The persecution was generally moderate and spiritually orientated – for example, through the refusal of deathbed sacraments.[62] He was not torturing or burning heretics, unlike the inquisition in neighbouring Spain. Nor did he follow the example of his immediate predecessor Louis XIV, who inflicted the notorious *dragonnades* – forced billeting of rowdy troops – on his Protestant subjects. Nevertheless, for many *philosophes* and much of the political and aristocratic elite, Louis XV's actions were beyond the pale, intolerable. By the time of his death he was one of the least popular monarchs ever to die peacefully on the French throne. His grandson, Louis XVI, glowed in comparison. The *libelles* were daring in referring to Louis XV's private life and in the outspokenness of their criticisms, but the annals of the thousand-year-old French monarchy were full of such tales.[63] Louis XVI was long celebrated, by contrast, as the restorer of the *Parlements* and – well into the Revolution – of French liberties.

Moreover, as Louis XVI's reign progressed, STN sales of political *libelles* to France flagged then slumped. Why? Perhaps the material no longer seemed so current? Perhaps the market was saturated? But there was another much more significant factor: the impact of the decrees of 30 August 1777 and 12 June 1783, which squeezed the *libelles* and other *livres philosophiques* out of the French market. As we have noted, the 1777 decrees impacted severely on the entire foreign import trade, not just the pirate sector. But paradoxically they hit the trade in clandestine *livres philosophiques* hardest of all. Once every *chambre syndicale de la librairie* in the realm was equipped with a centrally appointed inspector, it became much more difficult to smuggle books into the country. In fact, the STN data shows that after 1777, the only people in France to continue to trade in libertine works were specialist dealers such as Malherbe in Loudun, on whom, in an incident unique in their history, the STN dumped a large consignment of near unsellable cut-price pornographic and philosophic works in April 1779, and the fly-by-night Mauvelain, who ran a hole-in-the-wall operation out of Troyes and Tonnerre.[64] When these two dealers are excluded, it is evident that established French dealers fled the pornographic trade almost entirely (see Chart 9.2 below).

Conversely, the 12 June 1783 decree against the illegal sector emasculated the pirate industry. That decree's stipulation that every book entering the kingdom must be inspected at Paris provoked a litany of complaints to the French authorities. From Geneva, François de Bassompierre admitted that 'plusieurs libraires de Suisse sembloient avoir nécessité cette rigueur par leur licence excessive', but complained that the decree's blanket provisions also hit those who wished to conduct a licit trade. It was, he argued, driving innocent Swiss dealers and booksellers in the French provinces to the wall.[65] From Lyon, Piestre et Cormon insisted that their trade in foreign books would be ruined.[66] This claim was echoed by Jean-Marie Bruyset, *père et fils*, who complained that the Parisian booksellers' stranglehold on the trade meant that importing from abroad was the only legitimate option open to Lyonnais dealers.[67] And from the *Chambre syndicale* de Lille came protests that because the city was situated in the bishopric of Tournay, all religious works for diocesan use were printed in the

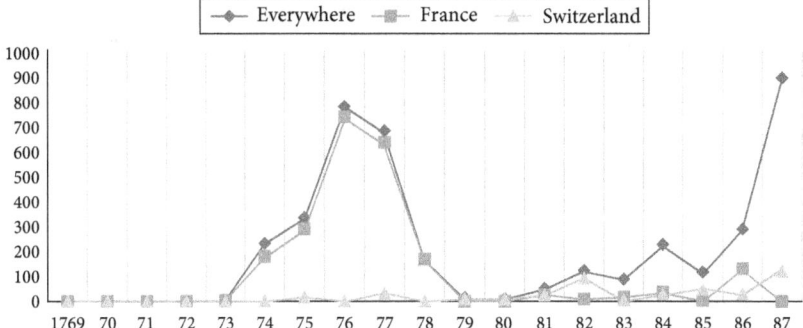

Chart 9.2 Comparative sales of pornographic works by the STN, 1769–87. NB. Before 1777 France comprised the vast majority of a buoyant market. From 1780, the STN reorientated its trade in such works eastward. (The STN's four 'foreign wholesale' clients including Mauvelain and Malherbe have been excluded.)

Austrian Netherlands (Belgium), and the cost of importation was now prohibitive.[68] In the face of such criticisms the government stood firm.

However, the revolutionary crisis opened the floodgates to a torrent of subversive literature. It included the *Mémoires justificatifs* of Madame de La Motte, published in February 1789, the first printed pornographic *libelle* against Queen Marie-Antoinette to circulate among the French public.[69] It finally appears in the STN registers on 31 May 1790.[70] Before the Revolution, despite its expertise in the illegal trade, the STN did not handle a single copy of a single *libelle* against the French queen. Thus the STN archive provided grist for my claims that pornographic pamphlets targeting Marie-Antoinette were not available prior to the Revolution.[71]

Hence by concentrating their attentions on a handful of lewd works from Hell, historians have stumbled into error about the entire illegal sector. The French illegal book trade indeed deserves all the priapic epithets that scholars have used to describe it. It was indeed 'vast', 'huge', 'enormous' in scale. Birn, Chartier and Darnton were almost certainly right that it comprised around half of the French book market. France was, moreover, the destination for a disproportionate volume of the STN's pornographic, materialist and anticlerical wares. But the typical illegal book was neither erotic, nor anticlerical, nor philosophic in nature, nor even political. Nor was it part of Darnton's hardcore clandestine trade or a likely denizen of the confiscation registers studied by Dawson. It was instead an unlicensed work or a pirated copy of a title that circulated licitly within the kingdom. The most popular subject matter for such works will become clear in the next chapter.

This is not to say that radical philosophic, libertine, pornographic or political texts should have no place in our narratives of the illegal sector, just that we should keep them in perspective. It is probable, moreover, that such radical works deserve attention as motors and reflectors of cultural change. But there were countervailing tendencies in popular culture, too, and by the late 1770s the authorities were becoming far more effective at regulating the trade and excluding subversive or heterodox texts from the market. Viewed in that way, it is even possible that the French Revolution, which made such a virtue of free speech, was not the result of an uncontrolled and uncontrollable public sphere, or even a torrent of smut and political invective. It was instead perhaps a reaction to the constriction of public discussion by an increasingly robust censorship and inspection apparatus. That might explain why in 1789 so many privileged printers and publishers turned against the royal authorities that had nurtured and enriched them.[72] Such an analysis challenges fundamentally previous orthodoxies about the structure, chronology, workings and operational autonomy of the illegal sector. The chapters that follow explore whether similar reappraisals are required when we turn our attention to the sale and dissemination by the STN of philosophic, religious, political and scientific works.

10

Philosophie, Science, Faith

The French doctor and botanist, Jean-Emmanuel Gilibert, is not among the first names that spring to mind when we think of eighteenth-century science. Nor are his credentials improved by his vociferous proselytizing for the popular pseudoscience of animal magnetism. However, he does stand out as a medical whistle-blower.[1] For his book, *L'Anarchie médicinale, ou La Médicine considérée comme nuisable à la société* (1772), blew the lid on the largely unregulated medical world of his day, castigating the cupidity, ignorance and charlatanry of many of its practitioners. In three hefty volumes, Gilibert called for sweeping changes in the medical and pharmaceutical professions; denounced the inadequacy of university medical training; and demanded reforms in medical administration. It was an agenda guaranteed to make powerful enemies. Not surprisingly, Gilibert was unable to publish his book in France. Fortunately, this made it attractive to the STN, who detected a potential *succès de scandale*. Nor was Gilibert alone in his attacks on medical charlatanry – Louis-Sébastien Mercier, for example, took swipes at the medical establishment in his *Tableau de Paris*. His scathing article 'Médecins' alleges members of the medical faculty habitually and knowingly supported one another's fatal misdiagnoses out of a murderous, self-serving esprit de corps.[2] Yet however in tune Gilibert may have been with the zeitgeist it comes as a surprise to see his 1,000-page medical blockbuster at the apex of the STN's 'trade list' of bestselling scientific monographs and reference works.[3]

Nor are most of the other authors who appear near the summit of the list household names in the history of science: Jacques-Christophe Valmont de Bomare, Jonas Gélieu, Pierre-Joseph Macquer, Elie Bertrand, Pons-Augustin Alletz.[4] Only the popular medical writer, Samuel Tissot, four of whose books appear in the top ten, might boast a certain name recognition beyond specialist historians of science. However, except for his study *L'Onanisme* (1760), which reached traditional conclusions about the harmful effects of masturbation from scientific rather than religious premises, even he is known primarily as a popularizer.[5] Yet these men, whose works span the fields of medicine, epidemiology, chemistry, palaeontology, astronomy and natural history, accounted for a large portion of the scientific works sold by the STN.

A rather more familiar directory of 'great men of science' can be found in Jean le Rond d'Alembert's account of the history of science in the 'Discours préliminaire' to the *Encyclopédie* (1751). To be fair, d'Alembert's tale of the driving forces of human progress allowed for environmental factors and institutional infrastructure. Men of genius, he insisted, had existed in similar proportions in every age, but in Europe's medieval past they were isolated and had little exposure to ideas, which 'sont le germe de presque toutes les découvertes'.[6] According to d'Alembert, medieval intellectual activity took place under the shackles of sterile scholasticism, 'une admiration aveugle pour l'antiquité',[7] the religious dogma developed by ambitious priests, and prejudice.[8] The heroes of d'Alembert's narrative were thus the handful of 'philosophers' who even 'sans avoir l'ambition dangereuse d'arracher le bandeau des yeux de leurs contemporains, préparoient de loin dans l'ombre & le silence la lumière dont le monde devoit être éclairé, peu à peu'.[9] D'Alembert thereby inverted traditional religious thinking, by substituting philosophers for the Hebrew prophets. It was philosophers who gradually prepared the way for the coming of the light of scientific truth. In this secular tale, it is the Christian religion and its priestly acolytes who represent the powers of darkness. Science and religion, philosophy and faith are become incompatible, diametric opposites. D'Alembert was thus expounding both a revolution in thinking and the foundational myth of late modern secularizers. He placed his faith in the progressive power of science to overcome religious superstition. The remainder of this chapter examines the presentation and dissemination of scientific, metaphysical and religious texts, in order to explore the power and reception of d'Alembert's myth among his contemporaries.

D'Alembert's roll call includes the founders of scientific method and modern epistemological traditions, Bacon, Descartes, Locke and Newton, together with their forerunners, the algebrist Viète, Huygens, Kepler and Newton's great rival, Leibniz. There is also a veiled allusion to Condillac, one of the Enlightenment heroes immortalized by Leonard DeFrance in À l'Égide de Minerve. Finally, d'Alembert offers a list of 'lesser greats', while adding candidly that he lacks the space to discuss their contributions properly: Galileo, Harvey, Pascal, Malebranche, Boyle, Vesalius, Sydenham, Boerhaave.[10] D'Alembert's list, then, is geared heavily towards the scientific revolution of the seventeenth and early eighteenth centuries, although Viète and Vesalius are both sixteenth-century figures. The latest work to grab his attention is Condillac's Traité des systêmes, published in 1746 and mentioned in a footnote.[11] He therefore says nothing about the contribution of the comte de Buffon, whose Histoire naturelle, générale et particulière began to appear in 1749. Its first volume already contained important essays on how to study natural history and the geological history of the world. Nor does he mention the Swedish taxonomist Carl Linnaeus, whose Systema naturae first appeared in 1735 as a twelve-page pamphlet. By 1758 it had run through ten editions and been extended to two large volumes. Ironically, much of Linnaeus work was republished in abridged form by our bestselling scientific author, Gilibert, who is better remembered as a botanist than a doctor.[12]

Had d'Alembert been writing in the twilight of the STN's history, he might also have mentioned Antoine Lavoisier and other pioneers of the chemical revolution; the English natural philosopher, scientist and controversial dissenting minister Joseph Priestley; the American Founding Father Benjamin Franklin, who like Priestley was known for experiments with electricity; the surgeon John Hunter; the mathematician Leonard Euler, who had already published major works when d'Alembert wrote; or Joseph Banks, who from naturalist on Cook's Endeavour voyage rose to become president of the Royal Society. If he had been more expansive in his approach, a latterday d'Alembert might also have mentioned the authors of foundational texts in the many distinct scientific sub-disciplines that emerged around this time. He might have referenced Jean-André Venel's work in orthopaedics;[13] Charles de Saint-Yves ophthalmological treatise, *Nouveau traité des maladies des yeux*; or the authors of numerous other seminal contributions among the 456 works classified with the keyword 'Science' in the STN database. These covered topics as varied as obstetrics, palaeontology, paediatrics, hydrology, entomology, meteorology, mineralogy, optics and many more.

The names of most of the scientists listed above appear in the STN database, but their works barely register in its sales figures. Their publications were generally bought by the STN in miniscule numbers for local luminaries in and around Neuchâtel. The STN sold forty-four copies of works by Newton and just six copies of Condillac's *Traité des sensations*. They distributed twenty copies of works by Buffon, two copies of Linnaeus and nothing by Malebranche. Indeed, although 12.66 per cent of titles sold by the STN were classified as science, they accounted for only 6.22 per cent of sales. Why was this? In part because as publishers the STN showed relatively little interest in science, perhaps reflecting their local context. As Alexandra Cook has noted, Neuchâtel society was far from fertile ground for the sciences or enlightened ideas, dominated as it was by Calvinist pastors and retired mercenaries, and lacking the theological seminaries, learned academies or universities found in other Swiss centres.[14] In this conservative atmostphere, what interest the STN did show in science was often parochial. Several of their bestselling scientific authors were Swiss scientists, polymaths and popularizers: Albrecht von Haller, Charles Bonnet, Samuel Formey, Abraham Trembley and Samuel Tissot. These men had respectable reputations, but with the exception of Haller, who is often seen as the father of experimental physiology, were decidedly second tier compared to the scientists name-checked by d'Alembert.

Our whistle-blower, Jean-Emmanuel Gilibert, a Frenchman who became the Girondin mayor of Lyon during the Revolution, is an exception to the STN's bias towards Swiss science. His was also one of the first scientific works published by the nascent STN and perhaps shaped their later business policy. As a result, the publishing history of *L'Anarchie médicinale* is instructive and reveals much about the STN's attitude to scientific publishing. The STN seems to have been attracted to Gilibert's work not so much for its content or novelty, but its clandestine marketability and 'high risk, high return' potential. Certainly Gilibert's first letter left the STN in no doubt that they were playing with fire. Having stressed the originality of his project, he went on to explain:

> je crois avoir démontré que la medécine considerée en general est nuisible a la societé, j'ai plus fait encor j'ai exposé les moiens de la rendre utile et je le scai, cenest [sic] pas la plus mauvaise partie de mon ouvrage.

However, Gilibert reassured the STN that his text avoided attacking individuals : 'ceux qui m'ont paru meriter le blame se trouvent condamné seulement dans les généralités'.[15]

When Gilibert first approached the STN in mid-1771, most of the company's directors still lacked publishing experience. Nevertheless, they probably spotted two key features of a potential sure-fire seller. The book's first attraction was that it addressed popular medicine, a subject genre that was in considerable demand. Second, it was likely to be highly controversial in France, the country where it would have most topical resonance: indeed, it had already fallen foul of the French censors and medical fraternity.

Gilibert was candid about his experience with the censorship. He explained that after submitting his work early in 1770, he had exchanged several missives with his appointed censor, M. Gardanne.[16] Gardanne admired the manuscript but was worried that its content would offend his colleagues in the medical fraternity, and hence compromise him as censor. Several of Gardanne's doctor friends confirmed his conclusion. Following accepted practice, rather than refuse a permission outright, Gardanne now offered a compromise solution: he proposed that Gilibert bowdlerize his work, removing all references containing anything 'desavantageux contre la medecine et les medecins'.[17]

Gilibert was not prepared to play this game and told Gardanne that 'si en France on ne pouvoit ni rélever les abus ni dire de la verité on pourroit s'adresser a letranger [sic]'. According to Gilibert, Gardanne quietly encouraged him to do just that, returning the manuscript and apologizing that as medical censor it was 'bien excusable de ne pas aprouver publiquement des verités qui publiées ne seroient pas avantageuses a ses confreres'.[18]

Nevertheless, the censor's attitude left Gilibert optimistic. If Gardanne was happy to see the work in print so long as he was not implicated in its production, perhaps higher officials might take a similar line and grant a *permission tacite*. Thus, once the STN agreed to publish the book, he mobilized friends and allies in Paris and Versailles to lobby for the desired permission. These efforts were redoubled when an old medical friend, Gabriel-François Venel of the University of Montpellier, a deputy in the Estates of Languedoc, assured Gilibert that Chancellor Maupeou would be pleased by the work.[19] The STN took the hint. They duly sent copies of *L'Anarchie médicinale* to Maupeou and the lieutenant of police, Sartine, who also had censorship responsibilities.[20] Meanwhile, Gilibert urged the STN to hurry the book to market.

> Les medecins de Paris sont seuls causes du refus, ils ont sottement imaginé que l'on vouloit devaster leur domaine, mais l'ouvrage ne contenant rien contre les mœurs et la religion, ni contre l'etat vous pourrés aisement vendre votre edition, meme plus rapidement parce que l'ouvrage est proscrit.[21]

Sadly, however, no permission was forthcoming. On the contrary, by June Gilibert was complaining of the Parisian 'inquisition litteraire', though he still believed that the ban would be lifted. In the interim, he arranged that two hundred copies be forwarded to his friend and fellow doctor and botanist, the abbé François Rozier. Rozier would orchestrate their clandestine distribution in Paris from a safe house in the countryside and try to promote *Anarchie médicinale* in his journal *Observations périodiques sur l'histoire naturelle, la physique et les arts*. This would require him to sneak copy past the journal's censor – the ever cautious Gardanne.[22] In the event, Rozier found this impossible. Gilibert lamented that the censors had prevented a single journal from mentioning his work.[23] He also warned the STN not to send the books to Rozier via Lyon, where the *Chambre syndicale de la librairie* was too vigilant.

Yet this particular game of cat and mouse proved a stalemate. It appears the book was never actually confiscated in France, which was the immediate destination for just over half of copies sold by the STN.[24] Nevertheless, the campaign of imposed press silence probably impeded sales. Between publication on 16 November 1772 and a stocktake of 18 October 1774, the STN shifted 1,274 copies, but that still left 206 copies in their magazine. On 30 November 1776 they still had eighty-three copies, and thereafter sales slowed to a trickle. The last recorded sale was in March 1788. Sluggish sales were not due initially to any competition. Although Gilibert had predicted that other publishers would hurry counterfeit editions onto the market, the sole known reprinting was a 1776 'édition revue et corrigée' bearing a (possibly false) Paris imprint.[25]

Gilibert's relations with the STN turned as sour as his sales. By 1774 the publisher was pursuing him before the courts for thirty-nine *livres* owing on a Latin edition of Haller's *Botanique* and a handful of other books. Gilibert counterclaimed, alleging improbably that the STN owed him at least one hundred *livres* for a supplement to *Anarchie medicinale*. The STN denied ever having requested the manuscript or promising to pay him an 'obole' for it. Their final verdict on the *Anarchie medicinale* affair was that 'nous avons malheureusement acheté et payé bien cher le manuscrit'.[26]

From a commercial point of view, the STN's first venture into popular scientific publishing was at best a mild success, but hardly enough to inspire a charge into that market. If anything, it showed that even a controversial work with the allure of clandestinity might meet with relatively limited sales. Perhaps this explains why the STN largely eschewed scientific publishing thereafter. Those scientific texts that it did publish tended to be aimed at niche audiences or the reference or school book markets. After *Anarchie médicinale*, the other bestselling STN editions on scientific subjects were Gélieu's short pamphlet *Réflexions d'un homme de bon sens sur les comètes & sur leur retour ou Préservatif contre la peur*; Macquer's *Dictionnaire de chymie*;[27] Elie Bertrand's *Elémens d'oryctologie, ou Distribution méthodique des fossils* and Valmont de Bomare's twelve-volume *Dictionnaire raisonné universel d'histoire naturelle*. To further reduce risk, both Macquer's chemical dictionary and Valmont's natural history were produced in partnership with the Sociétes typographiques de Berne and Lausanne.

The sales figures for these STN editions were challenged, however, by a set of authors and titles that were never published by the STN. Foremost among these were the popular medical works of Samuel Tissot and a household manual and pharmacopia, the *Albert moderne*, which was first published in 1768. It is usually attributed to the agronomist Pons-Augustin Alletz, who also published *L'Agronome, ou Dictionnaire portatif du cultivateur*. The *Albert moderne* presented itself as an eighteenth-century update of a popular corpus of medieval 'books of secrets' attributed to the medieval theologian Albrecht von Bollstädt. Otherwise known as 'Albert le Grand' or Albert of Cologne, von Bollstädt was reputedly a magician. Therein lay the difference between von Bollstädt and Alletz, as the preface to the *Albert moderne*. The *grimoires* associated with von Bollstädt, the *Secrets merveilleux de la magie naturelle et cabalistique du petit Albert*[28] and *Les Admirables Secrets d'Albert le Grand*, offered an anthology of astrological material, spells and recipes. Their subtitles variously promised to enlighten readers on the properties of plants and precious stones and the mysteries of human conception.[29] In contrast, Alletz's preface promised that his work had been stripped of anything that might offend common sense or decency, including magical spells, love philtres, magical amulets and astrological material. Instead he promised material compiled from the latest periodicals concerning discoveries confirmed by repeated empirical observation and experiment.[30] The STN shifted six hundred copies of the *Albert moderne*, together with almost three hundred copies of its medieval precursors the *Petit Albert* and *Albert le Grand*.[31] Tissot's works were more successful still: they sold 3,752 copies.

Other evidence reinforces the impression that Tissot's works and the *Albert moderne* were indeed bestsellers throughout the 1770s and 1780s. Worldcat lists at least thirteen French-language editions of the *Albert moderne* published between 1768 and 1789, six of them bearing the imprint of the *privilège* holder, *la veuve* Duchesne. Another French edition of 750 copies was produced at Rouen in 1782, following the grant of a *permission simple* to Pierre Machuel in December 1781.[32] The remaining six editions bore imprints from Basel, Liège, London and Neuchâtel, where Samuel Fauche apparently produced editions in 1776 and 1780.

Likewise, the surviving records of the *estampillage* inspectors indicate that the *Albert moderne* was readily available across France in 1778–80.[33] Inspectors found and stamped 704 copies *chez* Monoyer, père, in Neufchâteau; 125 copies on the premises of Rigaud and Pons in Montpellier; one hundred copies in Lehoucq's shop in Lille; and forty-four more with the veuve Leclerc in Nancy. They also found copies in Besançon, Châteaudun-en-Dunois, Montdidier, Orléans, Sens and Vendôme. In all they stamped some 1,046 copies, around one in four hundred of the total books legalized in this manner. In the small Normandy town of Dinan, they legalized 928 copies of another work of the Albert corpus, *Les Secrets de Nature, Extraits tant du petit Albert qu'autres Philosophes hébreux*.[34]

In the same exercise, Tissot's output proved even more popular. The inspectors stamped a grand total of 3,911 copies of his works, including *Onanisme* (1,355 copies); the *Santé des gens de lettres* (1,279 copies); the *Avis au peuple sur sa santé* (949 copies); and *Essai sur les maladies des gens du monde* (428 copies). Thus Tissot accounts for almost one in a hundred of all books stamped. Similarly, his works comprised almost 1 per cent of all STN sales.[35]

Popular scientific reading, when viewed through the prism of the STN looks rather distant from the secularizing model propounded by d'Alembert, and seems to have relatively little to do with his great men of science. Instead, it appears that scientific reading was applied to the practical purposes of an agrarian subsistence economy, albeit one that in the case of Neuchâtel, at least, was experiencing unprecedented rural industrialization, and an 'ingenious seasonal alternation of livestock-raising and proto-industrial production of high-tech goods'.[36] STN readers were preoccupied with the everyday business of living: being born, farming, preserving food, curing sick animals and people, and struggling to prolong life while preparing for death. This final preoccupation was also, of course, the domain of religion and, equally, of Enlightenment metaphysics.

It is today almost a commonplace to acknowledge that the seventeenth-century scientific revolution began largely as a religious quest. Indeed, God's existence was axiomatic to the founding figures of the main traditions of Enlightenment epistemology. Descartes entire theory of knowledge and material reality was based on the assertion that a (benevolent) God existed and therefore would not deceive his senses.[37] Without that certainty, Descartes' house of cards would come tumbling down. If John Locke is less forthcoming in his epistemological work, his political theory is steeped in theological argument: the starting point for the theory of property which underpins it is the assertion that God gave the world in common to all men.[38] Finally, with Newton's revelation that the physical world (creation) was governed by universal natural laws, the search was on to discover the purposes of the Creator through the laws He had ordained. For Newton (who was, ironically, one of d'Alembert's heroes), the scientific quest informed his religious quest. And increasingly, as he aged, it was the religious quest that consumed him and drove him to the study of scriptural forms of revelation.[39] In this respect he may not have been atypical of his era. Even Spinoza, whom Israel sees as the high priest of one substance materialism, presents his *Ethics* in the style of a medieval scholastic, and was famously described by Novalis as 'a God-intoxicated man'.[40]

What is less clear is how far popular scientific authors of a century later continued to perceive or portray science as the handiwork of divinity and, conversely, how far the 'light of science' – as d'Alembert would have it – was beginning to dispel the darkness of superstition. Robert Darnton has made much of the way in which *livres philosophiques* frequently mixed genres and subject matter that might, to more modern eyes, seem odd. His classic example was the novel *Thérèse philosophe*, which offered a heady brew of materialist philosophy, anticlericalism and sexual scandal spliced together with frequent pornographic interludes.[41] What has been less often been remarked is that heterodox works were not alone in playing this game: religious apologetics, for example, could rear their heads in unexpected places. Hence, a number of the 456 works labelled as 'Science' in the STN database also carry the subjective marker 'Work of Religiosity'. This indicates works 'which have been identified as having apparently been written or inspired in part through pious Christian motives'.[42] Some twenty-four works of 'Science' in the database carry this further keyword: they account for 4,365 out of 25,733 'scientific' sales. This certainly indicates a significant correlation between 'Science' and faith in the STN data, but not sufficient to draw firm conclusions. Nevertheless, statements of faith paying more than lip service to the divinity can be found across a range of scientific texts. One such occurs in a panegyric to his profession in the introduction of Tissot's *Santé des gens de lettres*. In it he declares:

> Supposons les hommes plongés dans l'oubli de la divinité, les Médecins les rappelleront bientôt aux notions sublime que leur science leur donnera de cet Être immortel, dont personne … n'a parlé avec plus de justesse & de grandeur qu'eux.[43]

The passage goes on to outline how ever since Hippocrates and Galen, scientists of the stature of Boyle, Sydenham, the 'immortel Locke' and Bohervaave [sic] have praised the divinity and defended faith against the unbelievers. Nor does Tissot forget his contemporaries, right down to Albrecht Haller who discussed and opposed 'les principes & les suites funestes de l'irréligion' and the obscure German physician Balthasar Ludwig Tralles 'qui a réfuté si victorieusement les sophismes de LA METTRIE'.[44] Coming from one of the STN's most prominent scientific authors, these words are revealing.[45] For Tissot, faith and the practice of science are inextricably linked.

According to Charles Bonnet's *Essai de psychologie*, there were equally inextricable links between the human soul and human body, for humans were in essence mixed beings composed of a corporal and a spiritual part. To emphasize this point against doubters, and implicitly refute materialist assertions to the contrary, he added:

> ce Principe est tellement celui de la REVELATION, que la Doctrine de la Résurrection des Corps en est la conséquence immédiate. Et loin de ce Dogme si clairement révélé dût revolter le Déiste Philosophe, il devroit, au contraire, lui paroitre une présomption favorable à la Vérité de la RELIGION, puisqu'il est si parfaitement conforme avec ce que nous connoissons de plus certain sur la nature de notre Etre.[46]

Here then, Bonnet is using the most fundamental truth propounded by Cartesian dualism to refute materialism, and he subverts it further by dressing up his arguments in the mechanistic language of La Mettrie.[47] Nor was he alone in using scientific means to refute incredulity. The Jesuit physics professor Aimé-Henri Paulian was another who jumped on the anti-materialist scientific bandwagon. In his *Dictionnaire des nouvelles découvertes faites en physique*, Paulian boldly announced that his work 'fait l'examen critique de ces nouvelles découvertes, et la réfutation de la partie physique du livre intitulé: *Système de la nature*'. If the individual titles cited here were not among their bestselling scientific works,[48] they demonstrate nevertheless that many of the STN's most popular scientific authors, including the Swiss luminaries Abraham Trembley, Haller, Bonnet and Tissot, were strident Christian apologists.[49] Moreover, if the Christianised science peddled by the STN was essentially Protestant and Swiss, it appears to have had widespread appeal across France.[50] But just how far does this revelation challenge d'Alembert's narrative of a sceptical science 'pulling the blindfolds' from the eyes of his contemporaries and dispelling priestly superstition?

Certainly other scientifically inclined writers were producing works of science antithetical to Christianity and many promoted a materialist metaphysics. First among them was d'Holbach, who in the *Système de la nature* cited Needham's (flawed!) observations that, given the right conditions, life could be spontaneously generated from flour and water, thereby obviating the need for a creator.[51] Such deicide is implied in d'Holbach's very title, for 'nature', a term that sceptics could conveniently substitute for the religious concept of 'creation', served as an Enlightenment euphemism for what we would call science. Science was conceived of as the study of nature; the 'laws of nature' were scientific laws. Such terminology had no need for a creator. D'Holbachean claims were also underwritten by the scientific and metaphysical work of figures such as Condillac, La Mettrie, Diderot, Naigeon and Boulanger. Their works, like the *Encyclopédie*, helped to inspire the secularization of modern science – seen by many as opposed to faith – and contain most of the philosophic arguments associated with militant modern scientific atheists such as Richard Dawkins. To understand their cultural impact, it is therefore important to get a close perspective on these works and their market.

How might we do this? One way might be to explore the trade of significant STN customers such as Charles-Antoine Charmet and his wife, who continued his business after his death in January 1783.[52] Theirs was, by their own accounts, a thriving enterprise based in Besançon, a large, bookish garrison town and religious centre overrun with military officers, clergymen, royal officials and university students, and boasting a small but not insubstantial Protestant minority.[53] Besançon was, moreover, a major centre of provincial Enlightenment, if we can judge by sales of the quarto edition of the *Encyclopédie*, a venture in which the STN were heavily invested. Charmet's arch-rival, Dominique Lépagnez, managed to find customers for no less than 338 copies. These sales made Besançon the quarto edition's fifth biggest outlet, although it was only the twenty-first most populous town in France.[54] Conversely, a survey of the publication of hagiographic texts from 1680 to 1788 found only six editions produced at Besançon, ranking it at twenty-eighth in the kingdom for this sort of religious work.[55] Besançon was, then, the sort of place we would expect to find all kinds of books, including radical materialist works. As purportedly the largest book dealers in town and clients of the STN, the Charmets were well placed to supply them.

Charles-Antoine Charmet and his wife were the STN's longest-serving and most prolific French customers: between 26 December 1771 and 16 July 1788 the STN sent them 7,064 copies of 393 works. According to Robert Darnton, the Charmet's were always avid for '*livres philosophiques*', and had a particular predilection for politically scandalous works. In short, their shop is just the sort of place we might expect to encounter the latest in materialist propaganda.[56] A close look at the Charmets' purchase list does not disappoint. It confirms that they did indeed have customers interested in this daring fare. In all, a little over 1 per cent of the books that Charles-Antoine and his wife received from the STN were atheist works, replete with a scientifically based materialist world view and highly hostile to Christianity. They included twenty-five copies of La Mettrie's *Œuvres*; nineteen copies of Condorcet's *Lettre d'un théologien à l'auteur du Dictionnaire des trois siècles*, a damning critique of clerical and judicial intolerance in the case of the Chevalier de La Barre, who was tortured and executed for allegedly blasphemous acts in 1765; twenty copies of *Le Christianisme dévoilé*; and a dozen of d'Holbach's *Système de la nature*. This constituted the bulk of the nineteen copies of *Système de la nature* that the STN supplied to Besançon, a total slightly lower than for other similarly sized towns along France's eastern frontier. Lunéville took seventy-eight copies, Nancy thirty-seven and Grenoble fifty.

Such numbers are perplexing. What do they imply about the size of the market for materialist works? And what does this indicate about the cultural penetration of religiously sceptical ideas in France, particularly in comparison to elsewhere? Are the numbers sufficient to constitute solid evidence that pre-revolutionary France was an increasingly sceptical country? Or were these relatively marginal texts sourced by a general book store from a specialist supplier to the illegal trade? Such questions strike at the heart of what the Enlightenment was all about, because as we have seen, the *Système de la nature* is in multiple ways a central text in a particular master-narrative of Enlightenment secularization and modernity, one which links the rise of a materialist, secular vision to advances in scientific understanding. Moreover, in Jonathan Israel's heavily contested version telling, such Spinozist materialist works inspired political radicalism as well.

Certainly much prima facie evidence suggests that the *Système de la nature* had a significant impact. The STN's own pirate edition, which was rushed to market shortly after the first edition in 1770, was rapidly followed by further editions in 1771, 1773,

1774, 1775, 1777, 1780 and 1781. Moreover, Robert Darnton identified d'Holbach (with collaborators) as France's second most ordered author in the STN's clandestine catalogue (2,903 copies from 28,212 ordered, including 768 orders for the *Système de la nature* itself).[57] The scale and vitality of the response to d'Holbach's *œuvre*, and particularly the Christian reaction, has also been underlined in a recent study which catalogues 122 works written exclusively or partially in response to d'Holbach, the majority of them by Christian apologists. A survey of the content of the *Journal encyclopédique, Journal historique et littéraire, Année littéraire, Journal ecclésiastique, Journal de Trévoux, Journal des Savants, Mercure de France* and miscellaneous other periodicals uncovered a further 222 occasions when authors engaged with d'Holbach's works.[58] This volume of interaction, it appears, exceeded that for any other Enlightenment author, even though d'Holbach's mask of anonymity prevented his contemporaries from identifying his rich and varied output with a single individual.

Yet d'Holbach does not fare quite so well on the STN global bestselling author rankings, charting at number twenty-two (3,071 sales). This equates to 0.75 per cent of total STN sales. Several authors of clandestine works appear above him, notably Mercier, Voltaire, Brissot, Raynal, Linguet and Rousseau, as does our Christian scientist, Tissot.[59] Moreover, although there are forty-one works associated with d'Holbach in the STN database, almost two thirds of his recorded sales are for the *Système de la nature*, which as an STN edition is over-represented in their global statistics. Other materialist authors were much less popular with the STN's audience. Altogether the STN shifted 3,326 copies of works carrying the keywords 'materialism' and 'atheist work' to ninety-nine different cities, including Bojnice, Lisbon, Prague, Cadiz, Dublin, Stockholm, Genoa, Naples, Moscow, St Petersburg and Warsaw. Clearly atheistic materialist works were being read in all the major centres of Europe and many obscurer towns, albeit in relatively small numbers. Yet well over half of these works (1,972 copies) were the *Système de la nature*. Other d'Holbachean works – *La Contagion sacrée, Le Christianisme dévoilé, Le Bon Sens, Abrégé du code de la nature, Lettre de Thrasibule à Leucippe, Lettres à Eugénie* and *Le Vrai Sens du Système de la nature* (a digest of d'Holbach's most celebrated work attributed to Helvétius) accounted for 337 more. The only other major materialist authors to achieve even moderate STN sales were Helvétius and La Mettrie. Helvétius' *Œuvres complètes* notched up 311 sales with *De L'Homme* close behind on 233 and *De L'Esprit* on sixty-six. The STN sold 155 copies of La Mettrie's *Œuvres* and four copies of his *L'Homme machine*. Fréret's *Œuvres* also sold a respectable 114 copies. Thus, once the one-time pirated house author d'Holbach is removed from the equation, atheist works only accounted for one in four hundred books sold by the STN. Nevertheless, these initial bibliometric soundings suggest that materialism, and particularly the d'Holbach corpus and the secularization narrative of which it forms a part, need to be taken seriously. Their impact among a sceptical intellectual elite and upon careerist Christian apologists deserves serious consideration in any mainstream intellectual history of the Enlightenment.

Yet doubts remain about the extent and meaning of the dissemination patterns these figures reveal. What was the real penetration of these atheist works, compared to, say apologetic works or general religious literature? Unfortunately, the STN database cannot really help us to answer such questions, because as a Protestant publishing house in a Protestant Swiss canton it traded only a handful of Catholic religious books. To be sure, the STN entered the lists on both sides of the materialist debate, publishing and selling significant volumes of a range of refutations of d'Holbach. These included the Protestant Georg-Jonathan Holland's *Réflexions philosophiques sur le Système de la nature* and Giovanni Francesco Mauro Melchior Salvemini da Castiglione's *Observations sur le livre intitulé Système de la nature*; as well as the deist Voltaire's *Dieu*.[60] They also sold anti-materialist novels, again regardless of the confessional loyalty of their authors, though in much smaller numbers. One-hundred twenty copies of the Genevan Protestant pastor Jacob Vernes's *Confidence philosophique* were matched by forty-two copies of abbé Augustin Barruel's *Les Helviennes*.[61]

However, very few copies of bestselling French devotional or pious works ever passed through the STN's magazines. They sold just fifty-eight copies of *L'Imitation de Jésus Christ* and just a handful of such Counter-Reformation devotional classics as the Jesuit Jacques Coret's *L'Ange conducteur* – a work which Michel Vernus claims ran to five hundred editions or reprints between 1683 and the late nineteenth century – or Bouhours and Clément's *Journée du Chrétien*, which was possibly more popular still.[62] The vast majority of the STN's religious book sales were for Protestant books sold to the famed Protestant arc. So if we are to assess and contextualize the scale of the Catholic religious market, we need to look elsewhere. As a starting point, we might compare the trade of a well-established provincial dealer in banned books with that of a specialist in religious works in a city like Besançon. There, in the 1770s and 1780s, two brothers plied these different sections of the trade. The purveyor of religious literature was Jean-Félix Charmet. The specialist in illegal books was our old friend Charles-Antoine.

According to Robert Darnton's account, Charles-Antoine Charmet and his wife vied with their rival Dominique Lépagnez *cadet* to be the biggest book dealers in Besançon.[63] As we have noted, he contends that by following their trade with the STN month after month, year after year, we can understand the wider book trade in the town and their province.[64] Such a view is open to challenge, not least because beyond his STN dossier, Charmet has left little trace of his activities. He does not seem to have published any sales catalogues and does not appear in standard modern reference sources. He did, however, run a *cabinet de lecture* [subscription reading rooms] and publish several editions.[65] Those we can definitely link to him include Jean Baptiste d'Auxiron, *Observations sur les jurisdictions anciennes et modernes de la ville de Besançon* published 'à Besançon, Chez Charmet, libraire, grand'rue, 1777' and a couple of military ordinances from the previous year, which give his address as 'Grand'rue, près la Place Saint Pierre'. He can be identified as probable or certain publisher for nine further secular works, although the online library records for several bear the ambiguous (and probably abbreviated) imprint details 'Besançon, Charmet'. They include three further military ordonnances published between 1776 and 1778 and a series of panegyrics by the abbé François Xavier Talbert published in 1777.[66] They also include a medical thesis and a lecture by the journalist–pamphleteer Claude-François-Adrien Lézay de Marnézia to the Academy de Besançon entitled *Essai sur la minéralogie du bailliage d'Orgelet, en Franche-Comté* (1777). A final work, the second edition of Philippe Bertrand's *Lettre à M. le comte de Buffon: Ou critique et nouvel essai sur la théorie générale de la terre* bears the date 1782. Works such as these generally had print runs of around 500 to 750 copies: this reflected the limited, and often merely local, interest they aroused. They are unlikely to have made Charles-Antoine rich.[67] However, it is not entirely clear that they were all his outputs, since his brother Jean-Félix also appears to have used the 'Besançon, Charmet' imprint.

What we know of Charles-Antoine's business raises the possibility that his correspondence with the STN exaggerates his success. A survey of the publishing trade in 1764 reveals that he had recently gone bankrupt, and in 1770 to 1772, when he first corresponded with the STN, he contemplated moving to Neuchâtel to work for them.[68] Moreover, on 11 August 1778, when Modeste Monnot, *Inspecteur de la librairie*, and his adjunct, the bookseller Nicolas-Anne de Sainte-Agathe, visited Charmet's shop seeking to legalize counterfeit works, he declared only thirty-two copies of six titles. All six were secular works. They included Pierre Baume's four volume *Chimie expérimentale*; the abbé Roger de Schabol's *La Pratique du jardinage*; and slightly more controversially, eight copies of the STN's edition of Brydone's *Voyage en Sicile et à Malthe*.[69] Charmet thus presented significantly less copies for stamping than any other bookseller in Besançon. Indeed, the majority declared at least 100 times as many (see Appendix 3.23). The *estampillage* evidence also hints at slow turnover, since the STN had not sent him copies of Brydone's *Voyage* since July 1776. Nevertheless, there were probably few other works sourced from the STN in his shop at the time of the inspection. In the year to August 1778, the STN only sent Charmet twenty-five sets of William Robertson's *Histoire d'Amérique* and twenty copies of a *Fragment sur les colonies* by Adam Smith, a work extracted from the *Wealth of Nations*.[70]

While Charles-Antoine Charmet's business appears to have been relatively stable during the years he corresponded with the STN, it seems unlikely that he was really the biggest dealer in Besançon. That accolade may instead belong to his younger brother, Jean-Félix Charmet, the holder of a coveted printer's licence and a position as printer to the Archbishop of Besançon. The books Jean-Félix presented for stamping were very different in nature to those declared by his older sibling and far more numerous. In total, the inspectors stamped 7,150 books on his premises.

The Charmet brothers may have colluded to dominate the Besançon trade by specializing in different market sectors. Certainly they had a history of working closely together – so closely that scholarship published prior to 2016 consistently confused their identities.[71] In the wake of Charles-Antoine's bankruptcy in the late 1760s and early 1770s, the brothers formed a family partnership under the name *Charmet frères et sœurs*, describing themselves as *imprimeurs* and *papetiers* and publishing a number of editions.[72] It was as a representative of this partnership that Charles-Antoine and Jean-Félix first corresponded with the STN, signing their names as Charmet *l'aîné* and Charmet *cadet* respectively. However, in the mid-1770s the brothers dissolved the partnership, and Charles-Antoine started signing his letters 'Charmet, *libraire*', thus distinguishing himself from Jean-Félix Charmet, *imprimeur*. Nevertheless, both seem to have used the imprint 'Besançon: Charmet'. There can be little doubt that it was the printer to the Archbishop of Besançon, Jean-Félix, who published the *Instructions chrétiennes pour les jeunes gens ... corrigées de nouveau & réimprimées par ordre de Monseigneur l'Archevêque de Besançon* (Besançon: Charmet 1774). He was also the only brother to apply for publishing licences under the *permission simple* legislation. Both they and the *estampillage* records testify to his specialism in religious works.

The 7,150 pirated books Jean-Félix Charmet presented for stamping to Inspector Monnot and his adjunct Monsieur de Sainte-Agathe on 7 September 1778 and succeeding days were all religious.[73] In fact, they comprised just three editions of two familiar titles, both popular devotional manuals. There were 1,875 copies of a single edition of *La Journée du chrétien* and a staggering 5,250 copies of in-12° and in-18° editions of *L'Ange conducteur*, a work whose distinctive characteristic was the prayers to the believer's guardian angel which accompanied each office. All three editions had been published recently by Jean-Félix himself, but both works are unfamiliar territory to most historians of the Enlightenment. Their presence in such numbers gives an indication of the scale of the religious book trade. The works Jean-Félix had stamped in 1778 exceed by volume the STN's entire trade with his brother Charles-Antoine and the latter's widow over almost two decades. The print runs of these three editions alone may also have exceeded those for all thirteen editions we have tentatively linked to Charles-Antoine. In terms of sales volumes, religious books were clearly big business.

But how big? To answer that question, we might begin by reconstructing Jean-Félix Charmet's business in more detail. Fortunately, we can do this through Worldcat and the registers of the *permissions simples*. From Worldcat we learn that Charmet published an octavo volume of *Instructions familières en forme de catéchisme sur les preuves de la religion* in 1778; an edition of Gonnelieu's much-admired translation of Thomas à Kempis, *L'Imitation de Jésus-Christ* in 1784; and, in the same year Paul Signieri's *Considérations chrétiennes pour tous les jours de la semaine*. He also published an *Instruction pastorale ... pour le Carême de 1773*; *Instructions familières en forme de catéchisme sur les preuves de la religion* (Besançon: F. Charmet [sic!], 1778), and at least one edition of the abbé Claude-François Nonnotte's, *Dictionnaire philosophique de la religion, où l'on établit tous les points de la religion, attaqués par les incrédules, & où l'on répond à toutes leurs objections* (4 vols.) (1774).

The available evidence suggests editions of religious material tended to be produced in larger print runs but have much lower survival rates than secular works. The registers of licensed *permissions simples* further testify to Jean-Félix Charmet's commitment to religious printing. In total, he applied for nine *permissions simples* between 1779 and 1783: all were for religious texts. Besides two further editions of the *Ange conducteur* in April 1779, he applied to print *Le Chemin du Ciel* (1779); *Considérations chrétiennes en forme de méditations pendant tous les jours du mois* (1779); *Histoire de la sainte jeunesse de notre seigneur Jésus Christ* (1779); Gonnelieu's popular translation of *L'Imitation de Jésus Christ avec une pratique de prières* (1779); Pierre Humbert's *Pensées sur les plus importantes vérités de la religion et sur les principaux devoirs du christianisme* (1783); *Instructions abrégées sur les devoirs et les exercices du chrétien* (1783) and, almost inevitably, yet another edition of *La Journée du chrétien* (1779).[74] If he followed all these *permissions* to the letter, Jean-Félix Charmet would have printed 23,500 copies of these nine editions, yet only one, a Besançon edition of Pierre Humbert's *Pensées sur les plus importantes vérités de la religion* has been tentatively identified through Worldcat.[75]

The implication is clear. Cheap editions of popular pious works are rarely preserved in major research collections. In contrast almost every identifiable title and edition of *novelesque* works in the FBTEE database survives. Nevertheless, across the period 1771–84, at least seven editions of religious works in Worldcat can be directly attributed to Jean-Félix Charmet.[76] In all probability, they are indicative of many more religious editions which have not come down to us. In contrast, the only non-religious works we can definitely attribute to Jean-Félix Charmet are a pamphlet arising from a dispute between ecclesiastics; a textbook history of Burgundy, and an award-winning scientific lecture.[77]

Two main conclusions can be drawn from our tale of two Charmets. First, Robert Darnton's confidence that we can gain 'a reliable view of the book trade' by studying the orders in the dossiers of dealers like Charles-Antoine Charmet in the STN's archives was misplaced.[78] International publishers such as the STN only catered for a small specialized segment of the Besançon market. The same is true of similar dealers in other towns, including Letourmy, the most prosperous dealer in Orléans, whose STN orders, according to Darnton, 'can be taken to represent the demand for literature in Orléans as he understood it'.[79] The work of Gaël Rideau on Orléans will inventories has shown that even elite library owners there left substantial bequests of religious books. They comprised 38 per cent of books bequeathed by merchants, 33 per cent of 'bourgeois' libraries, 32 per cent of 'officiers' libraries, and 29 per cent of those of nobles.[80] Yet Letourmy's religious orders to the STN comprised only three *Bibles*, a couple of Protestant liturgies, ten sermons and two Psalters from a total of 1,142 books requested.[81] If this was Letourmy's understanding of demand, he knew little of his customers' religious tastes!

Subsequent to my previous critiques, Darnton, too, now seems to have concluded that dealers' orders to the STN only give us limited insights. His 2018 monograph *A Literary Tour de France*, which appeared as I was correcting the proofs of this book, continues to insist that his tables of the most frequently ordered STN books 'provide the best available guide to the preferences among the French for the literature that was available to them in bookshops'.[82] However, he now (re)defines 'literature' in narrow terms: 'What the STN sold was *literature*. It was an omnibus term covering many genres, but generally did not apply to what many small bookshops stocked .... mainly devotional works and tracts related to local affairs.'[83] Where formerly he argued that Charmet's STN dossiers could give 'a reliable view of the book trade' in its entirety, without caveats about genre or types of book, he now insists only that the STN archive can give us a view of the trade in the sorts of books that the STN actually sold. These, as has now been clarified, did not include Catholic religious books and many other of the most popular genres sold by dealers such as Charles-Antoine Charmet's brother Jean-Félix.

The question remains, however, was Jean-Félix Charmet typical of the trade? The wider example of Besançon suggests that he was. As the book police continued their tour of inspection, they discovered that an astonishing 90 per cent of all pirated books declared there were religious works. A third of them were *Anges conducteurs*, a work which most Besançon booksellers held by the thousand in multiple editions. In total, on their tour of inspection in August and September 1778 the book inspectors stamped 18,730 copies of this work (see Appendix 3.23).[84] This in a town of 32,000 souls serving a provincial hinterland, the Franche-Comté, of perhaps 800,000. Moreover, Besançon printers continued to pump out copies of popular religious works thousand upon thousand, year after year.[85] Foremost among them remained *L'Ange conducteur*. Between April 1779 and May 1788 Besançon printers, including Charmet, were licensed to print no less than 18,000 copies under the new *permission simple* licence.[86] In total, then, we can trace 36,700 copies of *L'Ange conducteur* passing through the hands of Besançon booksellers in the decade prior to the Revolution.

Furthermore, these copies are just the ones that remain visible to us. Our only surviving weekly inspection report for the Besançon *Chambre syndicale* suggests that many thousands more entered the city from elsewhere. It records that in the week of 24 August 1779 alone, *veuve* Tissot and Messieurs Sainte-Agathe, Bertrand, Faivre and Girard all received sizeable deliveries of *Anges conducteurs* from Bruyères, where the *veuve* Vivot produced devotional manuals on an industrial scale.[87] All these booksellers also received a selection of further religious titles: *L'Ange à table*; *Instructions de la jeunesse*; and *Office de l'église*.[88] In the same week, Madame Bertrand received four further crates of *Anges conducteurs* from Vesoul, together with further copies in a 'caisse' of religious works sent from Paris.[89] How many more, then, would be visible if the inspection reports for the rest of the decade had come down to us?

The *permission simple* registers offer further hints of a thriving religious trade. Although Jean-Félix Charmet's *confrères* in Besançon only applied for ten *permissions simples* for works other than the *Ange conducteur*, nine of them were for religious works, including several perennial bestsellers. Couché received a *permission* to print 3,000 copies of the *Journée du Chrétien* in November 1781 and in April 1786 Métoyer applied for another for 1,000. The *missionaires de la diocèse de Besançon* were given permission to publish a staggering 10,000 copies of *Pensées sur les plus importantes vérités de la religion et sur les principaux devoirs du Christianisme* on 20 July 1780. Charmet, too, sought permissions for both these bestselling works. Likewise, in August 1786, Simard [Simart] was granted a licence to print 2,000 copies of *Instructions chrétiennes pour les jeunes gens*, and in May 1788 *veuve* Bertrand was authorized to print 1,500 more. The *permission simple* records suggest that this, too, was a perennial bestseller.

However, some religious works for which Besançon publishers were granted *permissions simples* were reissued rather less frequently. They include the *Ferventes aspirations à Dieu: recueillies de l'écriture et des Saints Pères*. Jean Bertrand was licensed to print 3,000 copies in September 1781. Likewise Daclin applied to print 2,000 copies of the Jesuit Charles-Joseph Perrin's *Sermons choisis du révérend P.P.* in November 1779 and in April 1782 Bertrand was authorized to produce 2,000 copies of Alfonso Maria de' Liguori's *Visite au saint sacrement et à la sainte vierge*. Finally, Charles Lepagnez l'aîné, the brother of Charles-Antoine Charmet's great rival-*cum*-collaborator, was in October 1786 granted permission to print 1,500 copies of *Jésus Christ, le modèle des chrétiens*. This was a relatively modest print run for a religious work, but still three times that for the sole secular edition licensed to a Besançon printer under the *Permission simple* legislation, Métoyer's edition of François-Ignace Dunod de Charnage's legal treatise, *Traités de la main-morte et des retraits*.[90]

Nor was Besançon the sole supplier of religious works to the Franche-Comté. In 1781, the will inventory of the Dôle printer–bookseller Pierre-François Tonnet listed 15,679 copies of just five *livres de piété*, including an astonishing 7,000 *Ange conducteurs*.[91] In Vesoul, the printer Poirson had no less than 6,576 of the same work in September 1778.[02] Clearly the Franche-Comté was inundated with this book, which sold strongly wherever in France it enjoyed diocesan approval. In Amiens, for example, Charles Caron declared copies of twelve different editions of the *Ange conducteur* to book trade inspectors for stamping.[93]

Demand for *L'Ange conducteur* was driven by the laity. Under the *ancien régime* it was a favoured work among *colporteurs* across much of the kingdom.[94] In 1807, a survey of clergymen in the diocese of Metz suggests that lay readers bought the bulk of copies sold.[95] Our circulation data for *L'Ange conducteur* confirms that this phenomenon predates the Revolution. For although our sources are very incomplete, the available records supply glimpses of over 50,000 copies circulating in the Franche-Comté between 1778 and 1789. The *Chambre syndicale* records hint that in reality two to three times that number may have been circulating. This is highly significant. Inventory surveys of the Franche-Comté indicate that 6 per cent of the province's approximately 700,000 peasants left books and 80 per cent of those owned religious books.[96] This would suggest that there were in the region of 35,000 peasant owners of religious books. Yet *L'Ange conducteur* alone was present in the province in far greater numbers than that. Ownership undoubtedly extended well beyond the province's estimated 10,000 'educated citizens'. The will inventory evidence appears to grossly underestimate the social penetration of *L'Ange conducteur*. By the 1780s it may have permeated a majority of *Franche-Comtois* households.

Not for the first time, therefore, it is necessary to ask why previous surveys of book circulation seem to have produced such wayward results? Why, in particular, does the will inventory evidence so understate the prevalence of religious books? One hypothesis must be that religious books evaded notice – perhaps they were seen as family property and so often not recorded. Perhaps, because of their small format they tended to be spirited away or overlooked? Moreover, most pious or devotional works were mass-produced in cheap editions so quickly became worn. The compilers of inventories probably felt that they had no commercial value and thus did not need to be recorded. Conversely, sales volumes may have been inflated because flimsy *livres de piété* were habitually replaced when they eventually fell apart with overuse. Yet all these hypotheses tend to the conclusion that these spiritual works were used, cherished, and, more literally than many other books, consumed, in far greater numbers than any others. The most common and commonly pored-over books of the Enlightenment era were religious works.

Reduced to purely statistical terms, enlightened scepticism had made little inroad into a rapidly expanding popular market for religious works. They remained the dominant sector of the book trade by volume, and the books that performed best in the marketplace were traditional titles, traditional devotional forms – Thomas à Kempis' *L'Imitation de Jésus Christ*, books of hours and long-cherished devotional manuals such as the *Ange Conducteur* and the *Journée du chrétien*, works whose regional sales patterns nevertheless reflect their adoption at diocesan level. There had been a major shift in religious publishing and reading across the century-and-a-half before the Revolution, one that cannot be adequately measured by the means and methods of previous studies, or by edition counts in collective library databases, or indeed through the STN database. For the new religious publishing comprised cheap and ultimately disposable editions of established works that eventually decayed through use and wear. Such works cannot be detected in bibliographical guides organized around date of first publication and they did not show up among the new titles on offer at the Frankfurt book fair, nor travel down the arterial networks of the international booktrade. They were produced, like school books, in large editions, primarily to feed local demand. By the late eighteenth century, the Catholic populations of France and, it seems, Northern Europe more generally, were consuming religious works in industrial quantities, possibly in greater numbers than their Protestant co-religionists in the more latitudinarian societies of Britain, the Netherlands and Northern Germany.

Since the work of François Furet and his collaborators, few commentators have doubted that religious books and works of local interest were the mainstay of French provincial publishing.[97] What is at issue here is the scale of production and social penetration of religious products. Both significantly outstrip findings of previous historians, and may require us to substantially recalibrate our estimates of both the total supply of books in the French market and the extent of the French readership and its engagement with religious texts.

Viewed in this light, the d'Holbach corpus looks truly marginal to the concerns of most French readers, and the 122 book and pamphlet responses to it smack of a mixture of cynical careerism and heartfelt moral panic. In retrospect, viewed through the prism of the 1793–94 dechristianization and the Republican secularizing campaigns of the nineteenth century, the d'Holbachean moment would acquire new lustre, as evidence of a deeply sceptical religious climate that inspired the revolutionary campaigns against the Church and provided the fanaticism to drive them forward. The bibliometric historical evidence seems to point in the opposite direction, hinting that revolutionary dechristianization was born of the politics of polarization, a desperate last-ditch response by *enragé* extremists to clerically inspired religious opposition to the politics of the Convention during the Terror.[98] To be sure, the revolutionary dechristianizing movement drew on d'Holbachean ideas, and found fertile soil among some of the readers of the radical political works described in the following chapter. Yet for all the sound and thunder they provoked, materialist ideologies had less prominence in the cultural mainstream before 1789 than subsequent events would seem to imply.[99] Prior to the Revolution, a book-based Catholicism drove demand for a panoply of religious related texts, ranging from religious histories and polemical defences of faith through to saints' lives, catechisms and works of moral instruction.[100] But it was devotional and liturgical works, for use in both public and private devotions, that remained 'top of the pops'. In the century of the reading revolution, the dominant way of reading remained deep engagement and intensely devotional in purpose. Rather than gliding fluidly from text to text, Enlightenment-era religious readers remained static on their knees. As late as 1785 there was no reason to believe that was that was about to change any time soon.

This leaves us with one last question. If materialist and desacralizing works were so marginal to the market in unit terms, why were they so prized by the STN's French bookseller clients? We know that after 1777 the STN's illegal trade centred only on marginal men such as Mauvelain in Troyes and Malherbe in Loudun, who conducted a niche trade in clandestine 'philosophic' literature far from the metropolis. But before 1777, some established licensed booksellers in significant centres, men like Charles-Antoine Charmet in Besançon, also stressed how important these works were to their trade. Yet it is now clear that in simple unit terms these '*livres philosophiques*' were actually marginal to their businesses. Even if we allow for price differentials and higher profit margins on illegal books, they cannot have made a majority contribution to the bottom line. Indeed, the majority of provincial booksellers and printer-booksellers preferred to earn their 'bread and butter' in the same way as Charles-Antoine Charmet's younger brother, Jean-Félix, by concentrating on popular religious fare and diocesan liturgical works. These sold steadily, and generally safely, in vast numbers. By contrast, illegal books were frequently confiscated and those who dealt in them could face serious penalties.[101]

So why were so many booksellers so willing to run the risks associated with 'philosophic works', and why did they insist they needed them so much? This is a conundrum to which the available evidence does not offer a direct answer. Hence it is best tackled using the deductive method of Sherlock Holmes and eliminating all other possible factors to arrive at the truth. We know that these books were not prized primarily for their sales volume or their value to the bottom line, so why else might they be commercially important? Phrased thus, the question permits an obvious solution. They must have helped attract a certain sort of valued business. Presumably they helped to entice what would today be called 'high net worth customers', individuals who were likely to make repeated high-value purchases. In eighteenth-century terms, this means highly cultured, well-educated members of the local aristocracy, clergy and business elites, who read fashionably and widely and bought books to display their fashionable erudition and wealth. The same customers who bought the latest materialist works of d'Holbach's coterie would also be likely to buy the *Encyclopédie*, the thirty-volume Saillant et Nyon edition of Velly's *Histoire de France depuis l'établissement de la monarchie jusqu'au règne de Louis XIV*, or return to make repeat purchases of the latest *nouveautés* or lavishly illustrated scientific compendia. Snaring a handful of such customers would likely bring in significantly more money than many hundreds of pious readers making once-a-decade replacement purchases for the tatty, dog-eared, intensively read *livres de piété* disintegrating on their tiny, cottage-shelf libraries.

In order to secure the loyalty of such 'high net worth' customers, booksellers needed to ensure that they had the full range of fashionable and Enlightenment fare, from innocuous popular novels to hardcore *philosophie* and salacious *livres philosophiques*. Yet a well-diversified, stable business needed both sorts of customers, especially since *livres de piété* sold more regularly and occasionally attracted bulk purchases from schools, diocesan authorities, individual churches, monastic communities and other religious institutions. Such an analysis implies a two-tier model of the eighteenth-century French book trade, in which an extensive market for traditional reading and especially religious books coexisted alongside a much more limited but high-value trade in non-religious fare, including Enlightenment works. Unfortunately for our purposes, the STN generally exported religious fare to only a few Protestant towns in France – notably Nîmes, Ganges, La Rochelle and Rochefort – and most of that trade was necessarily clandestine. The STN's correspondence and business ledgers are at best revelatory of only one tier of the trade and thus provide few insights into the 'bread and butter' trade in Roman Catholic religious books inside France. This traditional trade was greater in extent and had deeper social penetration than has been hitherto realized. Despite more than two generations of *philosophe* propaganda, the French of the late *ancien régime* were – to a hitherto undocumented degree – a 'people of the book' in both meanings of the word.

11

From Swiss Politics to Revolutionary History

Religiously sceptical works were marginal to Charles-Antoine Charmet and his wife's trade with the STN. Political works were something else entirely. The six works the Charmet's took in greatest numbers all related to France's Genevan-born finance minister Necker and the fiscal debates he provoked; their favourite scandalous political fare was the *Anecdotes sur Madame la comtesse du Barri* (ninety sales) and the *Vie privée de Louis XV* (fifty-two sales). Both sets of works have been linked to the origins of the Revolution. Necker's financial pamphlets not only covered up the looming financial crisis, creating a false confidence in French government stocks, but also, paradoxically, were part of a progressive opening of royal affairs to public scrutiny. What had once been 'the King's Secret' was now public knowledge, his 'dirty laundry' open to public scrutiny and interpretation. Meanwhile, according to Darnton, scandalous pamphlets (*libelles*) about Louis XV and his final mistress became part of a proto-revolutionary political mythmaking that depicted the monarchy as decadent, sexually corrupt and inherently despotic. Moreover, the literary stratagems developed by the *libelle* genre fuelled the development of a politics of personal denigration that reached fruition in the internecine politics of the Terror. Pamphlet broadsides were a key arm of political trench-fighting, used with devastating effect to denounce, discredit and destroy political opponents with smears and allegations of financial and political corruption.[1] Increased transparency combined with political slanders may link to wider political developments. The heyday of the STN, the 1770s and 1780s, has been depicted by Israel as the key decades in which monarchic reformism became discredited and radical Enlightenment ideas began to spread beyond narrow intellectual elites to gain popular and political traction. Nevertheless, many leading authorities remain unconvinced by his attempts to link radical religious sceptics such as d'Holbach to political radicalism.[2] Nor is it clear how much currency radical ideas had beyond a narrow, sceptical, educated elite.

What does seem undeniable, however, is that political works were central to the Enlightenment as generally conceived, certainly in bibliometric terms. Indeed, as Gary Kates and his students at Pomona College have shown, across the eighteenth century and Europe as a whole, a couple of them may have achieved comparable edition counts, if not print runs, to *L'Ange conducteur* or *Comptes faits*.[3] Kates and his students undertook edition counts through Worldcat for fifty leading Enlightenment titles.[4] One work stood out, with some 450 editions across all major languages across the century. That work was Fénélon's *Telemarchus*, a didactic tale of princely education which advocated for constitutional monarchy tempered by a strong aristocratic element. It was first published in 1699, strongly influenced Montesquieu and sold consistently across the century. The only other work that scored remotely close to this total was another political novel, Madame de Graffigny's *Les Péruviennes*, with 282 editions. Five other works broke the one hundred edition barrier: Montesquieu's 'big three', that is to say *L'Esprit des Lois*, the *Lettres persanes* and the *Considérations sur le grandeur et décadence des romains*, plus Robertson's *History of Charles V* and Voltaire's *Histoire de Charles XII*, which at 148 editions was the third-ranked work in the survey. The *Social Contract*, *Emile* and *La Pucelle* all broke the seventy barrier to make the top ten, Raynal's *Histoire philosophique des Deux-Indes* notched up fifty-seven editions and Smith's *Wealth of Nations* thirty-nine.

Kates cautions against taking these figures as definitive – but it seems probable that they are broadly indicative. It is unlikely, for example, that many editions escaped Worldcat: FBTEE's researchers have discovered it contains over 99 per cent of the editions of novels or Enlightenment classics that we have encountered in our sources. We can safely conclude then that across Europe as a whole a handful of well-known Enlightenment works circulated in large numbers, although the edition count and print-run evidence suggests that their French circulations were probably only one tenth to one fifth those of the most popular religious bestsellers identified in the last chapter.[5] Tellingly, Kates' bestselling Enlightenment classics were overwhelmingly political in nature – political novels, political histories, political theory, political satire. They were works – if we except Raynal – that belonged overwhelmingly to what Jonathan Israel dismissively labels the 'moderate enlightenment'. On the level of bestsellers, it looks as if Annalien de Dijn's myth-busting was justified – the Enlightenment was politically focused, but it was moderate, urbane and, to judge from the prevalence of Fénélon and Montesquieu, enthralled by the possibilities of liberal monarchy.

The purpose of this chapter is to broaden our view 'on the ground' by asking what politics looks like when viewed through the lens of the STN? Above all, what did politics mean to their readers, who mostly lived in states where political participation was, at best, limited? Similar questions have been asked through studies of newspapers and the public sphere, or certain forms of pamphlets (including ephemeral pamphlets of sorts not generally those sold by the STN), but they have been less commonly asked of books, still less those spanning an entire literary field.[6] The shape of the STN's trade may thus give us important insights into how readers were introduced and related to political ideas in the twenty years before the French Revolution. Were readers interested in political theory; politics as biography; international relations; single issues? How parochial were their political interests? How detailed was their knowledge – did they read as insiders or outsiders to the political process? And how far were they exposed and receptive to dreams of change?

In the 1770s and early 1780s, the STN operated against the background of the continuing political turmoil in nearby Geneva. Moreover, the STN's own foundation in 1768 followed hard on the heels of major rioting in Neuchâtel itself against Prussian fiscal reforms, events in which the STN director, Frédéric-Samuel Ostervald, in his role as *banneret*, had played a leading and successful role. The reforms were abandoned.[7] Thus, whereas religious conservatism probably inhibited the STN from pushing further atheistical works after their ill-starred experiment publishing the *Système de la nature*, the logic of their position encouraged them to dabble in political tracts relating to Genevan factional politics, French political scandal and financial polemics. All three issues had, in different ways, a topical interest in Switzerland as well as France. They were inescapable for the STN. Perhaps it is not surprising, therefore, that the political pamphlet that the STN produced and distributed in greater quantities than any other intertwined Swiss, French and international politics. Like many pamphlets, it concerned a single, decisive political incident, and was commissioned by some of its central protagonists: Genevan patriots. The incident was the patriots' capitulation to forces besieging their city in July 1782. Decisions made at that moment would shape the lives of those patriots, and the political life of both Geneva and France, for many years to come. Here is how events unfolded.

Two hours after midnight on Tuesday 2 July 1782, the leaders of Geneva's democratic *représentant* party sent a response to the ultimatums of the French, Sardinian and Bernese generals encamped under their battlements. This final Declaration announced the intentions of the Genevans 'non à se soumettre, mais à céder aux conditions qui leur sont imposées par la contrainte, quelque dures qu'elles soient'.[8] Those conditions included the temporary occupation of their city by the allied powers; the release of imprisoned *négatif* leaders of the Council of Two-Hundred who had resisted *représentant* demands for even a tokenistic extension of the franchise; full restoration of Geneva's former oligarchic forms of government; and the exile of some twenty-one named persons. While relatively lenient to the rebel leaders, who would be allowed to leave the city in peace, these terms in every other sense represented total capitulation. They had been forced upon the Genevans by the poor state of the city's arsenal and defences and the overwhelming force ranged against them (the army camped at their gates was larger than the city's entire male population). Acquiescing to the allied conditions was the only realistic option open to the patriots if they wished 'épargner l'effusion du sang de tant d'hommes vertueux qui succcomberoient sur les ruines de leur Patrie'.[9]

Nevertheless, the Declaration was more than a surrender note. It was also a self-justification, manifesto and clarion call for the right of self-determination. Designed for a wider political audience, it also requested grace for all Genevans to be allowed to leave the city unmolested, explaining:

> ne pouvant plus envisager comme leur Patrie une Ville dont les meilleurs Citoyens sont forcés de s'éloigner, une Ville occupée par des troupes étrangères, dont les Loix cesseront d'être l'effet de la volunté libre de la pluralité de ses Citoyens, & dont le Gouvernement sera désormais entre les mains d'hommes pour lesquels ils ne pourront jamais avoir ni estime ni confiance, ils iront chercher sous un autre Ciel une terre où ils puissant respirer en paix l'air pur de la liberté.

With the death of Geneva's ancient republic, the Declaration aligned the patriots' cause with a more universal aspiration for freedom and self-determination.

As soon as the Declaration was sent, the *négatif* leaders were released and the gates of the city flung open for those wishing to leave. Significant numbers did so, and many *représentant* leaders fled to Neuchâtel. There they published their Declaration. It is the final document in a twenty-seven-page pamphlet entitled *Pièces importantes à la dernière révolution de Genève*, which the STN published and began distributing within weeks of Geneva's capitulation.

Despite its commercial significance – in terms of circulation at least – from a modern perspective the *Pièces importantes* appears curiously anodyne. It is merely a selection of documents with virtually no accompanying commentary except a handful of explanatory footnotes. As with ancien régime newspapers, readers were expected to make sense for themselves of the various documents it contained – the allied ultimatums, the Genevan responses, a deliberation on the poor state of Geneva's defences, and finally the 'Declaration' itself. Despite its propagandist and self-justificatory purposes, the pamphlet presents its political narrative through the documentary record rather than editorial comment. Moreover, although it used democratic language, it required of its readers significant prior knowledge and sophisticated critical tools, suggesting that its main audience was primarily to be found in the Swiss Romande, and perhaps also among Europe's *francophone* elite. The distribution pattern for the pamphlet, which was probably at least partially subsidized by leading *représentant* politicians, supports such a conclusion.[10]

That such a work should be the most highly disseminated of the STN's political pamphlets is revealing. It reinforces the view that most political pamphleteering was conducted locally, often clandestinely and in haste, frequently subsidized by authors and political factions. Particularly when taken in combination with the evidence on illegal pamphleteering presented above (Chapter 9), it is clear that much pamphleteering activity took place beyond the long-distance commercial circuits of the international book trade. Genevan patriot propaganda features in the STN's registers primarily because Neuchâtel offered the nearest safe haven for *représentant* refugees. The Prussian-ruled principality was the most convenient asylum from which they could publish their *apologia*.

Conversely, this analysis reconfirms that significant areas of pamphleteering are likely to have left few traces in the STN archive. Beyond the scandalous works of the 'Mairobert corpus', which aroused interest around Europe, few pamphlets relating to the French *parlements* passed through the STN's *magasin*. Nor, according to the surviving archival record, did they trade a single pamphlet concerning the Diamond Necklace Affair before the Revolution; and there is only one copy of one pamphlet relating to the notorious Kornmann affair.[11] Yet all these issues were well-represented among the confiscated titles found in the Bastille's secret *dépôt*.[12] The STN's political bestsellers might therefore be expected to include mainly works which commanded Swiss local interest or international appeal – whether genuinely political or primarily salacious – sufficiently enduring to justify production and distribution from Switzerland. Such works were far from the entire range of francophone political pamphlets circulating at the time.

Yet in hindsight, there are also significant international dimensions to the *Pièces importantes*, particularly the identities of the proscribed *représentant* activists listed within it. Several of these individuals would play prominent roles in French pamphleteering and political life both before and during the Revolution. Most notable among them are the financier-*cum*-politician Etienne Clavière, who in the 1780s bankrolled the propaganda campaigns of Brissot and Mirabeau – both of whom had STN connections – before becoming finance minister in the revolutionary Girondin ministry. Clavière's role as a Deus ex machina in pre-revolutionary agitation was perhaps no less significant than his political role after 1789. For several of Brissot and Mirabeau's pre-revolutionary pamphlets targeted state-financed economic initiatives, suggesting that Clavière systematically sought to undermine confidence in the Bourbon administration and finances.[13] In this Clavière, Mirabeau and Brissot were abetted by two other Genevan refugee scribblers, Etienne Dumont and Jacques-Antoine Duroveray.[14] Such connections illustrate, at the very least, important continuities between pre-revolutionary and revolutionary pamphleteering spanning personnel, patronage and performance. Similar connections and continuities are also evident in the celebrated Le Maître affair of 1786, which implicated several government ministers and much of France's power elite in the *parlementaire* pamphleteering campaigns of the previous twenty years.[15] Yet much of this activity was internal to France, and the pamphlets concerned rarely, if ever, found their way to the STN's warehouse. So what – given these caveats – can the range and nature of the political works encountered in the STN's trade records indicate?

Political works – defined in the STN database as those 'that cover the political life, administration, organization and/or relationships between one or more human societies etc. in theory or practice, including contemporary history and the conduct of "Current affairs"' – were of major interest to the STN's customers.[16] Altogether they account for some 72,248 copies of 477 political titles, that is to say 17.5 per cent of the books the STN distributed. Those they circulated in greatest numbers included the *Pièces importantes* (7,953 copies); Raynal's *Histoire philosophique des Deux Indes* (3,684 copies); Pidansat de Mairobert's *Anecdotes sur du Barri* (1,389 sales) and *Espion anglois* (1,186 sales); Büsching's *Introduction à la connoissance géographique et politique des Etats de l'Europe* (1,133 sales) and numerous pamphlets concerning Necker and French finances.[17]

A separate category of 'Political Fiction' contains twenty-eight further works and accounted for 3,385 'sales' (0.81 per cent of total STN sales). Although that category is statistically marginal, the STN's 'political fiction' includes such classics as Fénelon's *Aventures de Télémaque* (366 sales), Marmontel's *Bélisaire* (258 sales), Montesquieu's *Lettres persanes* (ten sales), the allegorical *Amours de Zéokinizul, Roi des Kofirans* (twenty-five sales), and translated masterpieces including Jonathan Swift's allegorical *Voyages de Gulliver* (thirty-two sales) and Albrecht von Haller's *Usong, histoire orientale* and *Alfred, roi des Anglo-Saxons* (266 and 177 sales respectively). Thus altogether, works that FBTEE has identified as political in content and purpose, that is, those ascribed the keywords 'political fiction' or 'politics', accounted for almost one fifth (18.3 per cent) of books disseminated by the STN. This political literature included many commissioned titles (including – as Appendix 3.24 shows – six of the STN's top twenty political works), but this was not unusual of the political genre. Moreover, the authors of commissioned works included such Enlightenment luminaries as Mably and Brissot, or the celebrated courtier–pamphleteer Lauraguais, as well as less well-known figures such as Louis-Valentin Goëzman or our anonymous Genevan patriots.

A long-established criticism of the French Enlightenment, growing out of the counter-revolutionary tradition, asserts that the *philosophes* offered dangerous and utopian theoretical abstractions to a people inexperienced in practical politics. More recently historians have emphasized the degree to which pre-revolutionary pamphlets and newspapers offered their readers 'coded messages'.[18] The evidence of the STN database suggests that these arguments might be overstated, despite the significance of some major works of political theory in Gary Kates' survey. A breakdown of sales of political works by type suggests that 'political theory' was of much less interest to the STN's customers than 'current affairs', which accounted for the vast bulk of political sales. Works classified as 'Political Theory' clocked up a mere 9,989 global sales compared with 59,663 sales for works concerning 'Current Affairs'.[19] Nor do these relativities change significantly if we only include 'Trade' sales, even though a relatively high proportion of political works were 'Commissioned' titles (30 per cent by volume).[20] It appears, then, that the STN's popular audience was more engaged with day-to-day, bread and butter politics than abstruse political ideas, as suggested by FBTEE's poor sales figures for Rousseau's political works. They were also more interested in heavyweight topics such as 'financial administration' and 'international affairs' than political scandal. Despite the appearance of two key *libelles*, the *Espion Anglois* and the *Anecdotes sur Madame du Barri*, among the STN's political top twenty, works classified as relating to both 'Politics' and 'Scandal' sold only 4,562 copies.

Given the political cataclysm that hit France in 1789, we should also ask how far French pre-revolutionary sales trends differ from the European norm. Certainly 'Trade Sales' to French customers included proportionately more political works than sales to other parts of Europe. That said, in general the STN's customers' political interests were aroused by similar issues and stimuli: annualized trends and fluctuations in political engagement in the STN's main markets were remarkably similar over time. The graph of their 'global', French and Swiss 'Trade' shows that 'sales' of political works peaked in all three in 1770, 1774, 1776–77, 1781, 1786 and 1788 (Chart 11.1). It also reveals that, even if we discount a spike associated with Neckerana in 1781, French customers were ordering proportionately greater quantities of political works in the 1780s than the 1770s. In short, political works held greater appeal to French customers than to readers elsewhere, and that tendency intensified as the Revolution approached. However, these trends do not lend themselves to an easy interpretation. A high proportion of works on 'Politics' sold by the STN dealt with 'France': 33,896 'sales' carry both keywords. The higher sales figures for France may therefore merely indicate a higher topical interest. That would not, however, be the full story. The sales history with regard to political sales to France – as captured by Chart 11.1 below – is complex and nuanced, shaped in part by state interventions and political events.

The biggest surprise in the political sales graph is the trough for the years 1771, 1772 and 1773 during the Maupeou crisis, a period when pro-*parlementaire* agitation and political pamphleteering has been characterized by some historians as a 'dress rehearsal' for the Revolution.[21] Such assertions might lead us to expect a boom in sales of political works. Yet we can find little evidence of *parlementaire* pamphleteering in the STN data. Such pamphleteering, it seems, must have been confined to the internal clandestine Jansenist-*Parlementaire* networks described in police chief Lenoir's

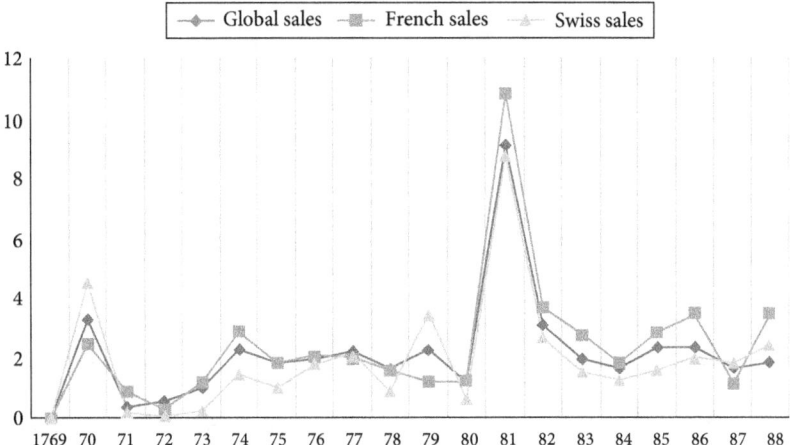

Chart 11.1 STN 'Trade Sales' of political works as a percentage of all STN 'Trade Sales' to France; Switzerland; and All Europe, 1769–88.

memoirs.[22] As Chapter 9 indicated, its products are much more likely to be found listed in the Bastille inventories than the trade ledgers of the cosmopolitan publishing industry. It is possible, too, that this success stemmed from a closing of French borders. We know from the work of Louise Seaward, that the French pursued Morande's *Gazetier cuirassé*, the most outspoken and obscene of the anti-Maupeou pamphlets, with unprecedented rigour both at home and abroad.[23] Jeroom Vercruysse has also shown how French diplomatic complaints were targeted at the Dutch-based French-language gazettes, and my own work has shown the success of such actions in muzzling the press, by excluding references to political agitation and publication of propagandist *parlementaire* declarations from early in the crisis.[24] In such circumstances, we might expect foreign publisher–wholesalers, who relied on French goodwill to circulate many of their products, to behave with circumspection.

Similar circumspection, it seems, was shown by would-be authors of political *libelles* and scandalous works concerning the court. As Chapter 9 highlighted, few such works seem to have circulated concerning royal mistresses in power. Instead they proliferated in the years immediately following a favourite's death or disgrace. This was true of the key scandalous works of the Mairobert corpus, notably the *Anecdotes sur Madame du Barri*, which was published in 1775 following the death of Louis XV and sold in significant numbers in 1776–77 (see Appendix 2.2). However, the market for such works collapsed in France following the decrees of 30 August 1777. An apparent flurry of sales in 1779 merely reflects the STN's desperate dumping unsaleable illegal stock on Malherbe *l'aîne* in Loudun.[25] His opportunistically smuggled consignment of contraband books contained 113 copies of the *Anecdotes*. However, if we ignore this one episode, sales of du Barri *libelles* to France were negligible in 1778–79, and remained relatively low thereafter (see Chart 11.2).

By the early 1780s, sales of such works were stagnant. Yet even at their height they only briefly accounted for one quarter of the STN's 'political' sales in France. Thereafter the figure was less than 5 per cent. All these issues – the timing of the publication and

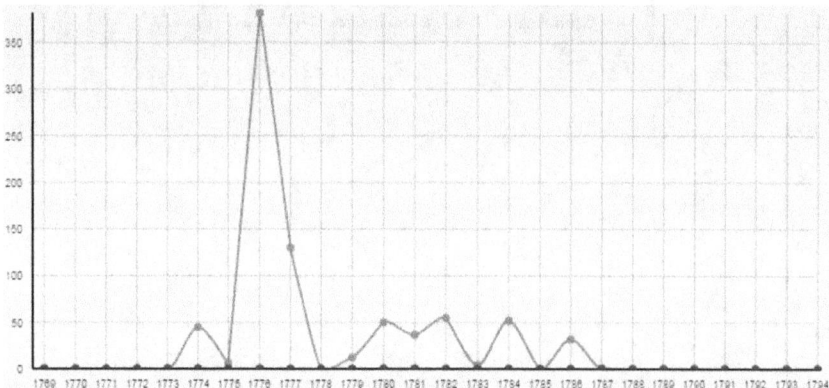

Chart 11.2 STN sales of works carrying keyword 'Du Barri' to France, 1769–94, adjusted to remove foreign wholesale clients (i.e. Malherbe *l'aîné* of Loudun).

the sales activity, the change in monarchic personnel – suggest that at the eve of the Revolution, the desacralizing mythologies contained in scandalous pamphlets were far from the dominant or most powerful political narratives available to French readers. As we have seen, works incorporating such narratives were marginal to the political trade of extraterritorial publishing houses, including the STN, which were probably the dominant players in the market for 'desacralizing' works. If we wish to discover these alternative narratives, we must look elsewhere. Nor are other sorts of defamatory works much in evidence.[26]

What political works, then, does the STN evidence suggest the French were reading in the decade before the Revolution? To answer this question, we might revisit the STN's trade with our old friend Charles-Antoine Charmet. For virtually all the works Charmet received in significant numbers from the STN were political in character. And they all concerned just one issue: French finances. Among the 393 titles that the STN sent to Charmet and his wife, those despatched in the greatest numbers were:

1. Necker, *Mémoire donné au roi … sur l'administration provincial*, 484 copies
2. = Grimouard, *Lettre du Marquis de Caraccioli à M. d'Alembert*, 400 copies
2. = Anon, *Requête au roi sur la retraite de Mr. Necker*, 400 copies
2. = *Réponse du sieur Bourboulon au Compte rendu au roi par M. Necker*, 400 copies
2. = Calonne, *Les Comments*, 400 copies
2. = Robert de Saint-Vincent, *Observations modestes d'un citoyen sur les opérations de finances de M. Necker*, 400 copies
7. Marmontel, *Les Incas*, 150 copies
8. *Lettres du Pape Clément XIV*, 122 copies
9. Beaumarchais, *Mémoires* [contre Goëzman?], 103 copies
10. Jean-Jacques Rutledge, *Bureau d'esprit*, 100 copies

The list needs some explanation, because Charles-Antoine Charmet did not order everything he was sent. Charmet's relationship with the STN directors was close and trusting, so they sometimes forwarded books unsolicited; he also occasionally received consignments of books ordered jointly with other local booksellers, notably Lépagnez cadet.[27] But Charmet would not have continued to permit such arrangements – which were not unusual – had he been dissatisfied with the results. The Necker pamphlets are a case in point. Usually, Charmet was a cautious trader purchasing works in lots of one to six copies, or just occasionally thirteen or twenty-five. As his wife later explained, he 'had as a principle to take a great many items and a small number of each'.[28] However, in June 1781, when Charmet placed an uncharacteristically large order for one hundred copies of the *Mémoire de Necker sur l'administration provincial* and *Lettre de Caraccioli à M. d'Alembert*, the STN sent him four hundred instead. They also sent a large consignment of Calonne's *Les Comments*, which he had not requested at all.[29] Far from being dissatisfied, Charmet complimented the STN. They had done well, he suggested, not to listen to him when he asked for only one hundred copies of the *Mémoire de Necker*.[30] The STN, it seems, understood its market. There are hints, however, that the affair did not end happily. When the STN tried to gauge Charmet's interest in a three-volume set of pamphlets for and against Necker the following October, he told them that the selection in question was past its use-by date: unless they added fresh materials, he would not be purchasing it.[31] The enthusiasm for such pamphlets was intense but short-lived, especially if they covered old ground. The same was true for more scandalous fare. For Charmet observed that the public's appetite for the leading *chroniques scandaleuses*, the *Mémoires secrets*, the *Espion français à Londres* and the *Espion anglois* was also wearing thin.[32]

The STN evidence suggests that the vogue for Neckerana was indeed short-lived, at least in terms of sales. It also shows that readers were yet more interested in the controversy surrounding the *Compte rendu* than Michael Kwass's wry observation that this 'accountant's memorandum' was the most sensational bestseller of the early 1780s would seem to imply.[33] For readers were consuming not only the *Compte rendu*, but also a whole series of related works. In all the STN alone shifted some 13,724 copies of pamphlets relating to the financial controversies of 1781, most of them in joint-editions with allied publishing houses, who probably sold as many again. Of the pamphlets the STN distributed relating to the controversy, barely one tenth (1,451) were copies of the *Compte rendu*, and less than two fifths (5,307) were by Necker himself. This implies impressive levels of public engagement with complex state financial issues. The *Compte rendu* alone ran to at least seventeen different editions and its sales have been estimated at 40–100,000.[34] In 1781, sales of pamphlets on French state finances clearly ran to several times that figure, both inside and outside France. In Besançon, Charles-Antoine Charmet and Dominique Lépagnez alone were able to offload the bulk of almost 2,500 pamphlets from the STN.[35] The town's other booksellers presumably sold many more, sourced doubtless from a range of publishers.

In October 1781, Charles-Antoine Charmet observed that market for financial pamphlets was exhausted, but interest in France's financial administration soon revived. There were further flurries of pamphleteering across the 1780s, particularly once the pre-revolutionary financial crisis broke. Again Necker and his arch-rival Calonne were the key protagonists. In 1791 another set of sensational accounts, the *Livre rouge*, which recorded the king's secret expenditures, became a revolutionary bestseller. It reportedly sold 2,000 copies within hours of going on sale in Paris.[36] Yet in terms of STN sales, works concerning France's financial administration never again had so much prominence after 1781. In part this was because thereafter the STN did not publish such works themselves. But it may also have been a consequence of their market reorientation away from France in the mid-1780s, since the Necker pamphlets never sold well beyond France and Switzerland.[37] But in place of financial pamphlets and scandalous *libelles*, other political fare sold well in France and the rest of Europe throughout the 1780s. Moreover, we can detect significant shifts from the 1770s to the 1780s. In this sense the Necker pamphlets seem to have been popular at a watershed moment. They mark a decisive shift of reader attention away from Maupeouana and court scandal towards more material political concerns.

This trend, which had already been evident for some time, was exemplified by one STN bestseller above all others. This was Raynal's sprawling, monumental multivolume account of the origins, history and current state of the European colonies and burgeoning global economy, the *Histoire philosophique des Deux Indes*.[38] Although the STN published their own edition in 1782–83, they had since 1773 bought in substantial volumes of Raynal's blockbuster from suppliers across Europe including Gabriel Decombaz in Lausanne, Gaudé, *père et fils* in Nîmes, J.S. Grabit in Lyon, Dufour and Roux in Maestricht and Pierre Gosse, junior, and Daniel Pinet in The Hague.[39]

The popularity of the *Histoire philosophique des Deux Indes* is beyond dispute. By the eve of the Revolution it had gone through forty French-language editions and numerous others in English, German, Italian and other European languages.[40] In all, we can trace somewhere between 3,491 and 4,973 sets leaving the STN's silos,[41] in addition to a handful of copies of abridgments and commentaries such as Jean-Baptiste Hedouin's *Esprit et génie de l'abbé Raynal* or the *Tableau de l'Europe, pour servir de supplément à l'histoire philosophique* by the *encyclopédiste* Alexandre Deleyre. Such was the *Histoire philosophique des Deux Indes*' success, that the *anti-philosophe journaliste* Simon Linguet estimated total sales at over 100,000.[42] The STN's own edition was a version of Raynal's third and final edition of the text, first published in 1780. This version was significantly more radical than the two previous ones, which had appeared in 1770 and 1774. A compilation by many hands besides Raynal, its authors included Alexandre Deleyre, d'Holbach and particularly Diderot, who wrote many of its most radical sections including the most cogent denunciations of slavery.[43]

Given such a provenance, it is not surprising that Jonathan Israel considers the *Histoire philosophique* to 'comprise the Radical Enlightenment's – indeed the whole Enlightenment's – most devastating single blow to the existing order'. According to Israel it infused political discourse across the European world with 'Diderot's rhetoric of universal basic human rights universally violated'.[44] Yet the book's fundamental appeal, as Israel himself notes, lay at least as much in the anodyne informational passages concerning the European colonies. This information, frequently gathered from royal officials and diplomatic informers, was simply unavailable to readers from other sources. Many doubtless used the *Histoire philosophique des Deux Indes* as their definitive work of reference, while avoiding, rejecting or ignoring the strident philosophic or moralizing narrative passages with which such valuable data was interlaced.[45] Yet as part of arguably the STN's most politically radical and widely disseminated political blockbusters of the 1780s, Diderot's most polemical passages are worth revisiting here.

The epic scale of Diderot's critique of the European colonial enterprise becomes clear at the opening of book eleven, as he sweepingly reviews the earlier chapters of Raynal's compilation:

> Nous avons vu – he wrote – d'immenses contrées envahies & dévastées; leurs innocens & tranquilles habitans, ou massacrés, ou chargés de chaînes; une affreuse solitude s'établir sur les ruines d'une population nombreuse; des usurpateurs féroces s'entr'égorger & entasser leurs cadavres sur les cadavres de leurs victimes.

Diderot reminds his readers that such crimes, the basis upon which Enlightenment Europe's commerce, civilization and prosperity were built, are far from over. They will be followed in his narrative by another 'moins sanglant peut-être, mais plus révoltant: le commerce de l'homme vendu & acheté par l'homme. Ce sont principalement les isles de l'Amérique qui ont excité à ce commerce abominable'.[46]

Thus, fully half way through Raynal's magnum opus, does Diderot introduce the theme for which it is best known. Yet even now readers must wade through a further sixty-five-page description of north and western Africa to reach his account of the origins of slavery in Guinea. Thereafter, Diderot warms to his theme, describing the sufferings and treatments of slaves. He even explores reasons for the prevalence of sexual relations between white masters and black slave women, which – in a finding echoed by recent historians – he considers to be rife.[47] Finally, he examines the arguments for and against slavery. His reproach to pro-slavers and their propagandists is withering and comprehensive.

Diderot begins by arguing 'qu'il n'est point de raison d'état qui puisse autoriser l'esclavage' and condemning before the 'tribunal de la lumiere & de la justice eternelles, les gouvernements qui tolerent ce cruauté'.[48] Then, one by one, Diderot takes apart arguments commonly used to justify slavery. That slavery was universal among ancient societies, even those presented to eighteenth-century school children as models, is no excuse.[49] Diderot indignantly derides claims based upon the 'droit du plus fort',[50] and condemns the inffectiveness of laws that supposedly 'enlightened' legislators had passed to protect those in servitude. Not one white slave–murderer, Diderot asserts, has ever expiated his sins on the scaffold under the *Code Noir*.[51] Besides, laws forbidding the killing of slaves do not prevent other forms of inhumanity, for 'le droit de l'esclavage est celui de commettre toutes sortes de crimes'.[52]

Diderot also condemns religious arguments for slavery on theological principles: 'Dieu est mon pere, & non mon maître. Je suis son enfant & non son esclave. Comment accorderois-je donc au pouvoir de la politique, ce que je refuse à la toute-puissance divine?'[53] Slavery is inconsistent with Christ's teachings, and attempts to justify slavery as a means of bringing black Africans to baptism are anathema: 'Si la religion chrétienne autorisoit ainsi l'avarice d'empires, il faudroit en proscrire à jamais ces dogmes sanguinaires'[54]

Finally, Diderot dissects arguments based upon racialist slurs and suggestions that Africans were born for slavery. If Europeans find them 'bornés, fourbes, méchans' and the slaves appear to recognize the whites' mastery and intelligence, it is because Europeans have forced them to behave thus. If slaves lie, for example, it is 'parce qu'on ne doit pas la vérité à ses tyrans'.[55] Nor do arguments that individuals have been born slaves, sold by the government or even wished to sell themselves into slavery stack up – the right to freedom is inalienable. Similarly, Diderot rejected claims that slavery saved prisoners taken in war from death, or was a just punishment for criminals, for the economics of the slave trade generated warfare and armed raids while judgements made in despots' courts lack validity.[56] Diderot likewise dismissed the slavery lobby's argument that the blacks were happier in the Americas. Why then did they universally pine for their homelands, escape to the wilderness or resort to suicide and self-abortions?[57]

Yet there was one slaver argument that Diderot accepted: 'en Europe, comme en Amérique, les peuples sont esclaves'.[58] This turns the debate on its head. What had been used hitherto as a justification for maintaining slavery in the Americas now becomes a call to extend political liberty in Europe. If Europeans are everywhere in chains, they, too, need to be liberated, for 'Partout des superstitions extravagantes, des coutumes barbares, des loix surannées étouffent la liberté'. Nevertheless, while awaiting the happy day when European political liberty would be reborn, there was no excuse for tolerating colonial slavery, for there was in truth no comparison between the lot of slaves and free Europeans: 'la condition de ces infortunées n'est pas le même que la nôtre'.[59]

In calling for the abolition of slavery, Diderot notes that Europeans need not give up the luxury commodities that fuel the slave trade. Tobacco, sugar, coffee, cotton, indigo could all be cultivated for cash in Africa by free Africans avid for European goods, or grown by black wage labourers in the Americas after a gradual process of liberation.[60] The alternative, in the long run, would be carnage. Already two colonies of runaway slaves had established their independence, '& il ne manque aux nègres qu'un chef assez courageux, pour les conduire à la vengeance & au carnage'.[61] Diderot's comments proved prophetic. The STN's last known sale of the *Histoire philosophique des Deux Indes* was to Jean-Baptiste Mangot in Vienna on 24 June 1790. Within fifteen months, the plantations of Saint-Domingue (Haiti), the jewel of France's Caribbean empire, were ablaze with bloody and ultimately successful slave insurrection.

Prophetic Diderot may have been, but his work did not help precipitate these events. Few black slaves probably ever read the *Histoire philosophique*, and the most systematic indictment of slavery was buried deep within the text. Readers either went looking for it, or encountered it only after penetrating deep into the work. It seems unlikely then that the *Histoire philosophique* changed many hearts and minds, for those readers who chose to read his critique were likely at least half-sympathetic to the abolitionist cause already. Much of the power of Diderot and Raynal's arguments, according to Israel, lay in the fact that most disciples of moderate Enlightenment agreed with most of what the *Histoire philosophique* had to say about trade liberalization, slavery and European serfdom. Sceptics among Israel's readers might take this throwaway line as evidence that his bifurcated model of Enlightenment is overdrawn.[62]

Yet something else is afoot here. For slavery is not the unique target of Raynal, Diderot and their collaborators. Book eleven offers scathing indictments of slavery and those who defend it – including the political, economic and, above all, religious leaders of European states. But it also contextualizes slavery within a broader system of European militarism, colonialism, brutality, exploitation and expropriation. These, it reveals, have been the drivers of the development of an increasingly global economy and a European civilization whose claims to refinement and politeness conceal the chilling ruthlessness at its heart.

Nevertheless, Diderot's response is by no means utopian. His moral argument is accompanied by an assessment and all-too-prophetic warning of impending cataclysm. This might be averted by limited practical political reforms to ameliorate and humanize the global system: end slavery in a measured way; acquire the products of the Indies through fairer trade; aspire to further political liberty in Europe. There is, then, in these passages on slavery a gap between the righteous, moralizing, absolute tone of the argument and the more measured, gradualist solutions that are propounded. This style of persuasion, steeped in classical antecedents, was not uncommon in influential writings of the era – one finds the same technique employed by the abbé Siéyès in his influential pamphlet, *Qu'est-ce que le tiers état?* which on the eve of the French Revolution called for political equality for the commoners or 'Third Estate'. 'What is the Third Estate?' He asks in his celebrated opening sentences – the answer 'Everything'. 'What has it been in the political order hitherto?' – 'Nothing'. 'What does it seek to become?' – 'Something'.[63] The shift in rhetorical key from outrage and [over] emphasis to moderation was a familiar one for educated contemporaries. The risk was that less sophisticated readers might take the rhetoric too literally. This was what the many contemporaries who vilified the *Histoire philosophique* for its denunciations of monarchic despotism, clerical complicity and the slave system feared most.

But perhaps the most compelling way to link the *Histoire philosophique des Deux Indes* with nascent rebellion is through its depiction of political issues as systemic problems tied to religious and political despotism. As such, they could potentially be remedied by systematic political and legal reform. This way of viewing the world, too, it seems, was part of a developing trend from the 1770s. As we have noted (above Chapter 9), the same decade witnessed a decisive shift in French prison narratives. Until 1774 they tended to depict the sufferings inflicted on prisoners in state prisons as the misfortunes of individuals, but following the appearance of the *Remarques historiques sur le château de la Bastille*, arbitrary arrests by *lettres de cachet* were presented as part of a vicious, despotic system.[64] Mirabeau and other commentators soon followed suit. A similar tendency is seen in the works of Louis-Sébastien Mercier. His *Tableau de Paris* repeatedly hints at the systematic despotism of a royal control that lines the theatres with troops, employs spies everywhere and has reduced Paris to a state where rebellion is unthinkable.[65] Reading his utopian novel *L'An 2440*, which imagines a morally perfected future world, alongside these descriptions is particularly instructive, since it suggests changes could be affected by a societal revolution in morality and political organization. The future citizens of 2,440 treat each other with respect and consideration; kings and princes throw open their homes and tables to the poor; and those who transgress by pursuing their own interests above the general good willingly submit themselves to re-education programmes.[66] Mercier's subtitle, *rêve s'il en fut jamais*, might suggest that even its author dismissed the book as a mere utopian thought experiment. A more subtle reading suggests that, like the *Histoire philosophique*, it supplied the STN's customers with a vision of programmatic change and a future pregnant with possibility.

Of course, Mercier's significance to our story transcends any single work. He was, as we have noted (above Chapter 2), the STN's most important house author by sales. In the 1780s, they distributed over 42,000 copies of his works. Although as an STN author, these figures doubtless exaggerate his popularity in the overall market place, they nevertheless give us a much surer statistical basis on which to reassess the influence of his *œuvre*, particularly the works containing political messages. Foremost among his political works are his historical dramas. Historical genres, both factual and fictional, offered ample opportunities to explore questions of power and how it was acquired, manipulated and used.[67] In terms of STN sales, the most important such work is Mercier's four-act historical melodrama, *La Destruction de la ligue*. The STN published the play's first edition in 1782 and it occupies third place on the STN's all-time bestseller list.[68] As an exemplar of many themes discussed in this book, it is well worth our attention.[69]

Set during the final episode of the French wars of religion, the action of *La Destruction de la ligue* spans just two days. The play's climax occurs on 22 March 1594, the momentous day when Paris came over to Henri IV. This event, as Mercier's title implied, marked the end of the French Catholic League as a political force. Since Henri had no legitimate rivals and had abjured Protestantism the previous July, the Leaguers had no ideological justification for opposing him as king. However, as the play begins, they and their foreign allies – the Spanish king Philip II and Swiss mercenary troops – are desperately trying to cling to power. Holding Paris is the key to their ambitions. Without the capital, further military resistance would be futile and the other Leaguer towns would capitulate.

Mercier's plot revolves around the fates of the Hilaire and Lancy families in the besieged city. The heads of these clans had been friends until Lancy defected to the heretic Henri IV. Hilaire now holds Lancy a traitor to faith and country. However, Hilaire's son and Lancy's daughter remain sweethearts, and on 21 March the Hilaires allow her to take refuge with them.[70] Unfortunately, their food is long gone, and freebooting Swiss mercenaries roam the streets outside.[71] In desperation, the Hilaire household argue over whether father and son should risk going out to forage. Nevertheless, father Hilaire and his elderly mother remain convinced that providence will help the family. They are protecting the One True Faith from the heretic usurper Henri who has perjurously abjured his Protestant beliefs to gain a crown. Hilaire's wife and son have their doubts, but barely dare put them into words.[72]

The Hilaire household and Parisian populace draw comfort from the assurances of the Leaguer priests, who visit regularly.[73] During one such visit, however, Hilaire *mère* overhears some clerics discussing the need to spread falsehoods against Henri and invoke God to keep the people in check. This will buy them time to install a Spanish *infanta* as a puppet on the throne and, if necessary, murder Henri.[74] The old lady also learns that the priests are feasting on secret supplies of food while the population starve. Unfortunately, she is discovered, but is so weak with starvation that the priests spare her life, believing her to be at death's door.[75]

Meanwhile, Henri IV reveals himself a model of kingly virtues. He tells his advisers that he remains true to his Protestant beliefs in his heart but, in order to spare his people from interminable civil wars, has irrevocably embraced Catholicism.[76] Nor is he prepared to take Paris by storm or starve the population into submission. Instead, he will risk his victory by secretly supplying the city with food. Any of his troops who have relatives inside Paris will be allowed to smuggle supplies into the city.[77] Meanwhile, his fifth columnist, Brissac, seeks an opportunity to throw open the city gates.

Shortly afterwards, Lancy, *père*, arrives *chez* Hilaire with several large loaves.[78] He discovers and revives Hilaire *mère*, delivers the bread and tells of Henri's bounties. Hilaire remains hostile, convinced Henri's generosity is a subterfuge.[79] After Lancy leaves, Swiss troops burst into the house. They spotted Lancy sneaking in so know there is bread. They take every crumb.[80] Old Madame Hilaire *mère* now expires, but only after revealing what she overheard the priests saying. In his grief even Hilaire *père* now accepts he has been duped by the priests. The Hilaire family decide to join Henri. Hilaire *fils*, bent on avenging his grandmother, runs out ahead.[81] Unfortunately, the rest of the family are captured en route and thrown into the Bastille.[82] From prison, they hear tumult outside. The gates have been opened by night and Henri's army has furtively gained control. Lancy arrives with troops to rescue the captives, followed by Hilaire *fils*.[83] Lancy and Hilaire *père* are reconciled and their children finally betrothed.[84] We have the requisite happy ending – or so it seems.

On a textual level, Mercier's sentimental historical melodrama appears, like so many other eighteenth-century works, to burn incense to the cult of Henri IV. Henri was widely revered as a warrior king, peace-bringer and beacon of religious toleration who had ended decades of religious civil war and brought prosperity to his kingdom. Yet Mercier's text should not be understood as a staged drama, for he never expected to see it performed. His paratextual devices – the footnotes and particularly his long author's *Preface* – therefore merit particular attention. He expects his readers to absorb them alongside the play itself.

On this paratextual level, Mercier's play is more ambiguous, for his *Preface* counteracts his onstage eulogies of good king Henri. It makes clear that Mercier had a view quite contrary to the prevailing historical orthodoxy. In his analysis, the French wars of religion were an exception to an avowed general rule of civil wars. Elsewhere, whatever suffering they caused, Mercier was convinced that civil wars generally had positive long-term political outcomes. He believed that the Roman, British, Swiss and Dutch civil wars invigorated patriotic virtues and secured lasting political liberties. These advantages, he felt, were worth their blood-price. If the insurgents were victorious, the American Revolution – which in his view was essentially a British civil war – would have similar outcomes.[85] France alone, with her wars of religion, seemed an exception. Mercier's play set out to explore this French historical exceptionalism, explaining why, for France, civil war was followed within a generation by the establishment of a tyrannical system under Cardinal Richelieu.[86]

Mercier's answer to his central historical problem was beguilingly simple. The French, he argued, had been sidetracked by theological trivia. A momentary opportunity to establish political liberty at the changing of the dynasty had been squandered over an enduring obsession with the Mass.[87] Henri IV's adjuration of Protestantism was a long-term political disaster, forced upon him by the obduracy of his subjects, who clung tenaciously to their old religion.[88] Viewed in this light, the most important character in the play is Hilaire, *père*, who even when violently disabused of his reverence for the priestly leaders of the League, retains his devotion to their faith. The obstinate, credulous, near fanatical Hilaire *père* thus symbolizes the bulk of the French people. They are the material with which Henri had to work. Their successors remained influential in Mercier's own lifetime. Thus the best possible result for the short-term problem of civil war led to the worst possible outcome under Henri's successors, as Richelieu and then Louis XIV shored up the Catholic position and renounced Henri's religious settlement.[89]

These arguments were made in hard-hitting language. The play's almost republican tone is reminiscent of Marie-Joseph Chénier's early revolutionary masterpiece, *Charles IX, ou l'école des rois*, the most popular play of 1789, which also tackled a key episode in the wars of religion, the Saint-Bartholomew's day massacre.[90] Like Chénier's play, Mercier's work offers a full frontal attack on the French theocratic state, castigating the hypocrisy and ambition of the clergy, but also, through its Preface, the religious policy of the Bourbon dynasty, including its august founder. Protestantism, he suggested, was a purer religion, closer to the early church and free from Catholic accretions and a politically ambitious priesthood.[91] Such an argument was, of course, appealing to his Protestant Swiss publishers. However, it also chimes with Mercier's calls in *L'An 2440* for a purged, natural religion focused on morality and consideration towards fellow human beings.[92]

Can we say that Neckerana, the *Pièces importantes*, the *Destruction de la Ligue*, Mercier's œuvre as a whole, or Raynal's *Histoire philosophique des Deux Indes* were typical or exemplary of the political reading, ideological messages, or, dare we say, the political Zeitgeist of the 1780s? We do not yet know for certain. But the bibliometric evidence gives us some strong indications. On the eve of the French revolutionary era, the STN pumped these works into the arteries of the cosmopolitan book trade in significant and hitherto unsuspected numbers, while fellow publishers and booksellers exponentially inflated their output. The majority of these works, moreover, betray a sophisticated reading audience capable of engaging with complex political messages and economic information, and this was probably the same public that had consumed the *libelles* of the 1770s. But where the *libelles* depicted politics as the playground of individual ministers, mistresses and courtiers, and proposed no alternative political programme, Raynal, Mercier and the *Pièces importantes* offered both an image of liberty everywhere suppressed and more concrete visions for achieving progress than the political theories of Fénélon and Montesquieu. The Genevan patriots would strive to rebuild their ideal republic under friendlier skies; Mercier's French compatriots might gradually recover liberty under their kings if only they abandon their devotion to Catholicism; and Raynal and Diderot supply a dream of universal liberty, a political blueprint and an economic, moral and pragmatic rationale for slave emancipation. Meanwhile, as Mercier made clear, political events in America and the patriot revolution in the Dutch Republic were by the early 1780s supplying hopes for a brighter future.

Surprisingly few books in the STN database deal with the 'American Revolution' and 'Politics' or treat the patriot revolution in the United Provinces. Yet informed readers everywhere, and certainly those who read the newspaper press, could not but be aware of these events, and the political aspirations to which they had given birth. Indeed, by the mid-to-late 1780s, journalists on the cosmopolitan francophone press across Europe seem united in their depiction of European politics as a Manichean struggle between more democratic forms of liberty on the one hand and monarchic and religious despotism on the other. They were divided only on whether this was to be welcomed or deplored; neither side felt victory was assured.[93] Sales evidence suggests the STN's customers and their customers' clients were overwhelmingly on the side of the former. In the imaginations of the STN's reading public, at least, the dreams and aspirations of a politically progressive Enlightenment had increasing currency. For those readers, multiple revolutions were now thinkable.

Conclusion

So what have we learned about the Enlightenment from unpacking so many crates resembling those depicted *At the Shield of Minerva*? When I first imagined creating a database of the STN's trade; when I invited Mark Curran to join me on the pilot project; as our ideas gradually assumed a digital form; and even as we finalized the original blueprints for paired monographs in October 2010, I naïvely dreamed that our endeavours would give us some final answers about the dissemination of books and discourses in the late Enlightenment. Our study would be monumental, its findings representative and its nature definitive. In an unguarded moment on our pilot trip in 2006, as we contemplated the scale and potential significance of our project, we even dared to compare our ambitions with Robert Darnton's achievement, a conceit which surely ignored his foundational contribution to the discipline of book history. Yet much feedback on the STN database suggests that by bringing Darnton's methods and bibliometric approaches into the digital age, the FBTEE project has in its own way been just as pioneering as his *œuvre*.[1] However, our initial ambitions and expectations proved largely misplaced, and in place of a definitive set of answers, we have opened up a series of new questions for further research. Yet at the same time, *Enlightenment Bestsellers* has given us unprecedented insights into the print culture and popular reading of the later Enlightenment, and established them on firmer bibliometric foundations. To do so, it has often had to look well beyond the STN evidence and exploit new sources in new ways, but by doing so we now have a new, more rounded outline vision of *ancien régime* print culture. That vision is still a fuzzy snapshot, and there are corners where our light has as yet hardly shone, but further research for the Australian Research Council-funded 'Mapping Print, Charting Enlightenment' project by a rejuvenated FBTEE team promises to illuminate even those. Other teams, working collaboratively with us on other materials, promise to expand our knowledge exponentially further.[2]

It is now clear that although the STN archive by itself, whether studied through methods privileging cultural demand (booksellers' orders) or cultural supply (STN sales and purchases) gives a far from complete or representative picture of the late eighteenth-century international book trade. Indeed, it can provide even the wariest of historians with distorted or misleading views of even its largest customers. Nevertheless, the FBTEE database can lead us towards unprecedented insights. Its objective data allows us to form a proper appreciation of the scale and chronology of the trade in scurrilous *libelles* or highbrow enlightened *philosophie*. Both have been cut down to size, the former significantly more than the latter. In their place we are beginning to discern the true importance of religious reading matter; the nature of the market for school books; and the commercial and cultural value STN customers placed on accounting guides, almanacs, household manuals and popular medical texts; and how science and popular folk-beliefs became conflated in books of secrets. If the print culture that emerges and the literary field that sustained it now appear unexpectedly alien territory to readers, that must in part be put down to the scholarly obsessions of *dix-huitièmistes*, including the current author, who have tended to view the Enlightenment (howsoever defined) as a modernizing force for change, disruption and, more recently, desacralization. It is also a reflection on the nature of sources used for most book history research in the period, which tends to draw predominantly on elite or metropolitan records. But books were woven very deeply into the fabric of everyday life for many eighteenth-century readers, and they reflect a wide variety of their quotidian concerns and priorities. Not surprisingly, many of these concerns were light years away from those of the *philosophes*. The very greatest bestsellers of the *siècle des Lumières* generally contained precious little Enlightenment.

So was DeFrance's heroic Enlightenment a mere sideshow, or even worse, a myth or fabrication? Not if we look at authorial evidence. Perusal of the titles in the STN database indicated that authors of all stamps – including scientific or theological apologists for Christianity – claimed to be enlightened and invoked Enlightenment and reason. The concept of Enlightenment was as much contested, it seems, among contemporary writers as historians. If we then consider these competing claims, and the literary field in which they were made, as an entire cultural system, we can begin to re-envisage the Enlightenment. Printed texts should stand at the heart of that endeavour. The age of *francophone* Enlightenment, according to the evidence presented here, was still deeply steeped in religion and confessional loyalties, and reinvigorated Catholic devotion appears surprisingly bookish. But in many secular texts in many different genres, the Enlightenment system also embraced strong anticlerical and irreligious strains. Suggestions that such works stemmed from a politically, as well as religiously, radical Enlightenment, or achieved the desacralization of the monarchy, remain unproven or have been problematized. Indeed, in purely bibliometric terms the STN evidence disrupts the neat chronological flow of the desacralization argument and implies that the importance of literatures of defamation and the democratic reach of materialist works are both open to question. Not for nothing would Robespierre call atheism 'aristocratic'. In contrast, the political and geographic imagination of the Enlightenment appears to have been cosmopolitan indeed, though not always able to transcend confessional frontiers. And within the Enlightenment's cosmopolitan fantasies, readers were increasingly, by the late 1770s and 1780s, encountering widely divergent societies organized in myriad different ways, and envisaging a common humanity based on equal rights and possibilities for radical political change. Messy, complex, challenging, inventive, self-contradictory and vast, this Enlightenment cultural system was transformative, unstable, vital and organic as life itself. The FBTEE project is allowing us to unpack this system via the contents of book-crates entering hundreds of book stores resembling *A L'Egide de Minerve*, and to locate and analyse their wares spatially and temporally. Armed with such historical bibliometric data, we can take the pulse of Enlightenment as never before.

Afterword: The Future of FBTEE—Towards a Digital History of the Book[1]

Simon Burrows and Jason Ensor

Soon after the publication of the FBTEE-1.0 database in June 2012, other scholars began to suggest it was a game-changing digital resource. According to Jeremy Caradonna, in a comparison with Stanford University's much-discussed 'Mapping the Republic of Letters' digital project, FBTEE was 'one of the best and most cutting-edge digital tools that historians of early modernity now possess. … [It brings the] historical profession into the age of interactive digital technologies and GIS.'[2] Other accolades were similarly enthusiastic. Robert Darnton called the database and interface 'a prodigious achievement and a joy to use.'[3]

The effusiveness of this praise came as a surprise. The FBTEE project was born of a set of tightly organized research questions: a database approach had been chosen because it appeared the best means to answer them. At the start of the project, we had not considered our approach particularly novel. Databases were by the mid-noughties a mature technology and widely used in commercial and research organizations. The discipline formerly known as 'humanities computing' had a long and illustrious pedigree. Even the term 'Digital Humanities' had been in use among practitioners since before the turn of the millennium.

In retrospect, the excitement can be explained from multiple angles. While humanities scholars had long used computers, we were riding the cusp of a wave. On 17 November 2010, the *New York Times* coverage of a student-produced visualization of data from the 'Mapping the Republic of Letters' project took the term 'Digital Humanities' out of the hands of specialists and into the public consciousness. At around the same time, North American university search committees routinely began asking for applicants to have digital humanities skills, against the background of a debate over the rigour and implications of digital humanities as an emergent discipline. Projects such as FBTEE and 'Mapping the Republic of Letters' hinted at the considerable transformative potential of well-designed and conceptually sophisticated digital humanities research programmes. Equally, timely technological developments promoted our cause. FBTEE's interactive digital maps – produced by Vincent Hiribarren on a shoestring budget – benefitted from the application of new technologies that were for the first time stable enough to support the complexity we required. At the start of the project we had been advised that such online maps were not possible – but five years on we found ourselves first in field. Likewise, the advent of Eighteenth-Century Collections Online and free online digital book repositories such as the Hathi Trust, Project Gutenberg, Gallica, and, above all, Google Books, facilitated and enriched the process of book classification in ways unimaginable at the start of the project. However, it was not so much the strengths as the shortcomings of the original FBTEE-1.0 project that have catalysed our current research agenda.

As we have seen, for each rich insight that FBTEE-1.0 offered, there were fundamental challenges within the data. The most important should have been obvious to a bright student in History 101. The STN data was drawn from only one source, albeit supposedly the best extant archive for purpose. This meant that further verification of the data it contained was in time necessary. One way to achieve that might have been to add further data from a range of similar publishers' archives unearthed during our research, but there seemed to be two obstacles to this: (1) there was not obvious scope for significant further methodological development in merely bolting-on additional data, but most funders prefer to promote innovation; and (2), conversely, the amount of funding required would be large, as the other possible archives to correlate with are vast. Also, no other archive has the range of ancillary materials that assisted with the import of STN data into FBTEE-1.0 (for example, annotated client lists to identify persons in the records, or book trade catalogues to help identify the majority of works and editions traded). As a result, after the FBTEE resources were transferred from Leeds to Western Sydney University in 2013, such ideas were put 'on ice' until we could build the scholarly coalitions and capacity necessary to undertake such work. As we write, that goal is in the process of being realized. We have acquired digital copies of the *veuve* Desaint archive and the Bibliothèque historique de la ville de Paris has granted us permission to create a database of Desaint's trade. Equally, Western Sydney has contributed towards the digitization of the Luchtmans archive. Having scoped the archive in November 2016, we are now working towards a large-scale pilot project with a team based at Amsterdam and Radboud universities.[4] Substantial efforts and further funding will be required to create a database of that immense archive. However, while these initiatives have been in preparation, FBTEE has also been pursuing a second pathway.

The initial warm response to FBTEE-1.0 provoked the rejuvenated team at Western to ask new questions of the project and its possible directions. In December 2013 and January 2014, assisted by Vincent Hiribarren, we revisited and remodelled the data and an alternative approach began to emerge. This modelling helped us understand that the FBTEE-1.0 database was already doing much more than providing data on the 'dissemination and reception of books' – my original formulation for what the project was attempting – but that there were gaps which, if filled, could help move towards that elusive synchronic slice of book history: that is, understanding the forces shaping the literary field of a society, as well as the life cycle of individual printed works from manuscript to bookseller to reader to estate. In this way we hoped that the methodologies and technical approaches started in FBTEE-1.0 could be extended to correlate data on potentially any quantifiable aspect of the Production, Reception, Ownership, Marketing, Policing and Transmission of books and the messages they contained. This formulation gave rise to the acronym PROMPT to describe our new and revised data model. This capacity was certainly present in the original FBTEE database project, but it was underdeveloped. The value of PROMPT, however, was particularly brought home by graphs we produced showing how book trade regulations introduced by the French government in 1777 and 1783 significantly impacted on the STN's pirate and highly clandestine trades. This in turn encouraged us to work on expanding the range of sources for PROMPT data that might be included in the database and assist us test our theories.

As a result, much of our effort across the years 2013, 2014 and 2015 went into identifying and scoping a variety of new data-sources that might be suitable for integration into the FBTEE database – lists of publishing privileges and banned books; records of books declared during an amnesty over pirated works in 1778–81; licences to print works under the *permission simple* licence; lists of works confiscated by Parisian police and customs; and so forth. These are currently being added to the database through generous seed-corn funding from Western Sydney University and the Australian Research Council's funding for our Discovery Project 'Mapping Print, Charting Enlightenment'.

A data model like PROMPT is of course transferrable to other times and places, and dovetailed neatly with work already being undertaken by Jason Ensor when we formed our research partnership in the dying days of 2012. Since his arrival at Western Sydney in late 2013, we have been able to develop and accelerate progress on creating a form of book history that will hopefully not be ring-fenced to periods and geographic regions. Instead we hope it will eventually reveal ebbs and flows over borders, cultures and periods of time. We are fortunate that an Australian-focused branch to this work is now being developed with the assistance of Dr Helen Bones and funding from the Australian National Data Service.

In essence, this new work, which is being piloted on the archival records of the iconic Australian Publisher Angus & Robertson, seeks to model new ways of presenting and researching documentary history. Put simply, much archival data is treated in the style of museum objects, with each object being lovingly described as an individual item. Such rich description may help to bring together disparate but different objects, but lacks a system for rigorous searching and organization of the archival record.

The Australian National Data Service-funded ARCHivER initiative (2016–17) in collaboration with Western Sydney University and the State Library of New South Wales will present noteworthy parts of the Angus & Robertson archive relating to the book trade and publishing in Australia across the twentieth century. It will contain both the digitized archival records and metadata drawn from the archive, and new metadata enrichment across several thousand documents. By focusing on the diverse activities of Angus & Robertson's competition, cooperation and conflict with other Australian firms, individuals and government bodies during the twentieth century with regards to two key themes – educational publishing and parallel imports – it will make visible the interdependency of publishing organizations and players, in which each participant is part of a larger and complex whole. With so many interactions distributed among multiple volumes, understanding Angus & Robertson's total business through a historically tuned analysis requires a step change in how research exploits digital technologies. While seeking to tease out the complexities of Angus & Robertson's activities with authors, booksellers, government agencies and publishers, ARCHivER's key principle is to link diverse collections in new ways. An individual document's relationship to other items in a volume will be maintained but in addition its relationship to other volumes, collections and documents will be exposed in ways better suited to our networked, data-intensive knowledge landscape.

The core premise is this: instead of the need to physically review folder after folder of pages delivered via stack requests, imagine the ability to seek information on, for example, noted Australian author 'Miles Franklin' and have all correspondence by, about and to Miles Franklin displayed via a generous digital interface, enabling faceted searching across the multiple volumes for keywords, titles, people, places and dates. Such changes in the shape, content and interactivity of the traditional memory archive that take full advantage of the capabilities of digital technologies and richly networked infrastructures would not only reveal hidden stories but would make new questions possible and thinkable. Unless deliberate investment is taken, however, to curate boxed documentary archives for future use within these new and emerging digital knowledge systems, the fragile status of their paper-based nature may result in their inaccessibility, loss or slow disintegration as sources of evidence for the next generation of researchers and public scholars. The workflow developed therefore for applying linked-data concepts to traditional paper holdings will not only enhance the reuse value of the State Library's uniquely Australian collections; it will also initiate the development of a framework centred around growing the rich connections between, across and throughout archival holdings.

If our approach can create opportunities for the development of new research tools for library and archival collections, it equally holds promise for understanding the history of libraries and their collections, taking us beyond individual catalogues to offer much more detailed comparative insights. The key to realizing this promise is the availability of well-curated, FRBRised bibliographic data (that is to say data structured according to the principles of the Functional Requirements of Bibliographic Records). This has remained problematically out of reach until only recently.

FRBR is a system developed by librarians to deal with the provenance of published texts and ambiguities such provenance can create for bibliographic records. Put simply, the word 'book' operates on multiple levels. When we mention 'a new book', we may be referring to an object (whether physical or digital); a new edition; a new version of an existing work; or a discrete intellectual project. Equally the word 'book' may relate to a single volume, or a multivolume set. To get around these fluid uses of the term, the FRBR model conceives of four interrelated levels of 'book', each with its own precise descriptive vocabulary. Three of these, in particular, are important to FBTEE, which counts individual 'items' (or copies) by aggregating them into discreet 'manifestations' (that is to say 'editions') and combining editions into distinctive 'works' (also called 'Superbooks' in FBTEE parlance).

The library community is only at the beginning of FRBRising historical bibliographic data. Australia of course is a leader in this area with AustLit, the Australian Literary Gateway. But for others, including the French, British and Americans it remains aspirational. This is a challenge for the FBTEE methodology, because experience has shown that where we have developed our own FRBRised data, the task of researching and collating data linking works and editions can be cut by up to 95 per cent. FRBRised data, then, is enormously important to our research agenda if we wish to find coherent datasets that enable us to move beyond regionally fenced notions of book history.

Afterword

Where then might we turn for FRBRised data? One of the best resources for our purposes was discovered almost by accident following the introduction through mutual friends of FBTEE director Simon Burrows and Sydney University's Emeritus Professor of French, Angus Martin, in 2013. This resource was the database of eighteenth-century novels (henceforth MMF-2) prepared by Angus Martin and his late collaborators, professors Vivienne Mylne and Richard Frautschi. Developed across a period of fifty years, it was until recently sheltered in 1980s software. We have now almost completed the process of repatriating the MMF-2 data from old technology into newer digital formats. This invaluable data contains FRBRised bibliographic information on every known edition of every novel published in French between 1701 and 1800, as well as known earlier editions. Each record is also accompanied by genre and subject classifications broadly compatible with the FBTEE categorizations for novels, which were in turn drawn largely from Martin, Mylne and Frautschi's print era *Bibliographie du genre Romanesque français, 1751-1800* (see Chapter 6). Armed with this data, we hope to map the occurrence of novels in bookdealer and private library catalogues across Europe. Moreover, we will also, for the first time, be able to correlate data on modern library holdings with historical data about eighteenth-century dissemination patterns. Obviously, library collections develop according to a large number of variables, but using the new FBTEE/MMF-2 data, it will be possible for book historians to investigate the hitherto tantalizing possibility that library holdings may reflect, among other things, historical distribution patterns.

If FRBRised novels data might allow us such insights, let us imagine what FRBRised metadata on the published output of an entire society might tell us, particularly when backed up by the integral titles and texts of the books that metadata describes. This is what we dream of achieving with Gale-Cengage Learning's Eighteenth-Century Collections On line (ECCO) product, which contains a near comprehensive collection of British and English language publications across the period 1700–1800. We are very fortunate that Gale-Cengage Learning, one of the world's leading publishers of digital resources, has now released their metadata. This data comprises bibliographic metadata on book published in the eighteenth century, and the OCR text and related metadata for every word and image on the 300,000,000 published pages the resource contains. While this work is still in its infancy, since receiving this data we have been developing a prototype visualization and analysis tool for geolocating texts. Mapping cultural data of course seems rather ordinary these days in this decade-old era of Google Maps but its implementation on data about eighteenth-century works, with all their variations in referring to places of publication, has its challenges, not least due to the need to verify stated places of publication against material evidence. A picture in this instance would indeed be worth 200,000 books.

As we add new FRBRised bibliographic metadata to FBTEE, other opportunities open up. Already we are working with an international group of library historians towards comprehensive projects on eighteenth-century subscription and circulating libraries. They aim to create a database assembling the entire catalogued collections of over 120 libraries, together with all surviving borrower records, which account for about ten of these libraries. Allowing for data entry speeds of one catalogue or borrower record per minute, which is surprisingly feasible, and some research on borrowers, this enterprise is within grasp and at a price commensurate with two very large research grants. That is, through surviving library holdings and use records we might have an insight into an entire historical society, with all that this may reveal about reading trends and cultural formation.

Such work would dovetail with other large-scale allied projects. Hence the FBTEE-2.0 team at Western Sydney have entered into a bibliographic metadata-sharing partnership and knowledge exchange programme with Professor Alicia Montoya's Dutch-based MEDIATE project on the printed library catalogues of private individuals, which enjoys lavish European Research Council funding. In an initiative led by FBTEE researcher Dr Katie McDonough, the two teams have also collaborated in attempts to create a historical gazetteer for early modern France, an essential tool in our attempts to link places across different datasets, but one which we currently lack. And for those interested in how readers responded, Simon Burrows and Dr Glenn Roe of the Australian National University have proposed a pilot project using data from the Electronic Enlightenment to data-mine 70,000 items of eighteenth-century correspondence for what (mostly elite and well-connected) letter writers had to say about the books they read. This could potentially create an Enlightenment 'Reading Experience Database' and link it to the most up-to-date and comprehensive data about the circulation of books across Europe. Finally, using a linked-data approach, we are working with Professor Dan Edelstein and his team at Stanford to connect some of that data to information on the circulation of those other leading bearers of ideas – people themselves – drawn from the 'Mapping the Republic of Letters' database, as part of our existing 'Mapping Print, Charting Enlightenment' project. In this case, the most important group of people may be the grand tourists on whom that project has been gathering data assiduously.

Through linked 'big data' bibliometric datasets and carefully curated technologies, FBTEE and its partner projects, aided and abetted by funding agencies and stakeholders and partners across academic book history disciplines, the library community and the publishing industry, are developing resources that hold out the prospect for understanding the factors shaping the dissemination of ideas and cultural formation in past societies on a level and scale never before achievable. Such an endeavour was only a short while ago in the realm of pure fantasy. Within a few short years, it has become a dream within our collective grasp. We commend all who have helped to make this possible and await our future with excitement.

List of Online Appendices

The online appendices for this book can be downloaded as a PDF at Bloomsbury's website, at https://www.bloomsbury.com/uk/the-french-book-trade-in-enlightenment-europe-ii-9781441126016/. They comprise:

Appendix 1: Maps

Appendix 2: Graphs and Charts

Appendix 3: Tables

Appendix 4: Designer notes on the FBTEE database

Appendix 5: Calculating the production and market for *livres philosophiques*

Appendix 4 is also available through the FBTEE database via the website, at http://fbtee.uws.edu.au/stn/interface/dsgnotes.php

Notes

Preface

1 Mark Curran, *The French Book Trade in Enlightenment Europe*, vol. 1, *Selling Enlightenment* (London: Bloomsbury, 2018).
2 For my reasons, see below, Chapter 3, and Simon Burrows, *Blackmail, Scandal and Revolution: London's French Libellistes, 1758-1792* (Manchester: Manchester University Press, 2006), especially Chapter 5. See also Chapters 9 and 11 of this book.
3 Bibliothèque publique et universitaire de Neuchâtel [BPUN], MS 1000 A, 'Société typographique, correspondants, répértoire géographique'. This list was prepared by John Jeanprêtre.
4 See http://fbtee.uws.edu.au/main/project-history/ and http://fbtee.uws.edu.au/main/project-tasks/.
5 Robert Darnton, review of 'The French Book Trade in Enlightenment Europe, 1769-1794', (review no. 1355) http://www.history.ac.uk/reviews/review/1355 (Date accessed 12 April 2018).

Chapter 1

1 On historical bibliometrics, see Jean-Pierre V. M. Hérubel, 'Historical Bibliometrics: Its Purpose and Significance to the History of Disciplines', *Libraries & Culture* 34:4 (Fall 1999), 380–88. See also E. W. Hulme, *Statistical Bibliography in Relation to the Growth of Modern Civilisation: Two Lectures Delivered in the University of Cambridge in May 1922* (London: Grafton, 1922). Hérubel (p. 382) defines historical bibliometrics as 'bibliometric study of periodicals and books published in the framework of time and space'. Hence it involves (p. 380) 'quantitative analysis of publications for the purpose of ascertaining specific kinds of [cultural] phenomena'.
2 See John Lewis Mallet, *An Autobiographical Retrospective of the First Twenty-Five Years of his Life* (Windsor: Privately printed, 1890), p. 209.
3 Phillippe Henry, 'Le Pays de Neuchâtel à l'époque de la naissance de la STN', in Robert Darnton and Michel Schlup, eds, *Le Rayonnement d'une maison d'édition dans l'Europe des Lumières: la Société typographique de Neuchâtel 1769-1789* (Neuchâtel and Hauterive: B.P.U.N. and Editions Gilles Attinger, 2005), pp. 33–49, at pp. 41–43.
4 On these booksellers and their printed output, see Daniel Droixhe, *Une histoire des Lumières au pays de Liège: livre, idées, société* (Liège: Éditions de l'Université de Liège, 2007). According to Droixhe (p. 181), Leonard DeFrance depicted Plomteux's shop in his four *Visites à l'Imprimerie*.
5 Ibid.
6 On Brydone's work, see below, Chapter 8.

7   Droixhe, *Histoire des Lumières*.
8   A matching order for volumes 1–17 was sent on 3 July 1779. Volumes 36–39, the plates, were apparently never requested, perhaps because of the expense.
9   Robert Darnton, *The Business of Enlightenment: A Publishing History of the Encyclopédie* (Cambridge, MA: Harvard University Press, 1979).
10 Darrin M. MacMahon, *Enemies of Enlightenment* (Oxford: Oxford University Press, 2002), ch. 1.
11 Roger Chartier, *The Cultural Origins of the French Revolution* (Durham, NC: Duke University Press, 1991).
12 Mallet Du Pan, *The British Mercury* II:14 (15 March 1799), 335. The French edition of Mallet's paper, *Le Mercure britannique* appeared five days before the English.
13 See Jonathan Israel, *Radical Enlightenment: Philosophy and the Making of Modernity, 1650-1750* (Oxford and New York: Oxford University Press, 2001); *Enlightenment Contested: Philosophy, Modernity, and the Emancipation of Man* (Oxford and New York: Oxford University Press, 2006); Jonathan Israel, *Democratic Enlightenment: Philosophy, Revolution, and Human Rights 1750-1790* (Oxford and New York: Oxford University Press, 2011); *Revolutionary Ideas: An Intellectual History of the French Revolution from The Rights of Man to Robespierre* (Princeton, NJ: Princeton University Press, 2014). For a synopsis of Israel's case see Jonathan Israel, *A Revolution of the Mind: Radical Enlightenment and the Intellectual Origins of Modern Democracy* (Princeton, NJ: Princeton University Press, 2009). A debate between Israel and several of his critics appears in H-France review, Volume 9, Issue 1 (Winter 2014) at http://www.h-france.net/forum/forumvol9/.
14 Israel, *Democratic Enlightenment*, p. 10.
15 Jonathan Israel, 'A Reply to Four Critics', *H-France Review* 9:1 (Winter 2014) at http://www.h-france.net/forum/forumvol9/, pp. 77–97 at p. 81.
16 For Israel's assertion of the work's radicalism see esp. *Democratic Enlightenment*, p. 69. Expensive, unwieldy and lacking an index until 1780, the *Encyclopédie* was an unlikely tool for the political education of the masses. Moreover, in some editions, particularly the Italian ones, its tone was relatively moderate. I thank Professor David Adams for his contribution towards these comments.
17 Israel, *Democratic Enlightenment*, p. 413.
18 Michel Schlup, 'La Société typographique de Neuchatel (1769-1789): Points de repère', in Michel Schlup, ed., *L'Edition neuchâteloise au siècle des Lumières: la Société typographique de Neuchâtel (1769-1789)* (Neuchâtel: Bibliothèque publique et universitaire, 2002), pp. 61–105 at pp. 72–74; Mark Curran, *Atheism, Religion and Enlightenment in Pre-Revolutionary Europe* (Woodbridge: Boydell and Brewer/Royal Historical Society, 2012), p. 31.
19 Darnton, *Business of Enlightenment*.
20 See Robert Darnton, 'J.-P. Brissot and the Société Typographique de Neuchâtel (1779-1787)', *SVEC* 2001:10 (2001), pp. 1–47. This article, together with Brissot's correspondence with the STN and related documents, can now be found at Darnton's website, http://robertdarnton.org/literarytour/brissot and at the Voltaire Foundation website at http://www.voltaire.ox.ac.uk/www_vf/brissot/brissot_index.ssi. See also Curran, *Selling Enlightenment*, pp. 102–3, 191 n. 29 *passim*.
21 The FBTEE database contains several Neuchâtel editions of Mirabeau's works, notably Jonas Fauche's clandestine edition of *Des Lettres de Cachet et des prisons d'état* bearing the false imprint Hambourg, 1782, and the *Errotika Biblion* (Rome: Vatican [Neuchâtel, Fauche], 1783). For more on Mirabeau's STN editions see Curran, *Selling Enlightenment*, pp. 102–3.

22 See below Chapters 9 and 10.
23 Israel, *Democratic Enlightenment*, p. 26 ff.
24 Dan Edelstein, *The Enlightenment: A Genealogy* (Chicago: University of Chicago Press, 2010); Roy Porter and Mikuláš Teich, eds, *The Enlightenment in National Context* (Cambridge: Cambridge University Press, 1981).
25 Alan Kors, *D'Holbach's Coterie: An Enlightenment in Paris* (Princeton: Princeton University Press, 1976) argues that d'Holbach's circle had a long-established suspicion of popular political participation 'in the means of social change' (esp. p. 309). In 2014, Kors reaffirmed that d'Holbach was no radical in politics in a paper to the Society for French Historical Studies conference in Montreal. Harvey Chisick, 'Review Essay' [on Israel's *Democratic Enlightenment*], *H-France Forum* 9:1 (Winter 2013), 57–76, makes similar comments, noting Spinoza accepted the legitimacy of Dutch government; his popularizer Bayle was pro-absolutism; and that Enlightenment philosophers – following Spinoza and ultimately Plato – were deeply concerned about the implications of the rule of the people (p. 63). So were the French revolutionaries, who in 1791 limited the franchise to those paying three days' wages in direct taxes.
26 Chisick, 'Review Essay', p. 59
27 Ibid., p. 57.
28 See Pierre Bayle's article 'Spinoza' in his *Dictionnaire historique et critique*, 5th edn, 4 vols (Amsterdam, Leiden: The Hague and Utrecht, 1740), pp. IV, 253–71. This edition is available online in searchable form at ARTFL at http://artfl-project.uchicago.edu/node/74. While suggesting Spinoza was the first to reduce the system of Atheism into a geometric doctrine, Bayle adds (p. 253) 'son sentiment n'est point nouveau. Il y a long-tems que l'on a cru que tout l'univers n'est-qu'une substance, & que Dieu & le monde ne sont qu'un seul être'. I thank Professor David Adams for first drawing my attention to the similarity between Bayle's reading of Spinoza and my own.
29 Carolina Armenteros, 'Review Essay' [on Israel's *Democratic Enlightenment*], *H-France Forum* 9:1 (Winter 2013), 26–40, at pp. 34–35.
30 Keith Michael Baker, 'Review Essay' [on Israel's *Democratic Enlightenment*], ibid., pp. 41–56 at pp. 45–48.
31 Annelien de Dijn, 'The Politics of Enlightenment from Peter Gay to Jonathan Israel', *Historical Journal* 55:3 (2012), 785–805.
32 Peter Gay, *The Enlightenment: An Interpretation*, 2 vols (New York: Knopf, 1969), vol. II, *The Science of Freedom*, p. ix.
33 Gay, *The Enlightenment*, II, 3.
34 Robert Darnton, 'The high enlightenment and the low-life of literature in prerevolutionary France', *Past and Present* 51 (1971), 81–115, quote at p. 81.
35 Darnton, 'The high enlightenment'. For a reappraisal of Morande, see Simon Burrows, *A King's Ransom: The Life of Charles Théveneau de Morande, Blackmailer, Scandal-Monger and Master-Spy* (London: Continuum, 2010).
36 Robert Darnton, *The Devil in the Holy Water or the Art of Slander from Louis XIV to Napoleon* (Philadelphia: University of Pennsylvania Press, 2010).
37 Robert Darnton, *Forbidden Best-Sellers of Pre-Revolutionary France* (London: Harper Collins, 1996).
38 Darnton, *Forbidden Best-Sellers*, pp. 63–65. These tables are extended and supplemented in Robert Darnton, *The Corpus of Clandestine Literature in France 1769-1789* (New York: Norton, 1995).
39 Darnton offers his own answers to some of these questions in Robert Darnton, *A Literary Tour de France. The World of Books on the Eve of the French Revolution* (Oxford and New York: Oxford University Press, 2018), esp. Ch. 13. Since *A Literary Tour*

appeared while this volume was in the proof stages of production, it has been impossible to address it directly.

40   Harvey Chisick, 'Introduction', in Harvey Chisick, ed., *The Press in the French Revolution*, SVEC 287 (Oxford: Voltaire Foundation, 1991), p. 8; Jeremy D. Popkin, 'Robert Darnton's Alternative (to the) Enlightenment', in Haydn T. Mason, ed., *The Darnton Debate: Books and Revolution in the Eighteenth Century* (Oxford: Voltaire Foundation, 1998), pp. 105–28; Elizabeth L. Eisenstein, 'Bypassing the Enlightenment: Taking an Underground Route to Revolution', in Haydn T. Mason, ed., *The Darnton Debate: Books and Revolution in the Eighteenth Century* (Oxford: Voltaire Foundation, 1998), pp. 157–77.

41   See Chapter 9 and Simon Burrows, 'French Banned Books in International Perspective, 1770-1789', in David Andress, ed., *Experiencing the French Revolution*, vol. 5 (Oxford: SVEC 2013), pp. 19–45.

42   The argument was first expounded in Simon Burrows and Mark Curran, 'How Swiss was the Société Typographique de Neuchâtel? A Digital Case Study of French Book Trade Networks', *Journal of Digital Humanities* I:3 (Summer 2012), 56–65.

43   Extensive work by Anna-Maria Rimm on the STN's trade with Sweden and particularly the royal bookseller Elsa Fougt, remains available only in Swedish.

44   The main monograph studies and essay collections to draw on the STN archive are Schlup, ed., *L'Edition neuchâteloise;* Darnton and Schlup, eds., *Le Rayonnement d'une maison d'édition;* Darnton, *Forbidden Best-Sellers;* Jeffrey Freedman, *Books Without Borders in Enlightenment Europe: French Cosmopolitanism and German Literary Markets,* (Philadelphia, PA: University of Pennsylvania Press, 2012); and Robert Darnton, *The Literary Underground of the Old Regime* (Cambridge, MA and London: Harvard University Press, 1982).

45   Dorinda Outram, *The Enlightenment*, 1st edn (Cambridge: Cambridge University Press, 1995), p. 12.

46   The secularism of the Enlightenment had been questioned even before the emergence of the scholarship on the Christian enlightenment. Carl Becker, *The Heavenly City of the Eighteenth-Century Philosophers* (New Haven, CT: Yale University Press, 1932), suggests that many *philosophes* shared more intellectual assumptions with religious thinkers than they would care to admit. Peter Gay went further, insisting in the subtitle of his *The Enlightenment: an Interpretation* that the Enlightenment witnessed 'the rise of modern paganism'. For more recent treatments see Helena Rosenblatt, 'The Christian Enlightenment', in Stewart J. Brown and Timothy Tackett, eds, *The Cambridge History of Christianity*, vol. 7, *Enlightenment, Reawakening and Revolution 1660-1815* (Cambridge: Cambridge University Press, 2006), pp. 283–301; Curran, *Atheism, Religion and Enlightenment*.

47   Mark Curran, 'Mettons Toujours Londres: Enlightened Christianity and the Public Sphere in Pre-revolutionary Europe', *French History* 24 (2010), 40–59 at p. 59.

48   See, for example, Kingsley Martin, *French Liberal Thought in the 18th Century: A Study of Political Ideas from Bayle to Condorcet* (London: E. Benn, 1929). Martin is nevertheless primarily known as a journalist and novelist.

49   The classic statement of this view appears in the appendix to Georges Lefebvre, *The Coming of the French Revolution*, first published in French in 1939. However, not all Marxist historians ignored the Enlightenment. For further details, see Arnold Miller, 'The Annexation of a "Philosophe": Diderot in Soviet Criticism, 1917-1960', *Diderot Studies* 15 (1971), 5–464. I thank Professor David Adams for this reference and the next.

50   The older view of Diderot as radical is exemplified by Anthony Strugnell, *Diderot's Politics: A Study of the Evolution of Diderot's Politics after the Encyclopédie* (The Hague: Nijhoff, 1973).

51 Previously our best survey is perhaps Pierre M. Conlon's monumental, *Le siècle des Lumières: bibliographie chronologique*, 32 vols (Geneva: Droz, 1983–2009), which surveys publishing trends via a list of first editions.

Chapter 2

1 The STN records sometimes distinguish between their own editions ('*nos éditions*'), joint editions produced with other Swiss publishers ('*livres en société*'), and '*livres d'assortissement*' (miscellaneous editions produced by other publishers, usually held in small numbers). Many publishers and booksellers also made a distinction between *livres d'assortissement* and titles they bought from other suppliers and held in bulk – '*livres en nombre*'. Some STN records also separate out '*livres troqués*' – swapped titles from other publishers supplied in uncut, unbound sheet form.
2 For these and similar examples, see the surviving 'Visites des inspecteurs de l'Imprimerie' for Paris in 1769, 1770, and 1771 Bibliothèque nationale de France [BNF], MS Fr. 22,081 fos 338–54, pieces 188, 188 bis and 189.
3 Curran, *Selling Enlightenment*, p. 46.
4 Jürgen Habermas, *The Structural Transformation of the Public Sphere: An Inquiry into a Category of Bourgeois Society*, trans. Thomas Burger (Cambridge, MA: MIT Press, 1989).
5 For critical overviews, see Craig Calhoun, ed., *Habermas and the Public Sphere* (Cambridge, MA: MIT Press, 1989); editors' 'Introduction', in Hannah Barker and Simon Burrows, eds, *Press, Politics and Public Sphere in Europe and North America* (Cambridge: Cambridge University Press 2002), pp. 1–22.
6 This is the subject of the second half of Habermas' book.
7 Eltjo Buringh and Jan Luiten van Zanden, 'Charting the "Rise of the West": Manuscripts and Printed Books in Europe, A Long Term Perspective from the Sixth through Eighteenth Centuries', *Journal of Economic History* 69:2 (2009), 409–45, Table 2.
8 The 1,000 print-run figure is widely cited. According to Philip Gaskell, *New Introduction to Bibliography* (Oxford: Oxford University Press, 1972), p. 161, technical and economic constraints usually limited print runs to 500–2,000 copies.
9 Conlon, *Le siècle des Lumières*, lists 1,963 new works published in 1781 (adjusted figures); cf. just 523 regular and illegal titles in Robert Estivals, *La Statistique bibliographique de la France sous la monarchie au XVIIIe siècle* (Paris and The Hague: Mouton/De Gruyter, 1965), 405.
10 See Buringh and van Zanden, 'Charting the "Rise of the West"', Table 6. On revolutionary pamphlet output see: Antoine de Baecque, 'Pamphlets: Libel and Political Mythology', in Robert Darnton and Daniel Roche, eds, *Revolution in Print. The Press in France, 1775-1800* (Berkeley: University of California Press, 1999), pp. 165–76, at pp. 165–6. De Baecque's count of pamphlet titles in the BNF's *Catalogue de l'histoire de France* yielded 312 titles for the years 1774 to 1786; 1,036 for the pre-revolution (1787–8) and 12,360 for the revolutionary decade.
11 Gilles Feyel, 'La Diffusion des gazettes étrangères en France et la revolution postale des années 1750', in Henri Duranton, Claude Labrosse and Pierre Rétat, eds, *Les Gazettes européennes de langue française (XVIIe-XVIIIe siècles)* (Saint-Etienne: Presses Universitaires de Saint-Etienne, 1992), pp. 81–99. See also Simon Burrows, 'The Cosmopolitan Press', in Hannah Barker and Simon Burrows, eds, *Press, Politics and*

the Public Sphere in Europe and North America, 1760-1820 (Cambridge: Cambridge University Press, 2002), pp. 23–47, at pp. 26–7.

12 Andreas Wurgler, 'Censorship and Public Opinion. Press and Politics in the Helvetic Republic (1798-1803)', in Joris Oddens, Mart Rutjes and Erik Jacobs, eds, *The Political Culture of the Sister Republics, 1794-1806. France, the Netherlands, Switzerland and Italy* (Amsterdam: Amsterdam University Press, 2015), pp. 159–69, at pp. 162–3. The figures are taken from graph 3.

13 Michel Schlup, 'Diffusion et lecture du Journal helvétique au temps de la Société typographique de Neuchâtel', in Hans Bots, ed., *La Diffusion et lecture des journaux de langue française sous l'ancien régime* (Amsterdam: APA-Holland University Press, 1988), pp. 59–71. Circulation fell from 401 in 1769 to 200 in 1782.

14 See 'Introduction', in Barker and Burrows, *Press, Politics and the Public Sphere*.

15 For a discussion, see David Cressy, 'Literacy in Context: Meaning and Measurement in Early Modern England', in John Brewer and Roy Porter, eds, *Consumption and the World of Goods* (London: Routledge, 1993), pp. 305–19.

16 R. A. Houston, *Literacy in Early Modern Europe. Culture and Education 1500-1800* (Harlow: Longman, 1988), p. 151.

17 Houston, *Literacy*, pp. 125–6.

18 Michel Vovelle, *The Fall of the Monarchy, 1787-1792*, trans. Susan Burke (Cambridge: Cambridge University Press, 1984), pp. 60–3.

19 Houston, *Literacy*, p. 151.

20 Buringh and van Zanden, 'Charting the "Rise of the West", Table 6.' For 1751-1800 the authors calculate annual per capita output for Europe (excluding Russia) at 122.4 books per thousand inhabitants. For both 1701–50 and 1651–1700 it was 66.7. Buringh and van Zanden do not distinguish between book production in the Swiss Romand (where production was quite buoyant) and German, Italian and Romansch-speaking areas.

21 See Denis Metzger, 'Livres, bibliothèques et lecture, à Saint-Avold au XVIIIe siècle', *Mémoires de l'académie nationale de Metz*, année 1999 (2000), 89–111, at p. 92.

22 On German demand see Freedman, *Books without Borders*, ch. 4.

23 Daniel Roche, *The People of Paris* (Leamington Spa: Berg, 1987), p. 212.

24 Roger Chartier, *Lecture et lecteurs en France d'ancien régime* (Paris: Editions de Seuil, 1982), esp. ch. 5.

25 Gaël Rideau, *De la religion de tous à la religion de chacun. Croire et pratiquer à Orléans au XVIIIe siècle* (Rennes: Presses universitaires de Rennes, 2009), pp. 279–82.

26 See Metzger, 'Livres, bibliothèques et lecture, à Saint-Avold'.

27 Michel Vernus, 'A Provincial Perspective', in Robert Darnton and Daniel Roche, eds, *Revolution in Print. The Press in France, 1775-1800* (Berkeley: University of California Press, 1999).

28 See below Chapter 10 and Simon Burrows, 'Charmet and the Book Police: Clandestinity, Illegality and Popular Reading in Late Ancien Régime France', *French History and Civilisation: Papers from the George Rudé Seminar* 6 (2015), 32–55. Note also the confusions surrounding Charmet's identity discussed in Chapter 10 note 71.

29 See Ernst Anton Nikolai, *Programma de Gummi Ammoniaci virtute dissertationi inaugural*. Gum ammoniac, a product of the tropical plant *Heraclium gummiferum*, was used as a stimulant, an antispasmodic, an expectorant and to treat tumours.

30 The other works on venereal disease were Joseph-Jacques de Gardane's *Manière sûre et facile de traiter les maladies vénériennes*; Pierre Fabre's *Traité des maladies vénériennes*; and Bernard Peyrilhe, *Remède nouveau contre les maladies vénériennes*.

31 The works referred to in this sentence are respectively: Jacques-François de Villiers, *Manuel secret et analyse des remède de MM. Sutton pour l'inoculation de la petite vérole*; Joseph-Jacques de Gardane, *Le Secret de Suttons dévoilé*; Dupré de Lisle, *Traité sur le vice cancéreux*; the baron de Saint-Ildephont's *Remède éprouvé, pour guérir radicalement le cancer occulte*; John Burton, *Système nouveau et complet de l'art des accouchements*; Pierre Hunauld's rather obscure *Dissertation sur la dysenterie et ses remedes les plus specifiques*, the only extant edition of which was published in 1750; Hugues Gauthier, *Dissertation sur l'usage des caustiques pour la guérison radicale ... des hernies*; Peter Cavane, *Dissertation su l'huile de palma Christi, ou l'huile de ricin qu'on appelle communement l'huile de castor*; and Henri Fouquet, *Essai sur le pouls par rapport aux affections des principaux organes*, which contained appended essays by Fleming and Solano translated from Spanish and English.

32 The subtitle is *Précis d'une mémoire sur les causes de la mort subite et violente, dans lequel on prouve que ceux qui en sont les victims peuvent être rappelés à la vie*.

33 The STN supplied Vennes with Antoine Planchon, *Dissertation sur la fievre miliaire* (Tournai: Adrian Serré, 1772); Jean-Marie Gamet, *Théorie nouvelle sur les maladies cancéreuses* (Paris: Ruault, 1772); F. -M. C. Richard de Hautesierck, *Recueil d'observations de médecine des hôpitaux militaires* (Paris: Imprimerie Royale, 1766–72); Théophile de Bordeu, *Recherches sur le pouls* (unidentified edition); and Francis Home, *Principes de médecine de M. Home* (Paris: Vincent, 1772). See BPUN, MS 1030, *Main courante*, fo. 66.

34 See below Chapter 10.

35 The STN sold fifty-eight *L'Imitation de Jésus Christ*; seven *Anges conducteurs*; and three *Journées du Chrétien*. These titles feature prominently in Chapter 10 below.

36 This list combines purchases attributed to two separate persons in the STN database: abbé Joseph-Grellet Desprades at Versailles and the abbé de Prades in Paris. The possibility that these were separate people is remote. An abbé Jean-Martin de Prades existed (c. 1720–82), but from 1752 he lived in Silesian exile in Glogau having penned a scandalously liberal theological doctoral thesis: see Jeffery D. Burson, *The Rise and Fall of Theological Enlightenment. Jean-Martin de Prades and Ideological Polarization in Eighteenth-Century France* (Notre Dame, IN: University of Notre Dame Press, 2010).

37 On Lesenne see Robert Darnton, 'A Pamphleteer on the Run', in Robert Darnton, ed., *The Literary Underground of the Old Regime* (Cambridge, MA and London: Harvard University Press, 1982), pp. 70–121. Darnton argues Lesenne was the incarnation of Voltaire's 'pauvre diable', living by his wits and his pen, but his narrative offers little evidence that Lesenne wrote very much or was paid for his output.

38 See Freedman, *Books without Borders*, p. 214

39 These included ten copies of Cornelius de Pauw's *Recherches philosophiques sur les Américains*, ten copies of Millot's *Elémens de l'histoire générale* and seven of Roubaud's *Histoire générale de l'Asie, de l'Afrique et de l'Amérique*.

40 These figures have been derived by aggregating STN sales to French, Swiss and Belgian geographic zones, then deducting sales to major non-French-speaking towns in those regions. Given the imprecise and unstable nature of language and political frontiers they are necessarily approximate. Moreover, 4.3 per cent of books traded by the STN went to Berne, where there was a significant French population, and 96 per cent of those were for the francophone Société typographique de Berne (14,115 units) or Albrecht Haller (2,998).

41 See Rolf Engelsing, 'Die Perioden der Lesergeschichte in der Neuzeit. Das statische Ausmass und die soziokulturelle Bedeutung der Lektüre', *Archiv für Geschichte des Buchwesens* 10 (1969), cols. 944–1002.

42   A typical school book in form of catechism was Frédéric-Samuel Ostervald's *Cours abrégé de géographie historique, ancienne & moderne, et de sphère: par demandes & réponses*, one of the STN's bestselling historical titles.
43   Freedman, *Books without Borders*, pp. 132–3.
44   On Mercier's relations with the STN see also Curran, *Selling Enlightenment*, pp. 102–3 *passim*.
45   BPUN, MS 1180, fos 241–2, Mercier to STN, 19 January 1778.
46   On author payments see Michel Schlup, 'La STN et ses auteurs', in Robert Darnton and Michel Schlup, eds, *Le Rayonnement d'une maison d'édition dans l'Europe des Lumières: la Société typographique de Neuchâtel 1769-1789* (Neuchâtel and Hauterive: B.P.U.N. and Editions Gilles Attinger, 2005), pp. 139–60 at pp. 149–50. Schlup does not mention Gilibert, but evidence cited in Chapter 10 below suggests he was paid.
47   See Darnton, 'A Pamphleteer on the Run'.
48   Curran, *Selling Enlightenment*, pp. 102–3 *passim*.
49   1,000 copies Goëzman's *Discours préliminaire* were printed several months before his main text and sent to Paris. The FBTEE database treats them as 1,000 extra copies of the *Tableau de la monarchie*. However, since we have not found extant copies, and now suspect that they should have been treated as a separate work, rather than part of the *Tableau de la monarchie*. For the purposes of this book and its statistics they are therefore treated as two separate works.
50   BPUN, STN MS 1042, bilan, 1785.
51   For evidence of Brissot's innocence, see Simon Burrows, 'The Innocence of Jacques-Pierre Brissot', *Historical Journal* 46 (December 2003), 843–71; cf, Robert Darnton, 'The Grub Street Style of Revolution: J.-P. Brissot, Police Spy', *Journal of Modern History* 40:4 (1968), 301–27. On Brissot's business relations with the STN see Darnton, 'Brissot and the STN'.
52   Robert Darnton, 'The Life-Cycle of a Book: A Publishing History of d'Holbach's Système de la nature', in Carol Armbruster, ed., *Publishing and Readership in Revolutionary France and America* (Westport, CT: Praeger 1993), pp. 15–43.
53   Roger Chartier, 'Book Markets and Reading in France at the End of the Old Rregime', in Carol Armbruster, ed., *Publishing and Readership in Revolutionary France and America* (Westport, CT: Greenwood Press, 1993); Robert Darnton, 'Booksellers/Demand' in 'A Literary Tour of France', at http://robertdarnton.org/literarytour/booksellers on 8 March 2016, p. 1.
54   BNF, MS Fr 22,075 fol. 389-90 and 391-92, *Arrêt du conseil concernant les contrefaçons des livres: Du 30 août 1777* (Paris, 1777). For amnesty and stamping arrangements see articles VI to IX.
55   For the *estampillage* records see BNF, MS. Fr. 21,831-21,834. They are discussed in Anne Boës and Robert Dawson, 'The Legitimation of Piracies and the police stamp of 1777', *SVEC* 230 (Oxford: Voltaire foundation, 1985), pp. 461–84; Jeanne Veyrin-Forrer, 'Livres arrêtés, livres estampillés, traces parisiennes de la contrefaction', in François Moureau, ed., *Les Presses grises. La contrefaçon du livre (XVIe-XIXe siècles)* (Paris: Aux Amateurs de livres, 1988), pp. 101–12.
56   See pp. 71–2.
57   See pp. 108–10.
58   See Darnton, *The Business of Enlightenment*; Louise Seaward, 'Censorship Through Co-operation: The *Société typographique de Neuchâtel* (STN) and the French Government, 1769-1789', *French History* 28:1 (2014), 23–42; Louise Seaward, 'The Société Typographique de Neuchâtel (STN) and the Politics of the Book Trade in late Eighteenth-Century Europe, 1769-1789', *European History Quarterly* 44:3 (2014), 439–79.

59 See Raymond Birn, *Royal Censorship of Books in 18th-Century France* (Stanford: Stanford University Press, 2012).
60 The main works condemned were du Marsy's *La Christiade ou le Paradis reconquis* and Isaac-Joseph Berruyer's *Histoire du peuple de Dieu*.
61 For these events and a translation of the decree see Birn, *Royal Censorship*, pp. 26–7.
62 The main registers for 1771–89 are at BNF, MS Fr. 21,933 and 21,934, and entitled 'Journal des livres suspendus depuis le 4 janvier de l'année 1771 jusqu'au 11 janvier 1791'.
63 Henry, 'Le Pays de Neuchâtel', p. 39.
64 Michel Schlup, 'L'Edition neuchâteloise des lumières', in Darnton and Schlup, eds, *Le Rayonnement d'une maison d'édition*, pp. 69–86. Schlup notes (pp. 81–2) that prison sentences never exceeded three days and got lighter as the century progressed.
65 Freedman, *Books without Borders*, p. 64.
66 Ibid., p. 72.
67 See *Catalogue des livres défendus par la commission impériale et royale jusqu'à l'année 1786* (Brussels, 1788). Some data from this source appears in the FBTEE database.
68 For more details on these measures, see pp. 60, 134–5, 161.
69 Silvio Corsini, 'Un pour tous … et chacun pour soi? Petite histoire d'une alliance entre les Sociétés typographiques de Lausanne, Berne et Neuchâtel', in Robert Darnton and Michel Schlup, eds, *Le Rayonnement d'une maison d'édition dans l'Europe des Lumières: la Société typographique de Neuchâtel 1769-1789* (Neuchâtel and Hauterive: B.P.U.N. and Editions Gilles Attinger, 2005), pp. 115–37 at pp. 117–18.
70 See pp. 134–5.
71 *Almanach de la librairie* (Paris: Moutard, 1781), pp. 2–7.
72 Birn, *Royal Censorship*, pp. 58–9: between 1750 and 1763, 40 per cent of 2,759 works of '*Belles-Lettres* and History' were judged by just five of eighty-four available censors.
73 See Robert Darnton, *Censors at Work: How States Shaped Literature* (New York: Norton, 2014), esp. p. 9.
74 *Almanach de la librairie* (Paris: Moutard, 1781), pp. 11–14. A *privilège* cost thirty-six *livres* twelve *sous*.
75 Nicole Hermann-Mascard, *La Censure des livres à Paris à la fin de l'ancien régime (1750-1789)* (Paris: Presses universitaires de France, 1968), pp. 67–8. *L'Imitation de Jésus Christ* was probably written between 1418 and 1427.
76 Birn, *Royal Censorship*, p. 3.
77 On the Helvétius affair, see David Smith, *Helvétius: A Study in Persecution* (Oxford: Clarendon Press, 1965).
78 Darnton, *Censors at Work*, p. 25.
79 BNF, MS Fr 21,832 fos 1–22, 'Etat général des imprimeurs du royaume fait en 1777'.
80 Claude Marin Saugrain, *Code de la librairie et de l'Imprimerie de Paris* (Paris: aux dépens de la communauté, 1744; facsimile edition, Farnborough, Gregg International, 1971).
81 See Jane McLeod, *Licencing Loyalty. Printers, Patrons and the State in Early Modern France* (University Park, PA: Penn State University Press, 2011).

Chapter 3

1 Darnton, *Forbidden Best-Sellers*, pp. 52–9, esp. p. 59.
2 Robert Darnton, 'Booksellers/Demand' in 'A Literary Tour of France' at http://robert-darnton.org/literarytour/booksellers on 8 March 2016. See also Darnton, *A Literary Tour*, pp. 264–81.

3   Robert Darnton, 'Charmet' in 'A Literary Tour of France' at http://robertdarnton.org/literarytour/booksellers/charmet on 17 July 2017. See also Darnton, *A Literary Tour*, p. 262.
4   Thierry Rigogne, 'Librairie et réseaux commerciaux du livre en France', in Robert Darnton and Michel Schlup, eds, *Le Rayonnement d'une maison d'édition dans l'Europe des Lumières: la Société typographique de Neuchâtel 1769-1789* (Neuchâtel and Hauterive: B.P.U.N. and Editions Gilles Attinger, 2005), pp. 375–404 at pp. 399, 404, n. 41.
5   Freedman, *Books without Borders*, pp. 8–9. Cf. Curran, *Selling Enlightenment*, pp. 94–5.
6   My initial projections estimated that the STN sold 750,000 to 1,000,000 books.
7   The handlist, MS 1000A, 'Société typographique, correspondants, répértoire géographique' is now available at http://bpun.unine.ch/pdf/BPUN_typo_correspondants_repertoire_geo.pdf.
8   Michael Schmidt, 'Liste des impressions et éditions de la société typographique de Neuchâtel', in Schlup, ed., *L'Edition neuchâteloise* pp. 233–85. STN catalogues survive from 1779 to 1785, as well as handwritten lists of 'livres philosophiques' which have been linked to them. Louis Fauche-Borel's 1787 catalogue and supplements also appear to have listed STN stock. See also BPUN, MS 1231 'Catalogues de la STN, 1781'.
9   The other archives are summarized in Curran, *Selling Enlightenment*, pp. 34–5. I thank Erik Jacob, Wallace Kirsop, Thierry Rigogne and Simon Macdonald for first bringing the Luchtmans, Desaint, Emeric David and Hoffman's company materials mentioned there to my attention.
10 Henry, 'Le Pays de Neuchâtel', pp. 36, 37.
11 See Curran, *Selling Enlightenment*, pp. 123–4.
12 Schlup, 'La STN: points de repère', pp. 72–6. A copy of the order banning the *Système de la nature* is reproduced at p. 75. See also Charly Guyot, 'Imprimeurs et pasteurs neuchâtelois: l'affaire du système de la nature', *Musée neuchâtelois* (1946), 74–81, 108–16; Darnton, 'The Life-Cycle of a Book'; and Curran, *Selling Enlightenment*, pp. 27, 123–4.
13 Schlup, 'La STN: points de repère', pp. 76–8.
14 Burrows, *A King's Ransom*, ch. 2.
15 Louise Seaward, 'The Small Republic and the Great Power: Censorship between Geneva and France in the later Eighteenth Century', *The Library: Transactions of the Bibliographical Society* 18:2 (2017), 191–217.
16 My 'Designer Notes' in appendix four discuss mapping issues.
17 Henry, 'Le Pays de Neuchâtel', p. 46, notes that after a 150-year hiatus, Neuchâtel had a continuous tradition of printing dating back to 1688.
18 See http://fbtee.uws.edu.au/stn/interface/dsgnotes.php#_Toc327948853; Curran, *Selling Enlightenment*.
19 Pierre Girardeau, *L'Art de tenir les livres en parties doubles* describes the STN's accounting methods and uses the same vocabulary. First published in Geneva in 1756, it was reprinted in Lyon in 1769, the year the STN was founded. The STN's directors probably used it to guide their financial accounting.
20 See Curran, *Selling Enlightenment*, pp. 44–5.
21 I owe this term to Dan Edelstein.
22 See BNF, MS Fr 22,018 and 22,019. The data they contain is reproduced in the appendices of Robert L. Dawson, *The French Book Trade and the Permission Simple of 1777: Copyright and the Public Domain*, SVEC 301 (Oxford: Voltaire foundation, 1992). It will appear in revised form in the FBTEE-2.0 database. I thank Catherine Bishop and Louise Seaward for their work on this dataset. *Comptes faits* is the only secular work among the top twenty most-printed works licensed under the *permission simple*.

23 For a brief overview of the literature on Marie-Antoinette *libelles*, see Burrows, *Blackmail, Scandal and Revolution*. For a previous challenge to the dominant reading of the *libelles*, see Vivian R. Gruder, 'The Question of Marie-Antoinette: The Queen and Public Opinion Before the Revolution', *French History* 16:3 (2002), 269–98.

24 For more detail on this narrative, see Burrows, *Blackmail, Scandal and Revolution*, esp. ch. 5.

25 I first reported these findings in a chapter entitled 'The French Book Trade in Enlightenment Europe, 1769-1787', Voltaire Foundation, Oxford, 14 January 2008.

26 Louis-Sébastien Mercier was also in exile in Neuchâtel from 1781 to 1785.

27 On books with foreign origins see Curran, *Selling Enlightenment*, p. 51. Foreign editions comprise 5 per cent of known 'in' transactions, and 4.9 per cent of 'out' transactions. The analysis below suggests that, in total, 9 to 10 per cent of books traded by the STN were foreign editions.

28 This was the line we took in Burrows and Curran, 'How Swiss was the STN?'

29 On Mauvelain, see Robert Darnton, 'Trade in the Taboo: The Life of a Clandestine Book Dealer in Prerevolutionary France', in Paul J. Korshin, ed., *The Widening Circle: Essays on the Circulation of Literature in Eighteenth-Century Europe* (n. pl.: University of Pennsylvania Press, 1976), pp. 13–83. For an abbreviated version see 'A clandestine bookseller in the provinces', in Darnton, ed., *Literary Underground*, pp. 122–47. On the problems of Darnton's use of Mauvelain as a case study see Burrows, *Blackmail, Scandal, and Revolution*, pp. 150–1 and 'French Banned Books'; and Mark Curran, 'Beyond the Forbidden Best-sellers of Pre-Revolutionary France', *Historical Journal* 56 (2013), 89–112.

30 Compare this analysis with the dismissal of FBTEE in Robert Darnton, 'The Demand for Literature in France, 1769-1789, and the Launching of a Digital Archive', *Journal of Modern History* 87 (2015), 509–31, at, p. 517 and Darnton, 'Literary Demand: Sources and Methods''A Literary Tour de France' at http://robertdarnton.org/, on 11 May 2016, p. 9. The sole grounds given there for Darnton's disdain are specious: 'Consider' – Darnton says – 'the example of a great bestseller, Voltaire's *Candide*. The STN's accounts make it possible to plot every copy sold by the STN on a map of Europe, but the statistics are so trivial as to make the map useless'. This is a non sequitur. The main research purpose of the FBTEE database is not to explore the geographic sales distributions of individual works (which, as this book has shown, reflect multiple variables), and *Candide* is a particularly poor choice for a case study. First published ten years before the STN opened for business, it was well past peak sales. (Martin et al., *Bibliographie du genre romanesque*, lists forty-five pre-revolutionary editions of *Candide*, but only four date from the period after 1772, when the STN began trading in volume in *livres d'assortiment*.) *Candide* is, moreover, only one of 4,000 works in the database. To discover meaningful patterns, FBTEE's tools allow us to aggregate and analyse those 4,000 works by author, content, genre, and place of publication. This study and its companion volume suggest that, skilfully employed, the database can offer insights that are far from trivial, whether or not one accepts Darnton's claims about the representative value of the STN archive. These insights have stimulated and underpin a reconsideration of the book trade, popular reading and the Enlightenment itself. In the process, they have helped to refine or challenge the work of many leading Enlightenment scholars, above all Darnton himself.

31 Although spreadsheets itemizing booksellers orders can be downloaded at http://robertdarnton.org/ much further work would be needed to create chronological breakdowns from this raw data.

32 See Curran, *Selling Enlightenment*, ch. 1.

33 Burrows, 'French Banned Books', pp. 24–5.

34 Giles Barber, 'The Cramers of Geneva and Their Trade in Europe between 1755 and 1766', *SVEC* 30 (1964), 377–413.

35 On STN works advertised at the Leipzig fair see Freedman, *Books without Borders*, pp. 23–6.
36 The FBTEE database records 273,116 units from a total of 413,710 sent out were STN editions, joint-editions and commissioned works.
37 FBTEE's 'edition type' data is the most difficult terrain in the database. For example, where a library bibliographic record noted that an edition with a Paris imprint was produced in The Netherlands, we generally had to take it on trust. Occasionally, too, 'fleuron' or provenance evidence allowed us to confirm where an edition was (probably) produced. But usually we had to follow the imprint data: in these cases our 'stated' and 'actual' place of publication were the same.
38 The STN received 38,099 units directly from non-Swiss suppliers, but 7,788 units were 'returns' of unpaid, damaged or unwanted orders, mostly of Swiss-produced titles, so were deducted from the figures here. In total, we can identify 5,246 'Swiss-produced' books (including a handful of 'Swiss international' editions) among the STN's imports from abroad.
39 The database lists 115,875 units as coming from Swiss suppliers.
40 This assumption implies that two thirds of books the STN's Swiss partners supplied were their own editions, 20 per cent of the remainder were directly imported from abroad, and a small further portion (assuming similar proportions, about 6.7 per cent) of foreign printings came through their own local suppliers. This suggests that almost 9 per cent $((20 + 6.7) \times 0.33)$ of the books the STN acquired from their Swiss trading partners (i.e. just over 10,000 units) would have been foreign editions. NB. The 6.7 per cent figure was calculated according to our assumptions by multiplying 33 per cent (i.e. proportion of books that were brought in from other suppliers) by 80 per cent (i.e. the proportion of purchased books that were not directly imported) by 20 per cent (i.e. the proportion of indirect imports).
41 On this point see Curran, *Selling Enlightenment*, pp. 159–60.
42 Although some putative 'foreign editions' in the database may be Swiss piracies, this tendency is clearly reflected in the STN sales figures. The STN sold 321,517 copies of Swiss editions relating to 866 titles (an average of 371 copies per title); 68,116 copies of editions of 1,208 titles whose publication place is recorded as 'unknown'; and just just 20,441 copies of 'foreign editions' across 1,093 works.
43 A survey of pirate editions from 1778 to 1781, which will appear in the FBTEE-2.0 database, suggests that many piracies were high volume products produced primarily for local circulation.
44 See Chapter 9 below.
45 For analysis of the relative importance of luxury and popular markets, see Curran, *Selling Enlightenment*, ch. 1.
46 See above, this chapter.
47 See Burrows and Curran, 'How Swiss was the STN?', p. 59.
48 See especially Chapter 7 and online Appendix 3.9.
49 The extent of these networks was revealed when Brissot was interrogated in the Bastille in 1784 about his involvement in distributing *libelle* pamphlets. See Burrows, 'Innocence'.

Chapter 4

1 BPUN, MS 1181 fos 216–17, William Owen to STN, London, 20 October 1769.
2 BPUN, MS 1212 fos 30–1, Samuel Roulet to STN, London, 27 February 1770.

3 These are the booksellers listed in Roulet's letter. On Nourse, and the use of his name as a false imprint, see Elena Muceni, 'John/Jean Nourse: un masque anglais au service de la littérature clandestine francophone', *La Lettre clandestine* 24 (2016), 203–19. I thank the author for sending me a prepublication version.
4 BPUN, MS 1114, fos 194, 198–9, 202–3, d'Arnal to STN, London, 16 October 1781, 14 December 1781, 5 February 1782; BPUN MS 1168 fos 221–2, Huguenin du Mitand to STN, 16 December 1783 confirms Elmsley succeeded in placing several copies of the *Descriptions des arts et métiers*.
5 BPUN, MS 1113 fos 72–3, Agassiz et Rougement to STN, London, 1 October 1784.
6 'Luchtmans' Client list, 1781-1787' in Amsterdam University Library, Luchtmans' archive, vol. 454. This document is reproduced in *The International Booktrade in the Eighteenth Century: Booksellers' accounts 1697-1803 from the Luchtmans archive* (Amsterdam and Lisse: Bibliotheek van de Koninklijke Vereeniging ter bevordering van de belangen des Boekhandels & MMF publications), microfiche 267, and in the online version of the Luchtmans archive at https://www.flickr.com/photos/bookhistorian/albums/72157675866777503/page6 (consulted on 12 November 2017).
7 Barber, 'The Cramers of Geneva', pp. 393–4; Burrows, *Blackmail, Scandal, and Revolution*, p. 65.
8 Darnton, *Business of Enlightenment*, p. 309. The consortium was led by Lyon publisher Joseph Duplain and Parisian publishing baron Charles-Joseph Panckoucke. Darnton has painstakingly mapped the distribution of Duplain's 8,011 subscriptions, using Duplain's subscription register (BPUN MS 1220) and other documents (see Darnton, *Business of Enlightenment*, appendix B). The STN database methodology only records copies which went through the STN's regular accounts, so its picture of sales of the quarto edition is generally less complete (but see below note 20).
9 See Darnton, *Business of Enlightenment*, pp. 33–7 for a summary of editions, print runs and prices.
10 BPUN, MS 1169 fo. 173, d'Ivernois to STN, 5 Hay Street, Westminster, 12 September 1784. D'Ivernois considered the 240 *livres* that the STN was demanding for its quarto edition too much.
11 D'Ivernois traded with the STN while in Geneva as part of Boin and d'Ivernois; Boin, d'Ivernois et Bassompierre; and the Société typographique de Genève (1778–83).
12 De Winter's order, enclosed with his letter of 6 December 1785, can be found at BPUN, MS 1230 fo. 135.
13 BPUN, MS 1230 fo. 135, de Winter's order, enclosed in fos 134/136, de Winter to STN, London, 6 December 1785.
14 Gordon Goodwin, 'Du Mitand, Louis Huguenin (b. 1748, d. in or after 1816)', rev. S. J. Skedd, *Oxford Dictionary of National Biography* (Oxford University Press, 2004) [http://www.oxforddnb.com.rp.nla.gov.au/view/article/18826, date accessed 28 March 2014]
15 BPUN, MS 1168 fos 207–8, Huguenin du Mitand to STN, London, 5 November 1782.
16 D'Arnal's correspondence refers several times to the *Encyclopédie*: the STN database confirms that he handled six copies in all.
17 BPUN, MS 1168 fos 223–4, Huguenin du Mitand to STN, London, 6 January 1784.
18 BPUN, MS 1176 fos 279–94, Edward Lyde's correspondence with the STN.
19 BPUN, MS 1042, Bilans, 1785, 1792.
20 Intriguingly, the STN database records twenty sales of the *Encyclopédie* to England, whereas Darnton, *Business of Enlightenment*, appendix B, p. 592 records just thirteen through Durand.

21 Darnton, *Business of Enlightenment*, p. 309. On Luke White's trade with the STN see Hugh Gough, 'Book Imports from Continental Europe in late eighteenth-century Ireland: Luke White and the Société typographique de Neuchâtel', *The Long Room* 38 (1993), 35–48.
22 BPUN, MS 1114 fos 202–3, Arnal to STN, London, 5 February 1782.
23 See David Smith, 'The Publishers of d'Helvétius *De l'Homme*: the Société typographique de Londres', *Australian Journal of French Studies* 30:3 (1990), 311–23, and below this chapter. On Boissière, see also Burrows, *Blackmail, Scandal and Revolution*, pp. 63–74, pp. 123–8.
24 David Shaw, 'French-Language Publishing in London to 1900', in Barry Taylor, ed., *Foreign Language Printing in London* (Boston Spa and London: British Library, 2002), pp. 101–22 at p. 101.
25 Axtell, Brookes and Garrett were all listed in 1780.
26 See de Lorme's entry in the British Book Trade Index, http://bbti.bodleian.ox.ac.uk/details/?traderid=43752; Jeremy Boosey and Ernst Roth, *Boosey and Hawkes 150th Anniversary* (London: Boosey and Hawkes, 1966), pp. 1–2.
27 The Leeds Foreign Lending Library collections survive in the Leeds Library.
28 BPUN, MS 1176 fos 289–90, Lyde to STN, London, 8 January 1779.
29 On this point see also Curran, *Selling Enlightenment*, passim.
30 BPUN, MS 1007, 'Rencontre, 1785-7' records stocktakes involving around 1,500 titles on 1 June 1785 and 1 June 1786.
31 Anna-Maria Rimm, 'Book Routes. Imports of Foreign Books to Sweden, 1750-1800', *Publishing History* 68 (2011), 5–24.
32 BPUN, MS 1227 fos 14–15, Ulf to STN, 11 September 1787.
33 Anna-Maria Rimm has produced several articles in Swedish on Elsa Fougt based on her PhD dissertation, 'Elsa Fougt, Kungl. boktryckare. Aktör i det litterära systemet ca 1780–1810' (Uppsala, 2009). I thank the author for sending me the extended English summary of this work.
34 Fyrberg, on 2,921 books, was the STN's largest Swedish client by unit sales.
35 The translation, by Erik Zetterstén (1732-1801), appears in variant editions under two different titles: *Den bewäpnade tidninge-skrifwaren, eller anecdoter wid den förra franska ministeren* and *Anmärkningar öfwer en skrift kallad: Le gazetier cuirassé ou anecdotes scandaleuses de la cour de France. Första delen*. Both were printed and published by Wennberg & Nordström in Stockholm in 1772. I thank Anna-Maria Rimm for assistance researching this translation. Supplementary information is from a 2015 catalogue of the Stockholm rare books dealer Matt Rehnström Rare Books at http://rehnstroem.se/pdf/Olympia15.pdf on 17 May 2017.
36 BPUN, MS 1227 fos 14–15, Ulf to STN, 11 September 1787. The STN despatched most of the books listed here to Ulf before they received this letter. They appear never to have sent the Raynals.
37 BPUN, MS 1214 fos 306–7, Schön et Cie to STN, Stockholm, 22 January 1788.
38 Ibid., fos 317–18, Schön et Cie to STN, Stockholm, 26 September 1788. MS 1042, Bilan 1792, reveals that by 1792 Ulf's bad debt had risen to 9,969 *livres*.
39 BPUN, MS 1214 fos 306–7, Schön et Cie to STN, Stockholm, 22 January 1788.
40 BPUN, MS 1042, Bilan 1792.
41 These were Leprince de Beaumont's *Magasin nouveau des jeunes demoiselles*; an anonymous *Précieuse collection, ou Recueil des pensées les plus sublimes des anciens et modernes, avec un choix des plus beaux traits de l'Histoire, à l'usage des adolescens & des hommes faits* published at Verrières in 1786; Jérémie Witel's religiously sceptical

philosophic and pedagogic treatise, *Mon Elève ou Emile instituteur: nouvelle éducation morale* (Neuchâtl, 1786); and four works by Stephanie de Genlis: *Veillées du château ou Cours de morale à l'usage des enfants*; *Annales de la vertu, ou Cours d'histoire à l'usage des jeunes personnes*; *Théâtre à l'usage des jeunes personnes*; and *Théâtre de société par l'auteur du Théâtre à l'usage des jeunes*.

42 Alicia Montoya, 'French and English Women Writers in Dutch Library Catalogues, 1700-1800. Some Methodological Considerations and Preliminary Results', in Suzan van Dijk et al., eds, '*I Have Heard about You*'. *Foreign Women's Writing Crossing the Dutch Border: from Sappho to Selma Lagerlöf* (Hilversum 2004), pp. 182–216.

43 I first discussed this topic in a keynote address entitled 'Reference Books, Text Books and Enlightenment Cosmopolitan Culture, 1770-1790', at the 'Alphabetical Nation Colloquium: Dictionaries and Encyclopedias within and Across Borders', Copenhagen, 27 May 2010.

44 Michel Schlup, 'Coup-d'oeil sur les relations commerciales de la STN avec Moscou et Saint-Pétersbourg', in Michel Schlup, ed., *L'Edition neuchâteloise au siècle des Lumières: la Société typographique de Neuchâtel (1769-1789)* (Neuchâtel: B.P.U.N., 2002), pp. 107–13 at pp. 108–9.

45 There may be some confusion between the second and third items: our data is frequently ambiguous.

46 Schlup, 'Coup-d'oeil sur les relations commerciales de la STN avec Moscou et Saint-Pétersbourg', p. 107.

47 Ibid.

48 A letter from Weitbrecht to the STN (BPUN, Ms 1229 bis, fo. 111, St Petersburg, 28 May 1781), reproduced in ibid., p. 111, asks the STN to add any 'jolies nouveautés' to their next consignment.

49 BPUN, Ms 1229 bis, fo. 111, Weitbrecht to the STN, St Petersburg, 28 May 1781, cited in ibid., p. 110.

50 For example, 3.18 per cent of books recorded in the FBTEE database are listed as 'anticlerical works' as opposed to 2.89 per cent of those going to Russia. For pornography the stats are 1.95 and 1.25 per cent respectively.

51 On Swiss partner houses see Curran, *Selling Enlightenment*, Chapter 2, 'The Myth of the Mountain-Dwellers'.

52 Gosse took between twenty and 506 copies of each work listed by Boissière. On the Gosse-Boissière partnership see Smith, 'The Publishers of d'Helvétius *De l'Homme*', pp. 311–23, at p. 312. On the STN's relations with Gosse, see Robert Darnton, 'La Science de la contrefaction', in Robert Darnton and Michel Schlup, eds, *Le Rayonnement d'une maison d'édition dans l'Europe des Lumières: la Société typographique de Neuchâtel 1769-1789* (Neuchâtel and Hauterive: B.P.U.N. and Editions Gilles Attinger, 2005), 89–113 at pp. 92–104.

53 *Catalogue général des livres qui se trouvent chez la Société typographique à Londres* (undated, c. 1775). The catalogue is misdated to 1785 in ECCO. The catalogue imprints have been checked against Schmidt, 'Liste des Impressions'. The five non-STN Neuchâtel editions in Boissière's catalogue all date from 1748 to 1767. Smith, 'The Publishers of d'Helvétius *De l'Homme*', p. 312, identifies another catalogue of Boissière's stock produced by Gosse when they dissolved their partnership in 1792. A copy survives in Amsterdam University library.

54 See http://robertdarnton.org/literarytour/otherlocations/lyon.

55 Barber, 'The Cramers of Geneva', pp. 390–1, p. 394. Strangely, Barber does not quantify the Cramers' trade with their Swiss partners.

56 Ibid., p. 394
57 These figures derive from a data match between Parisian correspondents of the STN in the FBTEE-1.0 database and 322 Parisian printers and booksellers identified during data-entry work for the FBTEE-2.0. Only twenty-nine appear on both lists. The FBTEE-2.0 list, which drew on the *Almanach de la librairie* and records of stock sales at the *Chambre syndicale* is likely to include all major general book dealers.
58 The entire editions of both Goëzman's *Tableau de la monarchie française* and Desmaisons' *Contrat conjugal* were seized by the French authorities. The latter was impounded in the Bastille (see Chapter 9), but by an order of 18 September 1771 Goëzman's work was released to its distributor, the bookseller Edmé, just one day after being seized as a *nouveauté*. The *discours préliminaire* to Goëzman's work was also seized then released. (See BNF, MS Fr. 21,933 fo. 21; fo. 7).
59 On the Lacoré's protection see BPUN, MS 1134 fols. 98-9, [Charles-Antoine] Charmet to STN, 18 October 1775; Darnton, *Business of Enlightenment*, pp. 289-90 and *Forbidden Best-Sellers*, pp. 35-6. Darnton erroneously identifies the intendant as Pierre-Etienne Bourgeois de Boynes, whom Lacoré replaced in 1761. Lacoré was intendant of the Franche-Comté until his death in 1784.
60 BPUN MS 1134, fols. 140-1, [Charles-Antoine] Charmet to STN, 20 February 1778.
61 See below Chapter 9. The retreat from the illegal trade is demonstrated graphically in the podcast of Simon Burrows, '30 August 1777 and 12 June 1783 – A Digital Impact Assessment of Two Censorship Measures' – Around the World Online Digital Humanities Symposium, 22 May 2014, http://youtu.be/aC5eP0yKiDo. Last consulted 11 May 2016.
62 The registers of the new *permission simple* are held in BN, MS.Fr. 22,018 and MS.Fr. 22,019. For more details, see Chapter 3, note 22, above.
63 On Favarger's tour see Darnton, *A Literary Tour*, pp. 3-262, and http://robertdarnton.org/literarytour/favarger. This webpage has downloadable versions of Favarger's diary, correspondence (in both the original and English translation) and records of his earlier travels on behalf of the STN.
64 After 13 June 1783, the STN database records only 2,911 units despatched to Paris (although we only have piecemeal records for June 1787 to May 1790, and none at all for January 1789 to 2 May 1790). Over half these units were copies of the *Descriptions des arts et métiers* and just 120 were non-STN editions.
65 For petitions against the 12 June 1783 decree see BNF, MS Fr. 21,823 fos 68-71, 83-5. These documents are cited fully in Chapter 9 below.
66 See BN, Ms.Fr. 22,040, 'L', p.29, undated note on 'Livres venant de l'étranger', [June 1787]. This document was reproduced in the appendices to Robert L. Dawson, *Confiscations at Customs: Banned Books and the French Book Trade During the Last Years of the Ancien Régime* (Oxford: SVEC 2006:07), appendix H, which was formerly available online (only), at http://uts.cc.utexas.edu/~dawson1/Confs_appendixes.htm (last consulted 24 March 2016), pp. 234-5. Professor Dawson died in 2007: a decade later his website appears to have finally gone off-line. The Voltaire foundation and I both have downloaded copies.
67 This transaction is recorded in BPUN, MS 1043, 'Livre de Caisse', fo. 99. The consignment equated to 1,862 units of 181 titles, and included four hundred copies of Riccoboni's sentimental novel *Histoire de deux jeunes amies*, 110 copies of Elie Bertrand's *Thévenon ou les journées de la montagne* and seventy-one copies of Leprince de Beaumont's *Magasins des enfans*. Some of this stock was probably well past its use-by date, including twenty-four copies of the *Vie privée de Louis XV*.

68 Saugrain, *Code de la Librairie*, pp. 190–1.
69 See Chapters 9 and 10 below; Burrows, 'Charmet and the Book Police'.
70 This figure is for total STN sales to the German geographic zone, which excludes Austria, Bohemia and Hungary.
71 Freedman, *Books without Borders*, p. 9.
72 On the STN's exchanges with Italy see also Anne Machet, 'Clients Italiens de la Société typographique de Neuchâtel', in Jacques Rychner and Michel Schlup, eds, *Aspects du livre neuchâtelois* (Neuchâtel: Bibliotheque publique et universitaire, 1986), pp. 159–86; Renato Pasta, 'Les Echanges avec l'Italie', in Robert Darnton and Michel Schlup, eds, *Le Rayonnement d'une maison d'édition dans l'Europe des Lumières: la Société typographique de Neuchâtel 1769-1789* (Neuchâtel and Hauterive: B.P.U.N. and Editions Gilles Attinger, 2005), pp. 455–73.
73 STN database after Schmidt, 'Liste des impressions'. Google books has an edition of the *Discours oratoire contenant l'éloge de son excellence monsieur le chevalier André Tron* (Venice: Charles Palese, 1773). The 'Marquis de Fogliani' was Giovanni Fogliani Sforza d'Aragona, Marquis of Pellegrino, Viceroy of Sicily, 1755–75.
74 The sales can be identified using the 'client type' options menu in the FBTEE database. This provides a very different overview to the anecdotal, dossier-based approach to the STN's local clientele taken by André Bandelier, 'Le Clientèle neuchâteloise et jurasienne de la STN', in Darnton and Schlup, eds, *Le Rayonnement d'une maison d'édition*, pp. 317–40.
75 There are records of counter sales in the STN's *Rencontres*, *Brouillards* and, in some instances, petty cash books. I have excluded from the counter-sale figures 482 copies of *Palettes simples* and *Palettes doubles*: for further explanation, see Appendix 3.4, note.
76 BPUN, MS 1030, 'Main courante', fo. 34. The name 'Bondely' does not appear in the online *Dictionnaire historique de la Suisse* or Michel Schlup, ed., *Biographies neuchâteloises*, vol. I, *De Saint Guillaume à la fin des Lumières* (Hauterive: Editions Gilles Attinger, 1996).
77 Other examples of customers at the counter include the Banneret Jean-Jacques Deluze's purchase of Voltaire's *Questions sur l'Encyclopédie* on 2 May 1772 and a purchase of Cicero's works in Latin on 30 November 1791 on behalf of 'professeur Meuron'. Meuron appears to be Henry de Meuron (1752-1813), a teacher and librarian who bought sixty-eight copies of thirty-six other books from the STN in 1783–84. The *conseilleur* Jean-Jacques de Luze who bought a couple of books from the STN in 1787 was a relative of the Banneret.
78 Her purchases are recorded in BPUN, MS 1024, Journal C, fo. 232; MS 1026, Journal, p. 99.
79 On Julie Bondeli, see her article in the online *Dictionnaire historique de la Suisse* at http://www.hls-dhs-dss.ch/textes/f/F11582.php
80 The STN tended to only account for counter sales every few days, so entries generally represent sales over up to a week. Annotations reveal occasions when counter sales on different days were amalgamated into one record. For example, a 9 May 1774 entry records that separate sales of Ostervald's *Geographie élémentaire* were made on 30 April and 7 May.
81 Surviving accounts record counter sales of Bertrand's *Sermons* on twenty-eight occasions.
82 We have records for counter sales of ninety-eight copies of the *Abregé*.
83 Gottfried Adam, 'Protestantism and modernisation in German children's literature of the late 18th century', in Jan de Maeyer, ed., *Religion, Children's Literature and Modernity in Western Europe: 1750-2000* (Leuven: Leuven University Press, 2005), pp. 233–49 at pp. 237–9.

Chapter 5

1. Théodore Rilliet, *Inceste avoué à un mari, ou Exposé rapide de l'innocence & de l'honnêteté, tant absolue que relative, de spectable Théodore Rilliet* (n.pl. [Neuchâtel]: n.p. [Société typographique de Neuchâtel], 1782), p. vii.
2. Mark Curran, *Selling Enlightenment*, pp. 114, 122.
3. While preparing this table it was noticed that the authors anthologized in Berquin's *Lectures pour les enfans* had erroneously been recorded as primary authors in the database. Their sales figures were duly adjusted downwards by 1,378. Authors affected with regards to this table are Fénélon, Gessner, La Fontaine, Marmontel, Montesquieu and Voltaire.
4. Simon Macdonald, 'Identifying Mrs Meeke: Another Burney Family Novelist', *Review of English Studies* 26:265 (June 2013), 367–85.
5. Mark Curran, *Selling Enlightenment*, pp. 114–24; Mark Curran, 'What Killed Théodore Rilliet de Saussure? Censorship and the Old Regime in France, 1769–1789' in Daniel Bellingradt, Paul Nelles, Jeroen Salman, (eds), *Books in Motion in Early Modern Europe* (Basingstoke: Palgrave Macmillan, Cham, 2017), pp. 193–218.
6. Rilliet's dossier, BPUN, MS 1207 fos 7–66, which spans the period 20 August 1782 to 12 April 1783 (and thus post-dates the first edition of *Planta gagnant sa vie en honnête homme*) contains extensive discussions of the format and print run for the second edition, originally planned for 24,000 copies.
7. See Mark Curran, *Selling Enlightenment*, pp. 102–3; http://fbtee.uws.edu.au/stn/interface/browse.php?t=book&id=spbk0002272.
8. BPUN MS 1180, fos 241–2, Mercier to STN, 19 January 1779. For a discussion of the work, see below Chapter 11.
9. BPUN MS 1180 fo.240, Mercier to STN, Paris, 27 August 1782; Curran, *Selling Enlightenment*, p. 105; http://fbtee.uws.edu.au/stn/interface/query_events.php?t=book&id=spbk0000504&d1=01&m1=01&y1=1769&d2=31&m2=12&y2=1794&d=table
10. Pellet often allowed his name to be used as a cover for semi-clandestine works including the *Encyclopédie*: see Robert Darnton, 'Hidden Editions of the *Encyclopédie*', in Jean-Daniel Candaux and Bernard Lescaze, eds, *Cinq siècles de l'Imprimerie Genevoise*, 2 vols. (Genève: Société d'histoire et d'archéologie, 1980–81), II, pp. 71–101 at p. 73.
11. John Jeanprêtre, 'Histoire de la Société typographique de Neuchâtel', *Musée Neuchâtelois* (1949), 70–7, 115–20, 148–53 at p. 117, reveals that a receipt for 5,000 copies sent to Chauvet indicates that the *Mémoire apologétique des Génèvois* is in fact the *Pièces importantes à la dernière révolution de Genève*. I thank Robert Darnton for drawing this to my attention.
12. The eleventh to twentieth bestsellers are: 11. Frédéric-Samuel Ostervald's *Géographie élémentaire*; 12. Raynal's *Histoire philosophique et politique des Deux Indes*; 13. *Mémoire donné au roi par M. Necker en 1778*; 14. *Pseaumes*; 15. Rilliet's *Inceste avoué à un mari*; 16. Christin's *Dissertation sur l'établissement de l'abbaye de S. Claude*; 17. Millot's *Elemens de l'histoire générale*; 18. Mercier's *Le Philosophe du Port-au-Bled*; 19. Voltaire's *Questions sur l'Encyclopédie*; and 20. Dorat's *Oeuvres*.
13. The 'port au bled' (literally Grain Port) was one of many wharfs along the *rive droite* of the Seine.
14. On Raynal's work, see below Chapter 11.
15. Schlup, 'La STN: points de repère', p. 72.
16. The exact figure is 11,254 units out of 65,904, or approximately 17 per cent.
17. On this point, see Curran, 'Beyond the Forbidden Best-sellers of Pre-Revolutionary France', pp. 90, 99–100.

Chapter 6

1. On d'Hémery's files see Robert Darnton, 'A Police Inspector Sorts his Files', in Darnton, ed., *The Great Cat Massacre and Other Episodes in French Cultural History* (New York: Vintage, 1985), pp. 145–89. On his journal, see: Sabine Juratic and Jean-Pierre Vittu, 'Surveiller et connaître: *le Journal de la librairie* de Joseph d'Hémery, instrument de la police du livre à Paris au XVIIIe siècle', in Dominique Mellot and Sergei Karp, eds, *Le Siècle des Lumières. Statut et censure de l'imprimé en France et en Russie au Siècle des Lumières* (St Petersburg: Naouka, 2008), pp. 90–107.
2. Robert Darnton, 'Philosophers Trim the Tree of Knowledge', in Darnton, ed., *The Great Cat Massacre*, pp. 190–213.
3. Library professionals at the University of Leeds encouraged us to consider the Dewey or Library of Congress systems. However, Dewey was too general and non-specific for our purposes, while the LoC system appeared complex to master and liable to inconsistent application. Dewey was also overly focused on modern preoccupations.
4. On the lineage of the system, see Edward Edwards, *Memoirs of Libraries: Including a Handbook of Library Economy*, 2 vols (London: Trübner, 1859), II, pp. 772–82.
5. See especially various essays in François Furet, ed., *Livre et Société dans la France du XVIIIe Siècle*, 2 vols (Paris: Mouton, 1965) and Robert Darnton 'Reading, Writing and Publishing', in Darnton, ed., *Literary Underground*, pp. 167–208.
6. Edwards, *Memoirs of Libraries*, p. 773.
7. Ibid., p. 782.
8. Ibid., p. 782 (quote), 780.
9. See *Catalogue des livres de la bibliothèque d'Holbach*, pp. 17–19.
10. The main sources consulted for Mark Curran's iteration were *Catalogue des livres de la bibliothèque de feu M. Le baron d'Holbach* (Paris, 1789); *Catalogue des livres du cabinet du feu Louis Jean Gaignat* (Paris, 1769); *Catalogue des livres, imprimés et manuscrit de la bibliothèque de feu monseigneur le Prince de Soubise* (Paris, 1788); *Catalogue d'une fort riche et très belle collection de livres rares & choisis en tout genre* (Anvers, 1785); and Edwards, *Memoirs of Libraries*.
11. This paragraph and the passages that follow on the FBTEE keyword system have been adapted from my 'Designer notes' (see Appendix 4).
12. Definitions are in the FBTEE database under the 'browse keywords' function.
13. These are defined in the FBTEE database as 'works designed to have an erotic charge, ranging from outright pornography (i.e. works which offer descriptions of genitals or the sexual act for the purposes of titillation) through to works which allude frequently to sexualized activities or pleasures, without necessarily offering graphic explicit passages'.
14. Lynn Hunt, 'Obscenity and the Origins of Modernity, 1500-1800', in Lynn Hunt, ed., *The Invention of pornography: Obscenity and the Origins of Modernity, 1500-1800* (New York: Zone Books, 1993), pp. 9–45, at p. 10.
15. Conlon, *Le siècle des Lumières*.
16. Martin and his collaborators list genre, historical and national setting, names of principal protagonists and certain themes or aspects or stylistic features. Although they warn that the system was neither entirely uniform nor satisfactory, it was more consistent than most other bibliographic sources consulted, and much of their information could feed directly into our categorization scheme.
17. http://www.cesar.org.uk/cesar2/index.php
18. See my 'Remarks on Taxonomic Systems for Future Projects' in the 'Designer Notes' in Appendix 4. In particular, I proposed adding a database field for categorization notes;

a standardized means of recording the basis on which each work was categorized; and the adoption of customizable 'keyword strings'.
19 On scandalous and subversive aspects of novel reading, see William Warner, 'Licencing Pleasure: Literary History and the Novel in Early Modern Britain', in John Richetti, ed., *The Columbia History of the British Novel* (New York: Columbia University Press, 1994), pp. 1–22.
20 *Catalogue général des livres qui se trouvent chez la Société typographique à Londres*. Boissière traded under several names between c. 1771 and c. 1787, including the *Société typographique de Londres*.
21 Edwards, *Memoirs of Libraries*, p. 782.
22 Statistics for *Belles-Lettres* here also include eleven works under the rubric 'Prix et travaux académiques'. *Science et Arts* includes the five rubrics 'Philosophie, métaphysique, morale' (212 works); Mathématique, physique, histoire naturelle, art militaire' (328); 'Agriculture, oeconomie, commerce' (127); Médécine, chirurgie, pharmacie, chymie, botanique, etc.' (163); 'Beaux arts, mécanique' (77). 479 works in all genres categorizsed as 'Bibliographie, Mélanges' have been excluded from my statistics.
23 This paragraph and those that follow are adapted from Simon Burrows, 'БИБЛИОМЕТРИЯ, ПОПУЛЯРНОЕ ЧТЕНИЕ И ЛИТЕРАТУРНОЕ ПОЛЕ ИЗДАТЕЛЯ ЭПОХИ ПРОСВЕЩЕНИЯ', ['Bibliometrics, Popular Reading, and the Literary Field of an Enlightenment Publisher'], *Annuaire d'études françaises*, special edition *Le 225e anniversaire de la Révolution française*, ed. Alexandre Tchoudinov et Dmitri Bovykine (Moscow, 2015), pp. 15–43. I thank the editors for permission to republish this material in English.
24 On Boissière's coterie, see Burrows, *Blackmail, Scandal, and Revolution*, pp. 63–4.
25 But note that some religious sure-fire sellers were printed in large runs to sell over several years.
26 See Darnton, 'Reading, Writing and Publishing', pp. 173–82. See also Daniel Mornet, 'Les enseignements des bibliothèques privées (1750-1781)', *Revue d'histoire littéraire de la France* 17 (1910), 449-96; Furet, ed., *Livre et société*.
27 The original survey is in Mornet, 'Les enseignements des bibliothèques privées'.

Chapter 7

1 The treatment of Parisian category data in this chapter draws extensively on Burrows, 'БИБЛИОМЕТРИЯ, ПОПУЛЯРНОЕ ЧТЕНИЕ И ЛИТЕРАТУРНОЕ ПОЛЕ ИЗДАТЕЛЯ ЭПОХИ ПРОСВЕЩЕНИЯ'.
2 *Romans* [novels] accounted for 8.6 per cent of STN editions sold (including commissioned works and joint editions) as opposed to 18.38 per cent of other Swiss and Neuchâtelois editions.
3 See Darnton's review of The French Book Trade in Enlightenment Europe.
4 See especially Darnton, *Forbidden Best-Sellers*, pp. 71–82; Darnton, 'High Enlightenment'.
5 The quote is taken from the written version of Popkin's comments to the ASECS-sponsored panel devoted to the FBTEE project at the American Historical Association conference in Chicago, January 2012. I thank Professor Popkin for supplying his comments and proposing the panel.
6 A summary of how this affects the most significant keywords is provided in online Appendix 3.9; see also online appendices 3.6 and 3.7. An alternative approach to compensating for 'commissioned works' would be to count the number of times a title was sent

out in a consignment of books, rather than the number of books. As this functionality is not currently available in the FBTEE online interface, I have preferred to use the options menus to filter out commissioned works. This method can be replicated by casual users.
7   See especially Robert Darnton, *The Devil in the Holy Water*.
8   The options menus are accessible from http://fbtee.uws.edu.au/stn/interface/option_summary.php
9   This is not, of course, discernible from the undifferentiated category 'Science et Arts': it can be discovered by digging into the second-level Parisian categories or exploring the project keyword 'Science'.
10 These appeared under several variant titles.
11 See above Chapter 4.
12 Our Helvetic or Swiss zone comprises areas found inside modern Switzerland, including perpetual allies which were not technically part of the eighteenth-century Swiss confederation, notably Geneva, the Bishopric of Basel and Neuchâtel itself. [Bourbon] France includes all territories within French borders immediately prior to 1789, including exclaves. Enclaves such as Avignon (even under the French occupation of 1770–75), Montbéliard, Mulhouse or Mandeure are not part of Bourbon France for the purposes of our analysis.
13 On textbook markets, see Chapter 4.
14 The term *Catechumène* – here signifying one being instructed in the catechism in preparation for [Protestant and therefore mature] Baptism – does not precisely match its English equivalent.
15 One important exception is Jean-Frédéric Ostervald's *Abrégé de l'histoire sainte et du catéchisme*, which appears second on the STN's global clandestine bestseller list in Chapter 9.
16 Of 16,636 unit sales tagged with the keyword 'financial administration', 14,706 also bear the keyword 'Necker, Jacques'.
17 On the Necker pamphlets and politics, see also Chapter 11.
18 16,636 out of a global total of 30,302 unit sales for 'Economics' also bear the classification 'Financial Adminstration'.
19 Altogether 13,907 out of 23,351 unit sales for 'Geography' also bear the tag for 'School Book'.
20 Only 2.04 per cent of unit sales of the STN's own (non-commissioned) editions have been tagged as 'Erotic works'.
21 Some 9.08 per cent of unit sales of the STN's (non-commissioned) editions have been tagged as 'Philosophie': this compares with 11.64 per cent for the 'trade' sector as a whole.
22 See Chapter 9.
23 9,188 out of 27,615 'global' unit sales for 'Lives and Letters' were also tagged 'History' and 10,337 were tagged 'Politics'. All three words were applied to works with a total of 1,082 unit sales.
24 Three year rolling averages of edition counts for new and reprinted novels given in Martin et al., *Bibliographie du genre romanesque*, pp. xxxvi–xxxvii rise across the period from the range 110 to 129 for the years 1771–73 to 156 to 172 in the period 1785–87.

Chapter 8

1   I thank participants in the international symposium on 'Enlightenment Cosmopolitanisms and Sensibilities' at Sydney University, 11–12 June 2014, for feedback on early draft material for this chapter.

2. Freedman, *Books without Borders*, p. 1. Similar concerns lay behind FBTEE and the Leeds University Centre for the Comparative History of Print, which I co-founded.
3. Freedman, *Books without Borders*, pp. 3-4.
4. Ibid., p. 1. See also Elizabeth L. Eisenstein, *Grub Street Abroad: Aspects of the French Cosmopolitan Press from the Age of Louis XIV to the Enlightenment* (Oxford: Clarendon Press, 1992).
5. Freedman, *Books without Borders*, p. 4.
6. This statement is based on extensive soundings in the Luchtmans archives in the University of Amsterdam Library special collections, and in its microfilmed and online versions (see List of Sources below).
7. These works can be isolated using the languages options menu and 'rank books' search query in the FBTEE database.
8. Only 2.8 per cent of non-STN editions in the database were printed in languages other than French.
9. For a full listing, see online Appendix 3.13.
10. For more details on sales of travel literature by region see online Appendix 3.14.
11. France took 471 out of 1792 sales.
12. BPUN, MS 1129, fos 200-1, Brydone to STN, 1 July 1775.
13. See esp. ibid., fos 218-19, Brydone to STN, Lausanne, 10 October 1775.
14. Ibid., fos 204-5, Brydone to STN, Lausanne, 11 July 1775.
15. Ibid., fos 218-19, Brydone to STN, Lausanne, 10 October 1775.
16. Ibid., fos 220-1, Brydone to STN, Vienna, 2 April 1776.
17. Ibid., fos 212-13, Brydone to STN, Lausanne, 14 August 1775.
18. Patrick Brydone, *Voyage en Sicile et à Malthe*, 2 vols (Londres [Neuchâtel] et se trouve à Neuchâtel au magasin de la Société typographique, 1776), vol. I, p. i. The title page advertised it was translated by M. Demeunier and had been 'soigneusement corrigée sur la seconde edition angloise, par M. B. P. A. N.'
19. Brydone, *Voyage en Sicile et à Malthe*, I, p. i.
20. Ibid., I, pp. i-ii.
21. Ibid., I, p. ii.
22. Ibid., p. 43.
23. Ibid., I, 43-4.
24. Ibid., I, 62-3.
25. Ibid., I, 81.
26. Ibid., I, 97.
27. Ibid., I, 98.
28. Ibid., I, 110.
29. Ibid., I, 100.
30. Ibid., I, 2.
31. Ibid., I, 51-7; 69-76.
32. Ibid., I, 9.
33. Mark Towsey, 'First Steps in Associational Reading: Book Use and Sociability at the Wigtown Subscription Library, 1795-9', *Proceedings of the Bibliographical Society of America* 103:4 (2009), 455-95.
34. The forty-four original members included eight clergymen, eight lawyers, four doctors and several prominent landlords.
35. Towsey, 'First Steps in Associational Reading', pp. 457-60.
36. A sixth woman, Lady Maxwell, was, with her husband, among the original library subscribers, but apparently never borrowed a book. The women borrowers were all

apparently less affluent, and probably widows. Wigtown was unusual, though far from unique, in having women subscribers. Towsey, 'First Steps in Associational Reading', p. 461.

37 The only works first appearing entirely after 1791 were *Bell's British Theatre* (1797), John Gillies, *The History of Ancient Greece* (1792–3); Robert Heron's *A New General History of Scotland* (1794–9); Adam Smith's *Essays on Philosophical Subjects* (1795); James Pettit Andrews, *History of Great Britain, from the death of Henry VIII, to the accession of James VI of Scotland to the crown of England* (1796); Dugald Stewart's *Elements of the Philosophy of the Human Mind* (published between 1792 and 1827) and Robert Watson's *The History of the Reign of Philip the Third, King of Spain* (1793).

38 These were the *Annual Register*, *Critical Review* and *Monthly Review*, *The Lounger* and *The Mirror*.

39 There is a minor discrepancy between Towsey's article, which lists Macpherson, *Ossian's Works*, in the loan records, and his spreadsheet which does not list Ossian but instead contains Cook's *A Compendious History of Captain Cook's Last Voyage*. The spreadsheet lists fifty-eight items but three are successive volumes of the *Annual Register*.

40 Towsey classifies Montesquieu's *Spirit of the Laws* and Adam Smith's *Wealth of Nations* as 'History'. Neither work has much impact on borrowing figures: Montesquieu was borrowed from Wigtown library four times by two readers, and Adam Smith taken out three times by just one. Some works in Towsey's spreadsheet carry a second classification, but the second, subsidiary, 'genre' is ignored here. Often this second classification was geographic (e.g. 'Britain'), but they also include 'Classics', '*Belles-Lettres*' and lone instances of 'Biography', 'Philosophy', 'History' and, in the case of Raynal, 'Travels' and, for Adam Smith, 'Economics'.

41 The STN sold thirty or more of each of these titles.

42 These included a fourteen-volume translation of James Bruce's *Travels to Discover the Source of the Nile*, published in London between 1790 and 1792.

43 Loan figures for these works were Henry Fielding's *Works* (53 loans, 226 equivalent unit STN sales); *Adventures of Roderick Random* (10 loans, 92 sales); *Adventures of Peregrine Pickle* (7 loans, 18 sales).

44 The STN did not trade in the two other most frequently borrowed novels, Henry Brooke's *The Fool of Quality, or, the History of Henry Earl of Moreland* (23 loans), which was first published in 1765–70, or John Moore's *Zeluco. Various Views of Human Nature, taken from Life and Manners, Foreign and Domestic* (20 loans), which first appeared in 1786.

45 The STN never handled Samuel Johnson's *The Prince of Abissinia* (1759), which was first published in French translation as *Histoire de Rasselas, Prince d'Abissinie, par M. Jhonnson* [sic] by Prault *fils* in Paris in 1760. It ran to three further editions by 1788. The final edition was supposedly published by Jean Mourer in Lausanne and de Bure *l'aîné* in Paris, and might therefore have been expected to appear in the STN data. However, the *Biblos 18* database does not list it as a Lausanne edition and Quérard and Rochedieu attribute the edition to de Bure alone. Neither did the STN deal in the French abridgement of Charles Johnstone's *Chrysal; or, the adventures of a guinea* (1760–5, transl. 1767). The publishing history of the French version, *Chrisal ou les aventures d'une guinée*, is complicated: the first French edition published by Grangé in 1767 provided a selection of episodes from volume one of the English work; episodes from volume two were published in 1769 in a *Supplément à Chrysal*. Between them these two versions seem to have run to six French editions (including an apparent

combined edition in 1774). Nor, as noted above, did the STN deal in Henry Brooke's *The Fool of Quality*, which was translated into French by Antoine-Gilbert Griffet de Labaume and published with a Bouillon/Paris imprint in 1789. The Paris publisher was named as Royer; the title was *Le Fou de qualité, ou histoire de Henry, comte de Moreland*. The translation of Moore's *Zeluco*, entitled *Zelucco ou le vice trouve en lui-même son chatiment* in 1796, appeared too late to feature in the STN's ledgers. On French editions of these works see Martin, Mylne and Frautschi, *Bibliographie du genre romanesque*, pp. 66, 120, 139–40, 335, 392.

46 The only work in more frequent demand was the library's 1797 edition of *Bell's British Theatre. Consisting of the Most Esteemed English Plays*, volumes of which were borrowed ninety times by thirty-four borrowers.

47 The Wigtown library edition was *A Philosophical and Political History of the Settlements and Trade of the Europeans in the East and West Indies* (6 vols., 1782).

48 The STN sold eighty-two copies of Robertson's *Histoire du règne de l'empereur Charles-Quint* and fifty copies of his *Histoire d'Ecosse sous les regnes de Marie Stuart et de Jacques VI* but just seven copies of Hume's history and two of Watson's.

49 *Histoire de l'ancienne Grèce, de ses colonies et de ses conquêtes*, traduite de l'anglois de John Gillies, par M. Carra, 6 vols (Paris: Chez Buisson, 1787).

50 Robert Watson, *Histoire du regne de Philippe III, roi d'Espagne*, trans. Guillaume Tomson (Paris: Cerioux, 1809).

51 Heron and Guthrie both drifted to London and spent time on the government payroll. On Heron see Simon Burrows, *French Exile Journalism and European Politics, 1792-1814* (Woodbridge: Boydell and Brewer for Royal Historical Society, 2000).

52 For a summary of history books borrowed from the Wigtown Library showing frequency of borrowing and availability in French-language editions, see Appendix 3.15.

53 Paul Kaufman, *Borrowings from the Bristol Library, 1773-1784. A Unique Record of Reading Vogues* (Charlottesville, VA: Bibliographical Society of the University of Virginia, 1960). I thank Mark Towsey for providing access to his copy of this rare work.

54 Kaufman, *Borrowings from the Bristol Library*, pp. 15–119.

55 Ibid., pp. 9, 121.

56 Kaufman (ibid., p. 121) tabulates the other categories in the Bristol Library records, in descending order of popularity, as 'Miscellanies' with 949 loans, 'Philosophy' (844); 'Natural History and Chemistry' (816); 'Theology and Ecclesiastical History' (607); 'Jurisprudence' (447); 'Mathematics, etc.' (276); 'Medicine and Anatomy' (124).

57 It appeared under the title *Relation des voyages entrepris par ordre de Sa Majesté britannique*.

58 The former was borrowed 137 times, the latter thirty-six.

59 They sold, respectively, twenty-three and seven copies.

60 I counted as translated any work identified, or describing itself as, a translation. The self-evidently spurious would have been excluded if encountered.

61 Kaufman, *Borrowings from the Bristol Library*, p. 9. The figure of 137 members relates to the year 1782. Membership was 132 in 1773 and 198 in 1798, by which time holdings had risen sharply to 4,987.

62 Hans Jürgen Lüsebrink, René Nohr and Rolf Reichardt, 'Kulturtransfer im Epochenumbruch – Entwicklung und Inhalte der französiche-deutschen übersetzungbibliothek 1770-1815 im Überblick' in Hans Jürgen Lüsebrink and Rolf Reichardt, eds, *Kulturtransfer im Epochenumbruch: Frankreich-Deutschland 1770 bis 1815* 2 vols. (Leipzig: Leipziger Universitätsverlag, 1997), I, 29–86, at p. 70, cited in Freedman, *Books without Borders*, p. 5.

63　As noted in Chapter 4, the 'Global Historical Bibliometrics' project estimated that approximately 117 million books appeared in German in the second half of the eighteenth century, and output accelerated over time. A figure of 10 per cent equates to the proportion of French-language editions among book advertised in the Leipzig book fair catalogues earlier in the century, a statistic also noted by Freedman. This proportion fell later in the century as German-language publishing expanded, but this wave of German publishing included many translations.

64　This impression is reinforced by the inclusion in the 1781 edition of the *Almanach de la librairie* of 261 German-based booksellers spread across ninety different cities, a sure sign that they were in contact with French book dealers. This compares with a total of 751 foreign-based booksellers listed altogether (my count).

65　I thank Gale-Cengage for kindly supplying the metadata for this collection.

66　I am grateful at Gale-Cengage to Craig Pett and Maryce Johnstone in Australia and company Vice-Presidents Jim Draper, Ray Abruzzi and Terry Robinson who have met with the FBTEE team.

67　In a meeting between FBTEE and Gale in June 2015, it was suggested that other Gale products contain files for perhaps 36,000 eighteenth-century volumes that do not appear in ECCO. This figure has not been verified. Work by the Helsinki digital humanities group, as reported by Mikko Tolonen in a seminar on 31 January 2018 at the University of Sydney entitled 'Tracing the Spheres of the Public in Europe, 1700–1910' reported that ECCO contains only 54% of eighteenth-century editions listed by the English Short Title Catalogue.

68　MARC records stands for Machine Readable Catalogue records, a system developed by the Library of Congress. It is now slowly being replaced by the LoC's Bibframe linked data model.

69　These comprised 676 out of the 2077 records.

70　In total these included fifty-six catalogues; twenty-two criminal biographies; twenty-four publishing prospectuses; eighty records of land alienations; one periodical volume; six street directories; seven published wills; and two genealogies

71　Precise totals were 192 foreign-language works; 189 works translated into English and 198 English works for which foreign-language editions exist.

72　Other editions in ECCO have imprints dated London, 1771 (3 vols); London, 1771 (4 vols); Dublin, 1771 (2 vols); Dublin, 1772 (2 vols); London, 1778 (2 vols); London, 1779 (3 vols); Dublin 1779 (3 vols); and Worcester, Mass., 1789 (5 vols), which was the first American edition.

73　The full English title was *A New and Impartial History of England, From the Invasion of Julius Cæsar, to the signing of the Preliminaries of Peace, in the Year 1762.*

74　The edition of Hume's history of the Stuarts bore the imprint (London, 1766). Both editions of Montesquieu's *Considérations* were published in Edinburgh. The publisher of the French edition of 1751 was Hamilton, Balfour and Neill; the English edition was published by Donaldson in 1775.

75　These editions were dated 1772 and 1788.

76　The ECCO sample's editions of William Robertson's *History of the Reign of the Emperor Charles V* were published by Robert Bell in Philadelphia in 1770–1 and (in English) by Tourneisen in Basel in 1788.

77　The Vienna edition of Robertson's *History of America* was printed for F.A. (Franz Anton) Schræmbl, corner in the Karnthner-Street, No. 1053, in 1787, and the Leipzig edition by E. B. Schwickert in 1786. Scraembl, a celebrated cartographer, also published English-language editions of Robertson's *History of Scotland* and *History of Charles V*. These seem to have been the only works he published in English. The

History of America was published by the STN as a joint edition in partnership with the Société typographique de Lausanne.
78 The ECCO metadata include parallel text versions of two editions each of two popular teaching texts *Eutropii historiæ Romanæ breviarium* (1755 and 1774) and *Cornelius Nepos de vitis excellentium imperatorum* (1768 and 1797). All four editions were published in London. There are also an edition of Sallust's works and two of Plutarch's *Lives*. The STN sold a couple of dozen copies of the latter.
79 They include *The Life of Baron Frederic Trenck*; Duvernet's *Life of Voltaire* (in English and French), Jacques-Vincent Delacroix's *The Memoirs of an American*; the *Vie de David Hume, écrite par lui-même*; and the *Mémoires de Maximilien de Bethune*.
80 Published in London in 1779 and 1780 respectively.
81 Crébillon *fils*, *Les Heureux Orphélins*.
82 These comprised Alain René Le Sage, *The Bachelor of Salamanca* (Dublin, 1737); two editions of the abbé Prévost's *The Dean of Coleraine* (both Dublin, 1742); two editions of Jean-Jacques Barthélemi, *The Travels of Anacharsis the Younger, in Greece* (Dublin, 1795; London, 1800), and one of Crébillon *fils*' erotic masterpiece, *The Wanderings of the Heart and Mind: or Memoirs of Mr. de Meilcour*. The French title of the last is *Les Egaremens du coeur et de l'esprit, ou Mémoires de Mr de Meilcour*.
83 Another false imprint, probably wrongly included in ECCO, is three volumes of Mairobert's *Mémoires secrets*, published clandestinely under the improbable 'John Adamsohn' imprint. No such printer or publisher existed in London.
84 The ECCO data sample includes *A Voyage round the World, performed in His Britannic Majesty's Ships the Resolution and Adventure, in the years 1772, 1773, 1774, and 1775*, 4 vols (Dublin: Whitestone et al., 1777); *A Voyage towards the South Pole, and round the World. Performed in His Majesty's ships the Resolution and Adventure, in the years 1772, 1773, 1774, and 1775*, 2 vols (London: Strahan, 1777); and an abridgement of *Captain Cook's third and last voyage to the Pacific Ocean. In the years 1776, '77, '78, '79 and '80* (New York: Gomez, 1795).
85 *A Voyage round the World. Performed by Order of His Most Christian Majesty, in the years 1766, 1767, 1768, and 1769* (Dublin: J. Exshaw et al., 1772). The STN sold 790 copies, mostly of own 1772 edition, which was entitled *Voyage autour du monde, par le frégate du roi 'La Boudeuse', et la flûte 'L'Étoile', en 1766, 1767, 1768 & 1769*.
86 The STN traded the Berne-Lausanne edition entitled V*oyages autour du monde et vers les deux pôles, par terre et par mer, pendant les années 1767, 1768, 1769, 1770, 1771, 1773, 1774 & 1776*; the ECCO metadata lists, *Travels round the world, in the years 1767, 1768, 1769, 1770, 1771* (Dublin: P. Byrne et al., 1791).
87 The STN traded mostly an edition produced jointly with the Société typographique de Berne, *Voyage de M. Niebuhr en Arabie et en d'autres pays de l'Orient, avec l'extrait de sa description de l'Arabie; et des observations de Mr. Forskal*, 2 vols (Berne: Libraires associés, 1780).
88 The STN sold this work as *Essai sur l'état présent, naturel, civil et politique de la Suisse*.
89 See *Description topographique, historique, critique et nouvelle du pays et des environs de la Forêt noire, situés dans la province du Merryland*. A copy of this work is available on Gallica. Initial examination suggests it probably dates from the eighteenth century not 1866, the date proposed by Gay. In particular, the publisher's preface to the translation reads as broadly contemporary with the main text and lacks the pseudo-scholarly discussion of the text and its history commonly found in late-nineteenth-century and early twentieth-century re-editions of classic erotica, such as those published under the Coffret du Bibliophile imprint. The original English edition was published under a false imprint by the prolific London pornographer Edmund Curll in 1741.

Chapter 9

1. The *Journal de Middlesex* is briefly discussed in Simon Burrows, 'The French Exile Press in London, 1789-1814', Oxford D. Phil. Thesis (1992), pp. 41–4.
2. A *talon rouge* or 'red heel' was literally a fashionable man about town.
3. For a summary of the historical literature relating to scandalous pamphlet attacks on Marie-Antoinette see Burrows, *Blackmail, Scandal, and Revolution*, pp. 10–15. Key contributions by authors mentioned here include Darnton, *The Devil in the Holy Water*, which, as other commentators – above all Darrin McMahon – have noted, postdates my demolition of this literature but fails to address my arguments; de Baecque, 'Pamphlets: Libel and Political Mythology'; Chartier, *Cultural Origins*, pp. 73–87; Lynn Hunt, 'The Many Bodies of Marie-Antoinette: Political Pornography and the Problem of the Feminine in the French Revolution', in Lynn Hunt, ed., *Eroticism and the Body Politic* (Baltimore, MD and London: Johns Hopkins University Press, 1991), 108–30; Chantal Thomas, *The Wicked Queen: The Origins of the Myth of Marie-Antoinette*, trans. Julie Rose (New York: Zone, 1999).
4. Note however Lynn Hunt's observation ('Many Bodies', p. 116) that less than 10 per cent of pamphlet attacks on Marie-Antoinette predate the Revolution; likewise the scathing scepticism of Vivian Gruder, who in 'The Question of Marie-Antoinette' challenges what she provocatively styled 'the pornographic school' of French revolutionary interpretation.
5. The clearest statement of the problem is perhaps Chartier, *Cultural Origins*, pp. 73–7.
6. The despatch and crate numbers are recorded in BPUN, STN MS 1036, Brouillard D, fo. 358.
7. Arsenal, Bastille MS 10,305, fo. 376, Lenoir, lieutenant of police, to the governor of the Bastille, 25 November 1782. The letter makes clear the books were recently seized at Versailles.
8. Arsenal, Bastille MS 10,305, fo. 378, Order of Amelot and Louis XVI to the Governor of the Bastille, 28 March 1783. This letter names the *Contrat conjugal* and gives the STN crate numbers. An annotation records the books finally arrived on 4 April. The list of titles was reproduced in Dawson, *Confiscations at Customs*, appendix G, formerly available online at http://uts.cc.utexas.edu/~dawson1/Confs_appendixes.htm (and last viewed 24 March 2016), pp. 26–7.
9. Arsenal, Bastille MS 10,305, fo. 378, Order of Amelot and Louis XVI to the Governor of the Bastille, 28 March 1783.
10. Jacques Le Scène Desmaisons, *Contrat conjugal, ou loix du marriage, de la répudiation et du divorce, avec une dissertation sur l'origine et le droit de dispenses* (Neuchâtel: STN, 1781), p. 161.
11. Ibid., p. 183
12. This pulping is derived information. Dawson, *Consfiscations at Customs*, p. 262, reveals only four copies of the Neuchâtel edition of *Contrat conjugal* remained in the Bastille to be inventoried by the Versailles bookseller Poinçot. Many other documents in MS 10,305 concern books to be pulped.
13. See Darnton, *Forbidden Best-Sellers*, ch. 2.
14. The phrase again is Darnton's: see Robert Darnton, 'Blogging, Now and Then (250 Years Ago)', *European Romantic Review* 24:3 (2013), 255–70 at 264.
15. Darnton, *Forbidden Best-Sellers*, p. 8.
16. Ibid., p. 13.
17. Ibid., p. 8.

18 Ibid., p. 16. On price markups for illegal works, see Darnton, 'The Life-Cycle of a Book'.
19 Darnton, 'High Enlightenment', p. 110.
20 On decoding of complex political allusions, see Robert Darnton, 'Mademoiselle Bonafon et la vie privée de Louis XV', *Dix-Huitième Siècle* 35:2 (2003), 369–91.
21 On these estimates, see above, this chapter.
22 Birn, *Royal Censorship*, p. 4.
23 The comparison here is between Dawson, *Confiscations at Customs* and Darnton's *Corpus of Clandestine Literature*.
24 Darnton's list of works in the *Corpus of clandestine literature* ends at 720, but there is no entry number '25' and another item is double-counted under the titles *Essai historique sur la vie de Marie-Antoinette de France* and *Vie d'Antoinette*. As I and latterly Darnton have noted, some of the scandalous political works on the list probably never existed, notably the *Amours du vizir de Vergennes* and the *Passe-temps d'Antoinette*. Minor adjustments were made to the edition counts on the spreadsheet for a small number of works in light of new research.
25 Dawson, *Confiscations at Customs*. There were many reasons works could end up in the Bastille *dépôt*, including having been left by or confiscated from prisoners. Hence not all were illegal.
26 Works found in the Bastille account for only 21.9 per cent of titles, but 38.6 per cent of estimated editions, of works in Darnton's *Corpus of Clandestine Literature*.
27 The STN data records that between 1769 and 1789 only about 45.5 per cent of libertine works (defined as works in Darnton's *Corpus* or on the Bastille list) went directly to France. However, a further 35.9 per cent went to booksellers who may have served as *entrepôts* in Switzerland, the Netherlands and the principality of Neuwied. If we assume that these dealers and their own wholesale clients on-sold books to France in similar proportions to the STN, the figure of 67 per cent (two thirds) is more or less exact.
28 For figures on total book output, see Chapter 2.
29 BNF, MS Fr 21,831-21,834. There are a handful of ambiguous records. For these the FBTEE-2.0 database records the minimum number consistent with the record. Veyrin-Forrer, 'Livres arrêtés, livres estampillés' gives the number of books stamped as 387,209.
30 *Almanach de la Librairie* (1781), pp. 36–81 (nb. some bracketed entries are ambiguous); BNF, MS Fr 21,832 fos 1–22, 'Etat General des Imprimeurs du Royaume fait en 1777'. The total appears in the recapitulation on fo. 22 v., along with a stated target of reducing the number of printers in the kingdom to 266.
31 See BN, MS Fr. 22,018-22,019 and Chapter 3, note 22 above.
32 See Dawson, *French Booktrade*, esp. section 5, which deals with fraud, and his list of editions, which notes following the *permission* registers the many editions 'n'a pas eu lieu'. This data will also appear in FBTEE-2.0.
33 These penalties were stipulated in the decrees of 30 August 1777.
34 See Burrows, 'Charmet and the Book Police', p. 48.
35 The figure for pirate editions was arrived at by taking the 12,000,000 pirate editions and 3,000,000 legal editions of *permission simple* works and multiplying by 43.5/56.5 = 77 per cent, reflecting the proportions of *permission* simple to non-*permission simple* works in the 1778–80 survey.
36 Stock turnover was derived by taking our 23,550,000 items and dividing it by the derived number of items declared in the 1778–80 *estampillage* exercise, that is, around 3,200,000.

37 Estivals, *La Statistique bibliographique*, p. 288. I have taken the higher of Estival's annual figure for 'Autorisations' or 'Permissions tacites enregistrées à la Chambre syndicale'. Discrepancies between the two figures usually arise from supplementary authorizations.
38 On this point see also Chapters 10 and 11 below.
39 These figures assume a constant output of pirate works, and that the amnesty did not result in a disproportionate number of works being hurried into print in the months after the amnesty was declared.
40 Technically this column represents 'copies distributed': not quite every copy was sold or commissioned.
41 For more detailed breakdowns by subcategory see Appendix 3.17.
42 The spreadsheet workings on which this discussion is based will be made available on line through the FBTEE website.
43 See Jeremy D. Popkin, 'Pamphlet Journalism at the End of the Old Regime', *Eighteenth-Century Studies* 22:3 (1989), 351–67.
44 Simon Burrows, 'Police and Political Pamphleteering in Pre-Revolutionary France: The Testimony of J.-P. Lenoir, Lieutenant-Général of Police of Paris', in David Adams and Adrian Armstrong, eds, *Print and Power in France and England, 1500-1800* (Aldershot: Ashgate, 2006), pp. 99–112.
45 For full listings see Appendix 3.17.
46 Darnton's *Corpus* contains 131 from a total of 141 titles classified as 'M1: Pornography, erotica & sexual scandal' and found in the Bastille or his sources. This proportion is higher than for any other sizeable genre. See Appendix 3.16.
47 See Appendix 3.19 for complete statistics by category.
48 On *Thérèse philosophe* see Darnton, *Forbidden Best-Sellers*, Chapter 3.
49 These overlapping categories contained 7,640 and 7,202 units respectively.
50 See Appendix 3.16 for more details, especially the statistics for category 'R3: Metaphysics, Natural Religion, Materialism, Deism, & the Soul'. Of eighty-two identified R3 titles, the STN traded fifty-eight (70.7 per cent) in the period 1769–89. This is a much higher proportion than for the general run of libertine works (448/938 or 47.8 per cent).
51 The figures given here for global and commercial sales across Europe cover the entire period of the STN's existence, 1769–94. Sales for the revolutionary period 1789–94 however were negligible, comprising 834 out of 39,958 'commercial' and 1,250 out of 115,373 'global' sales
52 Darnton's bestseller list appears in *Forbidden Best-Sellers*, pp. 63–4. For an extended version see his *Corpus of Clandestine Literature*, pp. 194–7.
53 On the *Albert moderne* and its predecessors, see Chapter 10.
54 On our definition of pornography, see Chapter 6.
55 This is not to deny the presence of sexually assertive or aggressive women, including the heroines of d'Argen's *Thérèse philosophe* and Cleland's *Fille de joie*.
56 Among such commentators, Darnton in particular blurs the distinction, considering freethinking libertine works to embrace both political and sexual realms.
57 21.4 per cent of libertine books sold to France were classified as 'Sceptical Works' by the FBTEE team, compared with a European average of 16.5. The figures are almost identical for 'Anticlerical Works'. For 'Irreligious Works' the equivalent figures are respectively 9.4 and 6.5 per cent while for 'Atheist works' they are 6.5 and 4.9. See Appendix 3.22.
58 For more on this point, see below, this chapter.

59 See Simon Burrows, 'Les traductions: éditions anglaises des Vies privées françaises', in Olivier Ferret, Anne-Marie Mercier-Faivre and Chantal Thomas, eds, *Dictionnaire des vies privées (1722-1842)* (Oxford: SVEC, 2011:2), pp. 110-29.
60 See Arlette Farge and Michel Foucault, *Le Désordre des familles, lettres de cachet des Archives de la Bastille* (Paris: Gallimard Julliard, 1982).
61 Hans-Jürgen Lüsebrink and Rolf Reichardt, *The Bastille. A History of a Symbol of Despotism and Freedom* (Durham, NC and London: Duke University Press, 1997), pp. 18-19. For the case that Morande was author of the *Rémarques historiques*, see Burrows, *A King's Ransom*, p. 45 and p. 227, note 2.
62 On the refusal of sacraments and resultant crisis see John McManners, *Church and Society in Eighteenth-Century France Volume 2: The Religion of the People and the Politics of Religion* (Oxford: Oxford University Press, 1999), pp. 481-506.
63 Indeed, *libelles* cross reference to stories of Frédégonde, Catherine de Médicis, and various notorious kings, including Charles IX, who ordered the Saint-Bartholomew's Day massacre.
64 On Mauvelain see above Chapter 3. One key conclusion of the FBTEE project is that Mauvelain and Malherbe were quite atypical of the general trade. See Burrows, 'French Banned Books', p. 33; Curran, 'Beyond the Forbidden Best-Sellers'.
65 BN, MS Fr. 21,823 fos 83-85, François de Bassompierre, imprimeur-libraire de Genève to Vergennes, undated petition [1783].
66 Ibid., fos 68-9, 'Mémoire pour les sieurs Piestre et Cormon, Libraires à Lyon' [1783].
67 Ibid., fos 75-8, 'Mémoire of Jean-Marie Bruyset, père et fils', Lyon, 22 March 1784.
68 Ibid., fos 70-1: Mémoire to the procureur général du Parlement de Flandres on behalf of the *Syndics* and *adjoints* of the Chambre Syndicale de Lille and their *confrères* in Flanders, Hainault, Cambrèsis, Artois and Boulonois [1783].
69 See Burrows, *Blackmail, Scandal and Revolution*, ch. 5.
70 La Motte's *Mémoires justificatifs* were sourced from Louis Fauche-Borel. The FBTEE database records twelve sales. The STN sold one copy of another *libelle*, the *Essais historiques sur la vie de Marie-Antoinette* in 1793. None were sold to clients in France.
71 See above Chapter 3.
72 On the monarchy's relationship with its printers, see McLeod, *Licencing Loyalty*. See also Thierry Rigogne, *Between State and Market: Printing and Bookselling in Eighteenth-Century France*, SVEC 2007:5 (Oxford: Voltaire Foundation, 2007), esp. chs 1-3.

Chapter 10

1 Gilibert published two books on magnetism: *Aperçu sur le magnétisme animal ou résultat des observations faites à Lyon sur ce nouvel agent* (Geneva, 1784) and *L'autocratie de la nature, ou, Premier memoire sur l'énergie du principe vital pour la guérison des maladies chirurgicales* (1785).
2 Louis-Sébastien Mercier, 'Médecins', in Mercier, Jean-Claude Bonnet, ed., *Tableau de Paris*, 2 vols (Paris: Mercure de France, 1994), I, pp. 324-8, article CXXXV. This article is available in the abridged English translation edited by Jeremy D. Popkin under the title *Panorama of Paris*.
3 Note that this definition excludes several works carrying the keyword 'Science', notably Brissot's *De La Vérité* (1,930 sales), which dealt with scientific method but is removed as a commissioned edition, as are several works focussing primarily on top-

ics other than science: Elie Bertrand's *Thévenon, ou les journées de la montagne* (1,838 sales); Justin Girod-Chantrans, *Voyage d'un Suisse dans différentes colonies d'Amérique* (745 sales), which contains some meteorological observations; Abraham Trembley's moral guide *Instructions d'un père à ses enfans* (656 sales); and Carsten Niebuhr's *Voyage de M. Niebuhr en Arabie et en d'autres pays de l'Orient* (373 sales). Despite being excluded, *De La Vérité* has a complex sales history and some might consider it the STN's third bestselling science book. Brissot originally took 1,544 copies – more or less the entire print run – but eventually he returned 1,156 copies to the STN, who sold all or most between 1782 and 1792.

4 The full top ten list of the STN's bestselling scientific monographs and reference works reads: 1. Gilibert, *Anarchie médicinale* (1,430 copies); 2. Valmont de Bomare, *Dictionnaire raisonné universel d'histoire naturelle* (1119 copies); 3. Tissot, *Avis au peuple sur sa santé* (942 copies); 4. Gélieu, *Réflexions d'un homme de bon sens sur les comètes* (890 copies); 5. Macquer, *Dictionnaire de chymie* (748 copies); 6. Bertrand, *Elémens d'oryctologie* (666 copies); 7. Tissot, *Onanisme* (625 copies); 8. Alletz (attrib.), *Albert moderne* (600 copies); 9. Tissot, *Traité de l'épilepsie* (521 copies); and 10. Tissot, *Essai sur les maladies des gens du monde* (332 copies).

5 On Tissot as a popularizer, see Patrick Singy, 'The Popularization of Medicine in the Eighteenth Century: Writing, Reading, and Rewriting Samuel Auguste Tissot's Avis Au Peuple Sur Sa Santé,' *Journal of Modern History* 82:4 (2010): 769–800. Singy cites FBTEE data.

6 *Encyclopédie, ou dictionnaire raisonné des sciences, des arts et des métiers, etc.*, eds. Denis Diderot and Jean le Rond d'Alembert. University of Chicago: ARTFL Encyclopédie Project (Spring 2013 Edition), Robert Morrissey, ed., http://encyclopedie.uchicago.edu/, I, xx.

7 Ibid., I, xxiii.

8 Ibid., I, xxiii–xxiv.

9 Ibid., I, xxiv.

10 His discussion of all these figures spans ibid., I, xxiv–xxx.

11 Ibid., I, xxxi.

12 Gilibert's main contribution was *Caroli Linnaei botanicorum principis systema plantarum Europae exhibens characteres naturales generum, characteres essentiales generum & specierum, synonima antiquorum, phrases specificas recentiorum Halleri, Scopoli, etc.; Descriptiones rariorum, nec-non Floras tres novas, Lugduanaeam, Delphinalem, Lithuanicam, non omissis plantis exoticis in hortis Europae vulgo obviis* published by Piestre & Delamolliere in Geneva [Colonia Allobrogum] in 1786-87. One copy was purchased by Thomas Jefferson and is today in the Library of Congress.

13 Notably Venel's *Description de plusieurs nouveaux moyens méchaniques propres à prévenir, borner & même corriger dans certains cas les courbures latérales & la torsion de l'épine du dos* (Lausanne: Jean Mourer, 1788).

14 Alexandra Cook, 'An eighteenth-century plea for sustainable forestry: Ostervald's *Description des montagnes & vallées du pays de Neuchâtel*', *1650-1850, Ideas, Æsthetics and Inquiries in the Early Modern Era* 22 (2015), 257–78, 260–1. On Neuchâtelois science see also Alexandra Cook, *Jean-Jacques Rousseau and Botany: The Salutary Science*, SVEC 2012:12 (Oxford: Voltaire Society, 2012), Chapters 3 and 4. I thank Dr Cook for forwarding copies of these works.

15 BPUN, MS 1156 fos 180–1, Gilibert to STN, 16 August 1771, fo. 181.

16 Ibid. Jacques Gardanne or Gardane (1726-?) was a medical doctor and founder of the *Gazette de Santé*. On Gardanne see the article by Robert Favre in Jean Sgard, ed.,

Dictionnaire de Journalistes, 1600-1789, second edition, 2 vols (Oxford: Voltaire Foundation, 1999), at http://dictionnaire-journalistes.gazettes18e.fr/journaliste/331-jacques-gardanne.
17 BPUN, MS 1156 fos 180–1, Gilibert to STN, Lyon, 16 August 1771, fo. 180.
18 Ibid.
19 BPUN, MS 1156 fos 197–8, Gilibert to STN, Lyon, 26 October 1772; fos 199–200, Gilibert to STN, Lyon, 20 December 1772; fos 201–2, Gilibert to STN, Lyon, 20 January 1773. Gabriel-François Venel was himself author of an STN bestselling medical tract on female health and hygiene, *Essai sur la santé et sur l'éducation médicinale des filles destinées au marriage*, which sold 326 copies. He should not be confused with the aforementioned Jean-André Venel, the father of modern orthopaedics.
20 BPUN, MS 1156 fos 185–6, Gilibert to STN, Lyon, letter misdated 1771 in STN archive. Judging from the content, it was written in December 1772.
21 Ibid., fos 201–2, Gilibert to STN, Lyon, 20 January 1773.
22 Ibid., fo. 204, Gilibert to STN, Lyon, 15 June 1773. Gardanne is revealed as the censor by Anne-Marie Chouillet's article on Rozier's journal in Jean Sgard ed., *Dictionnaire des journaux* 2 vols (Paris and Oxford: Universitas/Voltaire Foundation, 1991), II, 996, available online at http://c18.net/dp/dp.php?no=1089. It is not clear from his correspondence whether Gilibert knew Rozier's censor was Gardanne.
23 BPUN, MS 1156 fos 206–7, Gilibert to STN, Lyon, 31 July 1773.
24 *Anarchie médicinale* does not appear in the index or appendices to Dawson, *Confiscations at Customs*, or in Darnton's *Corpus of Clandestine Literature*. The STN despatched 733 copies of the work to France, comprising 50.4 per cent of known 'sales'. The total press run was 1,480 copies.
25 For this prediction, see BPUN, MS 1156 fos 201–2, Gilibert to STN, Lyon, 20 January 1773.
26 Ibid., fo. 179, STN to Schaub & Cie, Neuchâtel, 3 January 1775.
27 The full title was *Dictionnaire de chymie: contenant la théorie et la pratique de cette science, son application à la physique, à l'histoire naturelle, à la médecine, & aux arts dépendans de la chymie*.
28 This work was first published in Latin in 1688 as *Lucii libellus de mirabilibus naturae arcanus*.
29 This work's full title was *Les Admirables Secrets d'Albert le Grand, contenant plusieurs traités sur la conception des femmes et les vertus des herbes, des pierres précieuses, etc*. It was first published in Latin in c.1483 as *Liber Secretorum Alberti Magni de virtutibus herbarum, lapidum et animalium quorumdam*.
30 Pons-Augustin Alletz (attrib.), *L'Albert moderne, ou nouveaux secrets éprouvés et licites, recueillis d'après les découvertes les plus récentes*, 2nd edition (Paris: Veuve Duchesne, 1769), pp. iv–vi.
31 Sales for these works were respectively 204 and 94.
32 BN, MS Fr. 22,019 fo. 4r.
33 As noted above, the *estampillage* data is taken from the FBTEE-2.0 database and based on BNF, MS Fr. 21,831-21,834.
34 Worldcat lists several copies under the title *Le Secret des secrets de nature. Extraits, tant du Petit Albert, & d'autres philosophes hébreux, grecs, arabes, caldéens, égyptiens, et autres modernes* (Troyes: P. Garnier, [1723?]). I thank Professor David Adams for drawing this edition to my attention.
35 Singy, 'The Popularization of Medicine', p. 792, suggests Tissot's *Avis au peuple* alone went through over forty French editions by 1800 and numerous translations.

36 Cook, 'An Eighteenth-Century Plea for Sustainable Forestry', p. 271.
37 See Descartes' statement in the final paragraph of Discourse 4 of the *Discourse on Method*: 'For reason ... does tell us that all our ideas and notions must have some basis in truth, for it would not be possible that God, who is all perfect and true, should have put them in us unless that were so' (Quote from F. E. Sutcliffe's 1968 Penguin Classics translation, p. 60).
38 John Locke, *An Essay Concerning the True Original, Extent and End of Civil Government*, Chapter V, 'Of Property', paragraph 25, in John Locke, *Two Treatises of Government* (London and Melbourne: J. M. Dent, 1924, reprinted 1984), p. 129.
39 Newton's views were not those of a conventional Christian. Rob Iliffe, *Priest of Nature: The Religious Worlds of Isaac Newton* (Oxford: Oxford University Press, 2014) depicts him as a devout layman for whom intellectual independence was a cardinal virtue.
40 Novalis [a.k.a. Friedrich von Hardenberg], *Schriften*, ed. Richard Samuel et al., 6 vols (Stuttgart: W. Kohlhammer, 1977–99), III, pp. 562, 651.
41 Darnton, *Forbidden Best-Sellers*, ch. 3.
42 The full keyword definition reads, 'Works which have been identified as having apparently been written or inspired in part through pious Christian motives. These may include works of fiction or history as well as works that are explicitly religious in purpose. This category is necessarily more subjective than some other keyword categories.' See http://fbtee.uws.edu.au/stn/interface/browse.php?t=keyword&id=k1067&r1.
43 Samuel Tissot, *De La Santé des gens de lettres* (Lausanne: François Grasset, 1770), p. 2.
44 Ibid., p.4. See Balthasar Ludwig Tralles, *De Machina et anima humana prorsus a se invicem distinctis commentatio* (Leipzig and Breslau: Hubert, 1749).
45 Tissot ranks seventeenth on the STN all-time global bestselling authors list. Others who wrote on scientific matters rank above him, notably Brissot and Elie Bertrand, but unlike Tissot both these authors published primarily on other subjects.
46 Charles Bonnet, *Essai de psychologie; ou considérations sur les opérations de l'âme sur l'habitude et sur l'éducation* (London: n.p., 1755), pp. 3–4.
47 N.B. In his 'Préface', Bonnet felt it necessary to make a profession of faith and religious orthodoxy.
48 Aimé-Henri Paulian, *Dictionnaire des nouvelles découvertes faites en physique* (Nîmes and Avignon: Gaudé/J. J. Niel, 1787). The *Santé des gens de lettres* notched up 248 STN sales; the *Essai de psychologie* forty-three, and Paulian's work just nine.
49 On Trembley, see above Chapter 5.
50 Ths FBTEE database records 1,145 sales to forty-seven centres across France of works ascribed the twin keywords 'Science' and 'Work of Religiosity', as opposed to 1,817 to Switzerland (Helvetic zone) and 1,333 to the rest of Europe. Works tagged with just 'Science' sold 9,204 to France and 7,474 to Switzerland.
51 See Curran, *Atheism, Religion and Enlightenment*, pp. 98–9. As Curran points out, Needham's observations were erroneous: he had observed fermentation. They were however underwritten by other apparent discoveries, notably Abraham Trembley's observations on the freshwater polyp, published in 1744, which equally purported to show 'self-generation and asexual reproduction'.
52 Charles-Antoine Charmet's death is recorded in BPUN, MS 1174 fos 221–2, Dominique Lépagnez to the STN, dated 5 January 1782 but annotated '5 January 1783'. Other correspondence from the Charmet and Lépagnez dossiers makes clear that Charmet was still alive through 1782.
53 The Protestant population of Besançon was about 1,000 at this time, or around 3 per cent of the population.

54 Darnton, *Business of Enlightenment*, p. 595.
55 Éric Suire, *Sainteté et lumières. Hagiographie, spiritualité et propagande religieuse dans la France des lumières* (Paris: Honoré Champion, 2011), Annexe 4, pp. 425–7.
56 Darnton, *Forbidden Best-Sellers*, p. 34. NB. In *Forbidden Best-Sellers* Darnton wrongly identifies Charmet as his brother Jean-Félix, the *imprimeur*. See below, this chapter, note 71.
57 Darnton, *The Corpus of Clandestine Literature*, p. 199.
58 Curran, *Atheism, Religion and Enlightenment*, appendices 2 and 3.
59 The same authors all appear above him also if we limit our query to works with illegality markers.
60 On Holland and his *Réflexions*, see Curran 'Mettons toujours Londres'.
61 On these novels, see Curran, *Atheism, Religion and Enlightenment*, esp. pp. 126–8, 153–4. Of the other Christian-apologist novels discussed by Curran, the STN sold seventy-two copies of Philippe-Louis Gérard, *Le Comte de Valmont* and one of the abbé Crillon's, *Mémoires philosophiques du baron de ****, first published in 1774 and 1777 respectively. Though some titles ran to several editions, this genre of Christian-apologist anti-materialist novel comprised just a handful of works and its impact was consequently limited.
62 The STN sold seven copies of the former and three of the latter. On sales of *L'Ange conducteur* see Michel Vernus, 'Un Best-seller de la littérature religieuse: *L'Ange Conducteur* (du XVIIe au XIXe siècle)', in *Transmettre la foi: XVIe-XXe siècles*, 2 vols (Paris: C.T.H.S., 1984), I, pp. 231–43. The *permission simple* register at BN, MS Fr. 22,019 suggest that production of the *Journée du chrétien* significantly outstripped that of the *Ange conducteur* during the 1780s.
63 See Robert Darnton, 'Lépagnez', in Darnton, ed., 'A Literary Tour' at http://robert-darnton.org/literarytour/booksellers/lépagnez on 23 March 2017.
64 See Chapter 3, and Darnton, 'Charmet'.
65 A 182-page catalogue for Charmet's *cabinet de lecture* survives: see *Catalogue des livres qui se trouvent dans le cabinet littéraire établi par abonnement, à raison de trente sols par mois* (Besançon: chez Charmet, libraire, 1777).
66 These panegyrics were entitled *Eloge de Michel de l'Hôpital*; *Eloge historique du Cardinal d'Amboise*; and *Eloge de Philippe d'Orléans*.
67 Vernus, 'A Provincial Perspective', p. 125.
68 BNF, MS Fr. 22,184: entries for Besançon are at fol. 60; BPUN, MS 1134 fol. 54–5, [Charles-Antoine] 'Charmet *l'aîné*' to STN, 1 October 1772.
69 The inspection records are at BNF, MS Fr. 21,834 fos 118–19.
70 Burrows and Curran, French Book Trade Database: browse client: Charmet.
71 Darnton's *Forbidden Best-Sellers* (1996) and the original version of his online monograph 'Charmet' (as published on 1 September 2014) both wrongly identified the STN's correspondent Charmet *l'aîné* (or 'Charmet *libraire*') as Jean-Félix Charmet (who was not a *libraire* but an *imprimeur*). So, following Darnton, does my 2015 essay 'Charmet and the Book Police', which first raised the possibility that Charmet *l'aîné*'s identity might be subject to doubt. Alerted by my essay, Professor Darnton traced the brothers' birth records and corrected his essay in the spring of 2016. For a history of this case of mistaken identity, see Simon Burrows, 'Omissions and Revisions in Eighteenth-Century Book History: A Rejoinder to Robert Darnton', *French History and Civilisation: Papers from the George Rudé Seminar* 7 (2017), 209–17.
72 The Charmet family first contacted the STN as papermakers not booksellers: see BPUN, MS 1134 fol. 1, [Jean-Félix] Charmet *cadet* to STN, Besançon 14 July 1769. Letters in Charmet's STN dossier often describe the family as '*imprimeurs*' and

not infrequently '*papetiers*'. I have traced ten editions in Worldcat from the period 1765–73 to Charmet, *frères et sœurs*.
73 For Charmet's inspection, see BNF, MS Fr. 21,834, 'Etat de la Librairie, 1778', fo. 167.
74 BN, MS Fr 22,019 fols. 11, 41, 51, 52, 56, 86.
75 Worldcat advanced searches for the keyword combination 'Charmet' and 'Besançon' for the years 1750–90 were conducted between August 24 and September 10, 2014.
76 All these titles are listed in the discussion above.
77 These works were respectively: *Mémoire pour M. le cardinal de Choiseul, archevêque de Besançon, … contre le sieur de Chaffois, … le chanoine Ribaud* (1771); Pierre-Philippe Grappin, *Histoire abrégée du comté de Bourgogne, à l'usage des collèges* (nouvelle édition, 1780); and M. Thomassin, *Dissertation sur le charbon malin de la Bourgogne, ou la pustule maligne: ouvrage couronné par l'Académie des sciences, arts & belles-lettres de Dijon, le 14 février 1780* (1780).
78 Darnton, 'Charmet'.
79 Robert Darnton, 'Letourmy' in 'A Literary Tour de France' at http://robertdarnton.org/literarytour/booksellers/letourmy.
80 Rideau, *De la religion de tous à la religion de chacun*, p. 288.
81 Darnton lists Letourmy's orders at file://ad.uws.edu.au/dfshare/Homes-BNK$/30035303/Downloads/letourmy-orders.pdf.
82 Darnton, *A Literary Tour*, p. 278. For my earlier critiques see Burrows, 'Charmet and the Book Police'; Burrows, 'Omissions and Revisions', p. 215.
83 Darnton, *A Literary Tour*, pp. 46–7.
84 For the full *estampillage* inspections records for Besançon, see BNF, MS Fr. 21,834 fols. 118–93.
85 See also Burrows, 'Charmet and the Book Police'.
86 BN, MS Fr. 22,019 fols. 1, 3, 5, 7, 8.
87 Between 1779 and 1789, *veuve* Vivot applied for eighty-three *permissions simples*, all for religious works. The combined authorized print run was 164,500. For details see MS Fr 22,018 and MS Fr 22,019 or the sources cited in Chapter 3, note 22.
88 BNF, MS 21,927, fol. 20, 'Etat des Balles, Ballots, Caissses et Malles qui ont passé à la Chambre syndicale de Besançon pendant la semaine derniere'.
89 Ibid.
90 This licence, for an edition of five hundred copies, was granted to Métoyer on 20 November 1786. *Main-morte* and *retrait* are specialized legal terms relating to inheritance. The former signifies the legal incapacity of serfs to bequeath their goods; the latter the restitution at law of an inheritance which had been sold.
91 Philippe Martin, *Une religion des livres, 1640-1850* (Paris: CERF, 2003), p. 132.
92 BNF, MS Fr 21,834 fos 194–5.
93 Ibid., fos 2–8. In all, Caron had seventy copies.
94 Anne Manevy, 'Le Droit Chemin. L'ange gardien, instrument de disciplinarisation après la Contre-Réforme', *Revue de l'histoire des religions* 223 (2006:2), 195–227 at 197.
95 Jacques Carel, 'La Dévotion à l'ange gardien dans la nord de la Lorraine', *Cahiers Lorrains* 1995 (1), 23–34, at 24.
96 See Vernus, 'A Provincial Perspective', pp. 125, 127.
97 See Furet, ed., *Livre et Société*.
98 I have elaborated on this point at workshops on 'Secularisation and the Intellectuals' held at Western Sydney in 2013 and 2014. A published version entitled 'Revolutionary DeChristianisation and the Secularizing Tradition: A Re-Reading' will appear in a volume of papers being edited by David Burchell and Sarah Irving.

99 Cf. Michel Vovelle, *The Revolution against the Church*, trans. Alan José (Columbus: Ohio State University Press, 1991).
100 The best study of this culture is Martin, *Une Religion des livres*. See also Suire, *Sainteté et lumières*; Rideau, *De La Religion de tous*.
101 In theory those who wrote, commissioned or printed such works were liable to the death penalty following a decree of 16 April 1757. *Colporteurs* and booksellers were not infrequently embastilled or, in rare cases, sent to the galleys.

Chapter 11

1 See Darnton, *The Devil in the Holy Water*.
2 See Chapter 1, note 25.
3 Gary Kates, 'The Popularization of Political thought in Enlightenment Europe', a paper delivered to the second 'Digitizing Enlightenment Symposium' at Radboud University (July 2017). I thank Professor Kates for permission to discuss this work.
4 A few works with complex edition histories, among them *Candide*, were excluded from Kate's initial survey. However, according to Martin, Mylne and Frautschi's *Bibliographie du genre romanesque* there were only forty-five stand alone editions of *Candide* in French by 1800, plus approximately thirty more in collections of his novels or *oeuvres*.
5 Unlike Enlightenment classics, where almost every edition appears to survive somewhere in the world's research collections, survival rates for *livres de piété* seem to be around one edition in three. Equally, cheap editions of pious works tended to have average print runs two to three times those of Enlightenment editions. Finally, Kates counts refer to all major European languages, whereas my edition counts relate only to French-language editions.
6 A rare exception to this neglect is Chartier, *Cultural Origins*. On pamphleteering see Maza, *Private Lives and Public Affairs*; Darnton, *The Devil in the Holy Water*.
7 Henry, 'Le Pays de Neuchâtel', p. 40.
8 *Pièces importantes à la dernière révolution de Genève* (Neuchâtel: STN, 1782), p. 26.
9 Ibid., p. 26.
10 For its distribution pattern, see Appendix 1.5 and above Chapter 5.
11 For the diamond necklace affair and public opinion, see Jonathan Beckman, *How to Ruin a Queen* (London: John Murray, 2014); on the Kornmann affair see Maza, *Private Lives and Public Affairs*, pp. 295–311.
12 On books in the secret *dépôt* see Chapter 9; Dawson, *Confiscations at Customs*, appendix K, pp. 243–76.
13 James Livesey and Richard Whatmore, 'Étienne Clavière, Jacques-Pierre Brissot et les fondations intellectuelles de la politique des Girondins', *Annales historiques de la Révolution française* 72:3 (2000), 1–26.
14 See J. Benetruy, *L'atelier de Mirabeau; quatre proscrits genevois dans la tourmente révolutionnaire* (Paris: Picard, 1962).
15 On the Le Maître affair see Popkin, 'Pamphlet Journalism'; Burrows, 'Police and Political Pamphleteering'.
16 The full definition, including notes on its application, reads: 'Works that cover political life, administration, organization and/or relationships between one or more human societies etc in theory or practice, including contemporary history and the conduct of 'Current affairs'. In this database, 'Current Affairs' designates events that

happened in the adult lives of readers yet living. In practice, this means that the reigns of Louis XV and Louis XVI belong under 'Politics' + 'Current Affairs' not 'History'. Hence 'History' in this database ends (approximately) at the death of Louis XIV in 1715. Note that the genre of fictional works carrying the keyword 'Political fiction' does NOT carry the keyword 'Politics'. The main subcategories of 'Politics' are 'Current Affairs', 'Political Theory', 'Political Rights' and 'Public Administration'. 'Political Institutions' serves as a subcategory of 'Politics' EXCEPT where it refers exclusively to institutions from past 'History' (as defined in this database). Cf. 'Political fiction', which is a separate category'. In addition, works narrowly associated with military affairs are generally excluded from the 'political' label.

17 For a full list of the twenty global bestselling works ascribed the keyword 'Politics' in the FBTEE database, see online Appendix 3.24. On sales of Necker pamphlets, see Chapter 7.
18 See, for example, Vivian R. Gruder, 'Political News as Coded Messages: The Parisian and Provincial Press in the Pre-Revolution, 1787-1788', *French History* 12 (1998), 1–24.
19 See Appendix 3.25. Works classified as 'Politics' had total global sales of 72,248.
20 The keyword 'Current Affairs' was ascribed to works with 39,706 'trade' sales out of a total of 50,655 'trade' sales of works carrying the keyword 'Politics'. 'Political theory' was ascribed to works with 7,199 'trade' sales.
21 Durand Echeverria, *The Maupeou Revolution: A Study in the History of Libertarianism: France, 1770-1774* (Baton Rouge, LA: Louisiana State University Press, 1985).
22 See Burrows, 'Police and Political Pamphleteering', pp. 104–7.
23 Seaward, 'The Small Republic'. See also Burrows, *A King's Ransom*, pp. 35–6.
24 Jeroom Vercruysse, 'La Réception politique des gazettes de Hollande: une lecture diplomatique' in Hans Bots, ed., *La Diffusion et lecture des journaux de langue française sous l'ancien régime* (Amsterdam: APA-Holland University Press, 1988), pp. 39–47; Burrows, *Cosmopolitan Press*, pp. 30–1.
25 See above Chapter 9. Mark Curran kindly drew my attention to a 1778 Romandy edition of Mairobert's *Anecdotes*, whose existence may challenge this narrative. However, since the *Anecdotes* continued to sell outside France after 1777, it remained commercially viable to produce them even after August 1777. Equally, since printers often post-dated books appearing late in the year, the '1778' edition may already have been in production before the 30 August 1777 decrees.
26 Of 2,840 unit sales carrying the keyword 'Personal Libel', three quarters (2,152) are *libelles* against Du Barri and Louis XV. Of the remainder, the bestsellers were the *Remontrances du Père Adam à Voltaire* (ninety-eight sales) and Charles Théveneau de Morande's *Ma Correspondance avec M. le Comte de Cagliostro* (sixty-nine sales).
27 BPUN, MS 1134 fol. 165–6, [Charles-Antoine] Charmet to STN, 23 December 1779, refers to Charmet receiving works for Lépagnez. Likewise, a letter of Lépagnez *cadet* to the STN, dated 26 June 1781 (BPUN, MS 1174 fol. 210–11), reveals that two hundred of the copies of Necker's *Mémoire sur l'administration provincial* sent to Charmet were intended for Lépagnez. Lépagnez's STN dossier can be consulted at www.robert-darnton.org.
28 Darnton, *Forbidden Best-Sellers*, 36.
29 See BPUN, MS 1134, fos. 199–200, [Charles-Antoine] Charmet to STN, Besançon, 29 June 1781; fol. 201–02, Charmet to STN, Besançon, 18 July 1781.
30 See BPUN, MS 1134, fos. 192–3, [Charles-Antoine] Charmet to STN, Besançon, 9 June 1781.

31 BPUN, MS 1134 fol. 209–10, [Charles-Antoine] Charmet to STN, Besançon, 12 October 1781.
32 Ibid.
33 Michael Kwass, *Privilege and the Politics of Taxation in Eighteenth-Century France: Liberté, Egalité, Fiscalité* (Cambridge: Cambridge University Press, 2000), p. 214.
34 Kwass, *Privilege and the Politics of Taxation in Eighteenth-Century France.*
35 Not all the *Compte rendus* sent to Besançon sold. The STN database shows that Dominique Lépagnez took some 750 copies in March 1781, but later returned 235. Two hundred more were 'transferred' to [Charles-Antoine] Charmet.
36 Nicolas Ruault, *Gazette d'un Parisien sous la revolution: lettres à son frère, 1783-1796*, ed. Christiane Rimbaud and Anne Vassal (Paris: Perrin, 1976), p. 193.
37 50.96 per cent of the STN's 14,506 'global' sales of works ascribed the keywords 'Necker' and 'Financial administration' went directly to France; 41.85 per cent more went to Switzerland. (NB. These figures refer to geographic zones rather than eighteenth-century political units.)
38 The *Histoire philosophique des Deux Indes* was the STN's second ranked work of 'politics' by sales, and their twelfth highest selling work of all time. A significant portion of copies sold by the STN (around 750 out of 3,694) were bought in from other suppliers.
39 As Jonathan Israel notes (*Democratic Enlightenment*, pp. 427, 433), at least two of these publishers, viz Jean-Edmé Dufour (1775, 1777) and Pierre Gosse *fils* (1774) produced editions of Raynal's *Histoire*. Some very large in-transactions from Poinçot in Versailles in July and November may be transfers or returns of unsold STN editions, but we lack evidence for the bulk of copies he originally received. There is a significant discrepancy in the database between 'in' and 'out' transactions of Raynal's *Histoire philosophique des Deux Indes*.
40 Israel, *Democratic Enlightenment*, p. 421. Kates, 'The Popularization of Political thought in Enlightenment Europe', reports fifty-seven editions in all European languages by 1800.
41 The discrepancy arises because we do not always know which set was traded, and sets tended to vary between six and ten volumes.
42 Israel, *Democratic Enlightenment*, p. 431.
43 The passages written by Diderot for the third edition can be precisely identified using the BNF's copy of Jean-Leonard Pellet's five-volume Geneva edition of Raynal's, *Histoire philosophique*. This copy, acquired in April 2015, contains pencil highlighting of passages by Diderot and, at the start of the first volume, a list of all these passages. The author of these annotations was apparently Diderot's daughter Madame de Vandeul. I thank Glenn Roe and Robert Morrissey for drawing my attention to this copy, which has been digitized by ARTFL at https://artflsrv03.uchicago.edu/philologic4/raynal/ and was used in the preparation of this chapter. It was discussed in their paper entitled 'ARTFL and the History of Complex Texts', presented at the second Digitizing Enlightenment Symposium at Radboud University (15–16 June 2017).
44 Israel, *Democratic Enlightenment*, p. 414.
45 Ibid, pp. 429–30.
46 Guillaume-Thomas Raynal, *Histoire philosophique et politique des établissemens et du commerce des Européens dans les Deux Indes*, 5 vols (Geneva: Jean-Leonard Pellet, 1780), III, 91–2.
47 Raynal, *Histoire philosophique*, III, 185–6. On sexually predatory behaviour in colonial society, see Trevor Burnard, *Mastery, Tyranny, and Desire: Thomas Thistlewood and His Slaves in the Anglo-Jamaican World* (Chapel Hill: University of North Carolina

Press, 2004). Based on a close study of Thistlewood's diaries, Burnard suggests that Thistlewood had sexual relations with every adult slave woman he encountered save the old and infirm.
48 Raynal, *Histoire philosophique*, III, 186–7.
49 Ibid., III, 193.
50 Ibid., III, 195.
51 Ibid., III, 196.
52 Ibid., III, 196.
53 Ibid., III, 194.
54 Ibid., III, 200.
55 Ibid., III, 197.
56 Ibid., III, 198–9.
57 Ibid., III, 199.
58 Ibid.
59 Ibid., III, 200.
60 Ibid., III, 201–3.
61 Ibid., III, 204.
62 Israel, *Democratic Enlightenment*, p. 430.
63 Emmanuel Sieyès, *Qu'est-ce que le Tiers Etat* (1789), p. 1.
64 See Lüsebrink and Reichardt, *The Bastille*, p. 19.
65 See, for example, the articles 'Spies', 'Hommes de la police', 'Portes des spectacles' in Mercier, *Tableau de Paris*, I, 156–8, 161–4, 1406–9.
66 See especially ch. 5 'Les Voitures' (c.f. Mercier's accounts of dangerous driving in *Le Tableau de Paris* in the articles 'Portes cochères' and 'Coureurs, chiens coureurs'); ch. 24 'Le Prince Aubergiste'; and ch. 10 'L'Homme au masque' in Louis-Sébastien Mercier, *L'An 2440* (Londres, 1774), pp. 23–6, 48–52 and 156–9. Mercier's text went through three versions. The first appeared in 1771 and others in 1786 and 1799.
67 In the FBTEE database, 'Politics' and 'History' (and its related genres) are to a large extent mutually exclusive terms. Thus the *Destruction de la Ligue*, as a historical drama, does not carry any political keywords.
68 Total print runs for French editions of the *Destruction de la ligue* were probably somewhere between 12,000 and 20,000. The majority were doubtless the STN edition printed primarily for Jonas-Samuel Fauche, Charles-S. Favre and Cie of Neuchâtel in March-April 1782. Fauche and Favre took 8,500 copies, but the STN shifted over 1,500 more on their own account. There was an Amsterdam edition (which I have consulted – see note 69) and possibly others in 1782. Worldcat lists a 1783 edition as well, besides two German editions. BPUN, MS 1180 fo.240, Louis-Sébastien Mercier to STN, Paris, 27 August 1782, reveals the French police intercepted at least some of Fauche's copies of the *Destruction de la Ligue*, but intended to return them. See Curran, *Selling Enlightenment*, p. 105.
69 The edition I consulted is an Amsterdam pirate edition, Louis-Sébastien Mercier, *La Destruction de la ligue, ou la Réduction de Paris: pièce nationale* (Amsterdam, 1782). Its preface occupies pp. v–xxxi, whereas the STN 1782 edition had forty-three pages of front matter.
70 Mercier, *La Destruction de la ligue*, Act I, scenes ii.
71 Ibid., Act I, scenes i–ii.
72 Ibid., Act I, scene iii. Hilaire *père* remains steadfast til Act III, scene vii.
73 Ibid., Act I, scene iv.
74 On the infanta plot, see also Act IV, scene iii.
75 Ibid., Act I, scene v.

76 Ibid., Act II, scene iii.
77 Ibid., Act I, scenes i–ii.
78 Ibid., Act III, scene i.
79 Ibid., Act III, scene iii.
80 Ibid., Act III, scene v.
81 Ibid., Act III, scene vii.
82 Ibid., Act III, scene ix; Act IV, scene vi.
83 Ibid., Act IV, scene x.
84 Ibid., Act IV, scene xii.
85 Ibid., preface, pp. vii, xiii–xiv.
86 Ibid., p. xv and passim
87 Ibid., p. xx.
88 Ibid., pp. xxi–xxiv, xxvii.
89 See also, for example, the note in Act II, scene iii, on the edict of Nantes and its revocation (p. 71 in the 1782 Amsterdam edition) which asks how the revocation can remain in place when detested by the 'saine partie de la nation'.
90 See Marie-Joseph Chénier, *Charles IX, ou l'école des rois* (1789).
91 This point is also made forcibly through Henri IV's discussions with Sully in Mercier, *Destruction de la Ligue*, Act II, scene iii.
92 See especially ch. XIX, 'Le Temple' in Mercier, *L'An 2440*, pp. 108–22.
93 On this point see Burrows, *Cosmopolitan Press*; Jeremy D. Popkin, *News and Politics in the Age of Revolution: Jean Luzac's Gazette de Leyde* (Ithaca, NY: Cornell University Press, 1989).

Conclusion

1 In a bizarre passage on methodology on his website, Darnton claims that he considered gathering data on the STN's trade across Europe at the start of his research in the STN archives, but dismissed it as premised on a 'flawed methodology'. It is hard to see how such a project would have been possible before digitization – nor could it be done in 1960s software. See the section 'Research Strategy: A Flawed Approach' in his unpaginated file://ad.uws.edu.au/dfshare/HomesBNK$/30035303/Downloads/Literary_Demand_Sources_And_Methods%20(3).pdf. A similar, more extensive passage appears in Darnton, *A Literary Tour*, pp. 272–4, which was published as the proofs of this book were going to press, too late to offer an extended critique. Professor Darnton's comments ignore the power of digital analysis tools to compensate for the weaknesses inherent in the STN dataset and are premised on the absurd assumption that to offer meaningful insights the database must be based on sources representative of the wider trade. He therefore tries to establish that his methods, based on a sampling of the orders of French booksellers cherry-picked for their (perceived) representative value, is more valid means of measuring 'diffusion' than an approach based on recording all the books the STN actually despatched. Even were that demonstrably the case, which is questionable, this book and its companion volume have demonstrated the value of a proper appreciation and digital analysis of the accounting data for our understanding of the book trade and dissemination of print culture.
2 See 'Afterword' below. In 2016 a new FBTEE team (Simon Burrows, Dan Edelstein, Jason Ensor, Rachel Hendery, Katherine McDonough, Angus Martin, Laure Philip and Juliette Reboul) embarked on a new Australian Research Council grant-funded

project entitled 'Mapping Print, Charting Enlightenment'. FBTEE is also collaborating closely on Alicia Montoya's ambitious ERC-funded MEDIATE project on private library auction catalogues and helping to develop a comprehensive project on subscription and circulating libraries in the British Atlantic world that has grown out of the AHRC-funded Community Libraries network. The success of these monumental projects depends in large part on the sharing of technologies and bibliographic metadata. For thoughts on how this might be done see Simon Burrows, Jason Ensor, Per Henningsgaard and Vincent Hiribarren, 'Mapping Print, Connecting Cultures', *Library and Information History* 32:4 (2016), 259–71; Simon Burrows, 'Locating the Minister's Looted Books: From Provenance and Library Histories to the Digital Reconstruction of Print Culture', *Library and Information History* 31:1 (2015), 1–17; and Mark Towsey, 'Book Use and Sociability in the Lost Libraries of the Eighteenth Century: Towards a Union Catalogue', in Flavia Bruni and Andrew Pettegree, eds, *Lost Books, Reconstructing the Print World of Pre-Industrial Europe* (Leiden: Brill, 2016), pp. 414–38.

Afterword

1 An earlier version of this afterword was presented as 'The Hidden Life of Data: Bridge-Building across Cultural Space' to a forum on 'The Digital Humanities and the Role of the Library' organized by Gale-Cengage Australia at the University of Sydney on 29 June 2016. We thank Craig Pett for inviting us to address the forum.
2 Jeremy Caradonna, review of 'The French Book Trade in Enlightenment Europe' *French History* 27:2 (June 2013), 286–7, www.jeremycaradonna.com/Review%20of%20Simon%20Burrows%20et%20al.doc on 21 March 2017.
3 Darnton, review of 'The French Book Trade in Enlightenment Europe'.
4 I wish to thank Professors Alicia Montoya of Radboud University and Paul Dijstelberge and Lisa Kuitert of the University of Amsterdam, as well as their colleagues Dr Menno Polak and Ms Marike van Roon in the Special Collections of the Amsterdam University Library, for embracing and facilitating the Luchtmans' project. We also thank the University of Amsterdam research office and Dr Rindert Jagersma and Mr Erik Jacobs for their support and participation during the project's scoping exercise in November 2016.

Bibliography

Manuscripts

France

Bibliothèque Nationale de France, Paris
MS Fr. 21,081, fos 336-54, 'Visites des inspecteurs de l'Imprimerie', May 1769, May 1770, May 1771
MS Fr. 21,831, Estampillage, 1777-81
MS Fr. 21,832, Estampillage, 1777-81; 'Etat General des Imprimeurs du Royaume fait en 1777'
Ms Fr. 21,833, Estampillage, 1777-81; Correspondence relating to the *Arrêt* of 12 June 1783
Ms Fr. 21,834, Estampillage, 1777-81
MS 21,927, Livres visités par la Chambre syndicale
MS Fr. 21,933 and 21,934, Journal des livres suspendus depuis le 4 janvier de l'année 1771 jusqu'au 11 janvier 1791
MS Fr. 22,018-22,019, permission simple registers
Ms Fr. 22,040, 'I', p.29, undated note on 'Livres venant de l'étranger', [June 1787]
MS Fr. 22,075, Livres contrefaits, 1731-87
Bibliothèque de l'Arsenal
Bastille MS 10,305

The Netherlands

Amsterdam University Library
The Luchtsmans' Archive
Vols 434-69: Booksellers' accounts
Vols 470-86: Accounts of private individuals with Luchtmans
Vols 487-9: Foreign booksellers' accounts
Vols 622-71: Trade catalogues, stocklists and warehouse books

Switzerland

Bibliothèque publique et Universitaire de Neuchâtel (BPUN)
The following Manuscripts from the Archives of the Sociéte typographique de Neuchâtel were used in the compilation of the FBTEE database:
MSS 1000, Rencontre, (18 February to 27 November 1773);
1000 A, Société typographique, correspondants, répértoire géographique;
1001, Rencontre, (30 November 1776 to 14 February 1778);
1002, Rencontre, (15 February 1778 to 9 January 1779);
1003, Rencontre, (January 1781 to December 1782);

1007, Rencontre, (1 June 1785 to 1 June 1787);
1010, Marchandises pour notre compte (1793);
1016, Livre de commissions B n.2. (27 December 1773 to 27 September 1775);
1017, Livre de commissions, (28 September 1775 to December 1776);
1018, Livre de commissions, (January–December 1777);
1021, Livre de commissions, (December 1782 to March 1785);
1022, Main Courante, (28 November 1775 to 2 January 1776; 30 November 1776 to 7 March 1777)/Livre de comptes des Menus D ['debiteurs'], (January 1770 to July 1772);
1024, Journal C, (4 September 1774 to 22 August 1775);
1025, Copie de Comptes C, (March 1779 to June 1783);
1026, Journal (March to November 1776);
1027, Comptes, December 1782, (December 1782 to January 1783);
1028, Journal Ci, (25 September 1783 to 23 November 1786);
1030, Main Courante, (2 May to 3 September 1774);
1031, Main Courante, (24 November 1786 to 2 April 1787);
1032, Main Courante, (May 1790–93) [Brouillard E, pt 1];
1033, Brouillard A, (27 July 1769 to 3 February 1773);
1034, Brouillard B, (January 1778 to March 1779);
1035, Brouillard C, (March 1779 to December 1780);
1036, Brouillard D, (December 1780 to November 1782);
1037, Divers, (1779–81);
1038, Livre de caisse n. 2. (28 November 1773 to 6 July 1776);
1042, Bilans;
1043 [livre de] Caisse (1793–4), [Brouillard E, pt. 2];
1044, Livre de menus-debiteurs A, (April 1783 to June 1787);
1050–55, Carnet pour les ouvriers/Banque des ouvriers;
1095, Copies des Lettres A1, July 1769 to December 1771;
1096, Copies des Lettres A2, August 1771 to January 1772;
1098, Copies des Lettres C1, March 1773 to April 1774;
1099, Copies des Lettres C2, February 1773 to April 1774;
1101, Copies des Lettres E, June 1775 to December 1776;
1103, Copies des Lettres F, January 1777 to February 1778;
1105, Copies des Lettres G2, February 1778 to July 1779;
1108, Copies des Lettres H, July 1779 to October 1780;
1109, Copies des Lettres I, October 1780 to December 1781;
1110, Copies des Lettres L, August 1784 to June 1787;
1112, Copies des Lettres M, November 1786 to January 1790;
1116, Correspondence: Barde, Manget et Cie.;
1117, Correspondence: Isaac Bardin;
1131, Correspondence: Jean-Samuel Cailler;
1134, Correspondence: (Charles-Antoine) Charmet, *l'aîné* (and others);
1135, Correspondence: Barthélemy Chirol;
1140, Correspondence: Gabriel Décombaz;
1143, Correspondence: François Dufart;
1144, Correspondence: J.-E. Dufour and Ph. Roux;
1145, Correspondence: Du Puget, fils; Dossier Durand;
1146, Correspondence: Duvillard and Scherrer;
1149, Correspondence: Samuel Fauche and Jonas-Samuel Fauche, Charles Favre et Cie;

1159, Correspondence: J.S. Grabit, Pierre Gosse, junior, et Daniel Pinet, Henri-Albert Gosse et Cie;
1160, Correspondence: François Grasset et Cie.;
1161, Correspondence: Gabriel Grasset;
1165, Correspondence: Albert-Emanuel [Albrecht Emanuel von] Haller;
1167, Correspondence: Jean-Pierre Heubach;
1168, Correspondence: Emanuel Hortin;
1169, Correspondence: Jean-Jacques Imhoof;
1171, Correspondence: Amand König;
1172, Correspondence: François Lacombe;
1175, Correspondence: Amable Le Roy;
1179, Correspondence: Marc-Michel Martin;
1186, Correspondence: Jean Mourer, cadet;
1187, Correspondence: Nouffer / Nouffer & Bassompierre / Nouffer de Rodon;
1191, Correspondence: Perisse frères;
1194, Correspondence: Etienne Pestre;
1195, Correspondence: Claude Philibert et Barthélemy Chirol;
1199, Correspondence: Jules-Henri Pott et Cie.;
1202, Correspondence: Pyre;
1203, Correspondence: Jean Racine;
1205, Correspondence: Reycends frères;
1209, Correspondence: Pierre J. Duplain, aîné;
1215, Correspondence: François Seizer and C. A. Serini;
1219, Correspondence: Société typographique de Lausanne, Société typographique de Neuwied et Münz, and Société Littéraire et typographique d'Yverdun;
1220, STN, Lettres à ses correspondants en voyage 2 January 1771 to 2 May 1784;
1221 Correspondence: the Société typographique de Berne;
1222, Correspondence: the Société typographique de Berne;
1223, Correspondence: Jacques-Benjamin Téron, l'aîné/Jean-Louis Téron;
1225, Correspondence: Jean-Jacques and Emmanuel Tourneisin;
1229, Correspondence: Abraham Wagner;
1231, Catalogues de la STN, 1781;
In addition, the following Manuscripts were consulted in the preparation of this book:
MSS 1113, Correspondence: Agassiz et Rougement;
1114, Correspondence: d'Arnal;
1129, Correspondence: Patrick Brydone;
1156, Correspondence: Jean-Emmanuel Gilibert; Schaub et Cie;
1168, Correspondence: Huguenin du Mitand;
1169, Correspondence: François d'Ivernois;
1176, Correspondence: Edward Lyde;
1180, Correspondence: Louis-Sébastien Mercier;
1181, Correspondence: William Owen;
1207, Correspondence: Théodore Rilliet de Saussure;
1212, Correpondence: Samuel Roulet;
1214, Correspondence: Schön et Cie;
1227, Correspondence: Charles Ulf;
1229, Correspondence: Weitbrecht;
1230, Correspondence: James de Winter.

Sources on microform

The International Booktrade in the Eighteenth Century: Booksellers' accounts 1697-1803 from the Luchtmans archive (Amsterdam and Lisse: Bibliotheek van de Koninklijke Vereeniging ter bevordering van de belangen des Boekhandels & MMF publications)

Digital sources

Burrows, Simon, '30 August 1777 and 12 June 1783 – A Digital Impact Assessment of Two Censorship Measures' – Around the World Online Digital Humanities Symposium, 22 May 2014, http://youtu.be/aC5eP0yKiDo

Burrows, Simon, and Mark Curran, The French Book Trade in Enlightenment Europe Database, 1769-1794 (http://fbtee.uws.edu.au/stn/interface/

Biblos 18. Les presses lausannoises au siècle des Lumières at http://dbserv1-bcu.unil.ch/biblos/intro.php

The British Book Trade Index at http://bbti.bodleian.ox.ac.uk/

Caradonna, Jeremy, review of 'The French Book Trade in Enlightenment Europe' for *French History* 27:2 (June 2013), 286–7, at www.jeremycaradonna.com/Review%20of%20Simon%20Burrows%20et%20al.doc

http://www.cesar.org.uk/cesar2/index.php

Darnton, Robert, 'A Literary Tour de France' at http://robertdarnton.org/

Darnton, Robert. review of The French Book Trade in Enlightenment Europe, 1769-1794, (review no. 1355) http://www.history.ac.uk/reviews/review/1355.

Dawson, Robert, *Confiscations at Customs*, appendices at http://uts.cc.utexas.edu/~dawson1/Confs_appendixes.htm (this source is no longer online)

Dictionnaire de Journalistes, 1600-1789, ed. Jean Sgard, at http://dictionnaire-journalistes.gazettes18e.fr/

Dictonnaire de Journaux, 1600-1789, ed. Jean Sgard, at *http://c18.net/dp/index.php*

Dictionnaire historique de la Suisse at http://www.hls-dhs-dss.ch/

Dictionnaires d'autrefois at https://artfl-project.uchicago.edu/content/dictionnaires-dautrefois

Eighteenth-Century Collections Online [ECCO]

Global Historical Bibliometrics at https://socialhistory.org/en/projects/global-historical-bibliometrics

H-France review, Volume 9, Issue 1 (Winter 2014) at http://www.h-france.net/forum/forumvol9/

The Luchtmans Archive at https://luchtmansarchive.com/

Raynal, Guillaume-Thomas, *Histoire philosophique et politique des établissemens et du commerce des Européens dans les Deux Indes*, 5 vols (Geneva: Jean-Leonard Pellet, 1780) at https://artflsrv03.uchicago.edu/philologic4/raynal/

Towsey, Mark, 'Wigtown Library Borrowing Records' database (unpublished digital resource)

Select primary printed sources

Note: I consulted copies (primarily in digital form) of the majority of the 3,601 works (and wherever possible one of the exact editions) known to have passed through the STN silos during the FBTEE database book classification. For reasons of space, only works from which passages have been cited or which have been discussed in detail are listed here; other book titles that appear in the text or footnotes are noted in the index.

Alletz, Pons-Augustin, (attrib.), *L'Albert moderne, ou nouveaux secrets éprouvés et licites, recueillis d'après les découvertes les plus récentes*, 2nd edition (Paris: Veuve Duchesne, 1769).
Almanach de la librairie (Paris: Moutard, 1781).
Arrêt du conseil concernant les contrefaçons des livres: Du 30 août 1777 (Paris, 1777)
Bayle, Pierre, *Dictionnaire historique et critique*, 5th edition, 4 vols (Amsterdam, Leiden, The Hague and Utrecht, 1740).
Bonnet, Charles, *Essai de psychologie; ou considérations sur les opérations de l'âme sur l'habitude et sur l'éducation* (London, 1755).
Brydone, Patrick, *Voyage en Sicile et à Malthe*, 2 vols (Londres [Neuchâtel] et se trouve à Neuchâtel au magasin de la Société typographique, 1776).
Catalogue des livres de la bibliothèque de feu M. Le baron d'Holbach (Paris, 1789).
Catalogue des livres défendus par la commission impériale et royale jusqu'à l'année 1786 (Brussels, 1788).
Catalogue général des livres qui se trouvent chez la Société typographique à Londres (undated, c. 1775).
Chénier, Marie-Joseph, *Charles IX, ou l'école des rois* (1789).
Descartes, René, *A Discourse on Method*, transl. F. E. Sutcliffe (Harmondsworth: Penguin, 1968).
Diderot, Denis and Jean le Rond d'Alembert, *Encyclopédie, ou dictionnaire raisonné des sciences, des arts et des métiers, etc.*, eds. University of Chicago: ARTFL Encyclopédie Project (Spring 2013 Edition), Robert Morrissey (ed.), http://encyclopedie.uchicago.edu/
Gilibert, Jean-Emmanuel, *Anarchie médicinale, ou La Médecine considérée comme nuisance à la société*, 3 vols (Neuchâtel: STN, 1772).
Girardeau, Pierre, *L'Art de tenir les livres en parties doubles* (Geneva, 1756).
Le Scène Desmaisons, Jacques, *Contrat conjugal, ou loix du marriage, de la répudiation et du divorce, avec une dissertation sur l'origine et le droit de dispenses* (Neuchâtel: STN, 1781).
Locke, John, *Two Treatises of Government* (London and Melbourne: J. M. Dent, 1924)
Mallet, John Lewis, *An Autobiographical Retrospective of the First Twenty-Five Years of his Life* (Windsor: Privately printed, 1890).
Mallet Du Pan, Jacques, *The British Mercury*, 5 vols (London, 1798–1800).
Mercier, Louis-Sébastien, *L'An 2440* (Londres, 1774).
Mercier, Louis-Sébastien, *La Destruction de la ligue, ou la Réduction de Paris: pièce nationale* (Amsterdam, 1782).
Mercier, Louis-Sébastien, *Tableau de Paris*, ed. Jean-Claude Bonnet, 2 vols (Paris: Mercure de France, 1994).
Mirabeau, Honoré-Gabriel de Riquetti de, attrib., *Le Rideau Levé ou l'Education de Laure*, 2 vols (Cythère: n.p., 1790).
Paulian, Aimé-Henri, *Dictionnaire des nouvelles découvertes faites en physique* (Nîmes and Avignon: Gaudé/J. J. Niel, 1787).
Pièces importantes à la dernière révolution de Genève (Neuchâtel: STN, 1782).
Raynal, Guillaume-Thomas, *Histoire philosophique et politique des établissemens et du commerce des Européens dans les Deux Indes*, 5 vols (Geneva: Jean-Leonard Pellet, 1780).

Raynal, Guillaume-Thomas, *A Philosophical and Political History of the Settlements and Trade of the Europeans in the East and West Indies*, trans. J. O. Justamond, 6 vols (London: Strahan/Cadell and Davies, 1798).

Rilliet, Théodore, *Inceste avoué à un mari, ou Exposé rapide de l'innocence & de l'honnêteté, tant absolue que relative, de spectable Théodore Rilliet* (n.pl. [Neuchâtel]: n.p. [Société typographique de Neuchâtel], 1782).

Ruault, Nicolas, *Gazette d'un Parisien sous la revolution: lettres à son frère, 1783-1796* ed. Christiane Rimbaud and Anne Vassal (Paris: Perrin, 1976).

Saugrain, Claude Marin, *Code de la librairie et de l'Imprimerie de Paris* (Paris: aux dépens de la communauté, 1744; facsimile edition, Farnborough, Gregg International, 1971).

Sieyès, Emmanuel, *Qu'est-ce que le Tiers Etat* (1789).

Tissot, Samuel, *De La Santé des gens de lettres* (Lausanne: François Grasset, 1770).

Secondary sources

Adam, Gottfried, 'Protestantism and Modernisation in German Children's Literature of the Late 18th Century', in Jan de Maeyer, ed., *Religion, Children's Literature and Modernity in Western Europe: 1750-2000*, pp. 233-49 (Leuven: Leuven University Press, 2005).

Adams, David, and Adrian Armstrong, eds, *Print and Power in France and England, 1500-1800* (Aldershot: Ashgate Publishing, 2006).

Andress, David, ed., *Experiencing the French Revolution*, SVEC 2013:5 (Oxford: Voltaire Foundation, 2013).

Armbruster, Carol, ed., *Publishing and Readership in Revolutionary France and America* (Westport, CT: Greenwood Press, 1993).

Armenteros, Carolina, 'Review Essay' [on Israel's *Democratic Enlightenment*], *H-France forum* 9:1 (Winter 2013), 26-40.

Baecque, Antoine de, 'Pamphlets: Libel and Political Mythology', in Robert Darnton and Daniel Roche, eds, *Revolution in Print. The Press in France, 1775-1800*, pp. 165-76 (Berkeley: University of California Press, 1999).

Baker, Keith Michael, 'Review Essay' [on Israel's *Democratic Enlightenment*], *H-France forum* 9:1 (Winter 2013), 41-56.

Bandelier, André, 'Le Clientèle neuchâteloise et jurasienne de la STN', in Robert Darnton and Michel Schlup, eds, *Le Rayonnement d'une maison d'édition dans l'Europe des Lumières: la Société typographique de Neuchâtel 1769-1789*, pp. 317-40 (Neuchâtel and Hauterive: B.P.U.N. and Editions Gilles Attinger, 2005).

Barber, Giles, 'The Cramers of Geneva and their Trade in Europe between 1755 and 1766', *SVEC* 30 (1964), 377-413.

Barker, Hannah, and Simon Burrows, eds, *Press, Politics and Public Sphere in Europe and North America* (Cambridge: Cambridge University Press, 2002).

Becker, Carl, *The Heavenly City of the Eighteenth-Century Philosophers* (New Haven, CT: Yale University Press, 1932).

Beckman, Jonathan, *How to Ruin a Queen* (London: John Murray, 2014).

Bellingradt, Daniel, Paul Nelles, and Jeroen Salman, eds, *Books in Motion in Early Modern Europe* (Basingstoke: Palgrave Macmillan, Cham, 2017).

Benetruy, J., *L'atelier de Mirabeau; quatre proscrits genevois dans la tourmente révolutionnaire* (Paris: Picard, 1962).

Birn, Raymond, *Royal Censorship of Books in 18th-Century France* (Stanford: Stanford University Press, 2012).

Boës, Anne, and Robert Dawson, 'The Legitimation of Piracies and the Police Stamp of 1777', *SVEC* 230 (1985), 461–84.

Boosey, Jeremy, and Ernst Roth, *Boosey and Hawkes 150th Anniversary* (London: Boosey and Hawkes, 1966).

Bots, Hans, ed., *La Diffusion et lecture des journaux de langue française sous l'ancien régime* (Amsterdam: APA-Holland University Press, 1988).

Brewer, John, and Roy Porter, eds, *Consumption and the World of Goods* (London: Routledge, 1993).

Brown, Stewart J., and Timothy Tackett, eds, *The Cambridge History of Christianity*, vol. 7, *Enlightenment, Reawakening and Revolution 1660–1815* (Cambridge: Cambridge University Press, 2006).

Bruni, Flavia, and Andrew Pettegree, eds, *Lost Books, Reconstructing the Print World of Pre-Industrial Europe* (Leiden: Brill, 2016).

Buringh, Eltjo, and Jan Luiten van Zanden, 'Charting the "Rise of the West": Manuscripts and Printed Books in Europe, A Long Term Perspective from the Sixth through Eighteenth Centuries', *Journal of Economic History* 69:2 (2009), 409–45.

Burnard, Trevor, *Mastery, Tyranny, and Desire: Thomas Thistlewood and His Slaves in the Anglo-Jamaican World* (Chapel Hill: University of North Carolina Press, 2004).

Burrows, Simon, *Blackmail, Scandal and Revolution: London's French Libellistes, 1758-1792* (Manchester: Manchester University Press, 2006).

Burrows, Simon, 'Charmet and the Book Police: Clandestinity, Illegality and Popular Reading in Late Ancien Régime France', *French History and Civilisation: Papers from the George Rudé Seminar* 6 (2015), 32–55.

Burrows, Simon, 'The Cosmopolitan Press', in Hannah Barker and Simon Burrows, eds, *Press, Politics and Public Sphere in Europe and North America*, pp. 23–47 (Cambridge: Cambridge University Press, 2002).

Burrows, Simon, 'French Banned Books in International Perspective, 1770-1789', in David Andress, ed., *Experiencing the French Revolution*, pp. 19–45 (Oxford: Voltaire Foundation, 2013).

Burrows, Simon, 'French Censorship on the Eve of the Revolution', in Nicole Moore, ed., *Censorship and the Limits of the Literary. A Global View*, pp. 13–31 (New York: Bloomsbury, 2015).

Burrows, Simon, *French Exile Journalism and European Politics, 1792-1814* (Woodbridge: Boydell and Brewer for Royal Historical Society, 2000).

Burrows, Simon, 'The French Exile Press in London, 1789-1814', Oxford D. Phil. Thesis (1992).

Burrows, Simon, 'The Innocence of Jacques-Pierre Brissot', *Historical Journal* 46 (December 2003), 843–71.

Burrows, Simon, *A King's Ransom: The Life of Charles Théveneau de Morande, Blackmailer, Scandal-Monger and Master-Spy* (London: Continuum, 2010).

Burrows, Simon, 'Locating the Minister's Looted Books: From Provenance and Library Histories to the Digital Reconstruction of Print Culture', *Library and Information History* 31:1 (February 2015), 1–17.

Burrows, Simon, 'Omissions and Revisions in Eighteenth-Century Book History: A Rejoinder to Robert Darnton', *French History and Civilisation: Papers from the George Rudé Seminar*, 7 (2017), 209–17.

Burrows, Simon, 'Police and Political Pamphleteering in Pre-Revolutionary France: The Testimony of J.-P. Lenoir, Lieutenant-Général of Police of Paris', in David Adams and Adrian Armstrong, eds, *Print and Power in France and England, 1500-1800*, pp. 99–112 (Aldershot: Ashgate Publishing, 2006).

Burrows, Simon, 'Les Traductions: éditions anglaises des Vies privées françaises', in Olivier Ferret, Anne-Marie Mercier-Faivre and Chantal Thomas, eds, *Dictionnaire des vies privées (1722-1842)*, pp. 110–29 (Oxford:Voltaire Foundation, 2011).

Burrows, Simon, 'БИБЛИОМЕТРИЯ, ПОПУЛЯРНОЕ ЧТЕНИЕ И ЛИТЕРАТУРНОЕ ПОЛЕ ИЗДАТЕЛЯ ЭПОХИ ПРОСВЕЩЕНИЯ', ['Bibliometrics, Popular Reading, and the Literary Field of an Enlightenment Publisher'], *Annuaire d'études françaises*, special edition *Le 225e anniversaire de la Révolution française*, ed. Alexandre Tchoudinov et Dmitri Bovykine (Moscow, 2015), pp. 15–43.

Burrows, Simon, and Mark Curran, 'How Swiss was the Société Typographique de Neuchâtel? A Digital Case Study of French Book Trade Networks', *Journal of Digital Humanities* 1:3 (2012), 56–65.

Burrows, Simon, Jason Ensor, Per Henningsgaard and Vincent Hiribarren, 'Mapping Print, Connecting Cultures', *Library and Information History* 32:4 (2016), 259–71.

Burson, Jeffery D., *The Rise and Fall of Theological Enlightenment. Jean-Martin de Prades and Ideological Polarization in Eighteenth-Century France* (Notre Dame, IN: University of Notre Dame Press, 2010).

Candaux, Jean-Daniel, and Bernard Lescaze, eds, *Cinq siècles de l'Imprimerie Genevoise*, 2 vols (Genève: Société d'histoire et d'archéologie, 1980–1).

Calhoun, Craig, ed., *Habermas and the Public Sphere* (Cambridge, MA: MIT Press, 1989).

Carel, Jacques, 'La dévotion à l'ange gardien dans la nord de la Lorraine', *Cahiers Lorrains* no. 1 (1995), 23–34.

Chartier, Roger, 'Book Markets and Reading in France at the End of the Old Regime', in Carol Armbruster, ed., *Publishing and Readership in Revolutionary France and America*, pp.117–37 (Westport, CT: Greenwood Press, 1993).

Chartier, Roger, *The Cultural Origins of the French Revolution* (Durham, NC: Duke University Press, 1991).

Chartier, Roger, *Lecture et lecteurs en France d'ancien régime* (Paris: Editions de Seuil, 1982).

Chisick, Harvey, ed., *The Press in the French Revolution*, SVEC 287 (Oxford: Voltaire Foundation, 1991).

Chisick, Harvey, 'Review Essay' [on Israel's *Democratic Enlightenment*] in *H-France Forum* 9:1 (Winter 2013), 57–76.

Conlon, Pierre M., *Le siècle des Lumières: bibliographie chronologique*, 32 vols (Geneva: Droz, 1983–2009).

Cook, Alexandra, 'An Eighteenth-Century Plea for Sustainable Forestry: Ostervald's', *Description des montagnes & vallées du pays de Neuchâtel*, *1650-1850, Ideas, Æsthetics and Inquiries in the Early Modern Era* 22 (2015), 257–78.

Cook, Alexandra, *Jean-Jacques Rousseau and Botany: The Salutary Science*, SVEC 2012:12 (Oxford: Voltaire Society, 2012).

Corsini, Silvio, 'Un pour tous … et chacun pour soi? Petite histoire d'une alliance entre les Sociétés typographiques de Lausanne, Berne et Neuchâtel', in Robert Darnton and Michel Schlup, eds, *Le Rayonnement d'une maison d'édition dans l'Europe des Lumières: la Société typographique de Neuchâtel 1769-1789*, pp. 115–37 (Neuchâtel and Hauterive: B.P.U.N. and Editions Gilles Attinger, 2005).

Cressy, David, 'Literacy in Context: Meaning and Measurement in Early Modern England', in John Brewer and Roy Porter, eds, *Consumption and the World of Goods*, pp. 305–19 (London: Routledge, 1993).

Curran, Mark, *Atheism, Religion and Enlightenment in Pre-Revolutionary Europe* (Woodbridge: Boydell and Brewer/Royal Historical Society, 2012).

Curran, Mark, 'Beyond the Forbidden Best-Sellers of Pre-Revolutionary France', *Historical Journal*, 56 (2013), 89–112.
Curran, Mark, *The French Book Trade in Enlightenment Europe*, vol. 1, *Selling Enlightenment* (London: Bloomsbury, 2018).
Curran, Mark, 'Mettons Toujours Londres: Enlightened Christianity and the Public Sphere in Pre-revolutionary Europe', *French History* 24 (2010), 40–59.
Curran, Mark, 'What Killed Théodore Rilliet de Saussure? Censorship and the Old Regime in France, 1769–1789' in Daniel Bellingradt, Paul Nelles, Jeroen Salman, (eds), *Books in Motion in Early Modern Europe*, pp.193–218 (Basingstoke: Palgrave Macmillan, Cham, 2017).
Darnton, Robert, 'Blogging, Now and Then (250 Years Ago)', *European Romantic Review* 24:3 (2013), 255–70.
Darnton, Robert, *The Business of Enlightenment: A Publishing History of the Encyclopédie* (Cambridge, MA: Harvard University Press, 1979).
Darnton, Robert, *Censors at Work: How States Shaped Literature* (New York: Norton, 2014).
Darnton, Robert, 'A Clandestine Bookseller in the Provinces', in Robert Darnton, *The Literary Underground of the Old Regime*, pp. 122–47 (Cambridge, MA and London: Harvard University Press, 1982).
Darnton, Robert, *The Corpus of Clandestine Literature in France 1769-1789* (New York: Norton, 1995).
Darnton, Robert, 'The Demand for Literature in France, 1769-1789, and the Launching of a Digital Archive', *Journal of Modern History* 87 (2015), 509–31.
Darnton, Robert, *The Devil in the Holy Water or the Art of Slander from Louis XIV to Napoleon* (Philadelphia: University of Pennsylvania Press, 2010).
Darnton, Robert, *Forbidden Best-Sellers of Pre-Revolutionary France* (London: Harper Collins, 1996).
Darnton, Robert *The Great Cat Massacre and Other Episodes in French Cultural History* (New York: Vintage, 1985).
Darnton, Robert, 'The Grub Street Style of Revolution: J.-P. Brissot, Police Spy', *Journal of Modern History*, 40:4 (1968), 301–27.
Darnton, Robert, 'Hidden Editions of the *Encyclopédie*', in Jean-Daniel Candaux and Bernard Lescaze, eds, *Cinq siècles de l'Imprimerie Genevoise*, vol. II, 71–101 (Genève: Société d'histoire et d'archéologie, 1980–1).
Darnton, Robert, 'The High Enlightenment and the Low-life of Literature in Prerevolutionary France', *Past and Present* 51 (1971), 81–115.
Darnton, Robert, 'J.-P. Brissot and the Société Typographique de Neuchâtel (1779-1787)', *SVEC* 10 (2001), 1–47.
Darnton, Robert, 'The Life-Cycle of a Book: A Publishing History of d'Holbach's Système de la Nature', in Carol Armbruster, ed., *Publishing and Readership in Revolutionary France and America*, pp. 15–43 (Westport, CT: Greenwood Press, 1993).
Darnton, Robert, *A Literary Tour de France. The World of Books on the Eve of the French Revolution* (Oxford and New York: Oxford University Press, 2018).
Darnton, Robert, *The Literary Underground of the Old Regime* (Cambridge, MA and London: Harvard University Press, 1982).
Darnton, Robert, 'Mademoiselle Bonafon et la vie privée de Louis XV', *Dix-Huitième Siècle* 35:2 (2003), 369–91.
Darnton, Robert, 'A Pamphleteer on the Run', in Robert Darnton, *The Literary Underground of the Old Regime*, pp. 70–121 (Cambridge, MA and London: Harvard University Press, 1982).

Darnton, Robert, 'Philosophers Trim the Tree of Knowledge', in Robert Darnton, *The Great Cat Massacre and Other Episodes in French Cultural History*, pp. 190–213 (New York: Vintage, 1985).

Darnton, Robert, 'A Police Inspector Sorts his Files', in Robert Darnton, *The Great Cat Massacre and Other Episodes in French Cultural History*, pp. 145–89 (New York: Vintage, 1985).

Darnton, Robert 'Reading, Writing and Publishing', in Robert Darnton, *The Literary Underground of the Old Regime*, pp. 167–208 (Cambridge, MA and London: Harvard University Press, 1982).

Darnton, Robert, 'La Science de la contrefaction', in Robert Darnton and Michel Schlup, eds, *Le Rayonnement d'une maison d'édition dans l'Europe des Lumières: la Société typographique de Neuchâtel 1769-1789*, pp. 89–113 (Neuchâtel and Hauterive: B.P.U.N. and Editions Gilles Attinger, 2005).

Darnton, Robert, 'Trade in the Taboo: The Life of a Clandestine Book Dealer in Prerevolutionary France', in Paul J. Korshin, ed., *The Widening Circle: Essays on the Circulation of Literature in Eighteenth-Century Europe*, pp. 13–83 (n. pl.: University of Pennsylvania Press, 1976).

Darnton, Robert, and Daniel Roche, eds, *Revolution in Print. The Press in France, 1775-1800* (Berkeley: University of California Press, 1999).

Darnton, Robert, and Michel Schlup, eds, *Le Rayonnement d'une maison d'édition dans l'Europe des Lumières: la Société typographique de Neuchâtel 1769-1789* (Neuchâtel and Hauterive: B.P.U.N. and Editions Gilles Attinger, 2005).

Dawson, Robert L., *Confiscations at Customs: Banned Books and the French Book Trade During the Last Years of the Ancien Régime*, SVEC 2006:07 (Oxford: Voltaire Foundation, 2006).

Dawson, Robert L., *The French Book Trade and the Permission Simple of 1777: Copyright and the Public Domain*, SVEC 301 (Oxford: Voltaire foundation, 1992).

Dijn, Annelien de, 'The Politics of Enlightenment from Peter Gay to Jonathan Israel', *Historical Journal* 55:3 (2012), 785–805.

Droixhe, Daniel, *Une Histoire des Lumières au pays de Liège: livre, idées, société* (Liège: Éditions de l'Université de Liège, 2007).

Duranton, Henri, Claude Labrosse and Pierre Rétat, eds, *Les Gazettes européennes de langue française (XVIIe-XVIIIe siècles)* (Saint-Etienne: Presses Universitaires de Saint-Etienne, 1992).

Echeverria, Durand, *The Maupeou Revolution: A Study in the History of Libertarianism: France, 1770-1774* (Baton Rouge, LA: Louisiana State University Press, 1985).

Edelstein, Dan, *The Enlightenment: A Genealogy* (Chicago: University of Chicago Press, 2010).

Edwards, Edward, *Memoirs of Libraries: Including a Handbook of Library Economy*, 2 vols (London: Trübner, 1859).

Eisenstein, Elizabeth L., 'Bypassing the Enlightenment: Taking an Underground Route to Revolution', in Haydn T. Mason, ed., *The Darnton Debate: Books and Revolution in the Eighteenth Century*, pp. 157–77 (Oxford: Voltaire Foundation, 1998).

Eisenstein, Elizabeth L., *Grub Street Abroad: Aspects of the French Cosmopolitan Press from the Age of Louis XIV to the Enlightenment* (Oxford: Clarendon Press, 1992).

Engelsing, Rolf, 'Die Perioden der Lesergeschichte in der Neuzeit. Das statische Ausmass und die soziokulturelle Bedeutung der Lektüre', *Archiv für Geschichte des Buchwesens* 10 (1969), cols. 944–1002.

Estivals, Robert, *La Statistique bibliographique de la France sous la monarchie au XVIIIe siècle* (Paris and The Hague: Mouton/De Gruyter, 1965).

Farge, Arlette, and Michel Foucault, *Le Désordre des familles, lettres de cachet des Archives de la Bastille* (Paris, Gallimard Julliard, 1982).
Ferret, Olivier, Anne-Marie Mercier-Faivre and Chantal Thomas, eds, *Dictionnaire des vies privées (1722-1842), SVEC* 2011:2 (Oxford: Voltaire Foundation, 2011).
Feyel, Gilles, 'La Diffusion des gazettes étrangères en France et la revolution postale des années 1750', in Henri Duranton, Claude Labrosse and Pierre Rétat, eds, *Les Gazettes européennes de langue française (XVIIe-XVIIIe siècles)*, 81–99 (Saint-Etienne: Presses Universitaires de Saint-Etienne, 1992).
Freedman, Jeffrey, *Books Without Borders in Enlightenment Europe: French Cosmopolitanism and German Literary Markets* (Philadelphia, PA: University of Pennsylvania Press, 2012).
Furet, François, ed., *Livre et Société dans la France du XVIIIe Siècle*, 2 vols (Paris: Mouton, 1965).
Gaskell, Philip, *New Introduction to Bibliography* (Oxford: Oxford University Press, 1972).
Gay, Peter, *The Enlightenment: An Interpretation*, 2 vols (New York: Knopf, 1969).
Gough, Hugh, 'Book Imports from Continental Europe in Late Eighteenth-Century Ireland: Luke White and the Société Typographique de Neuchâtel', *The Long Room* 38 (1993), 35–48.
Gruder, Vivian R., 'The Question of Marie-Antoinette: The Queen and Public Opinion before the Revolution', *French History* 16:3 (2002), 269–98.
Gruder, Vivian R., 'Political News as Coded Messages: The Parisian and Provincial Press in the Pre-Revolution, 1787-1788', *French History* 12 (1998), 1–24.
Guyot, Charly, 'Imprimeurs et pasteurs neuchâtelois: l'affaire du système de la nature', *Musée neuchâtelois* (1946), 74–81, 108–16.
Habermas, Jürgen, *The Structural Transformation of the Public Sphere: An Inquiry into a Category of Bourgeois Society*, transl. Thomas Burger (Cambridge, MA: MIT Press, 1989).
Hermann-Mascard, Nicole, *La Censure des livres à Paris à la fin de l'ancien régime (1750-1789)* (Paris: Presses Universitaires de France, 1968).
Hérubel, Jean-Pierre V.M., 'Historical Bibliometrics: Its Purpose and Significance to the History of Disciplines', *Libraries & Culture* 34:4 (Fall 1999), 380–88.
Houston, Robert Allan, *Literacy in Early Modern Europe. Culture and Education 1500-1800* (Harlow: Longman, 1988).
Hulme, Edward Wyndham, *Statistical Bibliography in Relation to the Growth of Modern Civilisation: Two Lectures Delivered in the University of Cambridge in May 1922* (London: Grafton, 1922).
Hunt, Lynn, ed., *Eroticism and the Body Politic* (Baltimore, MD and London: Johns Hopkins University Press, 1991).
Hunt, Lynn, ed., *The Invention of Pornography: Obscenity and the Origins of Modernity, 1500-1800* (New York: Zone Books, 1993).
Hunt, Lynn, 'The Many Bodies of Marie-Antoinette: Political Pornography and the Problem of the Feminine in the French Revolution', in Lynn Hunt, ed., *Eroticism and the Body Politic*, 108–30 (Baltimore, MD and London: Johns Hopkins University Press, 1991).
Hunt, Lynn, 'Obscenity and the Origins of Modernity, 1500-1800', in Lynn Hunt, ed., *The Invention of Pornography: Obscenity and the Origins of Modernity, 1500-1800*, pp. 9–45 (New York: Zone Books, 1993).
Iliffe, Rob, *Priest of Nature: The Religious Worlds of Isaac Newton* (forthcoming, Oxford: Oxford University Press, 2016).

Inderwildi, Frédéric, 'Géographie des correspondants de libraires dans la deuxième moitié du 18e siècle. La Société typographique de Neuchâtel Cramer et Gosse à Genève', *Dix-huitième siécle* 40 (2008), 503–22.
Israel, Jonathan, *Democratic Enlightenment: Philosophy, Revolution, and Human Rights 1750-1790* (Oxford and New York: Oxford University Press, 2011).
Israel, Jonathan, *Enlightenment Contested: Philosophy, Modernity, and the Emancipation of Man* (Oxford and New York: Oxford University Press, 2006).
Israel, Jonathan, *Radical Enlightenment: Philosophy and the Making of Modernity, 1650-1750* (Oxford and New York: Oxford University Press, 2001).
Israel, Jonathan, 'A Reply to Four Critics', *H-France Forum* 9:1 (Winter 2014), 77–97.
Israel, Jonathan, *A Revolution of the Mind: Radical Enlightenment and the Intellectual Origins of Modern Democracy* (Princeton, NJ: Princeton University Press, 2009).
Israel, Jonathan, *Revolutionary Ideas: An Intellectual History of the French Revolution from The Rights of Man to Robespierre* (Princeton, NJ: Princeton University Press, 2014).
Jeanprêtre, John, 'Histoire de la Société typographique de Neuchâtel', *Musée Neuchâtelois* (1949), 70–77, 115–20, 48–53.
Juratic, Sabine, and Jean-Pierre Vittu, 'Surveiller et connaître: *le Journal de la librairie* de Joseph d'Hémery, instrument de la police du livre à Paris au XVIIIe siècle', in Dominique Mellot and Sergei Karp, eds, *Le Siècle des Lumières. Statut et censure de l'imprimé en France et en Russie au Siècle des Lumières* , pp. 90–107 (St Petersburg: Naouka, 2008).
Kates, Gary, 'The Popularization of Political thought in Enlightenment Europe', unpublished conference paper, delivered to the second 'Digitizing Enlightenment Symposium' at Radboud University, Nijmegen (July 2017).
Kaufman, Paul, *Borrowings from the Bristol Library, 1773-1784. A Unique Record of Reading Vogues* (Charlottesville, VA: Bibliographical Society of the University of Virginia, 1960).
Kors, Alan, *D'Holbach's Coterie: An Enlightenment in Paris* (Princeton: Princeton University Press, 1976).
Korshin, Paul J., ed., *The Widening Circle: Essays on the Circulation of Literature in Eighteenth-Century Europe* (n. pl.: University of Pennsylvania Press, 1976).
Kwass, Michael, *Privilege and the Politics of Taxation in Eighteenth-Century France: Liberté, Egalité, Fiscalité* (Cambridge: Cambridge University Press, 2000).
Lefebvre, Georges, *The Coming of the French Revolution*, transl. Robert R. Palmer (Princeton, NJ: Princeton University Press, 1947).
Livesey, James, and Richard Whatmore, 'Étienne Clavière, Jacques-Pierre Brissot et les fondations intellectuelles de la politique des Girondins', *Annales historiques de la Révolution française* 72:3 (2000), 1–26.
Lüsebrink, Hans-Jürgen, René Nohr and Rolf Reichardt, 'Kulturtransfer im Epochenumbruch – Entwicklung und Inhalte der französiche-deutschen übersetzungbibliothek 1770-1815 im Überblick', in Hans Jürgen Lüsebrink and Rolf Reichardt, eds, *Kulturtransfer im Epochenumbruch: Frankreich-Deutschland 1770 bis 1815*, 2 vols (Leipzig, 1997), I, 29–86.
Lüsebrink, Hans-Jürgen, and Rolf Reichardt, *The Bastille. A History of a Symbol of Despotism and Freedom* (Durham, NC and London: Duke University Press, 1997).
Machet, Anne, 'Clients Italiens de la Société typographique de Neuchâtel', in Jacques Rychner and Michel Schlup, eds, *Aspects du livre neuchâtelois*, pp. 159–86 (Neuchâtel: Bibliotheque publique et universitaire, 1986).
Macdonald, Simon, 'Identifying Mrs Meeke: Another Burney Family Novelist', *Review of English Studies* 26:265 (June 2013), 367–85.

de Maeyer, Jan, ed., *Religion, Children's Literature and Modernity in Western Europe: 1750-2000* (Leuven: Leuven University Press, 2005).
McLeod, Jane, *Licencing Loyalty. Printers, Patrons and the State in Early Modern France*, (University Park, PA: Penn State University Press, 2011).
McMahon, Darrin M., *Enemies of Enlightenment* (Oxford: Oxford University Press., 2002).
McManners, John, *Church and Society in Eighteenth-Century France*, vol. 2, *The Religion of the People and the Politics of Religion* (Oxford: Oxford University Press, 1999).
Manevy, Anne, 'Le Droit Chemin. L'ange gardien, instrument de disciplinarisation après la Contre-Réforme', *Revue de l'histoire des religions*, no. 223 (2006: 2), 195–227.
Martin, Kingsley, *French Liberal Thought in the 18th Century: A Study of Political Ideas from Bayle to Condorcet* (London: E. Benn, 1929).
Martin, Philippe, *Une religion des livres, 1640-1850* (Paris: Central Emergency Response Fund, 2003).
Mason, Haydn T., ed., *The Darnton Debate: Books and Revolution in the Eighteenth Century* (Oxford: Voltaire Foundation, 1998).
Martin, Angus, Vivienne Mylne and Richard Frautschi, *Bibliographie du genre romanesque français, 1751-1800* (London and Paris: Mansell/Expansion, 1977).
Mellot, Dominique, and Sergei Karp, eds, *Le Siècle des Lumières. Statut et censure de l'imprimé en France et en Russie au Siècle des Lumières* (St Petersburg, Naouka, 2008).
Metzger, Denis, 'Livres, bibliothèques et lecture, à Saint-Avold au XVIIIe siècle', *Mémoires de l'académie nationale de Metz*, année 1999 (2000), 89–111.
Miller, Arnold, 'The Annexation of a "Philosophe": Diderot in Soviet Criticism, 1917-1960', *Diderot Studies* 15 (1971), 5–464.
Montoya, Alicia, 'French and English Women Writers in Dutch Library Catalogues, 1700-1800. Some Methodological Considerations and Preliminary Results', in Suzan van Dijk et al., eds, *"I Have Heard about You". Foreign Women's Writing Crossing the Dutch Border: From Sappho to Selma Lagerlöf*, pp. 182–216 (Hilversum: Uitgeverij Verloren, 2004).
Mornet, Daniel, 'Les enseignements des bibliothèques privées (1750-1781)', *Revue d'histoire littéraire de la France* 17 (1910), 449–96.
Moureau, François, ed., *Les Presses grises. La contrefaçon du livre (XVIe-XIXe siècles)* (Paris: Aux Amateurs de livres, 1988).
Muceni, Elena, 'John/Jean Nourse : un masque anglais au service de la littérature clandestine francophone', *La Lettre Clandestine* 24 (2016), 203–19.
Novalis [a.k.a. Friedrich von Hardenberg], *Schriften*, ed., Richard Samuel et al., 6 vols (Stuttgart: W. Kohlhammer, 1977–99).
Oddens, Joris, Mart Rutjes and Erik Jacobs, eds, *The Political Culture of the Sister Republics, 1794-1806. France, the Netherlands, Switzerland and Italy* (Amsterdam: Amsterdam University Press, 2015).
Outram, Dorinda, *The Enlightenment*, 1st edition (Cambridge: Cambridge University Press, 1995).
Oxford Dictionary of National Biography (Oxford: Oxford University Press, 2004).
Pasta, Renato, 'Les Echanges avec l'Italie', in Robert Darnton and Michel Schlup, eds, *Le Rayonnement d'une maison d'édition dans l'Europe des Lumières: la Société typographique de Neuchâtel 1769-1789*, pp. 455–73. (Neuchâtel and Hauterive: B.P.U.N. and Editions Gilles Attinger, 2005).
Popkin, Jeremy D., *News and Politics in the Age of Revolution: Jean Luzac's Gazette de Leyde* (Ithaca, NY: Cornell University Press, 1989).

Popkin, Jeremy D., 'Pamphlet journalism at the end of the old regime', *Eighteenth-Century Studies* 22:3 (1989), 351–67.
Popkin, Jeremy D., 'Robert Darnton's Alternative (to the) Enlightenment', in Haydn T. Mason, ed., *Darnton Debate*, 105–28 (Oxford: Voltaire Foundation, 1998).
Porter, Roy, and Mikuláš Teich, eds, *The Enlightenment in National Context* (Cambridge: Cambridge University Press 1981).
Richetti, John, ed., *The Columbia History of the British Novel* (New York: Columbia University Press, 1994).
Rideau, Gaël, *De la religion de tous à la religion de chacun. Croire et pratiquer à Orléans au XVIIIe siècle* (Rennes: Presses universitaires de Rennes, 2009).
Rigogne, Thierry, *Between State and Market: Printing and Bookselling in Eighteenth-Century France*, SVEC 2007:5 (Oxford: Voltaire foundation, 2007).
Rigogne, Thierry, 'Librairie et réseaux commerciaux du livre en France', in Robert Darnton and Michel Schlup, eds, *Le Rayonnement d'une maison d'édition dans l'Europe des Lumières: la Société typographique de Neuchâtel 1769-1789*, pp. 375–404 (Neuchâtel and Hauterive: B.P.U.N. and Editions Gilles Attinger, 2005).
Rimm, Anna-Maria, 'Book Routes. Imports of Foreign Books to Sweden, 1750-1800', *Publishing History* 68 (2011), 5–24.
Rimm, Anna-Maria, *Elsa Fougt, Kungl. boktryckare. Aktör i det litterära systemet ca 1780–1810* (Uppsala; Avdelningen för litteratursociologi vid Litteraturvetenskapliga institutionen i Uppsala, 2009).
Roche, Daniel, *The People of Paris* (Leamington Spa: Berg, 1987).
Rosenblatt, Helena 'The Christian Enlightenment', in Stewart J. Brown and Timothy Tackett, eds, *The Cambridge History of Christianity*, vol. 7, *Enlightenment, Reawakening and Revolution 1660-1815. The Cambridge History of Christianity*, vol. VII, pp. 283–301 (Cambridge: Cambridge University Press, 2006).
Rychner, Jacques, and Michel Schlup, eds, *Aspects du livre neuchâtelois* (Neuchâtel: Bibliotheque publique et universitaire, 1986).
Schlup, Michel, ed., *Biographies neuchâteloises*, vol. I, *De Saint Guillaume à la fin des Lumières*. (Hauterive: Editions Gilles Attinger, 1996).
Schlup, Michel, 'Coup-d'oeil sur les relations commerciales de la STN avec Moscou et Saint-Pétersbourg', in Michel Schlup, ed., *L'Edition neuchâteloise au siècle des Lumières: la Société typographique de Neuchâtel (1769-1789)*, pp. 107–13 (Neuchâtel: B.P.U.N., 2002).
Schlup, Michel, 'Diffusion et lecture du Journal helvétique au temps de la Société typographique de Neuchâtel', in Hans Bots, ed., *La Diffusion et lecture des journaux de langue française sous l'ancien régime*, pp. 59–71 (Amsterdam: APA-Holland University Press, 1988).
Schlup, Michel, 'L'Edition neuchâteloise des lumières', in Robert Darnton and Michel Schlup, eds, *Le Rayonnement d'une maison d'édition dans l'Europe des Lumières: la Société typographique de Neuchâtel 1769-1789*, pp. 69–86 (Neuchâtel and Hauterive: B.P.U.N. and Editions Gilles Attinger, 2005).
Schlup, Michel, ed., *L'Edition neuchâteloise au siècle des Lumières: la Société typographique de Neuchâtel (1769-1789)* (Neuchâtel: B.P.U.N., 2002).
Schlup, Michel 'La Société typographique de Neuchatel (1769-1789): Points de repère', in Michel Schlup, ed., *L'Edition neuchâteloise au siècle des Lumières: la Société typographique de Neuchâtel (1769-1789)*, pp. 61–105 (Neuchâtel: B.P.U.N., 2002).
Schlup, Michel, 'La STN et ses auteurs', in Robert Darnton and Michel Schlup, eds, *Le Rayonnement d'une maison d'édition dans l'Europe des Lumières: la Société typographique de Neuchâtel 1769-1789*, pp. 139–60 (Neuchâtel and Hauterive: B.P.U.N. and Editions Gilles Attinger, 2005).

Schmidt, Michael, 'Liste des impressions et éditions de la société typographique de Neuchâtel', in Michel Schlup, ed., *L'Edition neuchâteloise au siècle des Lumières: la Société typographique de Neuchâtel (1769-1789)*, pp. 233-85 (Neuchâtel: B.P.U.N., 2002).
Seaward, Louise, 'Censorship through co-operation: The *Société typographique de Neuchâtel* (STN) and the French Government, 1769-1789', *French History* 28:1 (2014), 23-42.
Seaward, Louise, 'The Small Republic and the Great Power: Censorship between Geneva and France in the later Eighteenth Century', *The Library: Transactions of the Bibliographical Society* 18:2 (2017), 191-217.
Seaward, Louise, 'The Société Typographique de Neuchâtel (STN) and the Politics of the Book Trade in late Eighteenth-Century Europe, 1769-1789', *European History Quarterly* 44:3 (2014), 439-79.
Sgard, Jean, ed., *Dictionnaire de Journalistes, 1600-1789*, second edition, 2 vols (Oxford: Voltaire Foundation, 1999).
Sgard, Jean, ed., *Dictionnaire des Journaux*, 1600-1789, 2 vols (Paris and Oxford: Universitas/Voltaire Foundation, 1991).
Shaw, David, 'French-Language Publishing in London to 1900', in Barry Taylor, ed., *Foreign Language Printing in London*, pp. 101-22 (Boston Spa and London: British Library, 2002).
Singy, Patrick, 'The Popularization of Medicine in the Eighteenth Century: Writing, Reading, and Rewriting Samuel Auguste Tissot's *Avis Au Peuple Sur Sa Santé*', *Journal of Modern History* 82:4 (2010), 769-800.
Smith, David, *Helvétius: A Study in Persecution* (Oxford: Clarendon Press, 1965).
Smith, David, 'The Publishers of d'Helvétius *De l'Homme*: The Société typographique de Londres', *Australian Journal of French Studies* 30:3 (1990), 311-23.
Strugnell, Anthony, *Diderot's Politics: A Study of the Evolution of Diderot's Politics after the Encyclopédie* (The Hague: Nijhoff, 1973).
Suire, Éric, *Sainteté et lumières. Hagiographie, spiritualité et propagande religieuse dans la France des lumières* (Paris: Honoré Champion, 2011).
Taylor, Barry, ed., *Foreign Language Printing in London* (Boston Spa and London: British Library, 2002).
Thomas, Chantal, *The Wicked Queen: The Origins of the Myth of Marie-Antoinette*, transl. Julie Rose (New York: Zone, 1999).
Towsey, Mark, 'Book Use and Sociability in the Lost Libraries of the Eighteenth Century: Towards a Union Catalogue', in Flavia Bruni and Andrew Pettegree, eds, *Lost Books, Reconstructing the Print World of Pre-Industrial Europe*, pp. 414-38 (Leiden: Brill, 2016).
Towsey, Mark, 'First Steps in Associational Reading: Book Use and Sociability at the Wigtown Subscription Library, 1795-9', *Proceedings of the Bibliographical Society of America* 103:4 (2009), 455-95.
Michel, Vernus, *Transmettre la foi: XVIe-XXe siècles*, 2 vols (Paris: CTHS, 1984).
van Dijk, Suzan, Petra Broomans, Janet van der Meulen and Pim van Oostrum, eds, *"I Have Heard about You". Foreign Women's Writing Crossing the Dutch Border: From Sappho to Selma Lagerlöf* (Hilversum: Uitgeverij Verloren, 2004).
Vernus, Michel, 'A Provincial Perspective', in Robert Darnton and Daniel Roche, eds, *Revolution in Print. The Press in France, 1775-1800*, pp. 124-38 (Berkeley: University of California Press, 1999).
Vernus, Michel, 'Un Best-seller de la littérature religieuse: *L'Ange Conducteur* (du XVIIe au XIXe siècle)', in *Transmettre la foi: XVIe-XXe siècles*, vol. I, 231-43 (Paris: CTHS, 1984).

Vercruysse, Jeroom, 'La Reception politique des gazettes de Hollande, une lecture diplomatique', in Hans Bots, ed., *La Diffusion et lecture des journaux de langue française sous l'ancien régime*, 39–47 (Amsterdam: APA-Holland University Press, 1988).

Veyrin-Forrer, Jeanne, 'Livres arrêtés, livres estampillés, traces parisiennes de la contrefaction', in François Moureau, ed., *Les Presses grises. La contrefaçon du livre (XVIe-XIXe siècles)*, pp. 101–12 (Paris: Aux Amateurs de livres, 1988).

Vovelle, Michel, *The Fall of the Monarchy, 1787-1792*, transl. Susan Burke (Cambridge: Cambridge University Press, 1984).

Vovelle, Michel, *The Revolution against the Church*, transl. Alan José (Columbus: Ohio State University Press, 1991).

Warner, William, 'Licencing Pleasure: Literary History and the Novel in Early Modern Britain', in John Richetti, ed., *The Columbia History of the British Novel*, pp. 1–22 (New York: Columbia University Press, 1994).

Wurgler, Andreas, 'Censorship and Public Opinion. Press and Politics in the Helvetic Republic (1798-1803)', in Joris Oddens, Mart Rutjes and Erik Jacobs, eds, *The Political Culture of the Sister Republics, 1794-1806. France, the Netherlands, Switzerland and Italy*, pp. 159–69 (Amsterdam: Amsterdam University Press, 2015).

Subject Index

Adams, David   183 n.16, 184 n.28, 185 n.48
Agassiz (merchant)   50, 52–3
agricultural manuals   59
Alemán, Mateo   53
Alembert, Jean le Rond d'   5, 8, 10, 28, 72, 78, 137–9, 142, 144
Alletz, Pons-Augustin   130, 137, 141
Almaviva, comte d'   4
American Historical Association   201 n.5
American Revolution   37, 47, 48, 78, 87, 169, 170
Amsterdam University   176
ancien régime   11, 29, 31, 37–8, 40, 69, 78–9, 91, 122, 131, 151, 154, 158, 173
Andrews, George Pettit   114
Angerville. *See*, Mouffle d'Angerville
Angus & Robertson   177
Annual Register   114
Anticlericalism, anti-clerical works   4, 11, 25, 30, 55, 56, 58, 97, 127–8, 129, 130, 132, 135, 143, 145, 174
anti-Enlightenment   8, 10, 12
anti-Marie-Antoinette pamphlets   xi, 28, 40–1, 119, 133, 135
ARCHivER initiative   177
Aretino, Pietro   75, 130, 131
Argens, Jean-Baptiste de Boyer, Marquis d'   56, 128
Armenteros, Carolina   10
Arnal, Jean-Baptiste d'   51, 52
Arts and Humanities Research Council   48
Australian Literary Gateway (AustLit)   178
Australian National Data Service   177
Australian National University   180
Australian Research Council   173, 177
Austrian Habsburg Empire   38
Auxiron, Jean Baptiste d'   147

Baecque, Antoine de   119, 186 n.10
Baker, Keith   10, 12
ballots (wooden crates)   xiv, 1, 5, 37
Banks, Joseph   138
Barber, Giles   59
Barrême, François-Bertrand de   39
Barrois, Louis François   60
Barrow, John   117
Barruel, abbé Augustin   6, 10, 14, 25, 147
Barthélemi, Jean-Jacques   118
Barthélemy, Girard   24
Bassompierre, Anne-Catherine   2, 4
Bastille   40–1, 71, 120–6 *passim*, 129, 133, 158, 161, 169
Baume, Pierre   148
Bayle, Pierre   9, 26, 28, 184 nn.25
Beaumarchais, Pierre-Augustin Caron de   3–4, 27
Beaumont, Leprince de   75–6, 195 n.41, 197 n.67
Becker, Carl   185 n.45
Belles-Lettres   75, 80–1, 87–9, 91–3, 96, 98–9, 115, 201 n.22
Bergier, Nicolas-Sylvestre, abbé   81
Berquin, Arnaud   76, 199 n.3
Bertrand, Jean-Elie   37, 64, 101, 137, 141, 151, 197 n.67
Bertrand, Madame   151
Bertrand, Philippe   148
Berwick, James FitzJames, Maréchal-Duc de   54
bestsellers lists   67–76 and *passim*
Bibframe linked data model   206 n.68
Bible   70, 74–5, 101, 103
'Biblical History & Criticism'   128
bibliographic metadata   179–80
bilingual texts   107
Birn, Raymond   122
Bishop, Catherine   191 n.22
Blanning, Tim   12
Boës, Anne   189 n.55

Boffe, Joseph de 1, 53
Boissière, David 52, 59, 88–9, 92, 96
Bollstädt, Albrecht von 141
Bondeli, Julie Suzanne 63
Bondely, Mademoiselle 63
Bones, Helen 177
Bonnet, Charles 139, 144
books
  and censorship systems 29–31
  classification of 77–89
  foreign 44–5
  literary piracy 28–9
  ownership 22–3
  and printers' licences 32
  production 19–20
  for professional practice 23–4
  reading habits 26–7
  for religious practice 25
  school book sales 56–8, 95
  and signature literacy 21–2
  tacitly permitted works 31
Bordeu, Théophile de 188 n.33
Boubers, Jean-Louis 4, 8, 28, 62
Bouhours, Dominique 25, 147
Bouillaud, Ishmael 80
Boulanger, Nicolas-Antoine 2, 6–7, 79, 144
Brissot, Jacques-Pierre 7–8, 23, 28, 42, 47, 60, 95–6, 129, 159, 211 n.3
Bristol Library 84, 115–16
Brooke, Henry 53, 204 n.45
Brossais du Perray 133
Bruyset, Jean-Marie 134
Brydone, Patrick 4, 29, 108–12, 115, 118, 148
Buchan, William 24
Buffon, George-Louis Leclerc, comte de 138, 139
Bure, Guillaume de 79–81
Buringh, Eltjo 186 n.7, 187 n.20
Burnard, Trevor 219 n.47
Burney, Fanny 118
Busching, Antoine-Friedrich 5, 102, 159

Calonne, Charles-Alexandre de 73, 163
Caradonna, Jeremy 175
Caron, Charles 151
Castiglione, Giovanni Francesco Mauro Melchior Salvemini da 147
catechism 27, 70, 153, 189 n.42, 202 n.14

Catholic League 168
Catholicism 168–9
censorship systems 29–31
César database 85
chambres syndicales de la librairie 59, 60, 123, 134, 140, 151, 152, 197 n.57
Charmet, Charles-Antoine 36, 60–1, 121, 144, 145, 147, 148, 150, 151, 153–4, 155, 162–3, 214 n.52, 215 n.65, 216 n.75, 219 n.35
Charmet frères et soeurs 148
Charmet, Jean-Félix 23, 147–51, 148, 149, 153–4, 187 n.28, 215 n.71
Charnage, François-Ignace Dunod de 151
Chartier, Roger 6, 12, 29, 119, 122, 183 n.11
Chastellux, François-Jean, Marquis de 118
Chauvet, David 70
Chénier, Marie-Joseph 170
Chesterfield, Lord. *See* Philip Stanhope, Earl of Chesterfield
Chisick, Harvey 9, 12, 184 n.39
Christian apologists 143–6, 215 n.61
Christian enlightenment 14, 174, 185 n.45
Christianity 14, 103, 111, 130, 138, 143–6, 174
Christin, Charles-Gabriel-Frédéric 71, 73, 103
Classe des pasteurs 30
Clavière, Etienne 159
Cleland, John 56, 130
Clément, Denis-Xavier 25, 147
'Client gender' menu 98
'client type' options 198 n.74
commercial bestseller list 73–5, 96
Community Libraries network 221 n.2
Condillac, Etienne-Bonnot de xiii, 10, 81, 138, 139
Condorcet, Jean-Antoine-Nicolas de Caritat, Marquis de 6–7, 10, 145
Conlon, Pierre M. 19, 83, 185 n.50, 186 n.9
Cook, Alexandra 139
Coret, Jacques 25, 147
Corsini, Silvio 190 n.69
cosmopolitan books 118, 170

cosmopolitan Enlightenment   xiii, 105, 108, 115, 116
cosmopolitanism   xiv, 4, 13, 42, 106, 109, 111–12, 115
Courier de l'Europe (newspaper)   53
Coxe, William   113, 118
Coyer, Gabriel-François, abbé de   25
Cramer brothers   50, 59, 71–2
Crébillon, Claude-Prosper-Jolyot de   51, 118
Crébillon, *fils*. *See* Crébillon, Claude-Prosper-Jolyot de
Curll, Edmund   207 n.89
Curran, Mark   1, 17, 28, 37–9, 41–3, 49, 67, 81, 173, 182 n.1, 185 n.41, 200 n.10, 214 n.51, 218 n.25

Damiens, Robert-François   29
Darnton, Robert   10–15, 20, 29, 30, 35–6, 42–3, 48, 61, 67, 75–6, 88, 94, 104, 119, 121, 122, 124–6, 127, 128–9, 130, 132, 135, 143, 145, 146, 147, 150, 155, 173, 175, 182 n.5, 183 nn.9, 188 n.37, 192 n.29, 192 n.30, 194 n.8, 209 n.24, 215 n.71, 221 n.1
databases. *See* FBTEE
data-mining   87
Davies, Thomas   50
Dawkins, Richard   144
Dawson, Robert L.   122, 189 n.55, 191 n.22
Declaration of the Rights of Man and Citizen   14, 79
Decombaz, Gabriel   164
DeFrance, Leonard   xi, xiii–xiv, 1–5, 25, 91, 105, 138, 174
deism/deist   6, 7, 72, 81, 128, 144, 147
Deleyre, Alexandre   164
Demazeau. *See* Orval-Demazeau
desacralization   13, 40, 127, 128, 130, 132, 133, 153, 162, 174
Desauges, Edme-Marie-Pierre   60
Descartes, René   68, 143
Desmaisons, Jacques Le Scène   28, 71, 119, 120–1, 197 n.58
Desprades, Joseph Grellet   25, 188 n.36
Dewey system   200 n.3
Diamond Necklace Affair   67, 158
Diderot, Denis   5–8, 10, 14, 72, 78–9, 164–7, 170, 219 n.43

digital humanities   xii, xiii, 13, 175
Dijn, Annalien de   10, 14, 156
Dijstelberge, Paul   222 n.4
Directeur de la librarie   31
divorce   120
Don Quixote   114
Dorat, Claude   3–4, 25, 71, 76, 86
Dufour, Jean-Edmé   4
Dumont, Etienne   159
Duplain, Joseph   194 n.8
Duplain, Pierre   119
Durand, D. H.   50, 60
Duroveray, Jacques-Antoine   159

Easter book fair   44
'Ecclesiastical history'   81
'Economics'-related books   102
Edelstein, Dan   9, 180, 184 n.24
'Edition Types' option menu   98, 193 n.37
Edwards, Edward   80
Eighteenth-Century Collections Online (ECCO)   116–17, 118, 175, 179, 207 n.78
Eisenstein, Elizabeth   12
Electronic Enlightenment   180
Elmsley, Peter   50
Endeavour   138
Enfer   119
Engelsing, Rolf   26
Enlightenment, *passim*
   anti-   8, 10, 12
   cosmopolitan   xiii, 105, 108
   definition of   6
   moderate   7–8, 10, 156, 166
   national   9, 12
   and print culture   17–33
   radical   7–10, 14, 128, 130, 155, 164, 174
Enlightenment Bestsellers   43, 173
Enlightenment classics   2, 4, 32, 114, 156
Ensor, Jason   177
Erotica, 'Erotic works'   3–5 *passim*, 25, 55, 58, 64, 75, 82, 83, 85–7, 97, 102–3, 104, 118–21 *passim*, 126, 128, 131–2, 135, 200 n.13, 202 n.20, 207 n.89, 210 n.46
Estivals, Robert   186 n.9
Euler, Leonard   138
European Research Council   180

Fabre, Pierre   187 n.30
Fauche, Jonas   70, 183 n.21, 220 n.68
Fauche, Pierre-François   6
Fauche, Samuel   30, 37, 142
Fauche-Borel, Louis   39, 191 n.8, 211 n.70
Favre, Charles-Samuel   70, 220 n.68
FBTEE-2.0   180, 191 n.22, 196 n.57
FBTEE database   xi, xiii, 12, 17, 23, 29, 33, 35, 38, 43–4, 47–8, 63, 79, 86, 94–5, 97, 101, 149, 173, 175–9, 183 n.21, 189 n.49,192 n.30, 193 n.37, 196 n.57,200 n.13, 214 n.50 and *passim*
FBTEE maps   38
Fénélon, François de Salignac de La Mothe   62, 114, 155, 156, 159, 170
Fielding, Henry   51, 114, 115, 118
FitzJames, James. *See* Berwick
financial administration   102
financial pamphlets   21, 73, 102, 159, 162, 163
Fleuriot, Jean-Marie-Jérôme   55
'floating stock' theory   35, 42–3, 46
foreign editions   44–5, 106, 192 n.27, 193 n.40, 193 n.42
foreign language titles   19, 106–7, 116, 117
foreign lending libraries   53
Formey, Samuel   139
Fougereux, Jean   64
Fougt, Elsa   55–6, 195 n.3
Franklin, Benjamin   138
Franklin, Miles   178
Frautschi, Richard   85, 179
FRBR. *See* Functional Requirements of Bibliographic Records
Frederick II, King of Prussia   76
Freedman, Jeffrey   27, 62, 105–6
French Enlightenment. *See* Enlightenment
French Revolution   6–11, 14–15, 20, 38, 40–1, 47, 97, 121, 132, 133, 135, 153, 155 *passim*
Fréret, Nicolas   146
Functional Requirements of Bibliographic Records (FRBR)   178–9
Furet, François   88, 104, 153
Fyrberg, Antoine Adolphe   55–6

Gale-Cengage Learning   116, 179
Galen   143
Gallica   84
Gamet, Jean-Marie   188 n.33
Gardanes, Joseph-Jacques   140, 187 n.30, 212 n.16, 213 n.22
Garnier, Jean-Jacques   79
Garrett (London bookseller)   53
Gaskell, Philip   186 n.8
Gaudé, *père et fils*   164
Gay, Peter   10, 12–15, 76, 94–5, 104, 185, 185 n.45
Gélieu, Jonas   137, 141
Genevan politics   157–9
Genlis, Félicité de   56, 75–6, 195 n.41
Geography   102
Gibbon, Edward   114
Gilibert, Jean-Emmanuel   23, 28, 137, 139–41, 211 n.1, 212 n.12
Gillies, John   114
Girardeau, Pierre   191 n.19
Global Historical Bibliometrics   19, 22, 116, 206 n.63
Godard, Louis   62
Goëzman, Louis-Valentin   28, 159, 189 n.49, 197 n.58
Gonnelieu, Jérome de   149
Goodman, Dena   12
Google Books   84, 175
Google Maps   179
Google Scholar   85
Gorani, Guiseppe   7
Gordon, Dan   12
Gosse, Pierre   59, 164
Gottsched, Johann Christoph   58, 75
Goudar, Ange   75
Gough, Hugh   194 n.21
Grabit, J. S.   164
Graffigny, Madame de   156
Grasset, François   46
Grégoire, abbé Henri   10
Gregory, John   64
Griffet, Antoine-Gilbert   205 n.45
Grimoard, Philippe-Henri   73
Grub Street   10–12
gum ammoniac   187 n.29
Guthrie, William   114, 205 n.51

Habermas, Jürgen 18-19
Haller, Albrecht von 139, 141, 143, 144, 159
Hautesierck, F. -M. C. Richard de 188 n.33
Hawkesworth, John 115
Haywood, Eliza 118
Hedouin, Jean-Baptiste 164
Hell. *See Enfer*
Helvétius, Claude-Adrien xiii, 2, 4, 7-8, 10, 31, 76, 79, 146
Hémery, Joseph d' 77-8
Henri IV 168, 169-70
Henry, Phillippe 182 n.3
Henry, Robert 114
Heraclium gummiferum. *See* gum ammoniac
Heron, Robert 114, 205 n.51
Hérubel, Jean-Pierre V. M. 182 n.3
Hippocrates 143
Hiribarren, Vincent 175, 176
Histoire 80-2, 87-9, 91, 93, 96, 98-9, 103
historical bibliometrics 1, 19, 22, 40, 105-6, 116, 174, 182 n.1
'History, Antiquities and Geography' 115
Holbach, Paul Henri Thiry, baron d' 2, 4, 6-9, 14, 37, 67, 72, 76, 79-81, 87-9, 103, 104, 144, 145, 146, 147, 153, 154, 155, 164, 184 n.25
Holland, Georg-Jonathan 14, 81, 103, 147
Home, Francis 188 n.33
Houston, Robert 187 n.16
Hübner, Johann 58, 64
Huguenin du Mitand, Louis 51-2
humanities computing 175
Humbert, Pierre 149, 150
Hume, David 114, 116, 117
Hunt, Lynn 12, 83, 119, 208 n.4
Hunter, John 138

illegal books 11-12, 13-14, 29-30, 37, 46, 48, 75, , 77, 88, 94-5, 98, 101-4, 108, 119-46, 153, 158, 161 and *passim*
Imbert, Guillaume 55
interactive digital maps 175
Israel, Jonathan 7-10, 12, 14-15, 15-16, 76, 128, 145, 183 nn.13, 219 n.39

Ivernois, François d' 50-1

Jacobs, Erik 222 n.4
Jagersma, Rindert 222 n.4
Jeanprêtre, John 23, 36, 199 n.11
Joan of Arc 3, 75, 130
Johnson, Samuel 204 n.45
Johnstone, Charles 204 n.45
Jones, Colin 12
Joseph II (emperor) xiii, 3, 30
journalism 19
Jurisprudence 80, 87-8, 96, 98

Kates, Gary 155, 156, 160, 217 n.3, 217 nn.3-4
Kaufman, Paul 115, 205 n.56
Kempis, Thomas à 25, 31, 149, 152
Keralio, Louise de 86
keyword system 79, 82-7, 95-6
keyword tags 107
Koppen, Karl-Friedrich 130
Kors, Alan 9, 184 n.25
Kuitert, Lisa 222 n.4
Kwass, Michael 163

La Barre, Chevalier de 145
Laclos, Chloderos de 55
Lacoré, Charles-André de 60
Lacroze, Mathurin Veyssière de 58
La Mettrie, Julien d'Offray de 9, 79, 143-6
La Motte, Jeanne de Saint-Rémy de 135, 211 n.70
Lavoisier, Antoine 138
Leeds University 176
Lefebvre, Georges 185 n.48
legal editions 209 n.35
Leibniz, Gottfried Wilhelm 7, 81, 138
Le Maître, Pierre-Jacques 159
Lemarié, François 2
Lenoir, Jean-Charles-Pierre 160
Lepagnez, Charles 151
Lépagnez, Dominique 147, 163
Leprince de Beaumont, Jeanne-Marie 56, 58, 75
Le Sage, Alain René 114, 118
Le Scène Desmaisons, Jacques. *See* Desmaisons
Lesenne, abbé 25, 28

liberalism 30, 120
libertine works 35, 55–6, 62, 64, 75, 83, 122–7, 130, 131, 132, 134, 135, 209 n.27, 210 n.57
libertinism 4, 46, 55–6, 97, 132
licensed editions 124
Liger, Louis 87
Liguori, Alfonso Maria de 151
Lilti, Antoine 12
Linguet, Simon-Nicolas-Henri 60, 64, 74, 146, 164
Linnaeus, Carl 77, 138, 139
literacy skills 21–2
literary piracy 28–9, 46, 123–4
'Lives and Letters' 103
livres d'assortissement 93, 96–7, 186 n.1
livres en nombre 186 n.1
livres philosophiques 11, 30, 32, 48, 58, 62, 121–4, 127–9, 131, 132, 134, 143, 145, 153–4
livres troqués 186 n.1
Locke, John 7, 138, 143
Library of Congress classification system 200 n.3
Logique et morale 80, 93
Lorme, M. de 53
Louis XIV 134, 170
Louis XV 3–4, 21, 29, 37, 63–4, 132, 133–4, 155, 161, 217 n.16, 218 n.36
Louis XVI 133, 134
Luchet, Jean-Pierre-Louis de La Roche du Marin, Marquis de 3, 4, 55
Luchtmans company 35, 42, 203 n.6
Lüsebrink, Hans Jürgen 116, 133
Luze, Jean-Jacques de 198 n.77
Lyde, Edward 51, 52, 54
Lyton, John Peter 53
Lyttelton, George 114

Mably, Gabriel Bonnot de, abbé 62
Machine Readable Catalogue (MARC) 206 n.68
Macintosh, William 87
McMahon, Darrin 6, 183 n.10, 208 n.3
Macquer, Pierre-Joseph 137, 141
Mairobert. *See* Pidansat de Mairobert
Malherbe, Paul 121, 134, 153, 161,
Mallet Du Pan, Jacques 6–7, 183 n.12
Mangot, Jean-Baptiste 166

Mapping Print, Charting Enlightenment project 173, 177, 180, 221 n.2
Mapping the Republic of Letters project 175, 180
Marchand, Prosper 79–80
Marie-Antoinette, Queen of France xi, 28, 40–1, 119, 133, 135
'Markers of illegality' menu 98
Marmontel, Jean-François 25, 53–4, 62, 64, 74, 76, 114, 159
Marnézia, Claude-François-Adrien Lézay de 148
marriage 120
Martin, Angus 85, 179
Martin, Gabriel 80
Martin, Kingsley 185 n.47
Maupeou, René-Charles-Augustin de 140, 160–1
Maupeouana 164
Mauvelain, Bruzard de 41, 42, 120, 121, 134, 153
MEDIATE project 180, 221 n.2
Meeke, Elizabeth 68
Mercier, Louis Sébastien 3–4, 27–8, 60, 62, 67, 69–73, 75–6, 86, 93, 96, 107, 129, 137, 146, 167–70, 189 n.44, 192 n.26, 220 n.66
Mercure de France 146
'Metaphysics, Natural Religion, Materialism, Deism, & the Soul' 128
Métaphysique 79, 81–2, 93–4
Mettra, Louis-François 30
Meuron, Henry de 198 n.77
Millot, Claude-François-Xavier 24, 53, 55–6, 58, 64, 71, 117
Mirabeau, Honoré-Gabriel Riqueti, comte de 7–8, 46, 120, 130, 159, 167, 183 n.21
missionaires de la diocèse de Besançon 151
MMF-2 data 179
moderate Enlightenment 7–8, 10, 156, 166
Molière 25
monasticism 110
Monnot, Modeste 148, 149
Montesquieu, Charles-Louis Secondat, baron de 2, 4, 10, 64, 94, 117, 156, 159, 204 n.40

Montoya, Alicia   180, 196 n.42, 221 n.2, 222 n.4
Moore, John   113
Morande, Charles Théveneau de. *See* Théveneau de Morande
Morellet, André   25
Mornet, Daniel   88-9, 91-2, 104
Mouffle d'Angerville, Barthélemy   21
Mourer, Jean   204 n.45
Moutard, Nicolas-Léger   60
Munck, Thomas   12
Mylne, Vivienne   85, 179
'Myth of Enlightenment'   10, 14

Naigeon, Jacques-André   7, 79, 144
national Enlightenments   9, 12
Necker, Jacques   21, 64, 71, 73, 102, 104, 155, 163-4
newspapers   20
New Testament   64, 74-5, 101
Newton, Isaac   7, 138-9, 143, 214 n.39
New York Times   175
Niebuhr, Carsten   118
Nikolai, Ernst Anton   24
Nikolai, Friedrich   58
Nodier, Charles   80
Nohr, René   116
Nonnotte, abbé Claude-François   149
Nourse, John   50

Old Regime. *See* ancien régime
one-substance materialism   7, 9
options menus   47, 74, 78, 97
Orval-Demazeau (Liège bookseller)   2, 4
Ostervald, Frédéric-Samuel   23, 37, 40, 64, 70, 98, 102, 156
Ostervald, Jean-Frédéric   23, 40, 64, 70-2, 101
Ostervald, Jean-Rudolphe   74, 101
Outram, Dorinda   12-13
Owen, William   49-50, 53

Pagès, Pierre-Marie-François   118
pamphlets, pamphleteering   xi, xvi, 2, 4-6, 15, 17-18, 20-1, 22, 23, 28, 29, 32, 37, 40-1, 55, 61, 64, 67, 69-71, 72, 73, 96, 102, 104, 126-7, 132, 135
Panckoucke, baron Charles-Joseph   194 n.8

Parlements, parlementaires   29, 88-9, 91-2, 126-7, 133-4, 158, 159, 160-1
Paulian, Aimé-Henri   144
Pauw, Cornelius de   130
Payne, Thomas   50
Pellet, Jean-Leonard   70
Permissions registers   92, 124, 149, 151
Perregaux, Jean-Frédéric   52
Perrin, Charles-Joseph   151
Peyrilhe, Bernard   187 n.30
philosophes. *See* individual philosophers
philosophic works   134
Philosophie   80-1, 87, 93-5, 97, 102-4
Pidansat de Mairobert, Mathieu-François   45-6, 75-6, 94, 127, 129, 132, 159
Pinet, Daniel   164
piracy. *See* literary piracy
pirate editions   193 n.43, 209 n.35
pirate trade   123
Piron, Alexis   25
Planchon, Antoine   188 n.33
Planta, Friedrich von   67
Planta, Ursula von   67
Plato   184 n.25
Plomteux, Clément   2, 4
Plutarch   107
Poétique (poetry)   80, 82, 93
Poinçot, Claude   47, 122, 129
Polak, Menno   222 n.4
Political Fiction   159
political pamphlets   20 and *passim*
political radicalism   9, 14, 120, 146, 155
Political theory   160
political works   127
Politics   103, 218 n.16
Polygraphes anciens et modernes   93, 96
Pomaret (pastor)   101
Pope, Alexander   3
Popkin, Jeremy D.   12, 94, 201 n.5
pornographic books   119, 129, 131, 132, 134, 200 n.13 and *passim*. *See also* erotica, libertine works
Porter, Roy   9, 106
Pourtalès and Cie   23
Prades, Jean-Martin, abbé de   188 n.36
Prévost, Antoine-François, abbé   118
Priestley, Joseph   24, 138
print culture   17-33. *See also* books
printers' licences   32

Production, Reception, Ownership, Marketing, Policing and Transmission (PROMPT)   176-7
Protestantism   169-70
Protestant texts   101, 104

Quatre-Ministraux   30

Radboud University   176
radical Enlightenment   7-10, 14, 128, 130, 155, 164, 174
Raynal, Guillaume-Thomas, abbé   4, 7-8, 25, 42, 43, 46, 47, 51, 56, 62, 64, 71, 73, 75-6, 114, 115, 117, 120, 130, 146, 156, 159, 164-6, 170, 199 n.12, 204 n.40, 219 nn.39
'Reading Experience Database'   180
reading habits   26-7
Reichardt, Rolf   116, 133
Renoz, C. J.   2
Restaut, Pierre   53, 57, 64
Rétif, Nicolas   131
Riccoboni, Madame   25, 67, 71-3, 197 n.67
Richard, Charles-Louis   6
Richardson, Samuel   118
Richelieu, Armand-Jean du Plessis, Cardinal   169
Rideau, Gaël   150
Rigogne, Thierry   36, 191 n.4
Rilliet de Saussure, Théodore   21, 28, 58, 67-8, 67-9, 71-2, 95-6, 98
Rimm, Anna-Maria   35, 185 n.42, 195 nn.33
Robertson, William   114, 115, 117, 148, 156, 206 nn.76-7
Robson, James   50
Roche, Daniel   12
Roe, Glenn   180
Rohan, Louis de, cardinal   67
Roman Catholicism   110, 111
Romantic fiction   103
Rondi, Guiseppe   62
Roon, Marike van   222 n.4
Rouelle, Hilaire-Marin   24
Rougemont (merchant)   50, 52-3
Roulet, Samuel   49, 52-3
Rousseau, Jean-Jacques   6, 10, 39, 51, 54, 67, 71, 73, 75-6, 94, 104, 114, 121, 130

Rozier, abbé François   140
Rozoi, Barnabé Farmian Du   3
Rüdiger, Christian   58

Sabatier de Castres, abbé Antoine   25
Sade, Donatien-Alphonse-François, marquis de   9
Saint-Claude, Abbaye de   71
Sainte-Agathe, Nicolas-Anne de   148, 149
Saint Ildephont, Réné Guillaume Lefébure de   24
Saint-Lambert, Jean-François de   7, 64
Saint-Vincent, Pierre-Augustin Robert de   73
Saint-Yves, Charles de   139
sans culottes   8, 11
Savary, Claude-Etienne   113
sceptical works   130
scepticism   xiv, 4, 105, 132, 152
Schabol, abbé Roger de   148
Schlup, Michel   36, 39, 57, 183 n.18, 187 n.13, 189 n.46, 190 n.64, 191 n.4, 196 n.44
Schön and Cie 56
School books   101, 102
Sciences et Arts   80, 82, 87-8, 92-4, 96, 98-9
Science works   143, 144
Seaward, Louise   29, 161, 191 n.22
Second World War   8, 53
Senebier, Jean   54
Sentimental fiction   103
Shaw, David   53
Siéyès, abbé Emmanuel-Joseph   7
signature literacy   21-2
Signieri, Paul   149
Simonin, (Cologne printer)   30
Sinner de Ballaigues, Rudolf   28
Smith, Adam   148, 156, 204 n.40
Smollett, Thomas   114, 114
sociétés littéraires (reading circles)   62
Société typographique de Berne   188 n.40
Société typographique de Lausanne   115, 207 n.77
Société typographique de Londres   201 n.20
Société typographique de Neuchâtel (STN)   2, and *passim*

Spinoza, Baruch   7, 13, 28, 81, 143, 184 nn.25
Spinozism   9–10
Stanford University   175
Stanhope, Philip, Earl of Chesterfield   116
State Library of New South Wales   177
Sterne, Laurence   113, 115, 118
STN. *See* Société typographique de Neuchâtel (STN)
Stretser, Thomas   118
subject taxonomies. *See* taxonomic systems
Sutton, Robert   24
Swift, Jonathan   159
Sydney University   179

Talbert, abbé François Xavier   148
taxonomic systems   77–89
Teich, Mikuláš   9, 106
Téron, Jacques-Benjamin   37
Théologie   80–2, 87–8, 96, 99
Théologie hétérodoxe   79, 81
Théologie polémique   81–2
Théveneau de Morande, Charles   11, 37, 56, 94, 133, 161, 184 n.35, 211 n.6
Thomas, Chantal   119
Tissot, Samuel   23–4, 51, 74–6, 139, 141, 142, 143, 144, 214 n.45
Tonnet, Pierre-François   151
topic-modelling   87
Toscanelli, Charles-Marie   63
Towsey, Mark   112, 204 n.40
Trade bestsellers list, STN   100
trade sales   160
travel literature. *See* voyages
Tralles, Balthasar Ludwig   143
Travel literature   103, 108, 113, 118
Trembley, Abraham   75, 139, 144, 214 n.51
Turgot, Anne-Robert-Jacques   7, 10
Tutot, Jean-Jacques   2

Ulf, Charles G.   54–6

Vaillant, Paul   50
Valade, Jacques-François   60
Valmont de Bomare, Jacques-Christophe   137, 141
Vatel, Emer   5, 74
Velly, Paul-François   154
Venel, Gabriel-François   140
Venel, Jean-André   139
Vercruysse, Jeroom   161
Vernes, Jacob   6, 147
Vernus, Michel   147
Vertot, abbé René-Aubert   117
Volney, Constantin-François de Chasseboeuf, comte de   113
Voltaire, François-Marie Arouet   xiii, 2–4, 10, 12, 26, 29, 50, 53, 56, 62, 64, 67, 71, 73, 75–6, 94–5, 103, 104, 111, 117, 130, 147, 156, 188 n.37, 192 n.30, 199 nn.3
Vovelle, Michel   187 n.18
voyages [travelogues]   25, 80, 82, 87, 93, 115

Watson, Robert   114
Weitbrecht, Johann-Jakob   58
Welbruck, François-Charles, comte de   4
Western Sydney University   176, 177
White, Luke   194 n.21
Wigtown borrower records   114
Wigtown Library (Scotland)   112–14
Winter, James de   51
Witel, Jérémie   55, 195 n.41
Wolff, Christian   7
Woolston, Thomas   81
Works of Religiosity   83, 94, 97, 103, 143
Worldcat   142, 149
Wurgler, Andreas   186 n.12

Xenophon   107

Zanden, Jan Luiten van   186 n.7, 187 n.20
Zettersten, Erik   195 n.35

Title Index

Abrégé de l'histoire poétique, ou Introduction à la mythologie par demandes et par réponses (Fougereux) 64
Abrégé de l'histoire sainte et du catéchisme (Ostervald) 23, 40, 63-4, 71, 101, 103
Abrégé des principes de la grammaire Françoise (Restaut) 53, 57, 64
Abrégé du code de la nature (Holbach) 146
Abrégé élémentaire de l'histoire universelle (Lacroze) 58
Académie des Dames 56, 120, 121
Adélaïde, ou mémoires de la marquise de M*** (Keralio) 86
Adèle et Théodore ou Lettres sur l'éducation (Genlis) 56, 75
Admirables Secrets d'Albert le Grand (Bollstädt) 141, 142
Adventures of Peregrine Pickle (Smollett) 114
Adventures of Roderick Random (Smollett) 114
Agronome, ou Dictionnaire portatif du cultivateur (Alletz) 141
Albert moderne (Alletz) 74-5, 130, 141-2
À l'Égide de Minerve (DeFrance) xiii-xiv, 4, 17, 25, 33, 49, 91, 105, 138, 173, 174,
Alfred, roi des Anglo-Saxons (Haller) 159
Almanach de la Librairie 54, 123
Almanach de Neuchâtel 63
Amours, ou lettres d'Alexis et Justine par M**** (Fleuriot) 55
Amours de Charlot et Toinette 119
Amours de Zeokinizul, roi des Kofirans 132, 133, 159
An 2440 (Mercier) 62, 75, 129, 167, 170
Anarchie médicinale, ou La Médicine considérée comme nuisable à la société (Gilibert) 23, 137-41, 213 n.24

Anecdotes de l'ancienne cour 133
Anecdotes sur Madame du Barri (Mairobert) 25, 46, 75, 127, 129-30, 131, 155, 159, 160, 161
Ange à table 151
Ange conducteur dans la devotion chrétienne (Coret) 25, 147, 149, 150-2, 155, 215 n.62
Année littéraire (Fréron) 25, 146
Apologie du marquis de Fogliani 62
Arretin. See Vie de l'Arretin 64
Art de faire le vin 59
Art de la Vigne 59
Art de tenir les livres en parties doubles (Girardeau) 191 n.19
Avantures de Télémaque (Fénélon) 62, 114, 155-6, 159
Avis au peuple sur sa santé (Tissot) 73, 142, 213 n.35

Bachelor of Salamanca (Le Sage) 118
Balai 120
Barbier de Séville (Beaumarchais) 3
Bélisaire (Marmontel) 54, 74, 114, 159
Belisarius (Marmontel). See *Bélisaire*
Belle Allemande ou les galanteries de Thérèse (Bret & Villaret) 130
Bibliographie du genre romanesque français (Martin, Mylne and Frautschi) 85, 179
Biblische Historien (Hübner). See *Histoires de la Bible*
Bon père (Pomaret) 101
Bon Sens (Holbach) 8, 146
Books without Borders (Freedman) 27, 36, 62, 105
Botanique (Haller) 141
Brouette de vinaigrier (Mercier) 3

Candide (Voltaire) 10, 192 n.30
Cantiques sacrés 63

Catalogue général des livres qui se trouvent chez la Société typographique à Londres (Boissière)   59, 88, 89, 96, 196 n.53
Catalogue raisonné des manuscrits conservés dans la Bibliothèque de la ville et république de Genève (Senebier)   54
Catéchumène instruit sous une forme nouvelle (Pomaret)   101
Cecilia, or memoirs of an heiress (Burney)   118
Chandelle d'Arras (Du Laurens)   120
Charles IX, ou l'école des rois (Chénier)   170
Chemin du Ciel   149
Chimie expérimentale (Baume)   148
Chrétien par conviction et sentiment (Pomaret)   101
Christianisme dévoilé (Holbach)   145, 146
Chronique scandaleuse (Imbert)   55, 120, 163
Chroniqueur ou l'Espion des Boulevards   120
Clarissa (Richardson)   118
Code de la Librarie et imprimerie   32
Collection complète des oeuvres de Madame Riccoboni   86
Collection de pièces intéressantes et authentiques concernant la vie et les derniers jours de Frédéric le Grand (Hertzberg)   64
Comments (Calonne)   73, 163
A Compendious History of Captain Cook's Last Voyage   204 n.39
Compère Mathieu (Du Laurens)   120
Compte rendu des finances (Necker)   64, 73, 102, 163, 219 n.35
Comptes faits (Barrême)   39, 155, 191 n.22
Confidence philosophique (Vernes)   147
Considérations chrétiennes en forme de méditations pendant tous les jours du mois   149
Considérations chrétiennes pour tous les jours de la semaine (Signieri)   149
Considérations sur le grandeur et décadence des romains (Montesquieu)   117, 156
Considérations sur les causes de l'ancienne foiblesse de l'Empire de Russie (Goudar)   75

Contagion sacrée (Holbach)   146
Contes moraux (Marmontel)   51
Continuation of the Complete History of England (Smollett)   114
Contrat conjugal (Desmaisons)   28, 71, 119, 120, 121, 129, 197 n.58
Corpus of Clandestine Literature (Darnton)   43, 122, 124–7, 129
Critical Review   114
Cyropaedia (Xenophon)   107

Dean of Coleraine (Prévost)   118
Decline and Fall of the Roman Empire (Gibbon)   114
De La Législation (Mably)   62
De La Vérité (Brissot)   129, 211 n.3
De L'Esprit des Lois (Montesquieu)   xiv, 10, 156, 204 n.40
De L'Esprit (Helvétius)   31, 146
De L'Homme (Helvétius)   8, 79, 146
Description des montagnes et des vallées qui font partie de la principauté de Neuchâtel et Valangin (Ostervald)   64
Descriptions des arts et métiers   3, 25, 27, 46, 50
Description topographique, historique, critique et nouvelle du pays et des environs de la Forêt noire, situés dans la province du Merryland (Stretser)   207 n.89
Destruction de la Ligue (Mercier)   27, 28, 62, 70–1, 107, 168–70, 220 n.68
The Devil in the Holy Water (Darnton)   11, 208 n.3
Dictionnaire de chymie (Macquer)   141
Dictionnaire de l'Académie   51
Dictionnaire des nouvelles découvertes faites en physique (Paulian)   144
Dictionnaire historique et critique (Bayle)   9, 26, 184 n.28
Dictionnaire philosophique de la religion, où l'on établit tous les points de la religion, attaqués par les incrédules, & où l'on répond à toutes leurs objections (Nonnotte)   149
Dictionnaire philosophique (Voltaire)   10, 26, 72, 111
Dictionnaire raisonné universel d'histoire naturelle (Bomare)   141

Dieu. Réponse de M. de Voltaire au Systême de la nature (Voltaire) 62, 72, 73, 95, 103, 129, 147
Discourse on Method (Descartes) 68
A Discourse on the Miracles of Our Saviour (Woolston) 81
Discours oratoire contenant l'éloge de S.E.M. le chevalier André Tron (Godard) 62
Discours préliminaire (Goëzman) 189 n.49
Dissertation de Gummi 24
Dissertation de Trisino 24
Dissertation sur l'établissement de l'Abbaye de S. Claude (Christin) 73, 103
Don Pèdre, roi de Castille (Voltaire) 3, 5
Doyen de Coleraine (Prévost). See *Dean of Coleraine*
Droit des gens portative (Vatel) 51, 62, 73
Du Contrat Social (Rousseau) 10
Dunciade (Pope) 3

Ecole des filles (Milot) 130, 131
Elémens d'histoire générale (Millot) Histoire de Dom 24, 55, 58, 64, 117
Elémens d'oryctologie, ou Distribution méthodique des fossils (Bertrand) 141
Eloge de Louis XV 64
Eloge funèbre de Louis XV 64
Eloisa (Rousseau) 114
Encyclopédie (Diderot and d'Alembert) 5, 8, 10, 29, 50, 52, 54, 72, 78, 144, 145, 154
The Enlightenment: A Genealogy (Edelstein) 9
The Enlightenment. An Interpretation (Gay) 10
The Enlightenment in National Context (Porter and Teich) 9, 106
Errotika Biblion (Mirabeau) 46
Espion anglois (Mairobert) 45, 159, 160, 163
Espion dévalisé (Baudouin de Guémadeuc) 120
Espion français à Londres (Goudar) 163
Esprit et génie de l'abbé Raynal (Hedouin) 164
Essai de psychologie (Bonnet) 144

Essai sur les maladies des gens du monde (Tissot) 142
Ethics (Spinoza) 7, 9
Evelina (Burney) 118
Examen important de Milord Bolingbroke (Voltaire) 75, 130
Expériences et observations sur les différentes espèces d'air (Priestley) 24
Extrait du journal d'un officier de la Marine de l'escadre de M. le comte d'Estaing 47

Fanny Hill (Cleland). See *Fille de joie*
Fastes de Louis XV (Mairobert) 132
Ferventes aspirations à Dieu: recueillies de l'écriture et des Saints Pères (Bona) 151
Fille de joie (Cleland) 56, 130, 131
Fille naturelle (Rétif) 131
Forbidden Best-Sellers of Pre-Revolutionary France (Darnton) 11, 43, 67, 75, 127, 129
Fortunate Foundlings (Haywood) 118
Fragment sur les colonies (Smith) 148

Galerie de l'ancienne cour 132
Gazetier cuirassé (Morande) 11, 37, 46, 56, 120, 121, 133, 161
Gazette de Cythère (Bernard) 132
General History of Scotland (Guthrie) 114
General History of Scotland (Heron) 114
Géographie (Busching) 5, 57, 93
Géographie elémentaire (Ostervald) 57, 63

Helviennes (Barruel) 147
Henri IV (Du Rozoi) 3
Histoire d'Amérique (Robertson) 148
Histoire de Charles XII (Voltaire) 156
Histoire de deux jeunes amies (Riccoboni) 197 n.67
Histoire de Dom Bougre, portier des Chartreux (Latouche) 56
Histoire de France depuis l'établissement de la monarchie jusqu'au règne de Louis XIV (Velly) 154

Histoire de Jonathan Wild le Grand (Fielding) 118
Histoire de la Maison de Stuart (Hume) 117
Histoire de la sainte jeunesse de notre seigneur Jésus Christ (Grisot) 149
Histoire de Marguerite fille de Suzon, nièce de Dxx Bxxxxx 55
Histoire du parlement d'Angleterre (Raynal) 117
Histoire et avantures de Gil Blas de Santillane (Le Sage). See *History and Adventures of Gil Blas of Santillane*
Histoire et vie de l'Aretin. See *Vie de l'Aretin*
Histoire naturelle, générale et particulière (Buffon) 138
Histoire philosophique des Deux Indes (Raynal) 8, 51, 56, 62, 64, 71, 73, 75, 114, 115, 130, 156, 159, 164–7, 168, 170, 219 n.38
Histoires de la Bible (Hübner) 58, 64
History and Adventures of Gil Blas of Santillane (Le Sage) 114
History of America (Robertson) 117
History of Ancient Greece, its Colonies, and Conquests (Gillies) 114
History of Charles V (Robertson). See *History of the Reign of the Emperor Charles V*
History of Edinburgh (Arnot) 114
History of England (Hume) 114, 116, 117
History of Great Britain (Andrews) 114
History of Great Britain (Henry) 114
History of Scotland, during the reigns of Queen Mary and of King James VI (Robertson) 114
History of Sir Charles Grandison (Richardson) 118
History of the Knights Hospitallers (Vertot) 117
History of the life of King Henry the Second (Lyttelton) 114
History of the Reign of Philip the Second, King of Spain (Watson) 114
History of the Reign of Philip the Third, King of Spain (Watson) 114
History of the Reign of the Emperor Charles V (Robertson) 114, 115, 117, 156

History of the Revolution in Sweden (Vertot) 117
History of the Russian Empire under Peter the Great (Voltaire) 117
Homme sauvage (Pfiel) 86

Imitation de Jésus-Christ (Kempis) 25, 31, 147, 149, 152
Incas (Marmontel) 25, 53, 62
Instruction pastorale ... pour le Carême de 1773 149
Instructions abrégées sur les devoirs et les exercices du chrétien 149
Instructions chrétiennes pour les jeunes gens (Humbert) 149, 151
Instructions d'un père à ses enfans, sur la religion naturelle et révélée (Trembley) 75
Instructions familières en forme de catéchisme sur les preuves de la religion 149
Intolérance ecclésiastique (Nikolai) 25, 58
Introduction à la connoissance géographique et politique des Etats de l'Europe (Busching) 102, 159

Jardin potager mis à la portée de tout le monde 59
Jésus Christ, le modèle des chrétiens 151
Jezzenemours (Mercier) 86
Journal de médecine, chirurgerie, pharmacie 24
Journal de Middlesex 119
Journal des Savants 88–9, 91–2, 146
Journal de Trévoux 146
Journal ecclésiastique 146
Journal encyclopédique 146
Journal Helvétique 20, 28, 108
Journal historique de la révolution opérée ... par M. de Maupeou (Mairobert) 45
Journal historique et littéraire 146
Journée du Chrétien sanctifiée par la prière (Bouhours and Clément) 25, 124, 147, 149, 151, 152
Julie, ou la nouvelle Héloïse. See *Eloisa*

Leçons du Clavecin 63
Lectures pour les enfans (Berquin) 64, 75, 199 n.3

Legs d'un père à ses filles (Gregory)   64
Letters on Egypt (Savary)   113
Letters to his Son (Chesterfield)   116
Lettre à M. le comte de Buffon: Ou critique et nouvel essai sur la théorie générale de la terre (Bertrand)   148
Lettre de M. Linguet à Monsieur de Vergennes (Linguet)   64
Lettre de Thrasibule à Leucippe (Freret)   146
Lettre du marquis de Caraccioli à M. d'Alembert (Grimoard)   73, 163
Lettre d'un théologien à l'auteur du Dictionnaire des trois siècles (Condorcet)   145
Lettres à Eugénie (Holbach)   146
Lettres de cachet (Mirabeau)   120
Lettres de Mme la marquise de Pompadour (Mairobert)   132
Lettres hollandaises ou Correspondance politique (Damiens de Gomicourt)   120
Lettres originales de Madame la comtesse du Barri (Mairobert)   132
Lettres persanes (Montesquieu)   156, 159
Liaisons dangereuses (Laclos)   55
Libertin de qualité (Mirabeau). See *Ma Conversion ou le libertin de qualité*
Life and Opinions of Tristram Shandy (Sterne)   115, 118
Livre et société (Furet)   88
Livre rouge   163
Lupiologie, ou traité des tumeurs (Barthélemy)   24
Lyre gaillarde   130, 131

Ma Conversion ou le libertin de qualité (Mirabeau)   55, 130
Magasin des enfans (Beaumont)   56, 75, 197 n.67
Maître de la langue Allemande (Gottsched)   58, 75
Malheurs de l'inconstance (Dorat)   3, 86
Manière sûre et facile de traiter les maladies vénériennes (Gardane)   187 n.30
Mariage de Figaro (Beaumarchais)   4
Médecine commentaires   24
Médecine domestique (Buchan)   24

Mémoire apologétique des Genevois. See *Pièces importantes à la dernière revolution de Genève*
Mémoire aux souverains de l'Europe   120
Mémoire de Necker sur l'administration provincial (Necker)   163
Mémoire donné au roi par M. Necker en 1778 (Necker)   73
Mémoires authentiques de Mme la comtesse du Barri (Nerciat?)   4, 132, 133
Mémoires de l'académie royale de chirurgie   24
Mémoires de Louis XV   132
Mémoires de Mme la marquise de Pompadour   132
Mémoires de Suzon, soeur de D... B... portier des Chartreux   55
Mémoires de Trévoux   89, 92
Mémoires justificatifs (La Motte)   135, 211 n.70
Mémoires pour server à l'histoire du jacobinisme français (Barruel)   6
Mémoires secrets (Bauchaumont, Mairobert)   163, 207 n.83
Mémoires sur l'Angleterre   3
Morale universelle (Holbach)   8

New and Impartial History of England (Barrow)   117
A new description of Merryland. Containing, a topographical, geographical, and natural history of that country (Stretser)   118, 207 n.89
New Introduction to Bibliography   186 n.8
A New Treatise on the Method of Teaching Languages (Huguenin du Mitand)   51
Nourriture de l'Ame (Ostervald)   74, 101
Nouvelle Héloise (Rousseau). See *Eloisa*
Nouveau traité des maladies des yeux (Saint-Yves)   139
Nouvelle maison rustique (Liger)   87

Observateur François à Amsterdam   120
Observations modestes d'un citoyen sur les opérations de finances de M. Necker (Saint-Vincent)   73

Observations périodiques sur l'histoire naturelle, la physique et les arts 140
Observations sur le livre intitulé Système de la nature (Castiglione) 147
Observations sur les jurisdictions anciennes et modernes de la ville de Besançon (Auxiron) 147
Œuvres (Freret) 146
Œuvres (Gessner) 3
Œuvres (La Mettrie) 145, 146
Œuvres (Rousseau) 53, 74, 75, 130, 131
Œuvres (Voltaire) 217 n.4
Œuvres complètes (Helvétius) 146
Office de l'église 151
Onanisme (Tissot) 75, 137, 142

Pensées sur les plus importantes vérités de la religion et sur les principaux devoirs du christianisme (Humbert) 149, 150, 151
Péruviennes (Graffigny) 156
Petit Albert 142
Philosophe au Port-au-Bled (Mercier) 71, 73
Philosophical Dictionary (Voltaire). See *Dictionnaire philosophique*
Pièces importantes à la dernière revolution de Genève 55, 58, 62, 70-1, 157-9, 170, 199 n.11
Planta gagnant sa vie en honnête homme (Rilliet) 55, 67-9, 71-2, 95-6, 98, 199 n.6
Politique naturelle (Holbach) 8
Portefeuille d'un talon rouge 119
Pratique du jardinage, La (Schabol) 148
Present state of Sicily and Malta, Extracted from Mr. Brydone, Mr. Swinburne, and other modern travellers 118
Prince of Abissinia (Johnson) 204 n.45
Procès du Comte du Barri avec Madame la comtesse de Tournon 120
Pseaumes. See Psalms
Psalms 64, 74-5
Pucelle d'Orléans (Voltaire) 75, 130, 156
Pucelle libertine, 120

Qu'est-ce que le tiers état? (Siéyès) 167
Questions de droit naturel (Vatel) 5

Questions sur l'Encyclopédie (Voltaire) 29, 62, 71-3, 95

Recherches philosophiques sur les Américains (Pauw) 130
Recueil de diverses pièces servant de supplément à l'Histoire philosophique (Raynal) 51
Recueil des passages du Nouveau Testament 63
Reflections on the causes of the rise and fall of the Roman Empire see *Considérations sur le grandeur et décadence des romains* (Montesquieu)
Réflexions d'un homme de bon sens sur les comètes & sur leur retour ou Préservatif contre la peur (Gélieu) 141
Réflexions philosophiques sur le Système de la nature (Holland) 14, 81, 103, 147
Réfutation d'Helvétius (Diderot) 10
Remarques historiques sur le Château de la Bastille (Morande?) 133, 167
Remède nouveau contre les maladies vénériennes (Peyrilhe) 187 n.30
Remonstrances du Père Adam à Voltaire pour être mises à la suite de sa confession 3
Rideau Levé ou l'Education de Laure (Mirabeau) 46
robertdarnton.org (Darnton) 36

Santé des gens de lettres (Tissot) 142
Secrets de Nature, Extraits tant du petit Albert qu'autres Philosophes hébreux 142
Secrets merveilleux de la magie naturelle et cabalistique du petit Albert 141
Selling Enlightenment (Curran) 1, 17, 28, 38, 41-3, 49
Sentimental Journey (Sterne) 113
Sermons choisis du révérend P.P. (Perrin) 151
Sermons sur différens textes de l'Ecriture Sainte (Bertrand) 63-4, 101
Spirit of the Laws (Montesquieu). See *De L'Esprit des Lois*

Statistique bibliographique de la France sous la monarchie au XVIIIe siècle, La 186 n.9
The Structural Transformation of the Public Sphere (Habermas) 18–19
Supplément à l'abbé Raynal 120
Systema naturae (Linnaeus) 77, 138
Système de la nature (Holbach) 8, 14, 28, 37, 39, 46, 62, 79, 81, 104, 121, 144, 145–6, 147, 157
Système social (Holbach) 8

Tableau de la monarchie française (Goëzman) 28, 189 n.49, 197 n.58
Tableau de l'analyse chymique (Rouelle) 24
Tableau de l'Europe, pour servir de supplément à l'histoire philosophique (Deleyre) 164
Tableau de Paris (Mercier) 28, 55, 58, 69–70, 96, 107, 129, 137, 167
Tableau historique de Laurent Ganganelli 120
Telemarchus (Fénélon). *See Avantures de Télémaque*
Testament politique de l'Angleterre (Brissot) 47
Théatre (Voltaire) 51
Thérèse philosophe (Argens) 56, 95, 120, 128, 143
Thévenon ou les journées de la montagne (Bertrand) 64, 197 n.67
Tom Jones (Fielding) 118
Tour through Sicily and Malta. See Voyage en Sicile et à Malthe (Brydone)
Tractatus theologico-politicus et alia opera (Spinoza) 81
Traité d'épilepsie (Tissot) 23
Traité des maladies vénériennes (Fabre) 187 n.30
Traité des sensations (Condillac) 139
Traité des systêmes (Condillac) 138
Traités de la main-morte et des retraits (Charnage) 151

Travels in North-America (Chastellux) 118
Travels in Switzerland (Coxe) 118
Travels into Poland, Russia, Sweden and Denmark (Coxe) 113
Travels of Anacharsis the Younger, in Greece (Barthélemi) 118
Travels through Arabia, and other countries in the East (Niebuhr) 118
Travels through Syria and Egypt (Volney) 113

Usong, histoire orientale (Haller) 159

Venus dans le cloître 130
Vicomte de Barjac (Luchet) 55, 130
Vie de l'Arretin 64, 75, 131
Vie et histoire de l'Arretin. See Vie de l'Arretin
Vie privée de Louis XV (Mouffle d'Angerville) 21, 53, 132, 155, 197 n.53
View of Society and Manners in France, Switzerland and Germany (Moore) 113
Visite au saint sacrement et à la sainte vierge (Liguori) 151
Voyage en Sicile et à Malthe (Brydone) 3–4, 29, 108–12, 115, 118, 148
Voyages de Gulliver (Swift) 159
Voyages en Europe, en Asie et en Afrique (Macintosh) 87
Voyages (Hawkesworth) 115
Vrai Sens du Systême de la nature 146

Wanderings of the Heart and Mind (Crébillon) 118
Wealth of Nations (Smith) 148, 156, 204 n.40
Works (Fielding) 114, 115